Voice Over!
Seiyu Academy

2

Vol.2

Story & Art by

Minami

TECHNICAL ADVISORS
Yoichi Kato, Kaori Kagami, Ayumi Hashidate,
Ayako Harino and Touko Fujitani

Voice Over!
Seiyu Academy

Vol.2

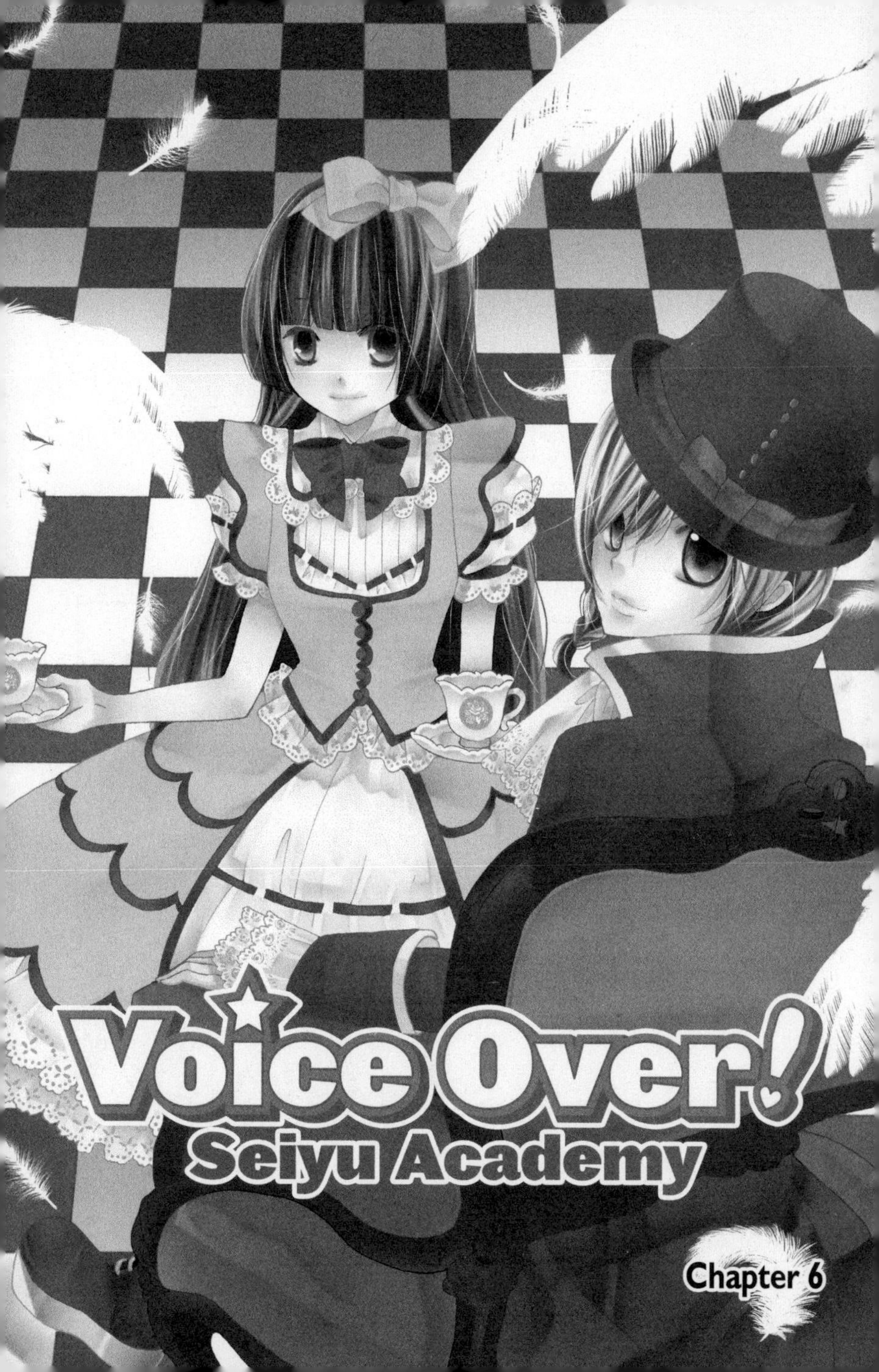
Voice Over!
Seiyu Academy
Chapter 6

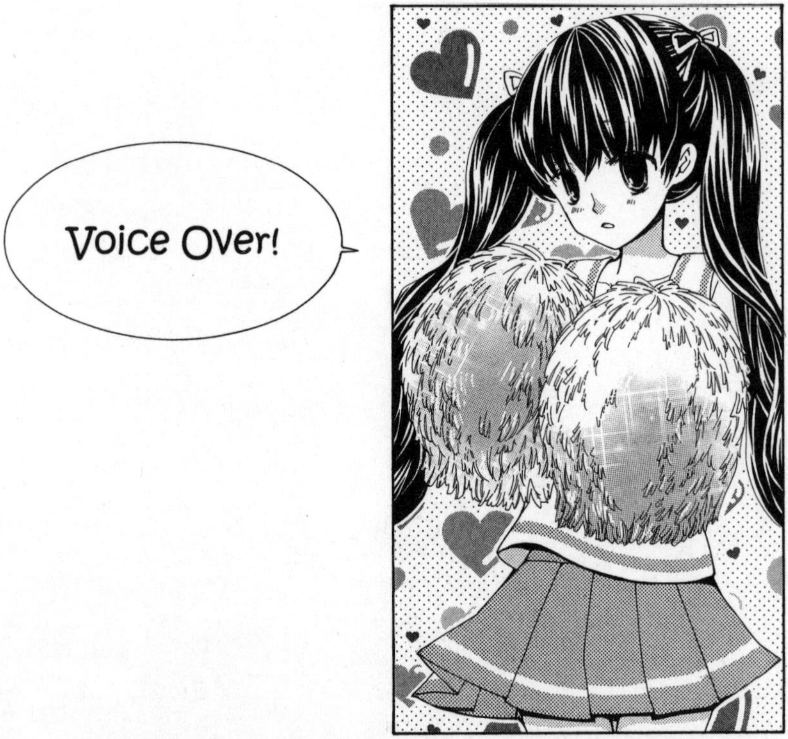
Voice Over!

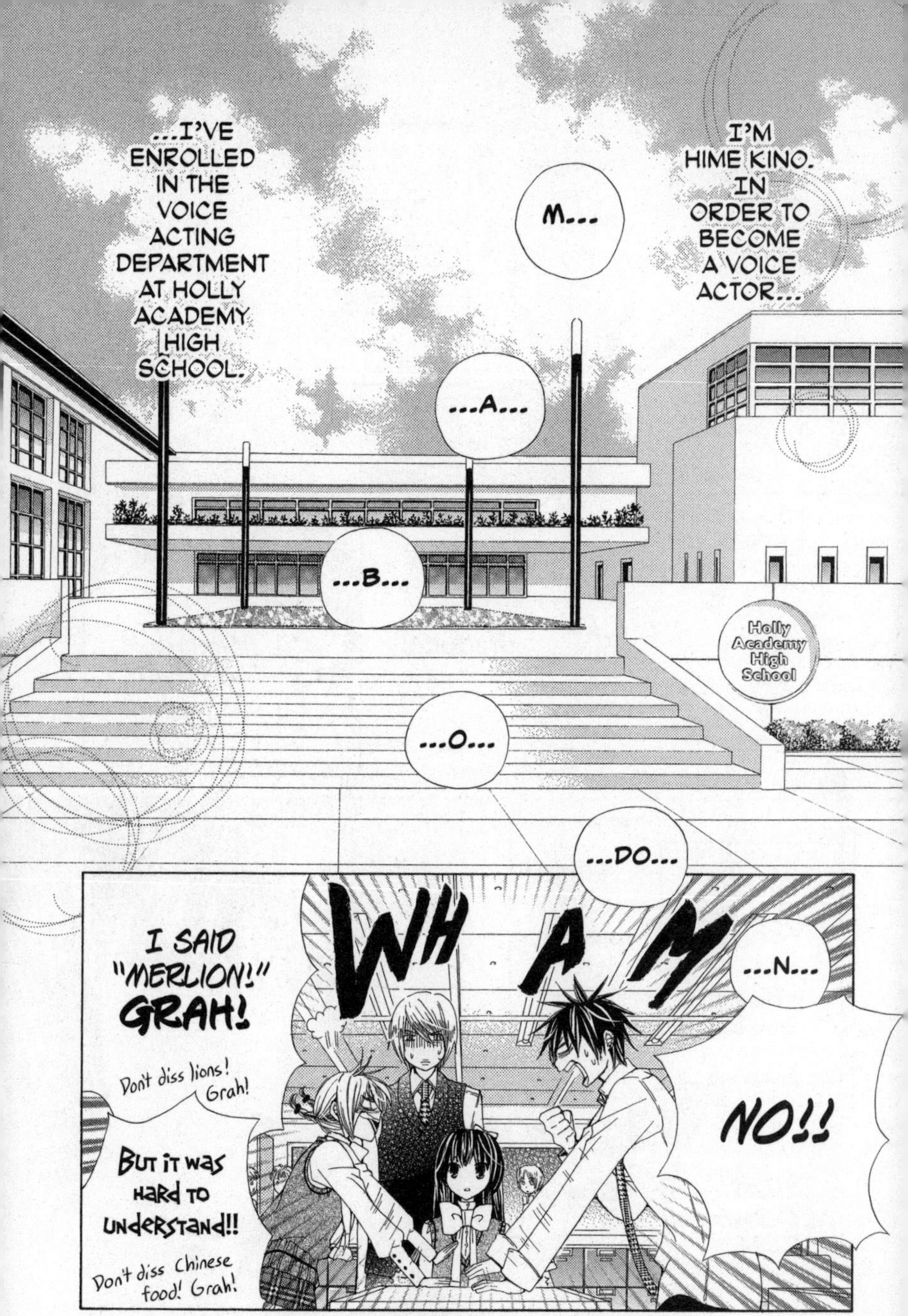
I'M HIME KINO. IN ORDER TO BECOME A VOICE ACTOR...
...I'VE ENROLLED IN THE VOICE ACTING DEPARTMENT AT HOLLY ACADEMY HIGH SCHOOL.
M...
...A...
...B...
Holly Academy High School
...O...
...DO...
WHAM
...N...
NO!!
I SAID "MERLION!" GRAH!
Don't diss lions! Grah!
BUT IT WAS HARD TO UNDERSTAND!!
Don't diss Chinese food! Grah!

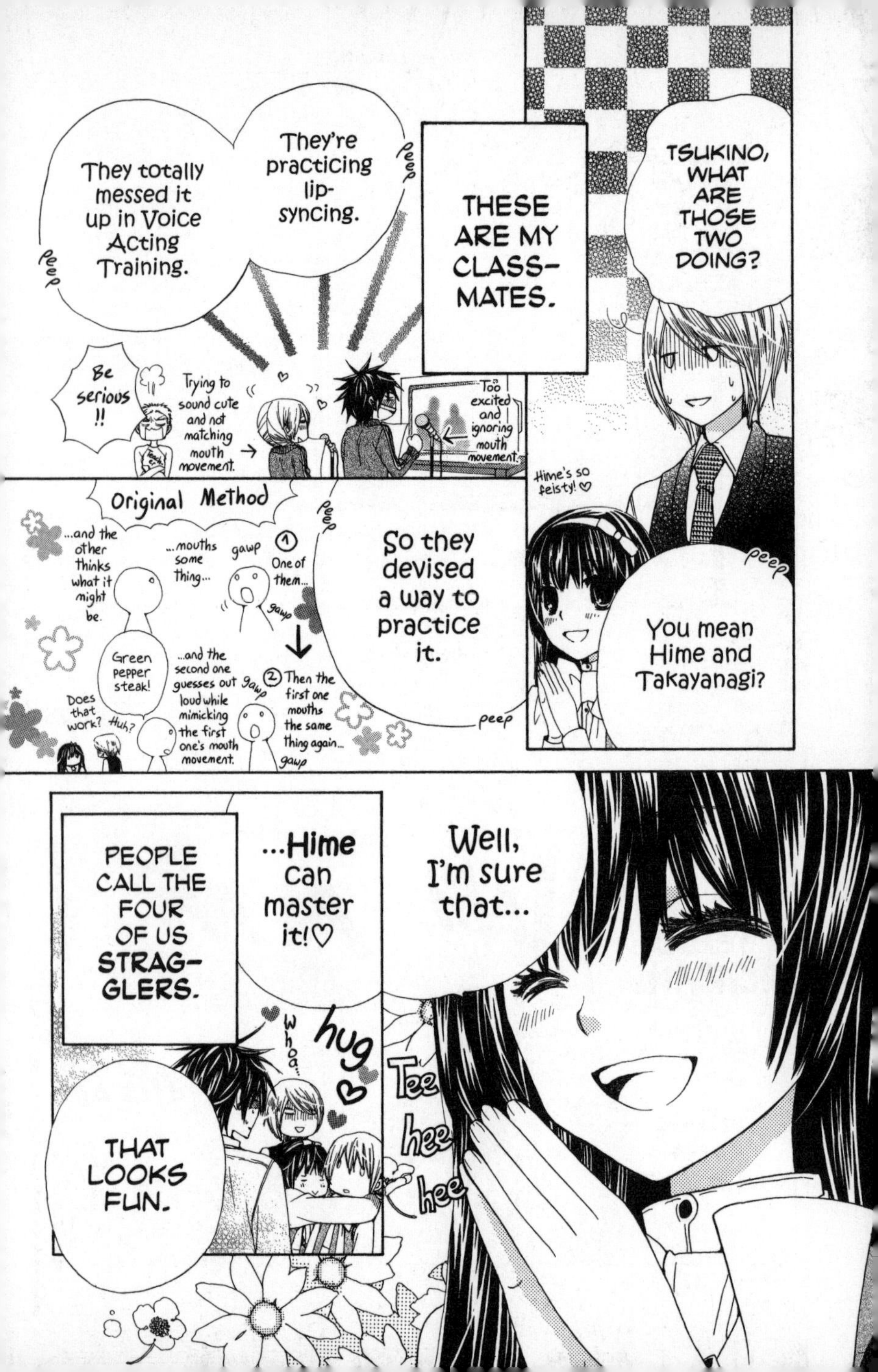
TSUKINO, WHAT ARE THOSE TWO DOING?
peep
You mean Hime and Takayanagi?
peep
Hime's so feisty! ♡
THESE ARE MY CLASSMATES.
peep
They're practicing lip-syncing.
peep
They totally messed it up in Voice Acting Training.
Too excited and ignoring mouth movement.
Trying to sound cute and not matching mouth movement.
Be serious!!
peep
So they devised a way to practice it.
Original Method
① One of them...
gawp
...mouths some thing...
gawp
...and the other thinks what it might be.
② Then the first one mouths the same thing again...
gawp
gawp
...and the second one guesses out loud while mimicking the first one's mouth movement.
Green pepper steak!
Does that work?
Huh?
Well, I'm sure that...
...Hime can master it! ♡
PEOPLE CALL THE FOUR OF US STRAGGLERS.
hug
Whoa...
Tee hee hee
THAT LOOKS FUN.

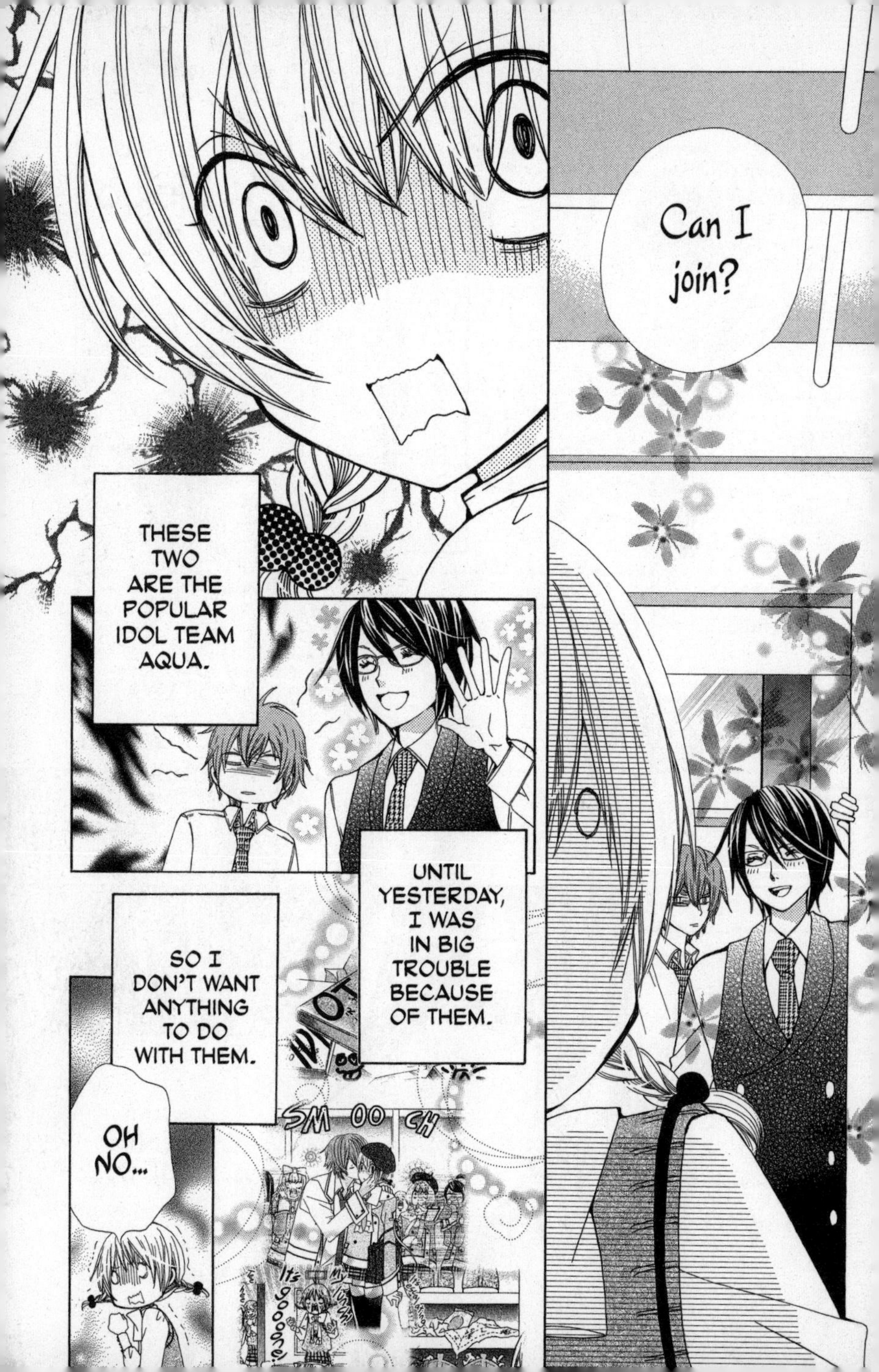
Can I join?
THESE TWO ARE THE POPULAR IDOL TEAM AQUA.
UNTIL YESTERDAY, I WAS IN BIG TROUBLE BECAUSE OF THEM.
SO I DON'T WANT ANYTHING TO DO WITH THEM.
SMOOCH
My lunch
It's goooone!
OH NO...

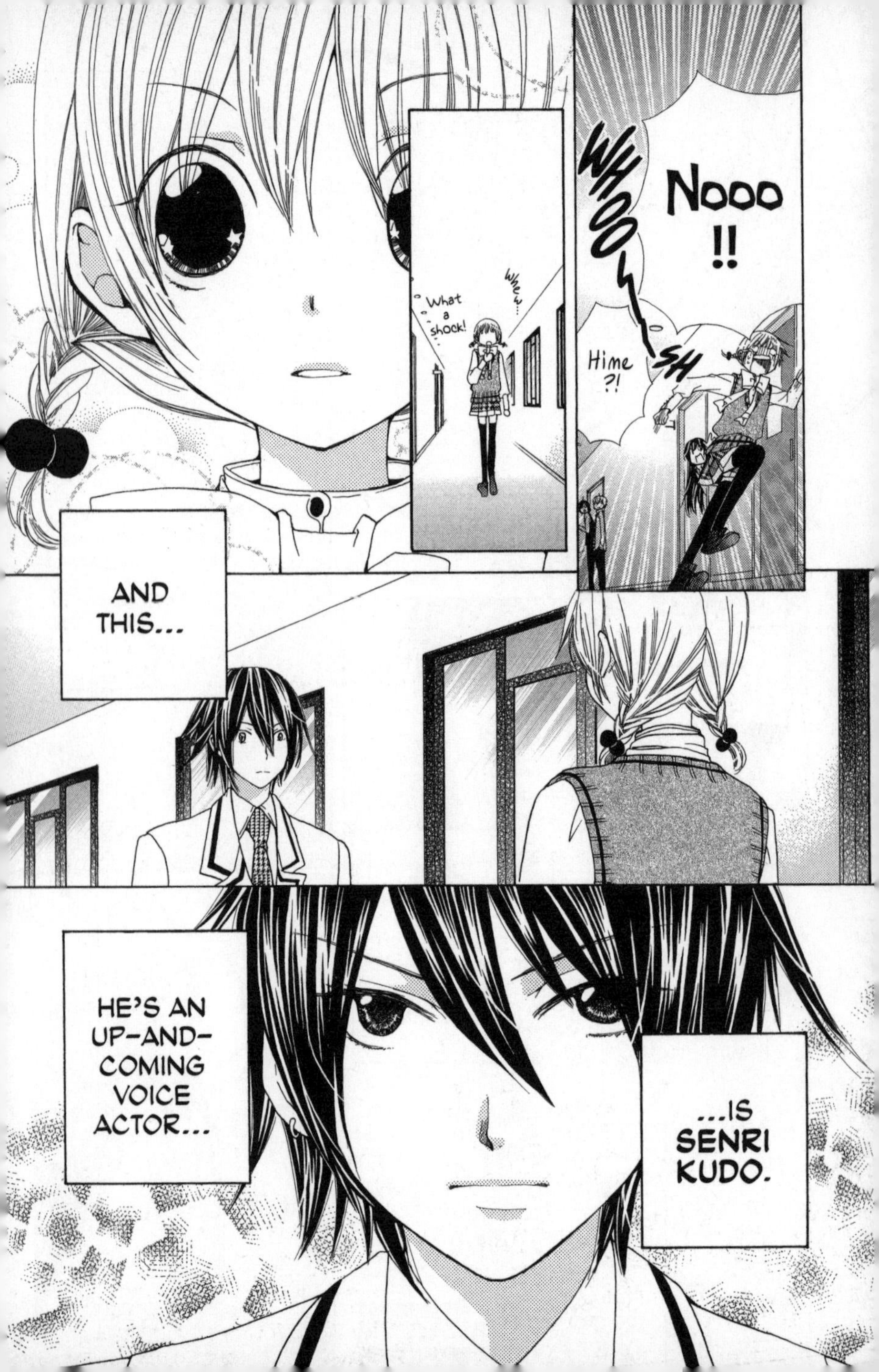
Nooo!!
WHOOOOOSH
Hime?!
Whew...
What a shock!
AND THIS...
HE'S AN UP-AND-COMING VOICE ACTOR...
...IS SENRI KUDO.

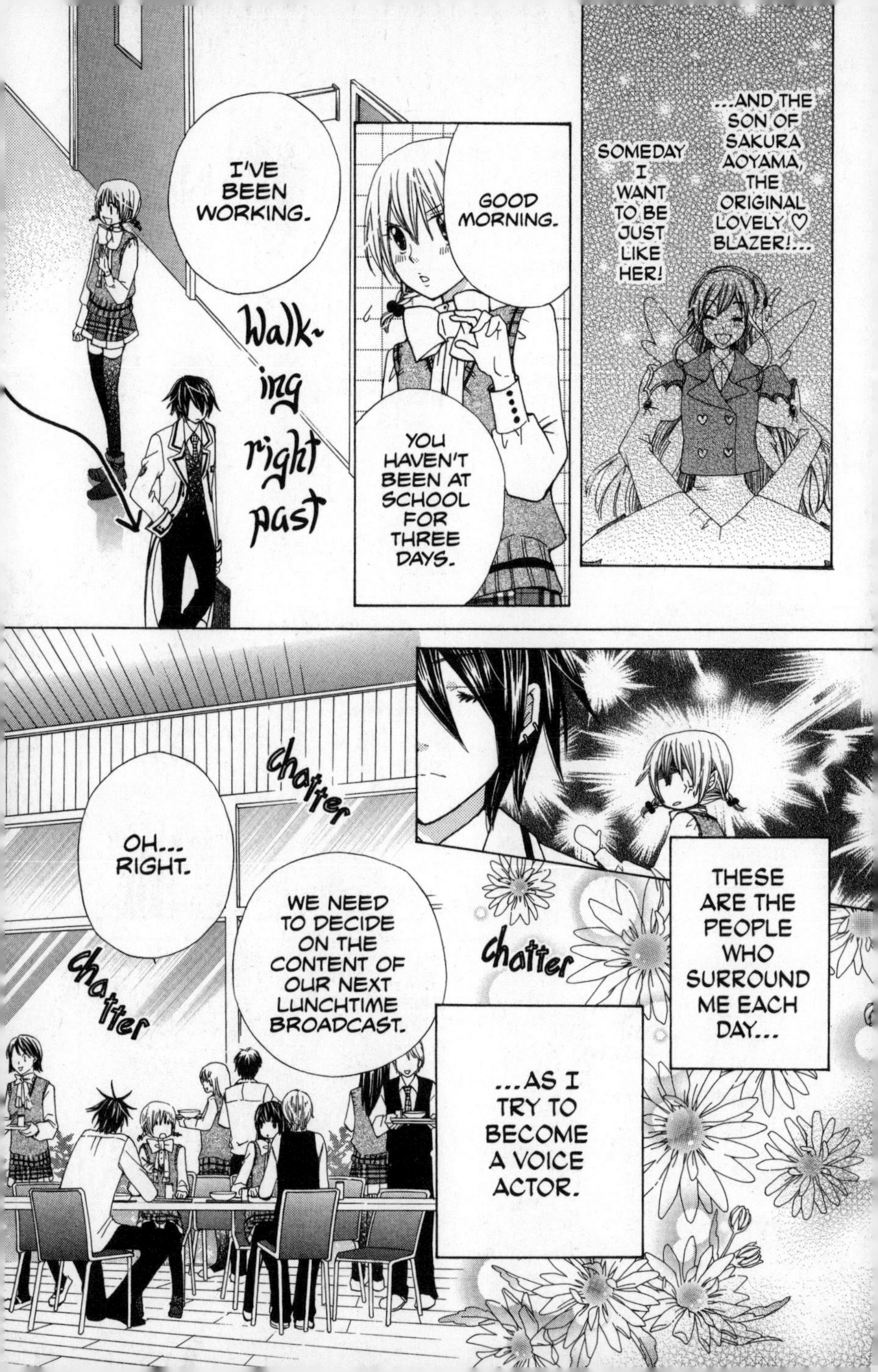
...AND THE SON OF SAKURA AOYAMA, THE ORIGINAL LOVELY ♡ BLAZER!...
SOMEDAY I WANT TO BE JUST LIKE HER!
GOOD MORNING.
YOU HAVEN'T BEEN AT SCHOOL FOR THREE DAYS.
I'VE BEEN WORKING.
Walking right past
THESE ARE THE PEOPLE WHO SURROUND ME EACH DAY...
...AS I TRY TO BECOME A VOICE ACTOR.
chatter
WE NEED TO DECIDE ON THE CONTENT OF OUR NEXT LUNCHTIME BROADCAST.
OH... RIGHT.
chatter
chatter

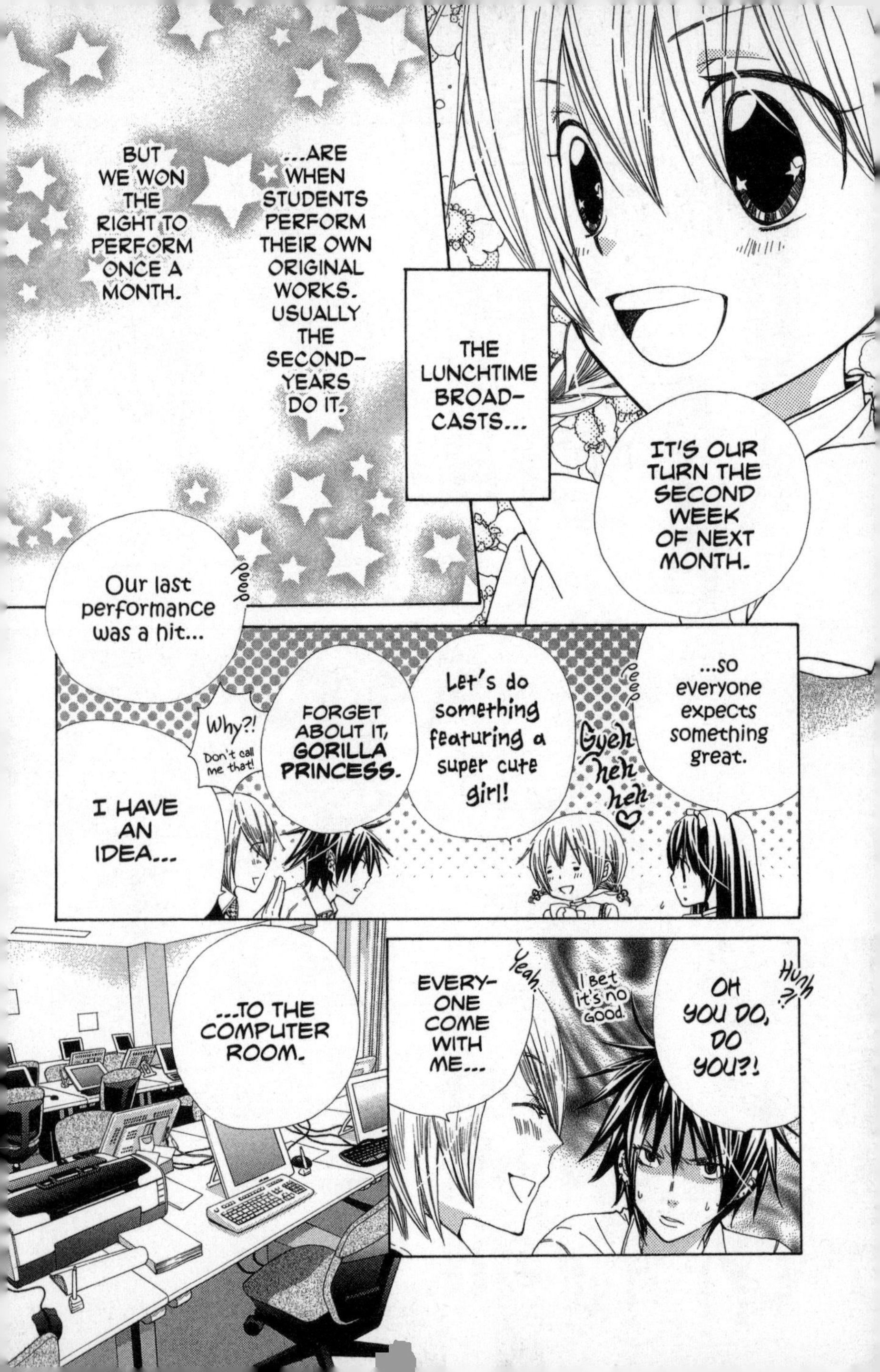

THE LUNCHTIME BROADCASTS...
...ARE WHEN STUDENTS PERFORM THEIR OWN ORIGINAL WORKS. USUALLY THE SECOND-YEARS DO IT.
BUT WE WON THE RIGHT TO PERFORM ONCE A MONTH.
IT'S OUR TURN THE SECOND WEEK OF NEXT MONTH.
peep
Our last performance was a hit...
peep
...so everyone expects something great.
Gyeh heh heh
Let's do something featuring a super cute girl!
FORGET ABOUT IT, GORILLA PRINCESS.
Why?!
Don't call me that!
I HAVE AN IDEA...
Huh ?!
OH YOU DO, DO YOU?!
I bet it's no good.
Yeah
EVERY-ONE COME WITH ME...
...TO THE COMPUTER ROOM.

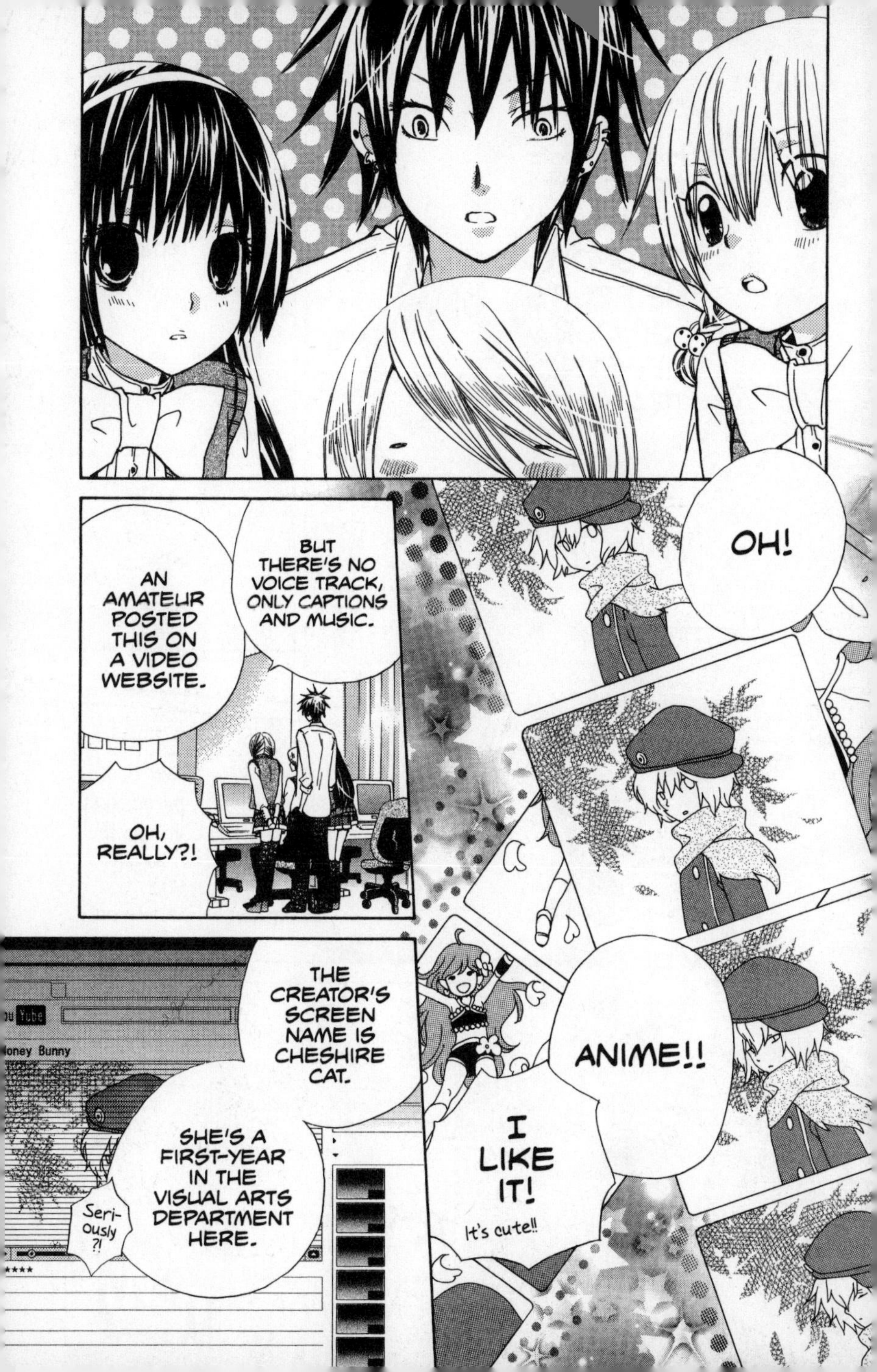
OH!
BUT THERE'S NO VOICE TRACK, ONLY CAPTIONS AND MUSIC.
AN AMATEUR POSTED THIS ON A VIDEO WEBSITE.
OH, REALLY?!
ANIME!!
I LIKE IT!
It's cute!!
THE CREATOR'S SCREEN NAME IS CHESHIRE CAT.
SHE'S A FIRST-YEAR IN THE VISUAL ARTS DEPARTMENT HERE.
Seri-ously?!

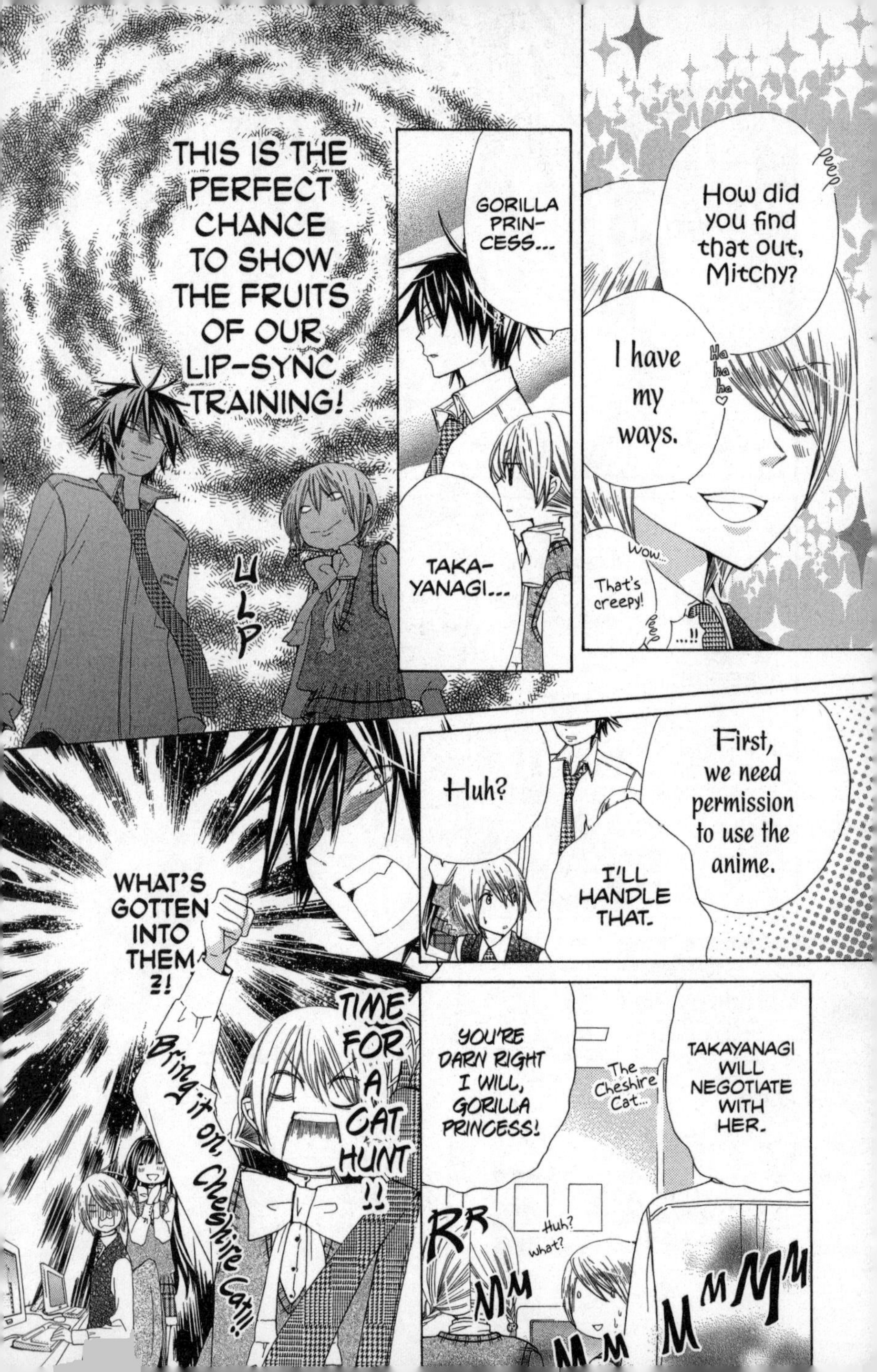
peep
How did you find that out, Mitchy?
Ha ha ha ♡
I have my ways.
Wow...
That's creepy!
peep
...!!
GORILLA PRINCESS...
TAKA-YANAGI...
THIS IS THE PERFECT CHANCE TO SHOW THE FRUITS OF OUR LIP-SYNC TRAINING!
ULP
First, we need permission to use the anime.
Huh?
I'LL HANDLE THAT.
TAKAYANAGI WILL NEGOTIATE WITH HER.
The Cheshire Cat...
YOU'RE DARN RIGHT I WILL, GORILLA PRINCESS!
Huh?
what?
RRMMMMMMMM
WHAT'S GOTTEN INTO THEM?!
TIME FOR A CAT HUNT!!
Bring it on, Cheshire Cat!!

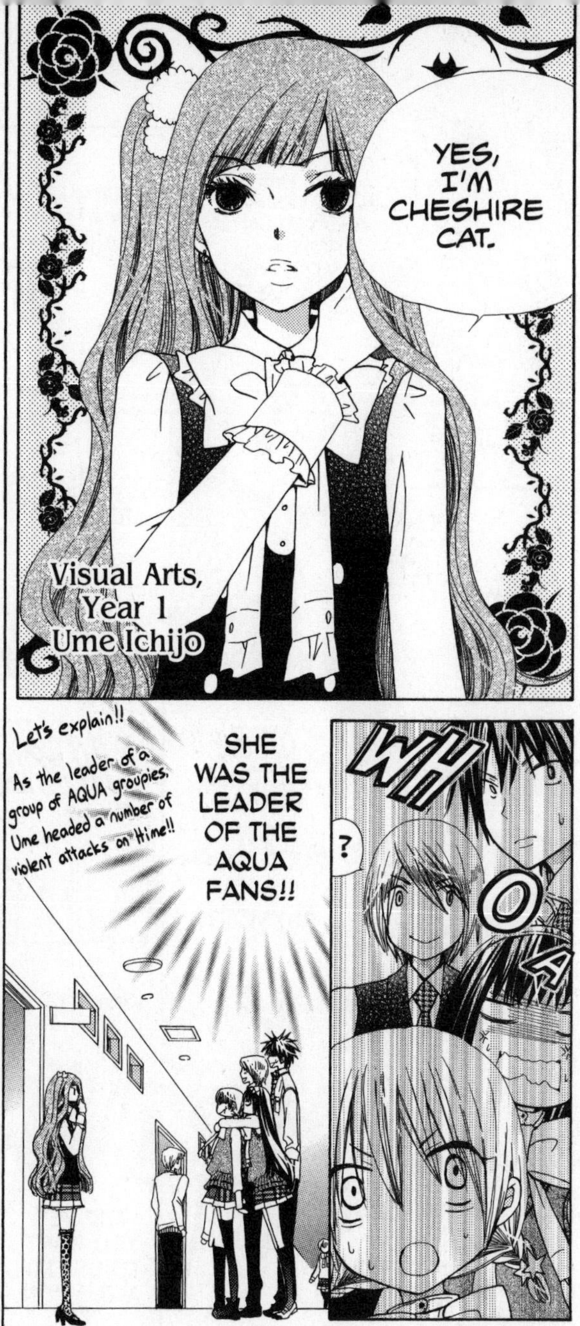
YES, I'M CHESHIRE CAT.
Visual Arts, Year 1
Ume Ichijo
WHOA
?
SHE WAS THE LEADER OF THE AQUA FANS!!
Let's explain!!
As the leader of a group of AQUA groupies, Ume headed a number of violent attacks on Hime!!

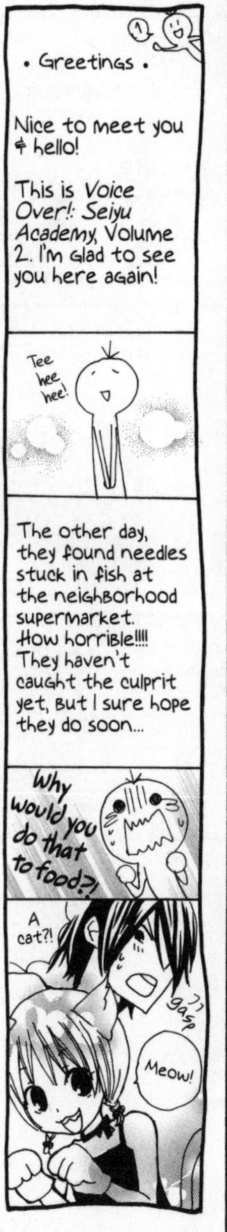
1
• Greetings •
Nice to meet you & hello!
This is *Voice Over!: Seiyu Academy*, Volume 2. I'm glad to see you here again!
Tee hee hee!
The other day, they found needles stuck in fish at the neighborhood supermarket. How horrible!!!! They haven't caught the culprit yet, but I sure hope they do soon...
Why would you do that to food?!
A cat?!
gasp
Meow!

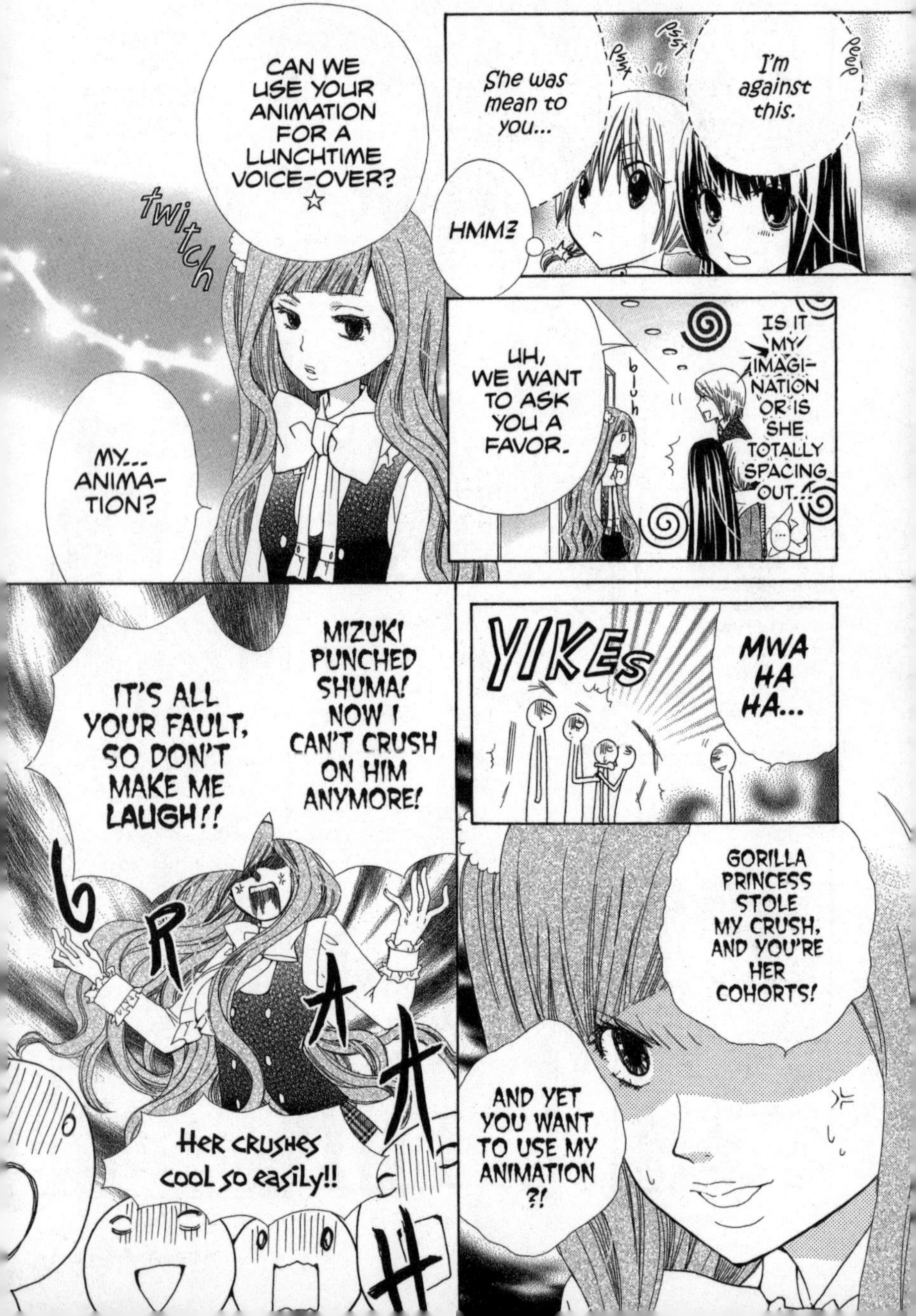
peep
I'm against this.
psst
psst
She was mean to you...
HMM?
IS IT MY IMAGINATION OR IS SHE TOTALLY SPACING OUT...?
UH, WE WANT TO ASK YOU A FAVOR.
bluh
CAN WE USE YOUR ANIMATION FOR A LUNCHTIME VOICE-OVER? ☆
twitch
MY... ANIMATION?
MWA HA HA...
YIKES
GORILLA PRINCESS STOLE MY CRUSH, AND YOU'RE HER COHORTS!
AND YET YOU WANT TO USE MY ANIMATION ?!
MIZUKI PUNCHED SHUMA! NOW I CAN'T CRUSH ON HIM ANYMORE!
IT'S ALL YOUR FAULT, SO DON'T MAKE ME LAUGH!!
GRAAH
Her crushes cool so easily!!

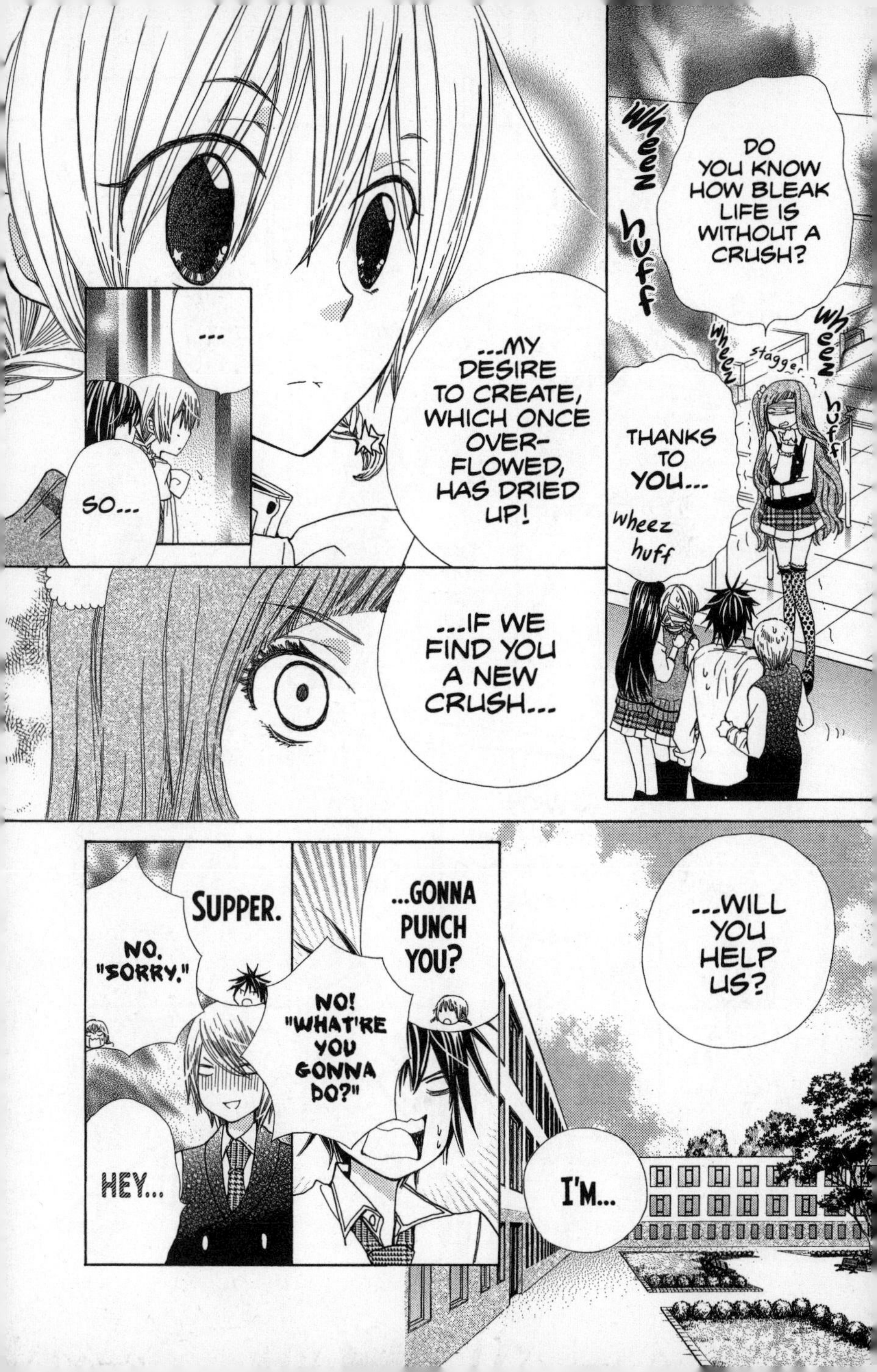
wheez
huff
DO YOU KNOW HOW BLEAK LIFE IS WITHOUT A CRUSH?
wheez
wheez
stagger
huff
THANKS TO YOU...
wheez huff
...MY DESIRE TO CREATE, WHICH ONCE OVER-FLOWED, HAS DRIED UP!
...
SO...
...IF WE FIND YOU A NEW CRUSH...
...WILL YOU HELP US?
I'M...
...GONNA PUNCH YOU?
NO! "WHAT'RE YOU GONNA DO?"
SUPPER.
NO. "SORRY."
HEY...

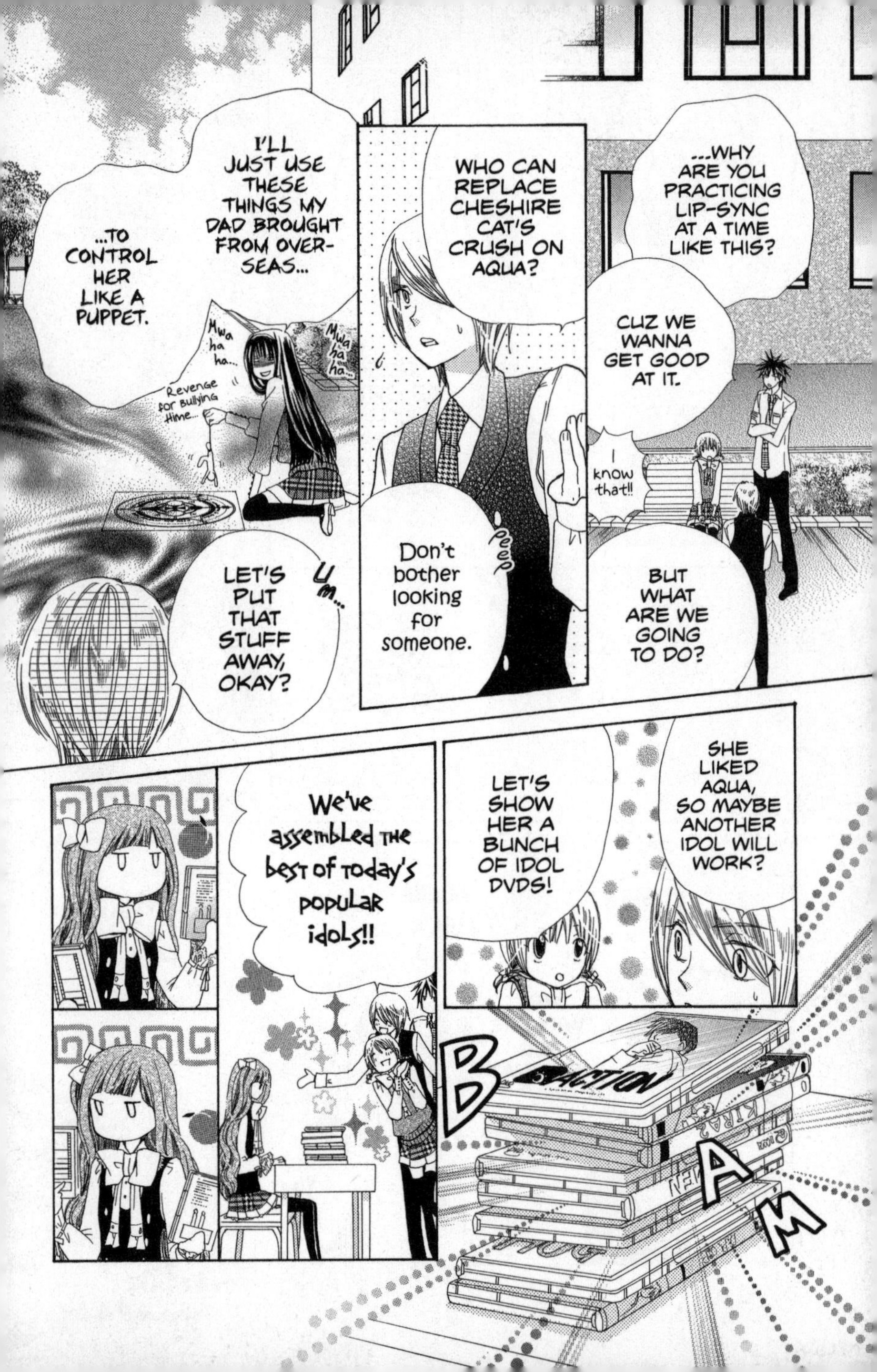
...WHY ARE YOU PRACTICING LIP-SYNC AT A TIME LIKE THIS?
CUZ WE WANNA GET GOOD AT IT.
I know that!!
BUT WHAT ARE WE GOING TO DO?
WHO CAN REPLACE CHESHIRE CAT'S CRUSH ON AQUA?
peep
Don't bother looking for someone.
I'LL JUST USE THESE THINGS MY DAD BROUGHT FROM OVERSEAS...
...TO CONTROL HER LIKE A PUPPET.
Mwa ha ha...
Mwa ha ha...
Revenge for bullying Hime...
Um...
LET'S PUT THAT STUFF AWAY, OKAY?
SHE LIKED AQUA, SO MAYBE ANOTHER IDOL WILL WORK?
LET'S SHOW HER A BUNCH OF IDOL DVDS!
BAM
We've assembled the best of today's popular idols!!

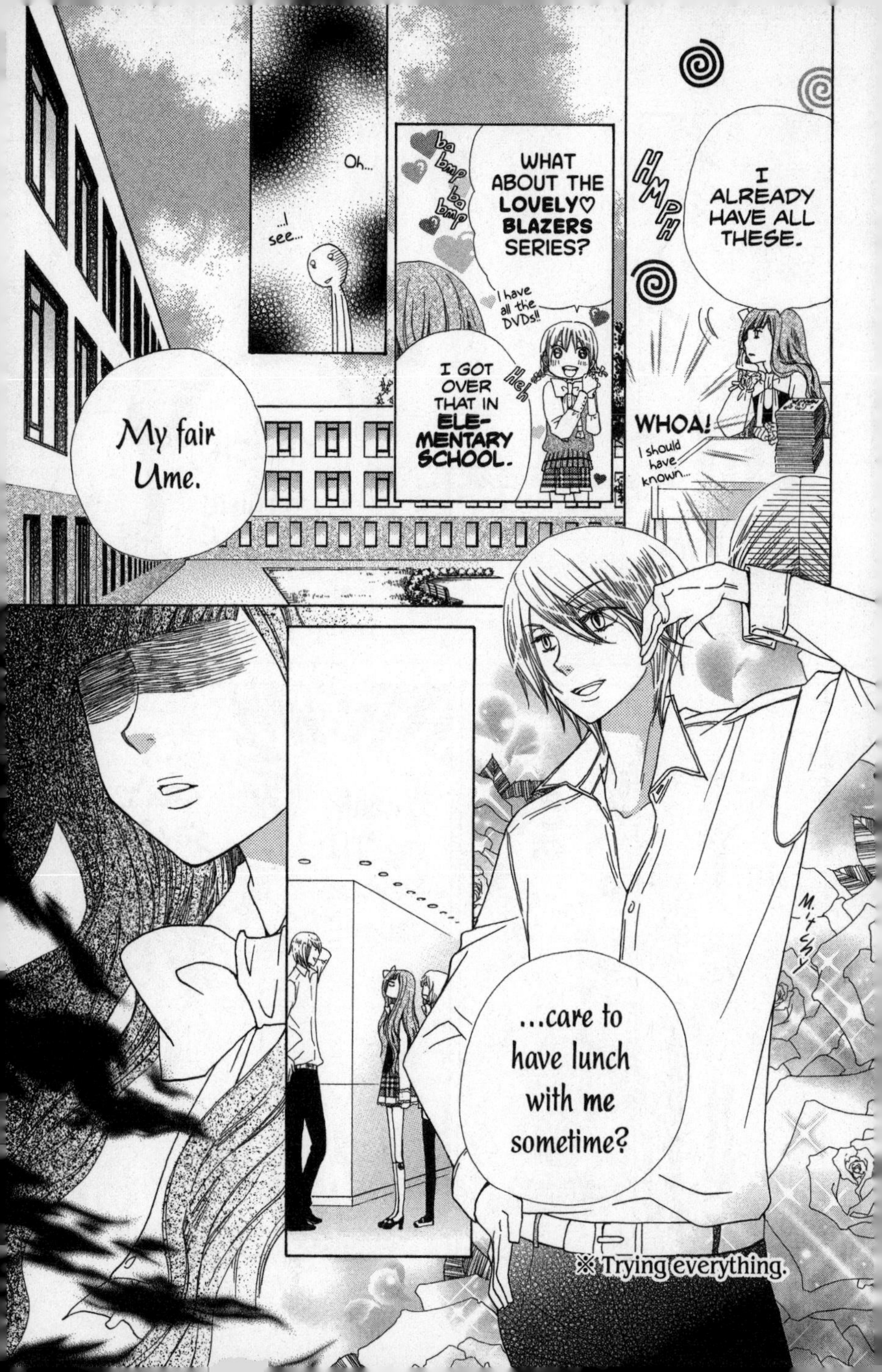
HMPH
I ALREADY HAVE ALL THESE.
WHOA!
I should have known...
ba bmp ba bmp
WHAT ABOUT THE LOVELY♡ BLAZERS SERIES?
I have all the DVDs!!
Heh
I GOT OVER THAT IN ELEMENTARY SCHOOL.
Oh...
...I see...
My fair Ume.
Mitchy
...care to have lunch with me sometime?
※ Trying everything.

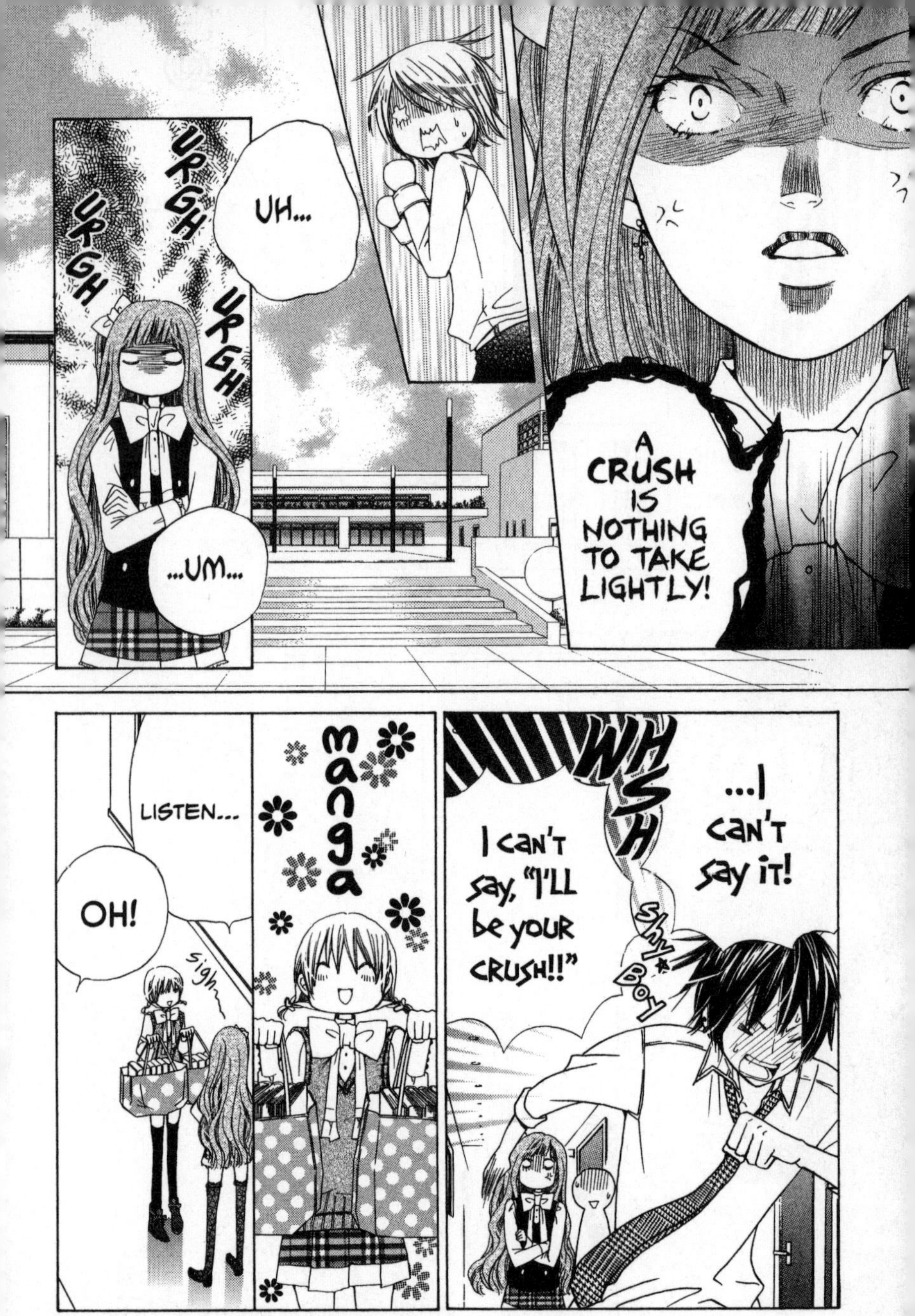
A CRUSH IS NOTHING TO TAKE LIGHTLY!
UH...
URGH URGH URGH
...UM...
WHSH
...I can't say it!
I can't say, "I'LL be your CRUSH!!"
SHY BOY
manga
LISTEN...
OH!
sigh

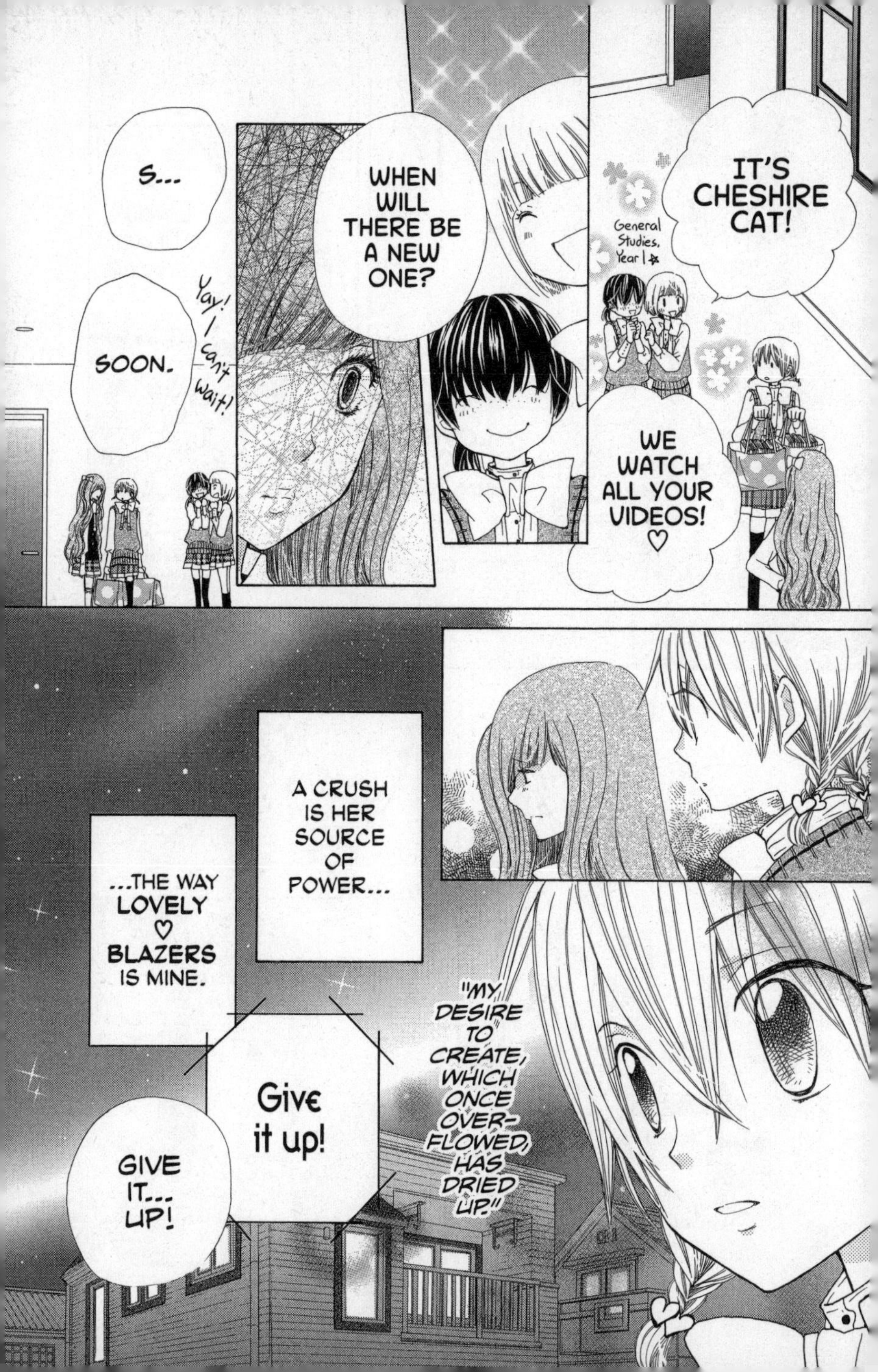
IT'S CHESHIRE CAT!
General Studies, Year 1 ☆
WE WATCH ALL YOUR VIDEOS! ♡
WHEN WILL THERE BE A NEW ONE?
S...
SOON.
Yay! I can't wait!
A CRUSH IS HER SOURCE OF POWER...
...THE WAY LOVELY ♡ BLAZERS IS MINE.
"MY DESIRE TO CREATE, WHICH ONCE OVER-FLOWED, HAS DRIED UP."
Give it up!
GIVE IT... UP!

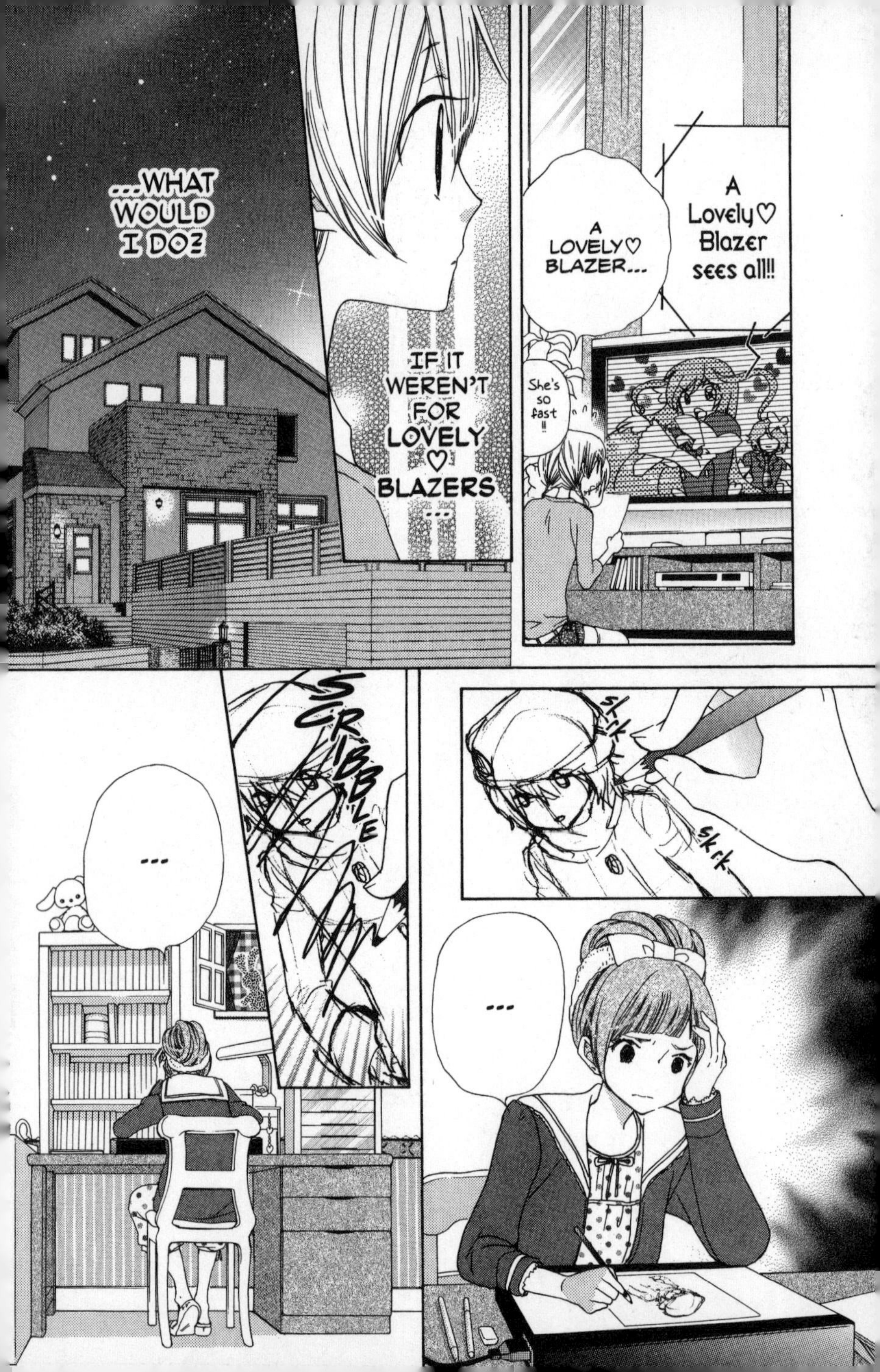
A Lovely♡ Blazer sees all!!
A LOVELY♡ BLAZER...
She's so fast!!
IF IT WEREN'T FOR LOVELY♡ BLAZERS...
...WHAT WOULD I DO?
skrk
skrk
SCRIBBLE
...
...

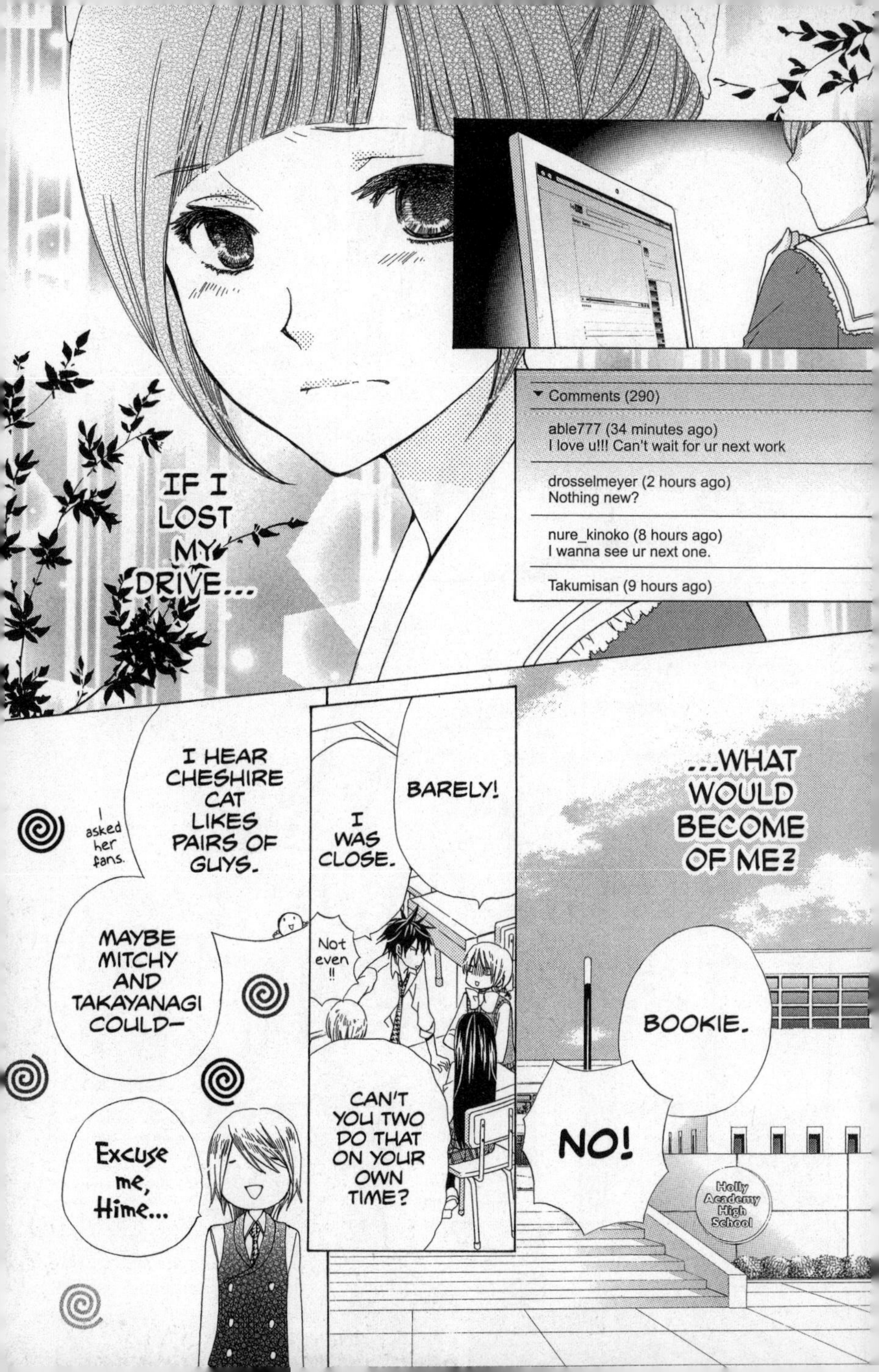

Comments (290)
able777 (34 minutes ago)
I love u!!! Can't wait for ur next work
drosselmeyer (2 hours ago)
Nothing new?
nure_kinoko (8 hours ago)
I wanna see ur next one.
Takumisan (9 hours ago)
IF I LOST MY DRIVE...
...WHAT WOULD BECOME OF ME?
BOOKIE.
NO!
Holly Academy High School
BARELY!
I WAS CLOSE.
Not even!!
CAN'T YOU TWO DO THAT ON YOUR OWN TIME?
I HEAR CHESHIRE CAT LIKES PAIRS OF GUYS.
I asked her fans.
MAYBE MITCHY AND TAKAYANAGI COULD—
Excuse me, Hime...

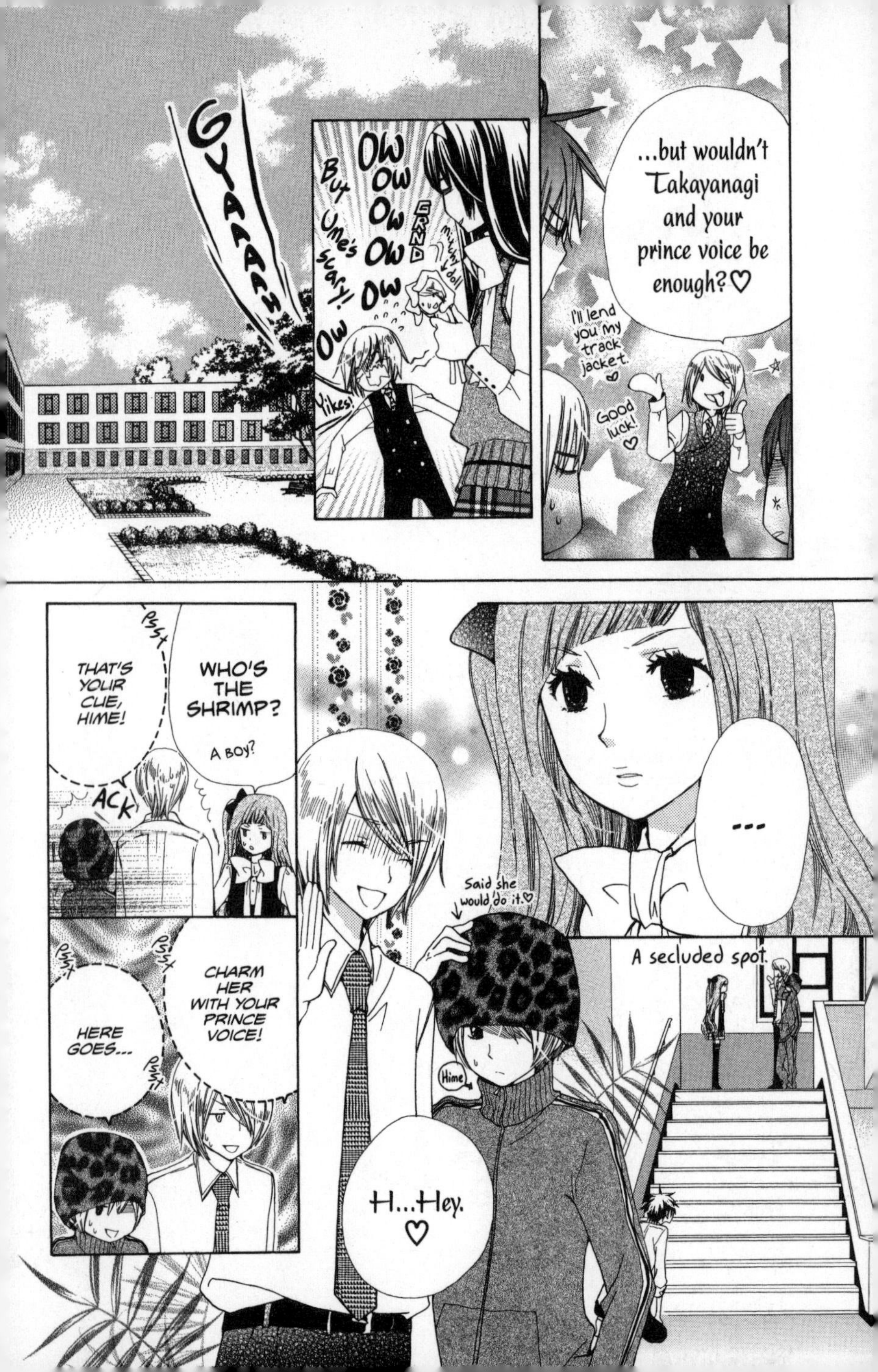
...but wouldn't Takayanagi and your prince voice be enough?♡
I'll lend you my track jacket.
Good luck!♡
OW OW OW OW OW OW OW
GRND
mitchy doll
But Ume's scary!!
Yikes!
GYAAAAAH
A secluded spot.
Said she would do it.♡
Hime
H...Hey. ♡
...
WHO'S THE SHRIMP?
A BOY?
PSST
THAT'S YOUR CUE, HIME!
ACK
PSST
CHARM HER WITH YOUR PRINCE VOICE!
PSST
HERE GOES...

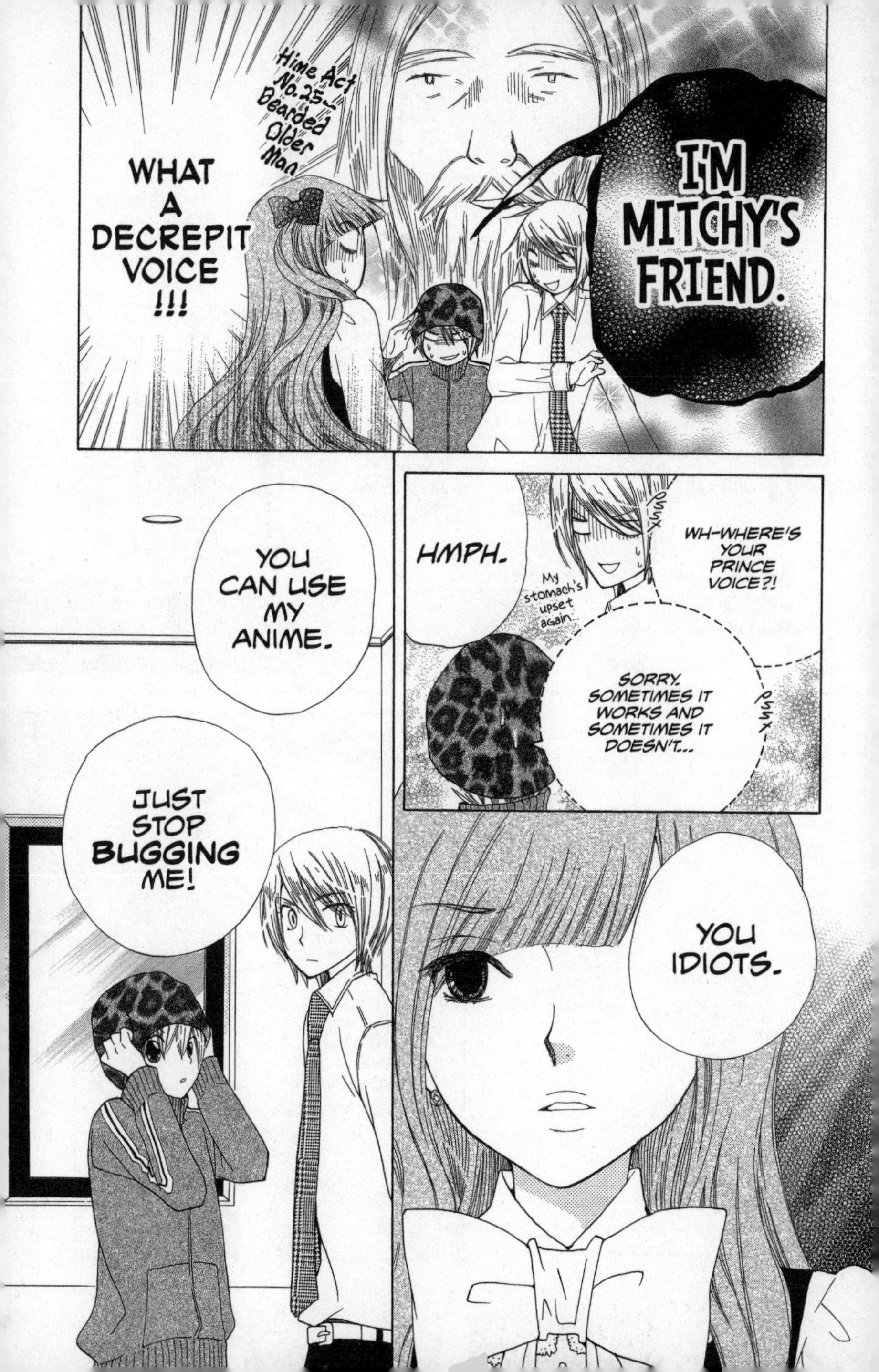
I'M MITCHY'S FRIEND.
Hime Act No.25 ~ Bearded Older Man
WHAT A DECREPIT VOICE!!!
PSST
WH-WHERE'S YOUR PRINCE VOICE?!
HMPH.
My stomach's upset again...
SORRY. SOMETIMES IT WORKS AND SOMETIMES IT DOESN'T...
PSST
YOU IDIOTS.
YOU CAN USE MY ANIME.
JUST STOP BUGGING ME!

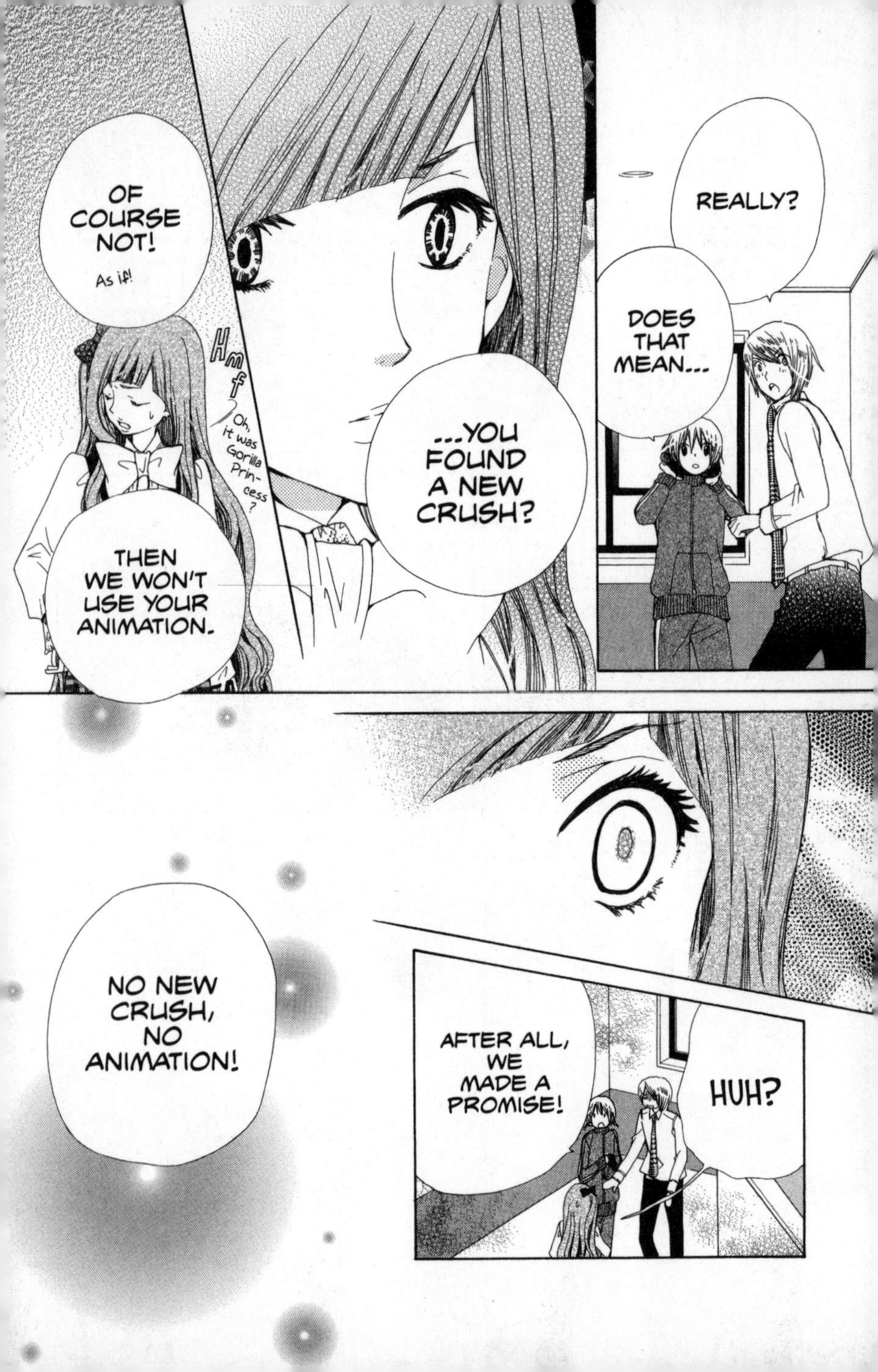
REALLY?
DOES THAT MEAN...
...YOU FOUND A NEW CRUSH?
OF COURSE NOT!
As if!
Hmf
Oh, it was Gorilla Prin-cess?
THEN WE WON'T USE YOUR ANIMATION.
HUH?
AFTER ALL, WE MADE A PROMISE!
NO NEW CRUSH, NO ANIMATION!

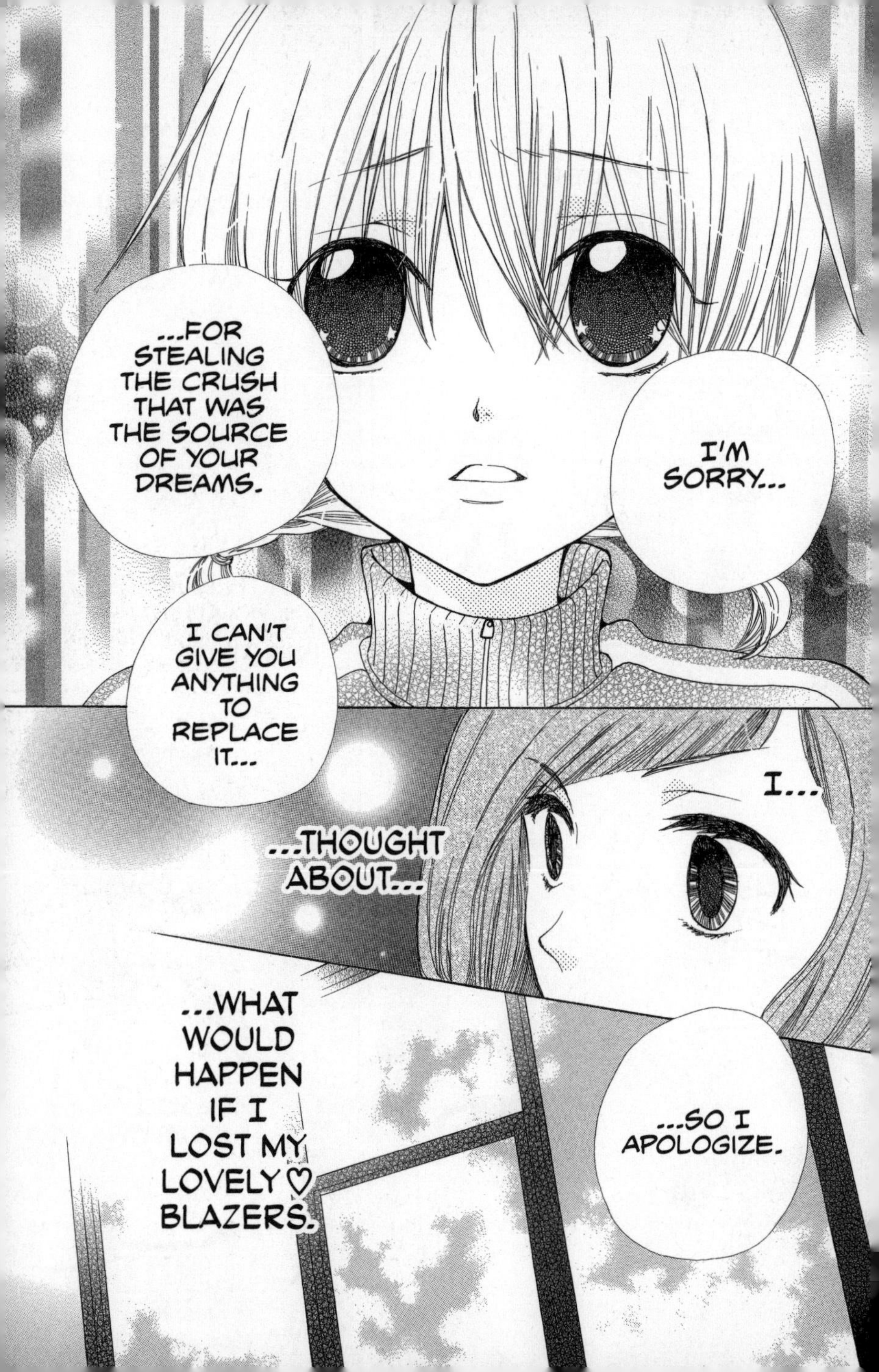
I'M SORRY...
...FOR STEALING THE CRUSH THAT WAS THE SOURCE OF YOUR DREAMS.
I CAN'T GIVE YOU ANYTHING TO REPLACE IT...
I...
...THOUGHT ABOUT...
...WHAT WOULD HAPPEN IF I LOST MY LOVELY ♡ BLAZERS.
...SO I APOLOGIZE.

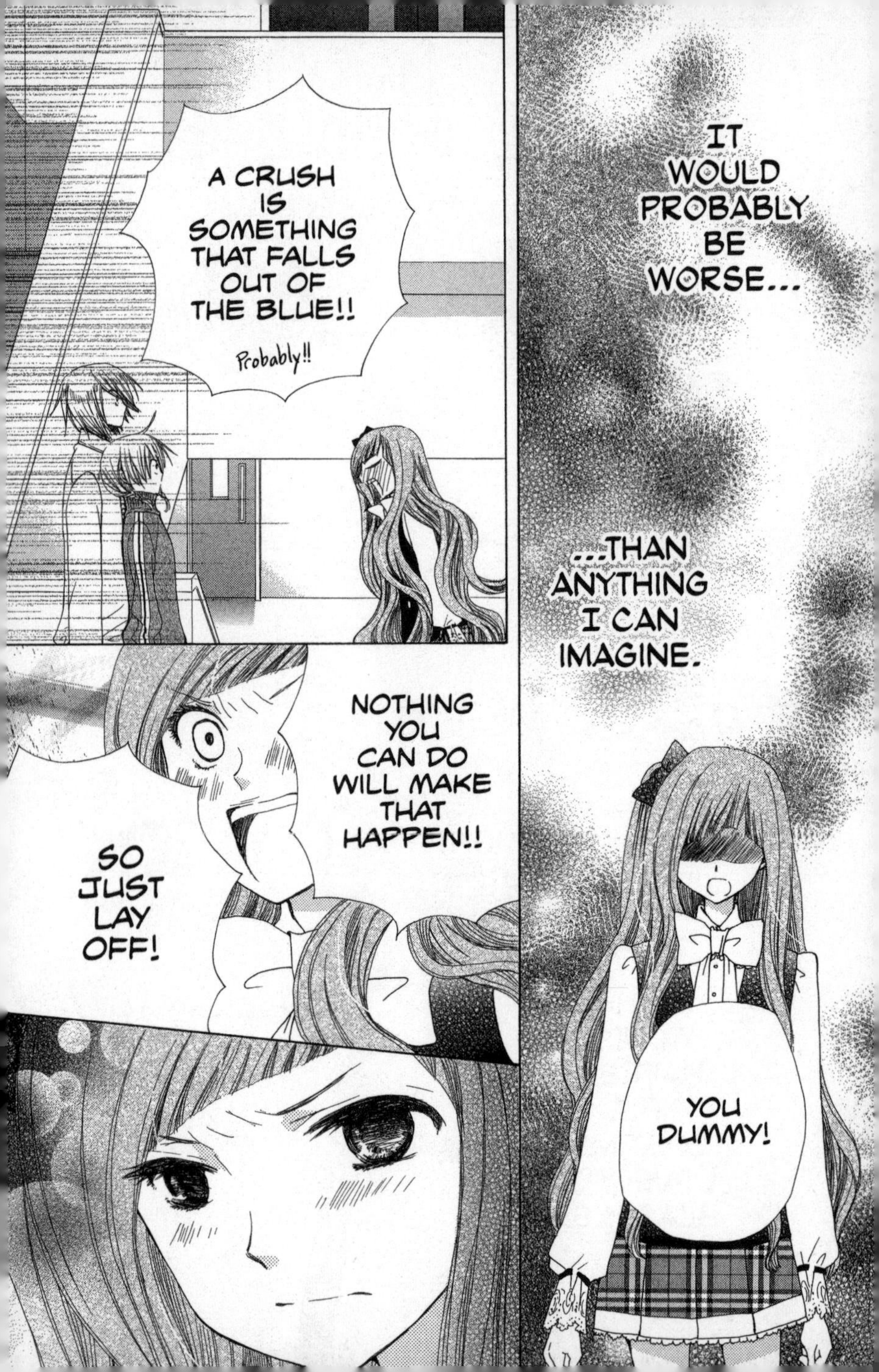
IT WOULD PROBABLY BE WORSE...
...THAN ANYTHING I CAN IMAGINE.
YOU DUMMY!
A CRUSH IS SOMETHING THAT FALLS OUT OF THE BLUE!!
Probably!!
NOTHING YOU CAN DO WILL MAKE THAT HAPPEN!!
SO JUST LAY OFF!

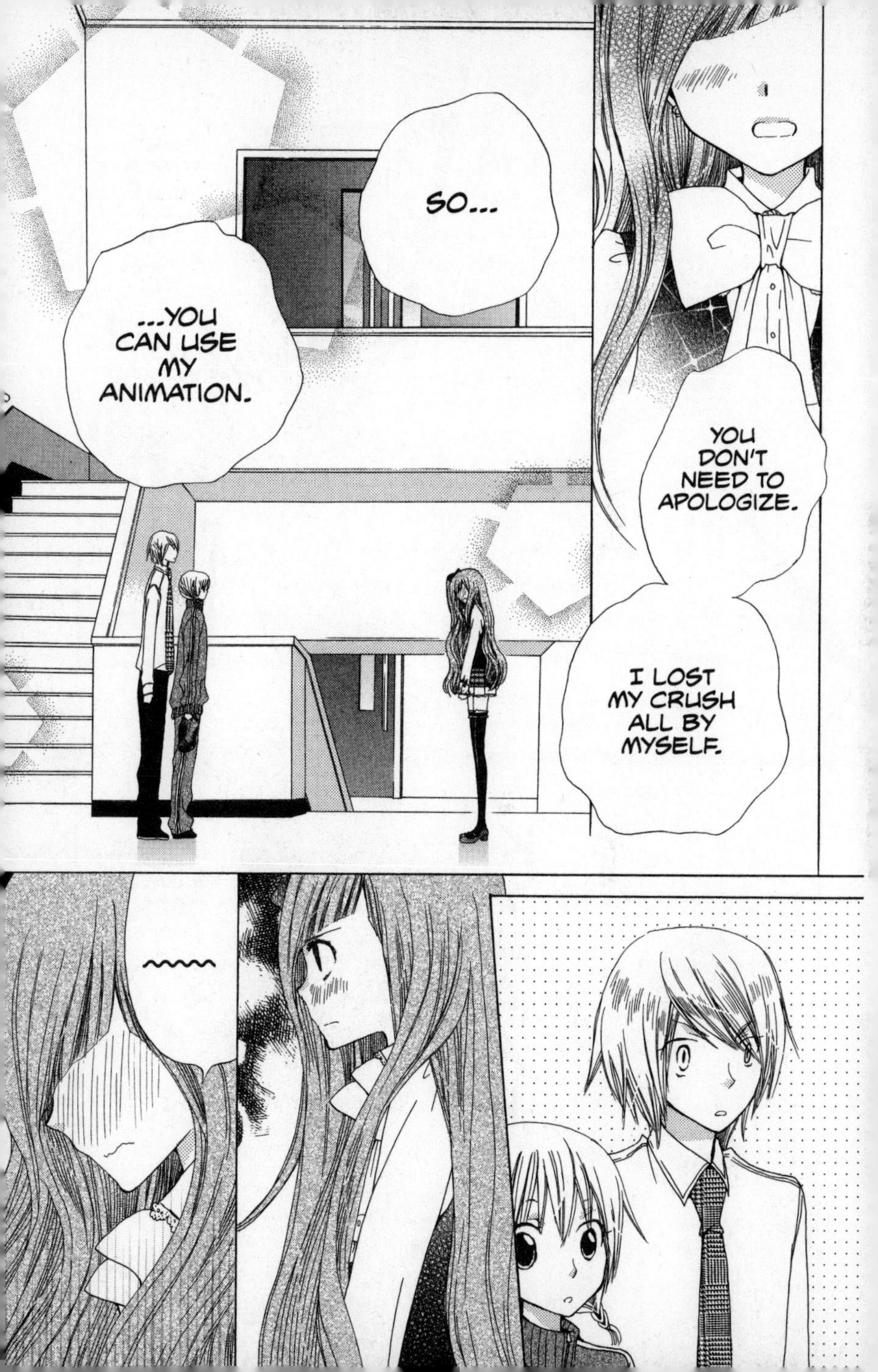
YOU DON'T NEED TO APOLOGIZE.
I LOST MY CRUSH ALL BY MYSELF.
SO...
...YOU CAN USE MY ANIMATION.
~~~
~~~

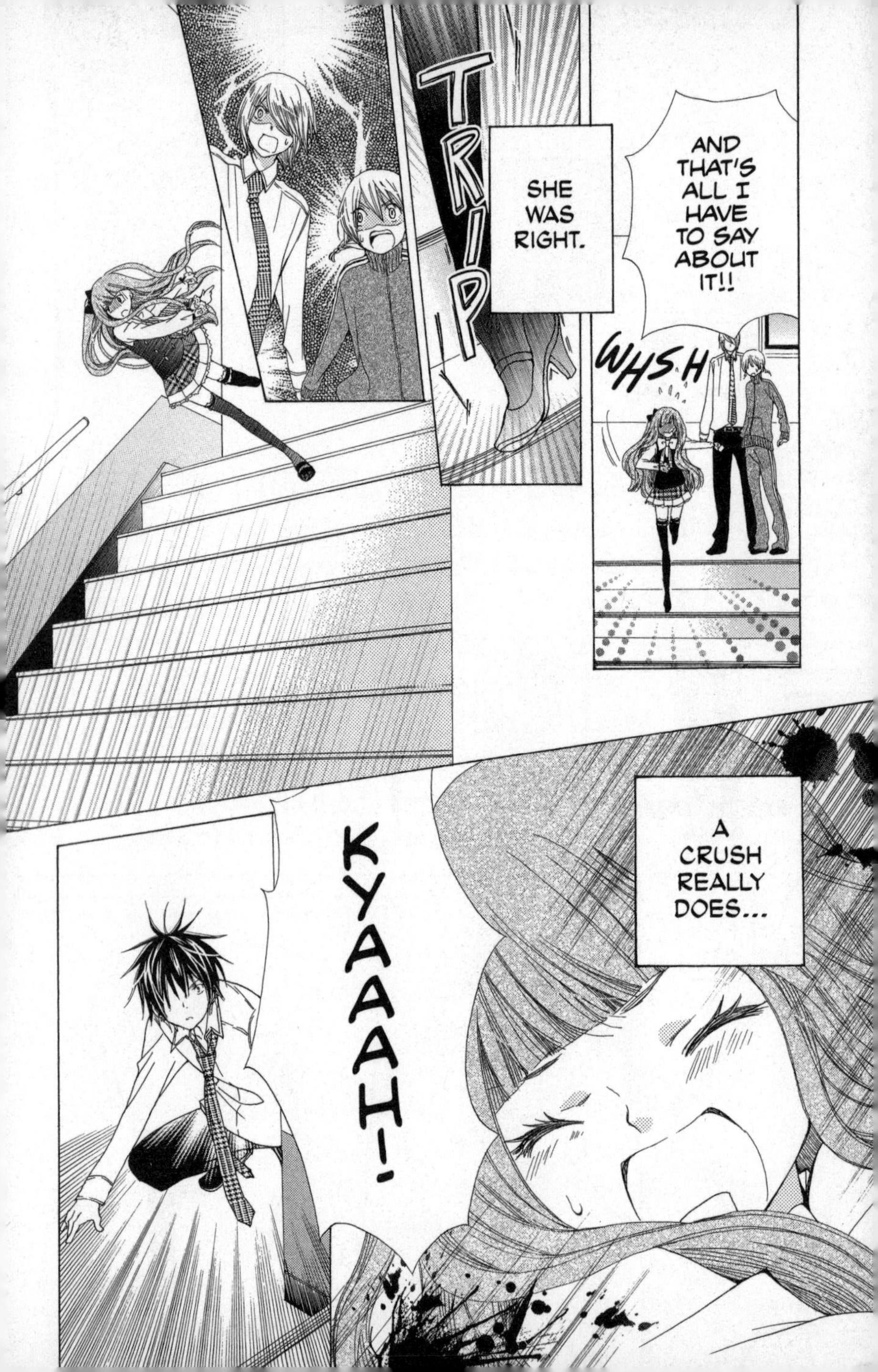
AND THAT'S ALL I HAVE TO SAY ABOUT IT!!
WHSH
SHE WAS RIGHT.
TRIP
A CRUSH REALLY DOES...
KYAAAH!

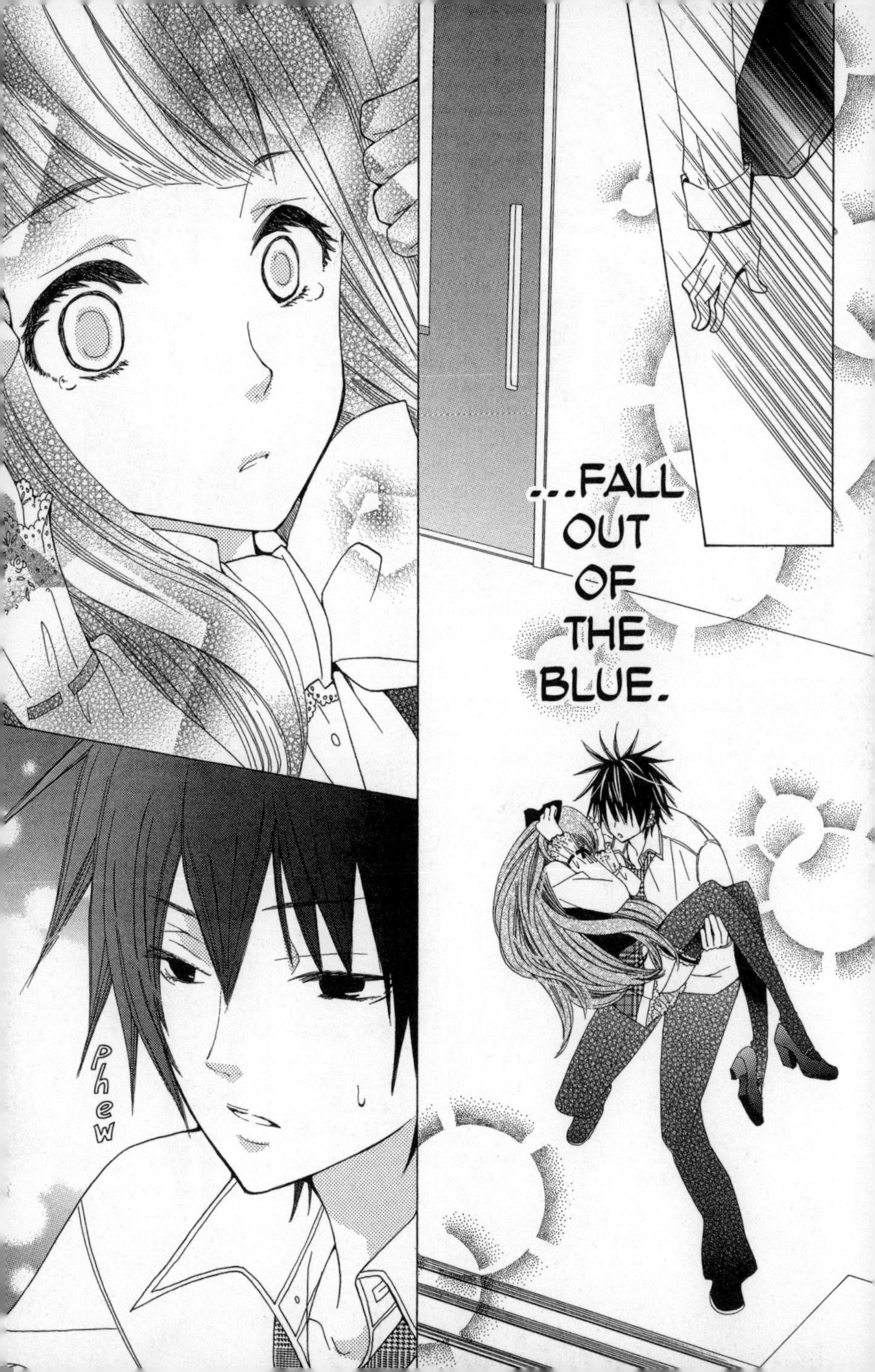
...FALL OUT OF THE BLUE.
Phew

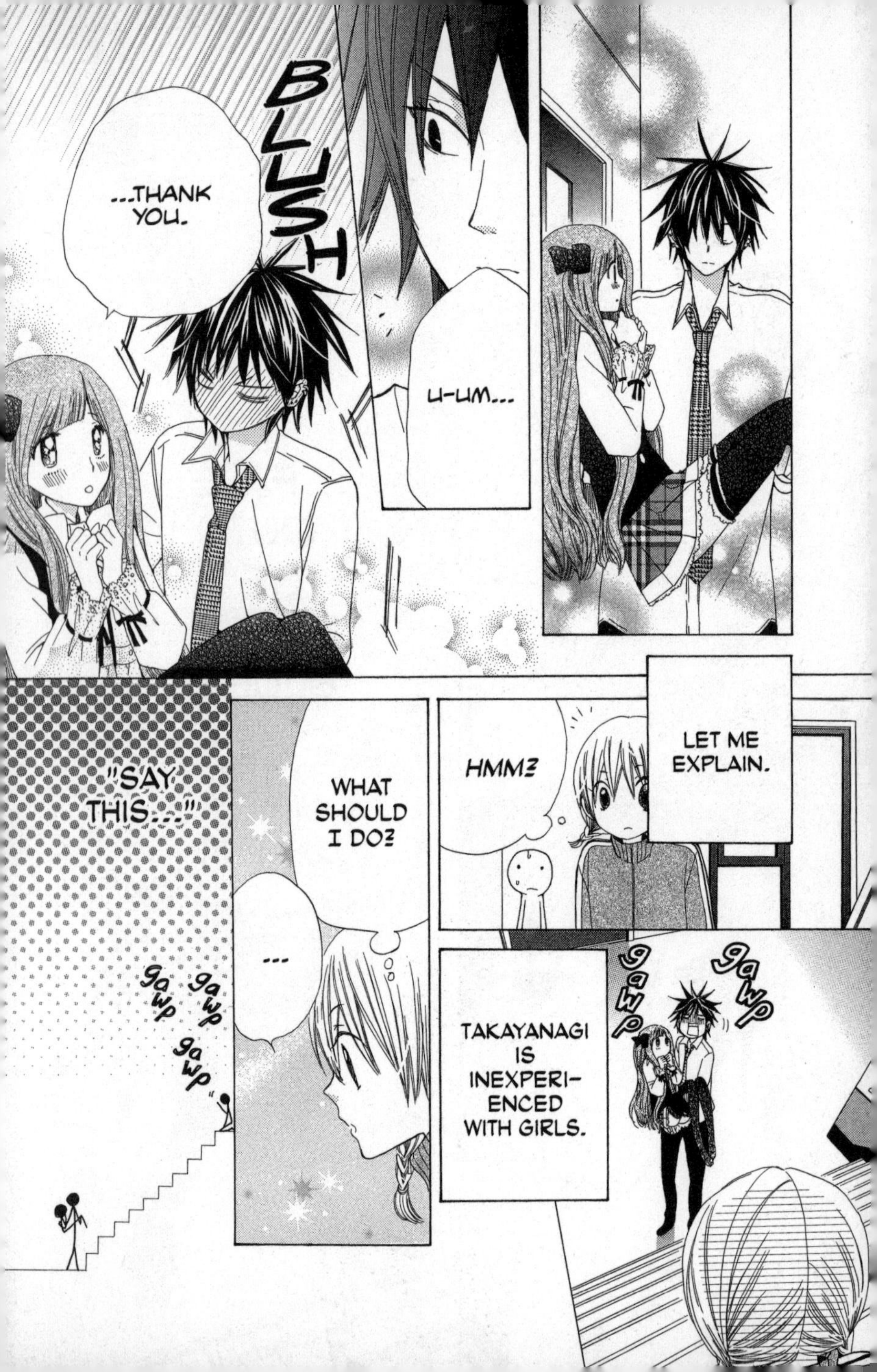
U-UM...
BLUSH
...THANK YOU.
LET ME EXPLAIN.
HMM?
gawp
gawp
TAKAYANAGI IS INEXPERI-ENCED WITH GIRLS.
WHAT SHOULD I DO?
...
"SAY THIS..."
gawp
gawp
gawp

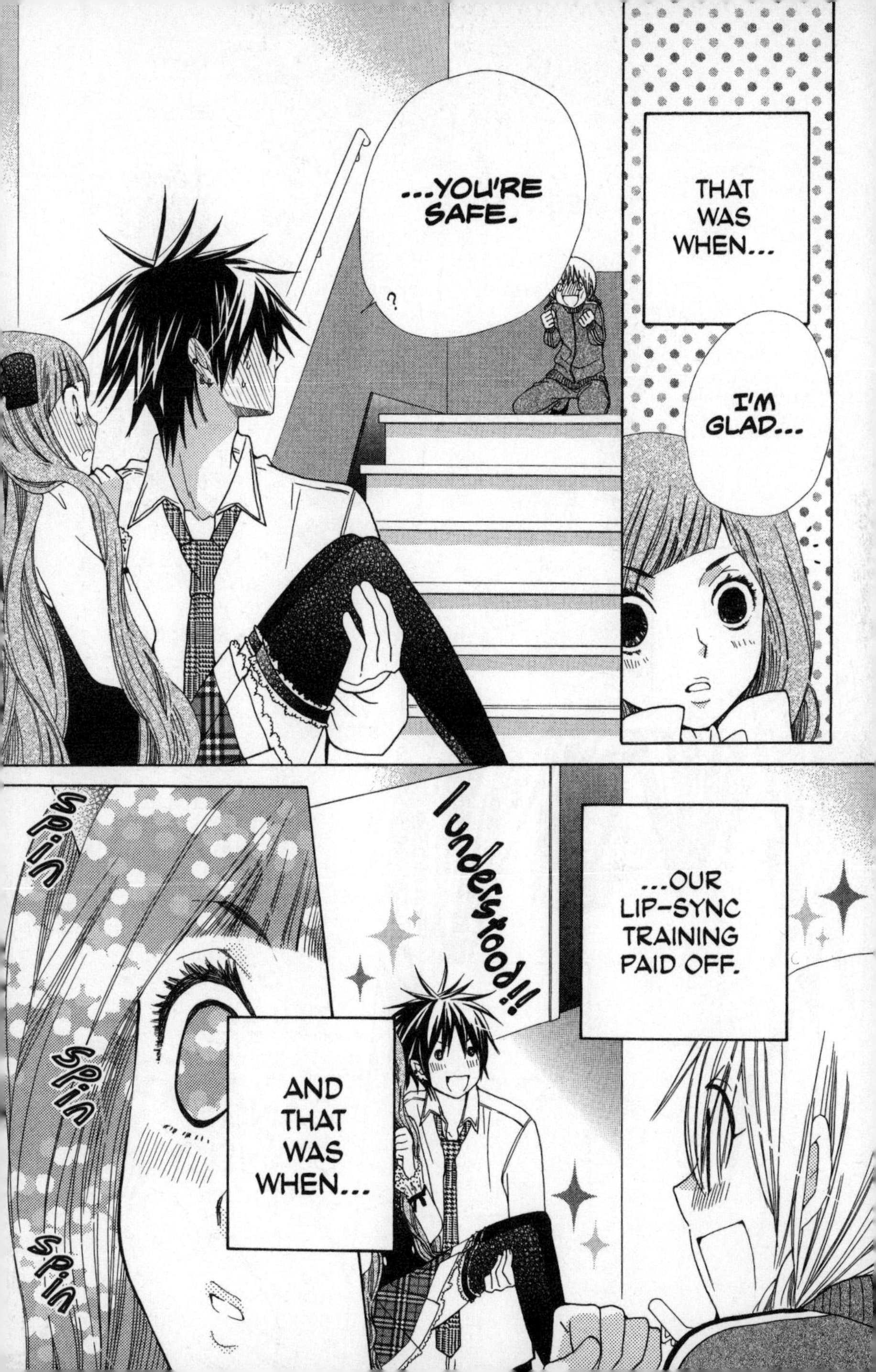
THAT WAS WHEN...
I'M GLAD...
...YOU'RE SAFE.
?
...OUR LIP-SYNC TRAINING PAID OFF.
I understood!!
AND THAT WAS WHEN...
spin
spin
spin

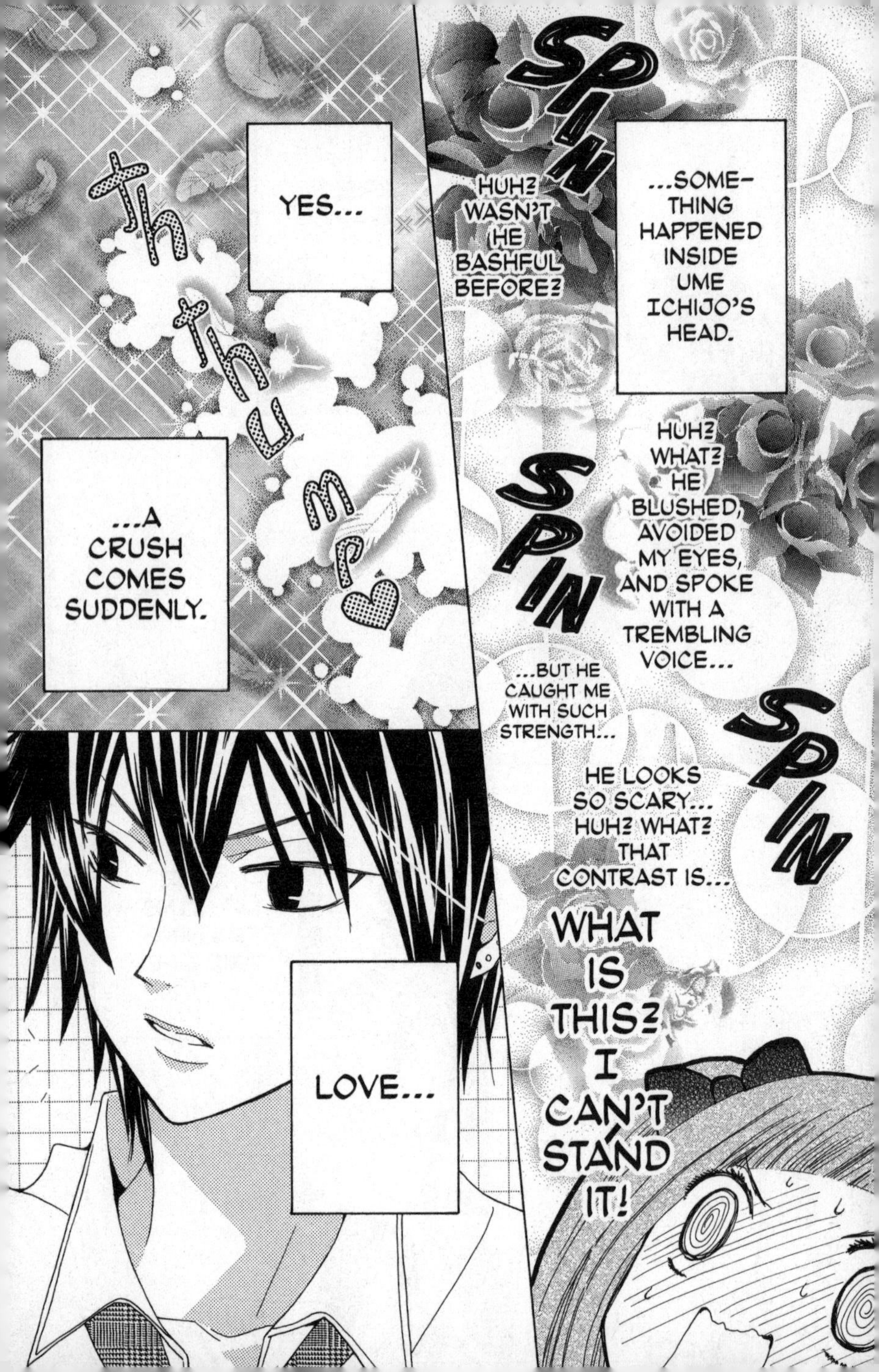
SPIN
...SOMETHING HAPPENED INSIDE UME ICHIJO'S HEAD.
HUH? WASN'T HE BASHFUL BEFORE?
HUH? WHAT? HE BLUSHED, AVOIDED MY EYES, AND SPOKE WITH A TREMBLING VOICE...
SPIN
SPIN
...BUT HE CAUGHT ME WITH SUCH STRENGTH...
HE LOOKS SO SCARY... HUH? WHAT? THAT CONTRAST IS...
WHAT IS THIS? I CAN'T STAND IT!
YES...
Ththump
...A CRUSH COMES SUDDENLY.
LOVE...

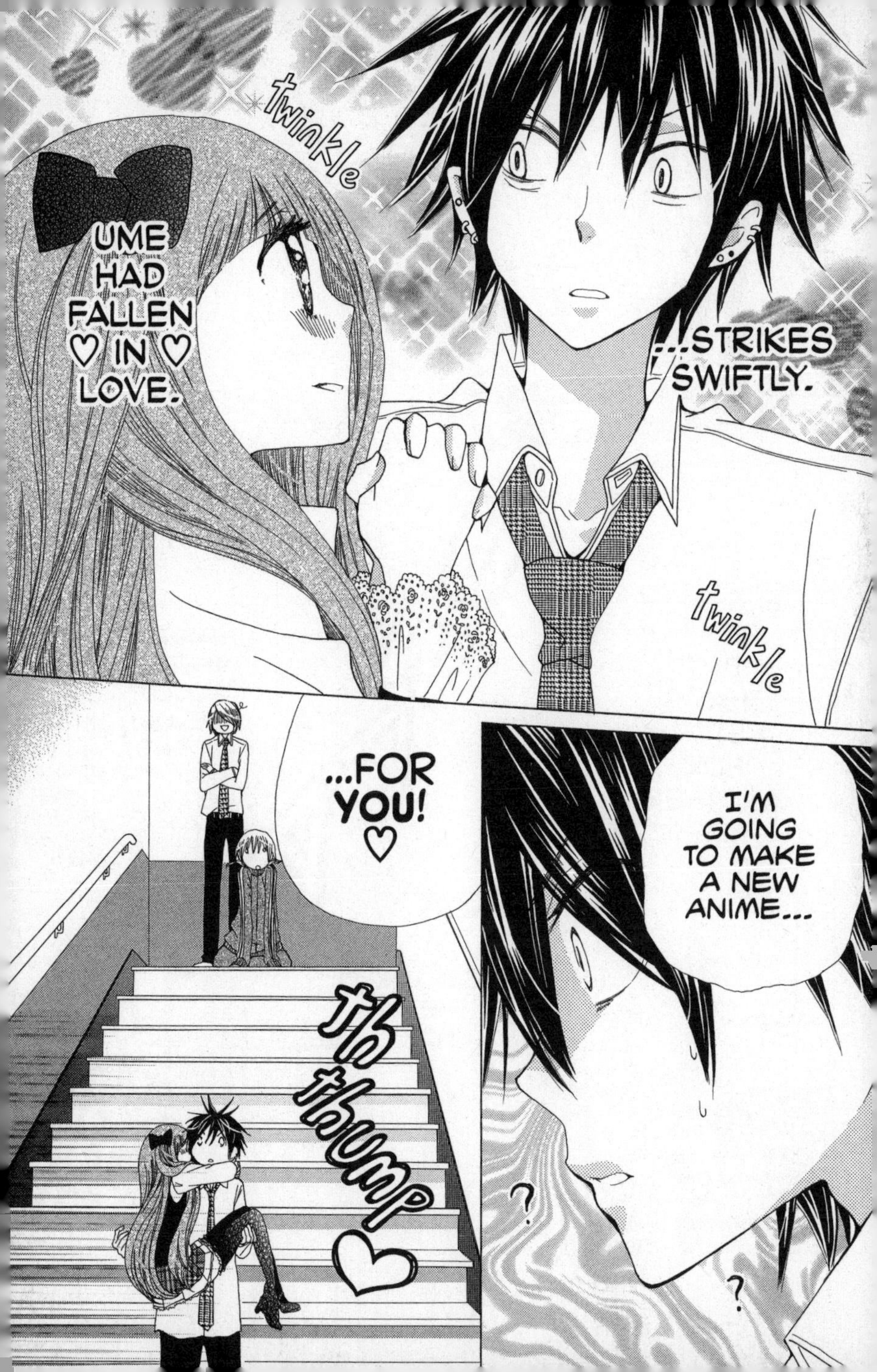
twinkle
...STRIKES SWIFTLY.
UME HAD FALLEN ♡ IN ♡ LOVE.
twinkle
I'M GOING TO MAKE A NEW ANIME...
...FOR YOU! ♡
?
?
th thump ♡

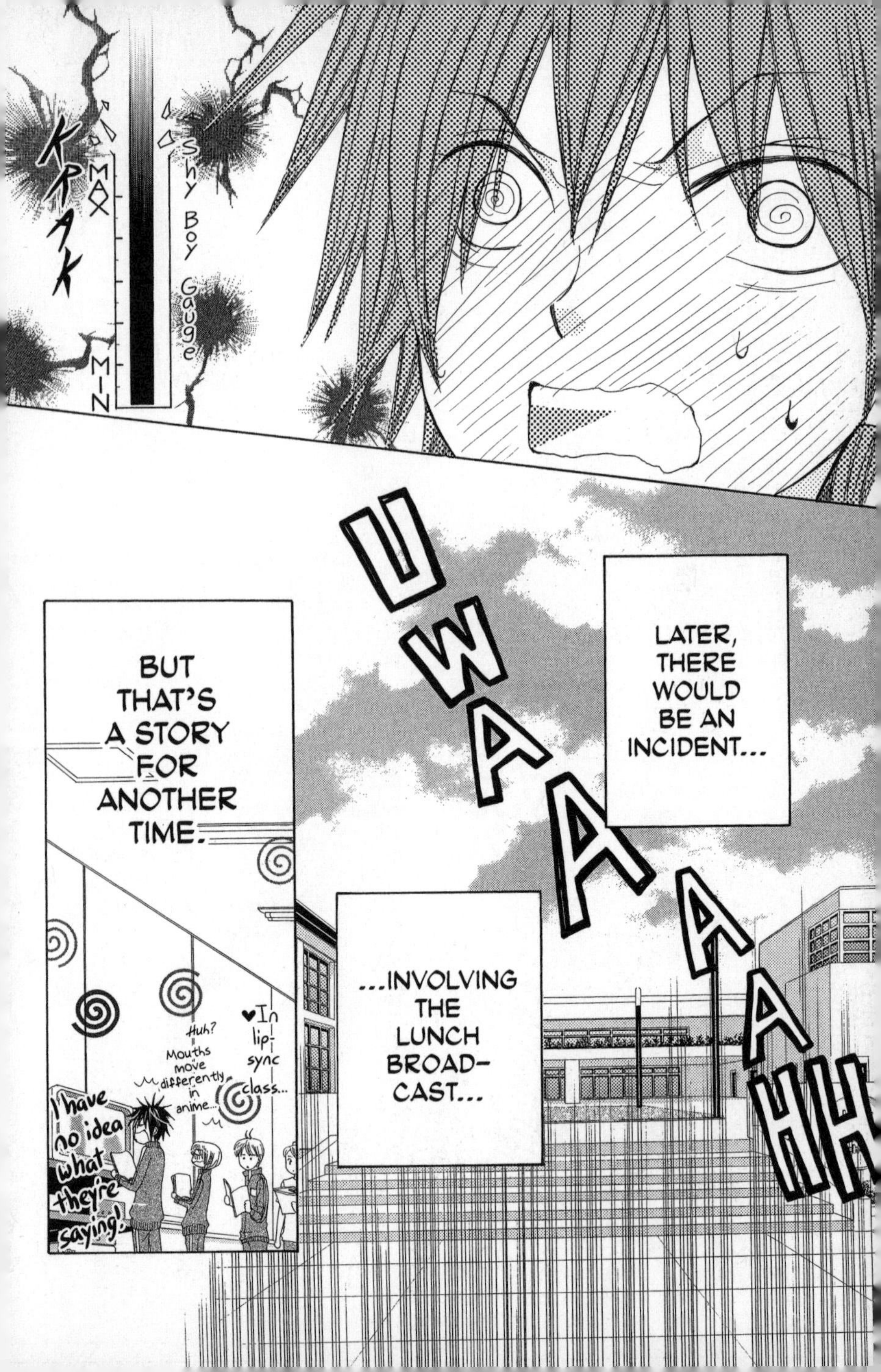
Shy Boy Gauge
MAX
MIN
KRAK
UWAAAAHH
LATER, THERE WOULD BE AN INCIDENT...
...INVOLVING THE LUNCH BROADCAST...
BUT THAT'S A STORY FOR ANOTHER TIME.
In lip-sync class...
Huh? Mouths move differently in anime...
I have no idea what they're saying!

Chapter 7

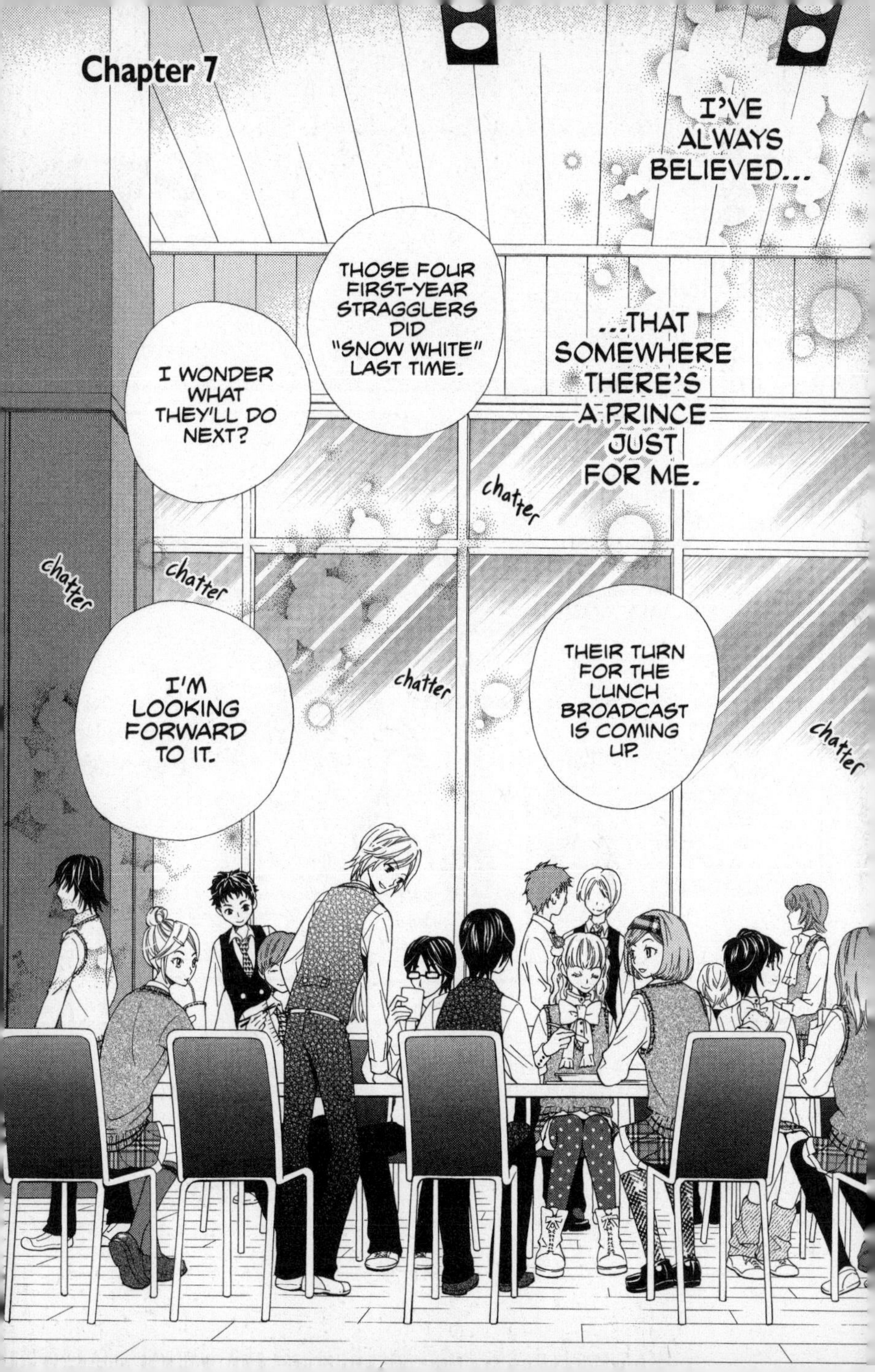
I'VE ALWAYS BELIEVED...
...THAT SOMEWHERE THERE'S A PRINCE JUST FOR ME.
THOSE FOUR FIRST-YEAR STRAGGLERS DID "SNOW WHITE" LAST TIME.
I WONDER WHAT THEY'LL DO NEXT?
chatter
THEIR TURN FOR THE LUNCH BROADCAST IS COMING UP.
I'M LOOKING FORWARD TO IT.
chatter
chatter
chatter
chatter

DON'T RUIN UME'S MOOD BEFORE THE BROAD-CAST!
GOT IT, YOU GUYS?
WHY NOT?!
NO WAY!
I hate her! She was mean to Hime!
Okay!!
Various Answers
GYAH
And you want to be entertainers?!
How can you fools ask why or refuse?!
GYAH
Someone who has to take a potty break in the middle of a performance has no right to talk.
I'm sorry about that!!
GYAH
She was against it at first.
UME IS GOING TO MAKE A NEW ANIMATION FOR OUR NEXT BROADCAST!!
IF WE RUIN HER MOOD, WE'LL BE THE ONES WHO SUFFER!
This is our chance to voice an anime!!

Voice Over! ②

This is volume 2 of *Voice Over!: Seiyu Academy*. This time is about another lunch broadcast. It was fun drawing the animator Ume and the shy boy Takayanagi.

I enjoy drawing such a close-knit group of characters.

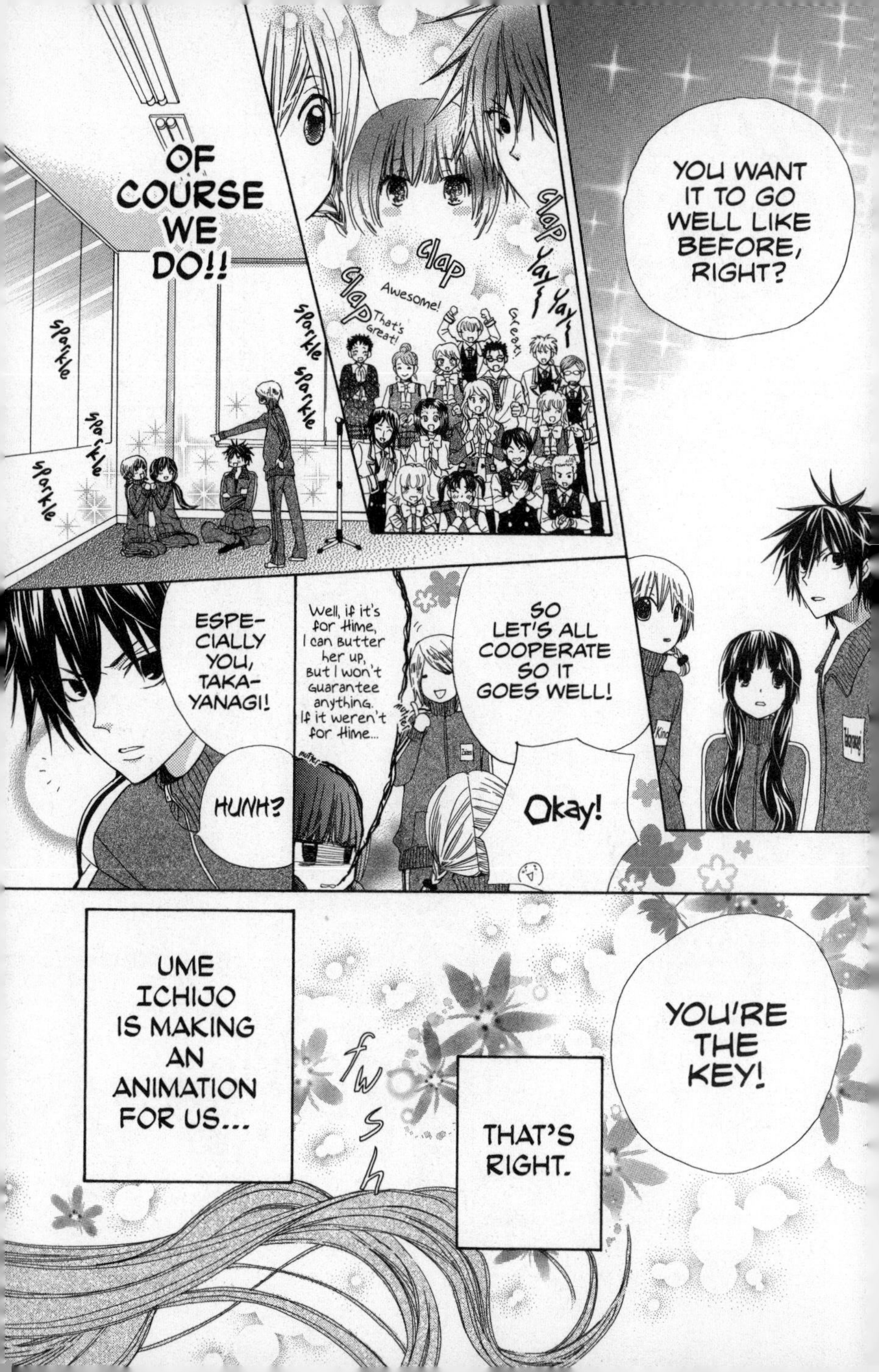
YOU WANT IT TO GO WELL LIKE BEFORE, RIGHT?
clap
Yay~ Yay~
clap clap
Awesome!
Great!
That's great!
OF COURSE WE DO!!
sparkle sparkle
sparkle sparkle
SO LET'S ALL COOPERATE SO IT GOES WELL!
Okay!
Well, if it's for Hime, I can butter her up, but I won't guarantee anything. If it weren't for Hime...
mutter
mutter
ESPE-CIALLY YOU, TAKA-YANAGI!
HUNH?
YOU'RE THE KEY!
THAT'S RIGHT.
fwsh
UME ICHIJO IS MAKING AN ANIMATION FOR US...

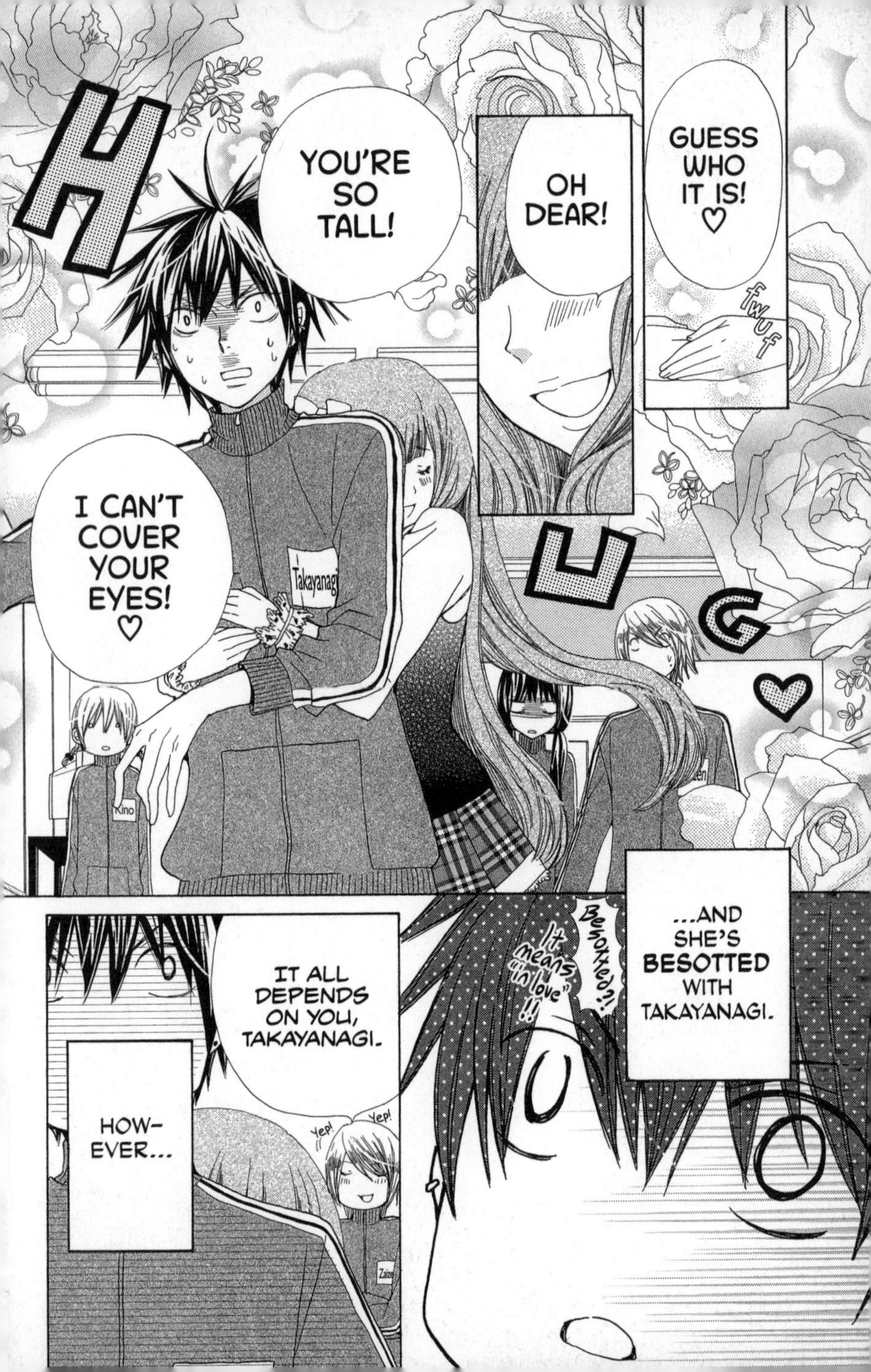
GUESS WHO IT IS! ♡
fwuf
OH DEAR!
YOU'RE SO TALL!
HUG ♥
Takayanagi
I CAN'T COVER YOUR EYES! ♡
Kino
...AND SHE'S BESOTTED WITH TAKAYANAGI.
Besotted?!
It means "in love"!!
IT ALL DEPENDS ON YOU, TAKAYANAGI.
Yep! Yep!
HOW-EVER...

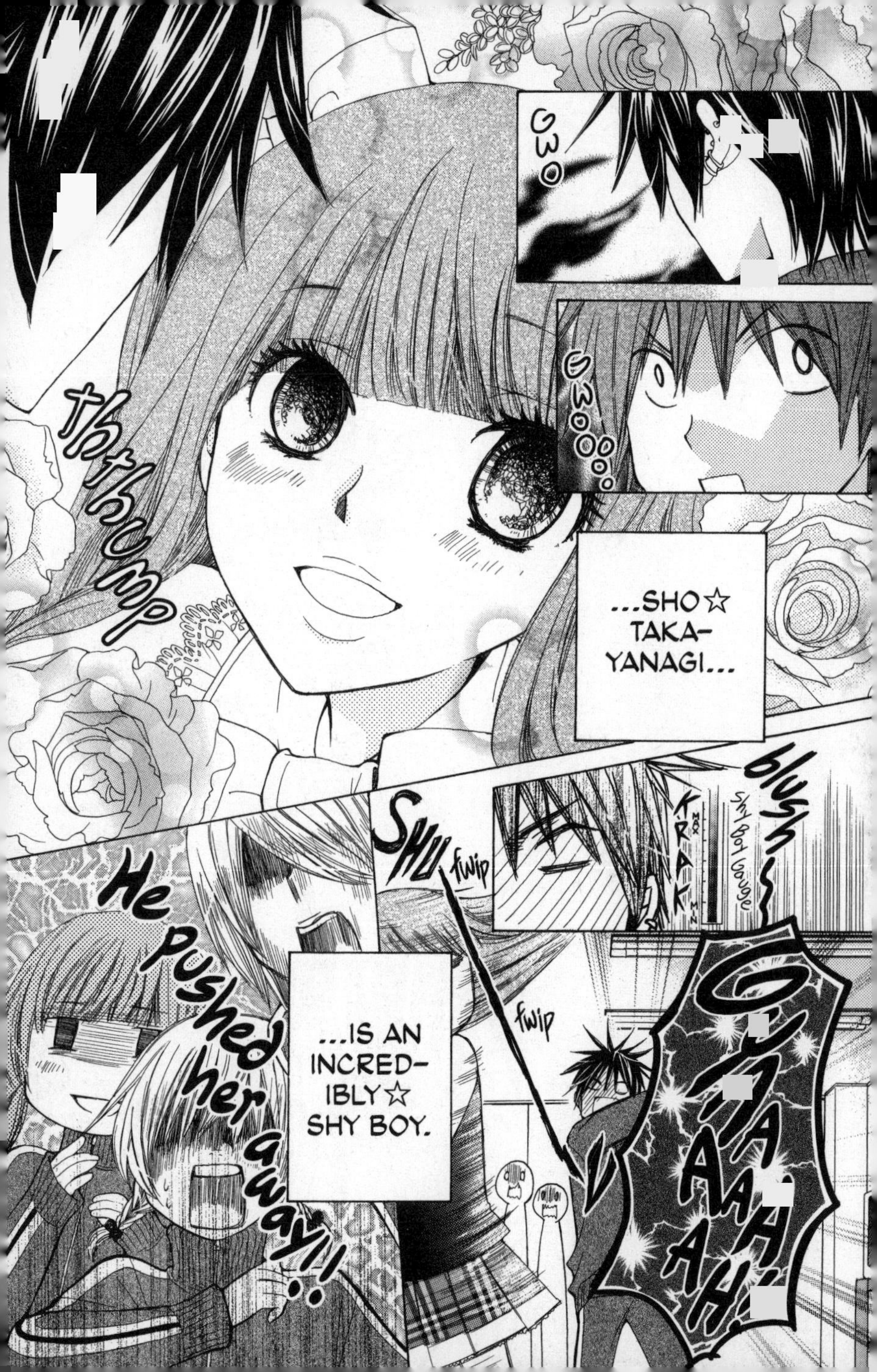
GWO
GWOOOOoo
ththump
...SHO☆ TAKA-YANAGI...
blush
Shy Boy Gauge
MAX
KRAK
MIN
SHU
fwip
GYAAAAH
fwip
...IS AN INCRED-IBLY☆ SHY BOY.
He pushed her away!!

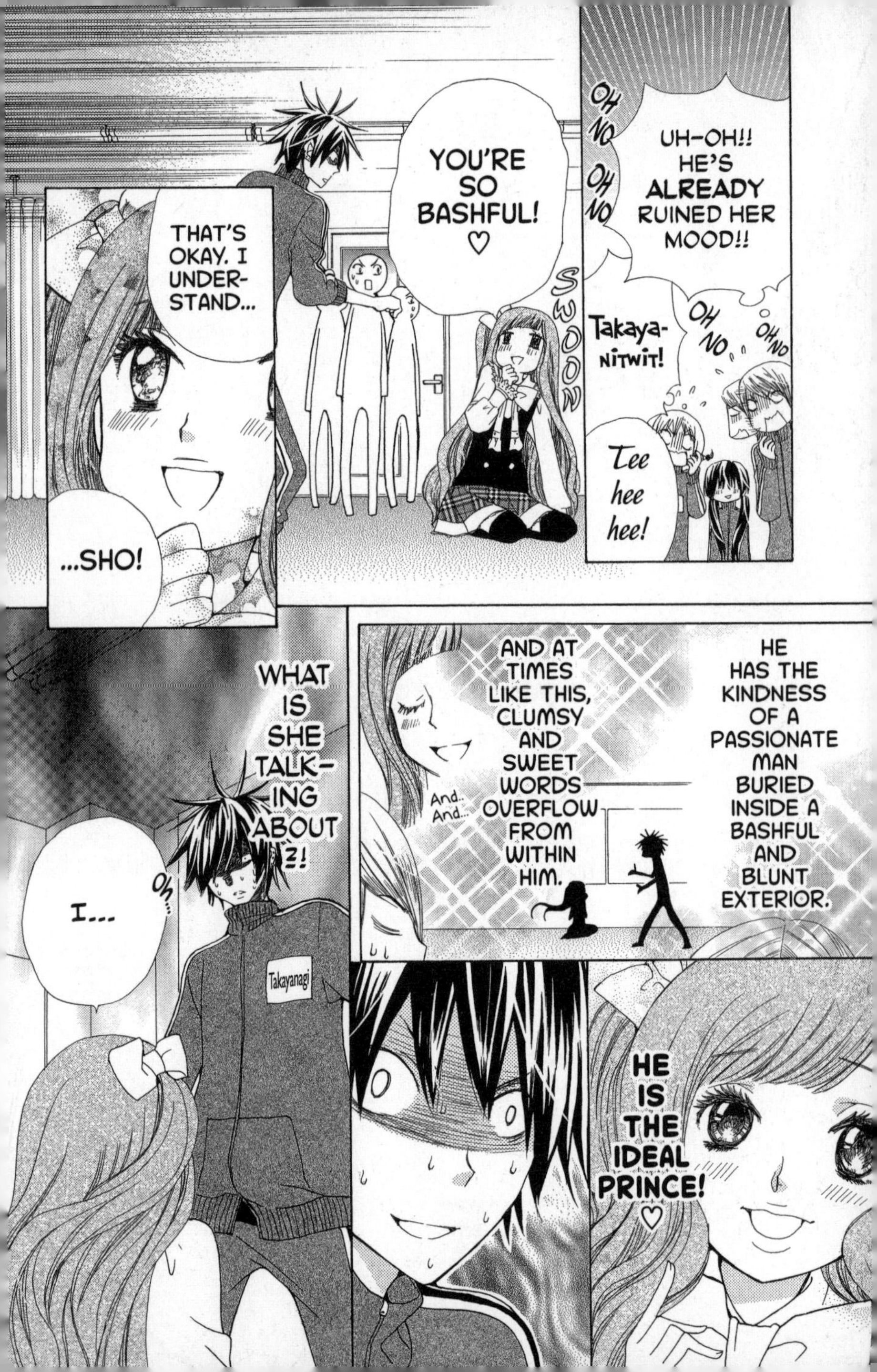
UH-OH!! HE'S ALREADY RUINED HER MOOD!!
OH NO OH NO
Takaya-NITWIT!
OH NO
OH NO
Tee hee hee!
YOU'RE SO BASHFUL! ♡
SWOON
THAT'S OKAY. I UNDERSTAND...
...SHO!
HE HAS THE KINDNESS OF A PASSIONATE MAN BURIED INSIDE A BASHFUL AND BLUNT EXTERIOR.
AND AT TIMES LIKE THIS, CLUMSY AND SWEET WORDS OVERFLOW FROM WITHIN HIM.
And.. And...
HE IS THE IDEAL PRINCE! ♡
WHAT IS SHE TALKING ABOUT?!
OH...
I...
Takayanagi

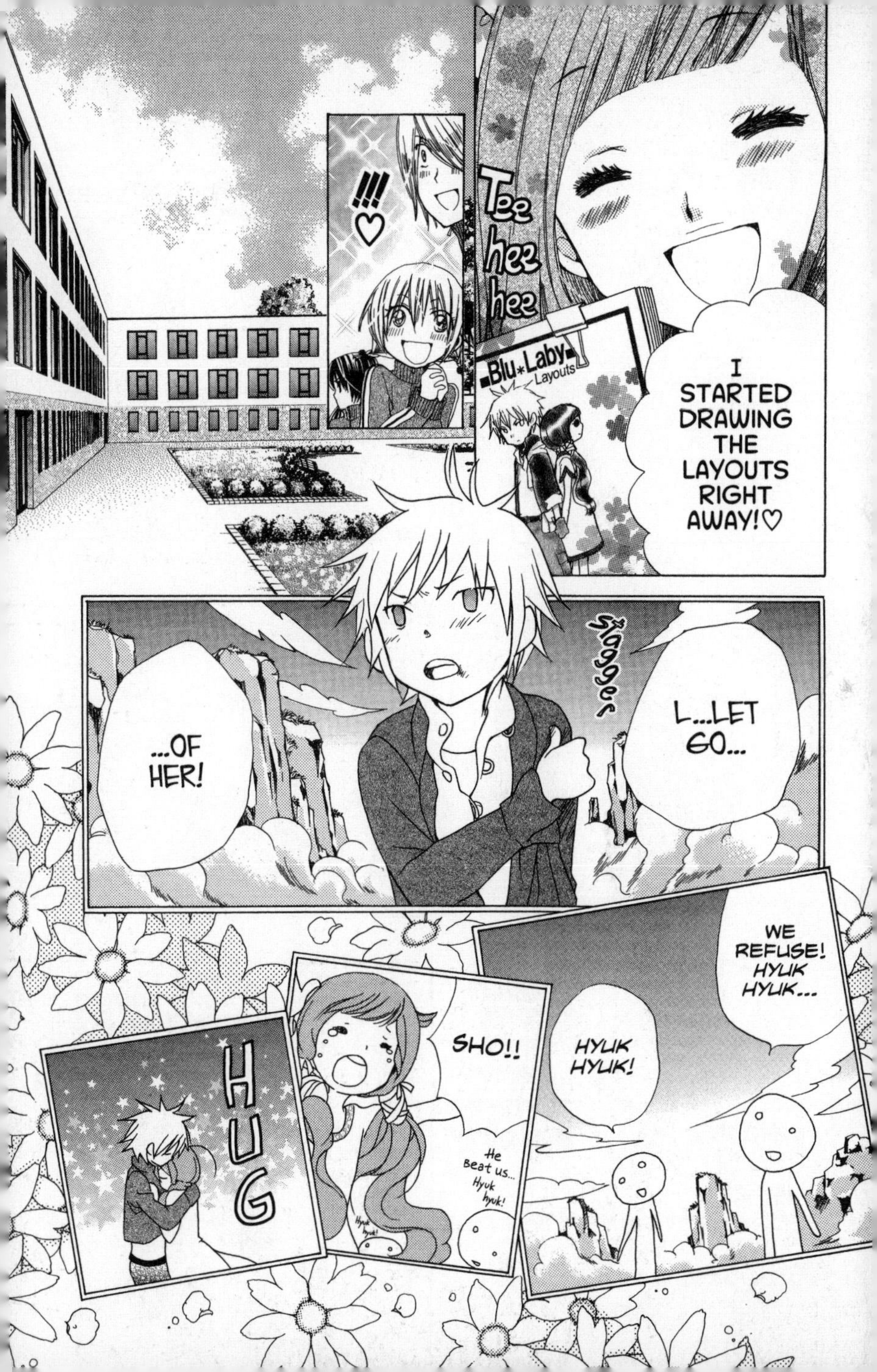
Tee hee hee
I STARTED DRAWING THE LAYOUTS RIGHT AWAY!♡
Blu*Laby Layouts
!!! ♡
L...LET GO...
Stagger
...OF HER!
WE REFUSE! HYUK HYUK...
HYUK HYUK!
SHO!!
He beat us... Hyuk hyuk!
HUG

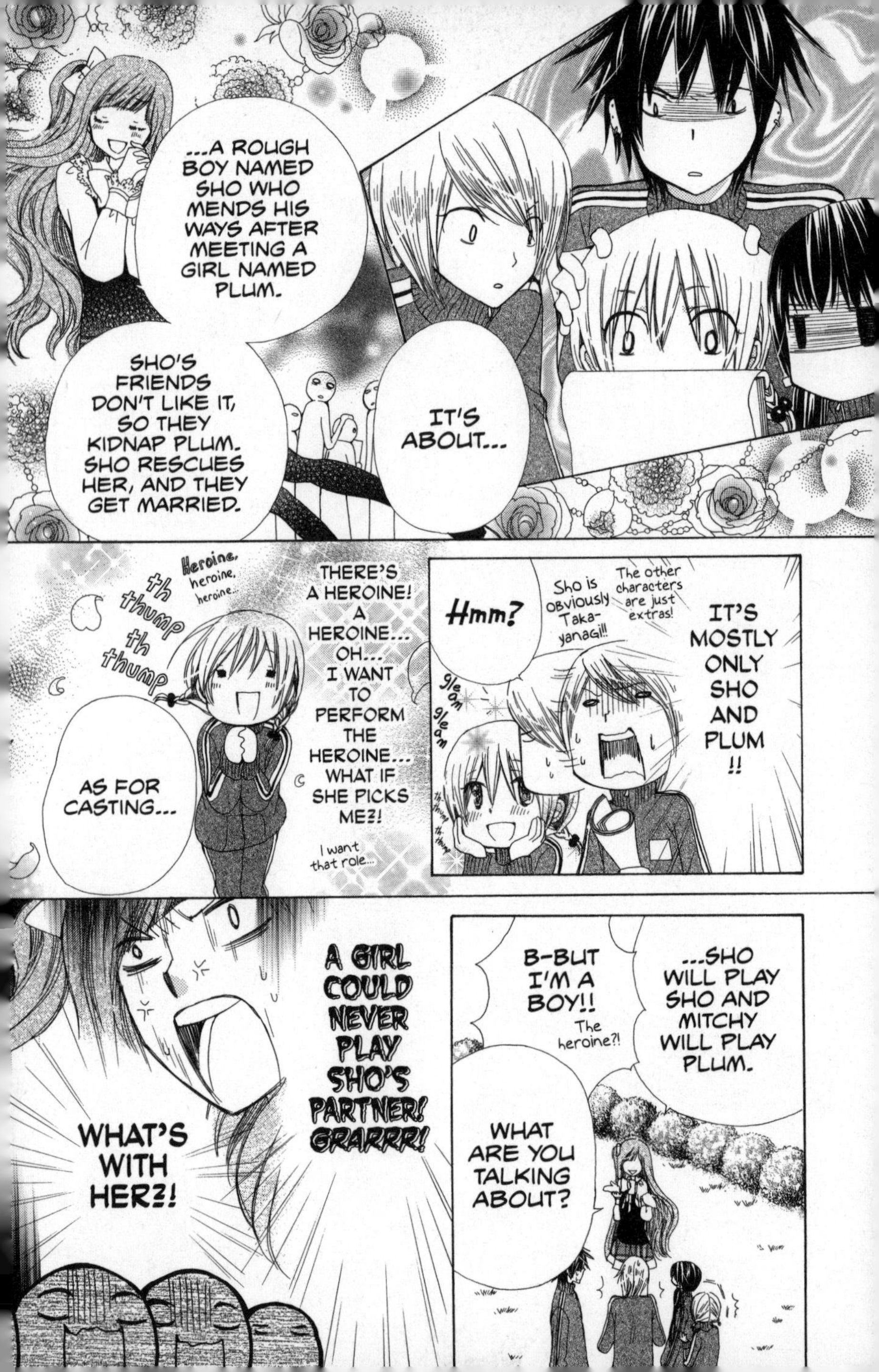
IT'S ABOUT...
...A ROUGH BOY NAMED SHO WHO MENDS HIS WAYS AFTER MEETING A GIRL NAMED PLUM.
SHO'S FRIENDS DON'T LIKE IT, SO THEY KIDNAP PLUM. SHO RESCUES HER, AND THEY GET MARRIED.
IT'S MOSTLY ONLY SHO AND PLUM!!
The other characters are just extras!
Sho is obviously Taka-yanagi!!
Hmm?
gleam gleam
th-thump th-thump
Heroine, heroine, heroine...
THERE'S A HEROINE! A HEROINE... OH... I WANT TO PERFORM THE HEROINE... WHAT IF SHE PICKS ME?!
th thump th thump
AS FOR CASTING...
I want that role...
...SHO WILL PLAY SHO AND MITCHY WILL PLAY PLUM.
B-BUT I'M A BOY!!
The heroine?!
WHAT ARE YOU TALKING ABOUT?
A GIRL COULD NEVER PLAY SHO'S PARTNER! GRARRR!
WHAT'S WITH HER?!

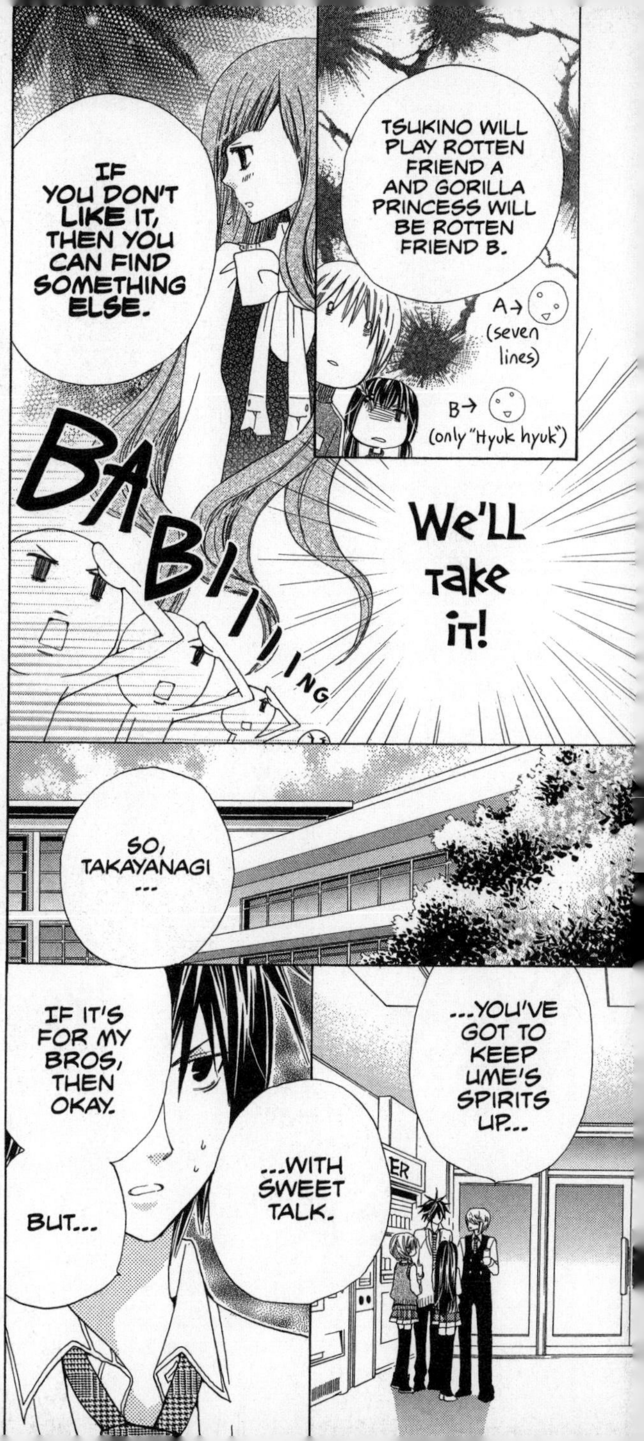
TSUKINO WILL PLAY ROTTEN FRIEND A AND GORILLA PRINCESS WILL BE ROTTEN FRIEND B.
A→ (seven lines)
B→ (only "Hyuk hyuk")
IF YOU DON'T LIKE IT, THEN YOU CAN FIND SOMETHING ELSE.
We'LL Take iT!
BABIIIING
SO, TAKAYANAGI...
...YOU'VE GOT TO KEEP UME'S SPIRITS UP...
...WITH SWEET TALK.
IF IT'S FOR MY BROS, THEN OKAY.
BUT...

• Concert •

A friend once invited me to a concert. Our seats were awesome, so I was in a great mood throughout the concert.

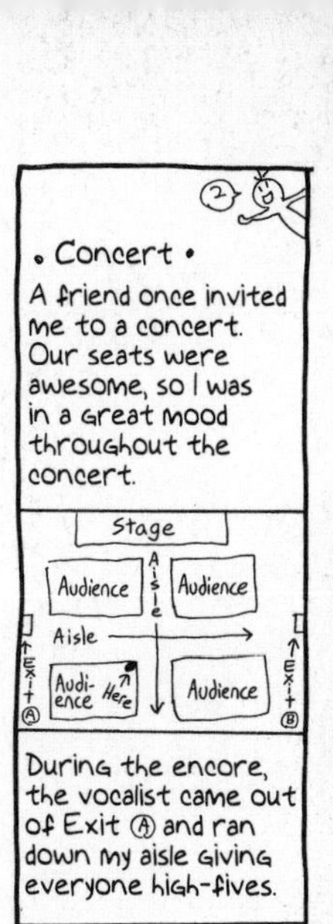
Stage
Audience
Aisle
Audience
Aisle
Exit Ⓐ
Exit Ⓑ
Audi-ence
Here
Audience

During the encore, the vocalist came out of Exit Ⓐ and ran down my aisle giving everyone high-fives.

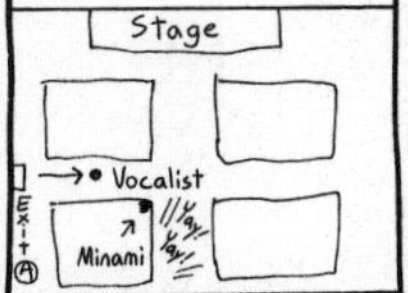
Stage
Vocalist
Exit Ⓐ
Minami
Yay
Yay

When it was my turn, I reached out, but three guards came forward and pinned my arms!!

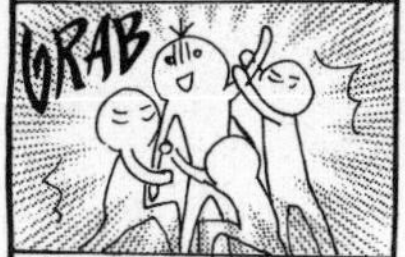
GRAB

The vocalist passed by and went up on stage. The guards acted like nothing had happened, let me go, and went back to their positions... But why did they do that?

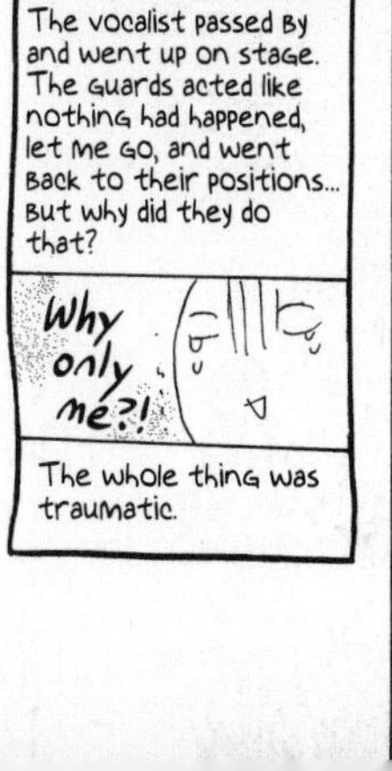
Why only me?!

The whole thing was traumatic.

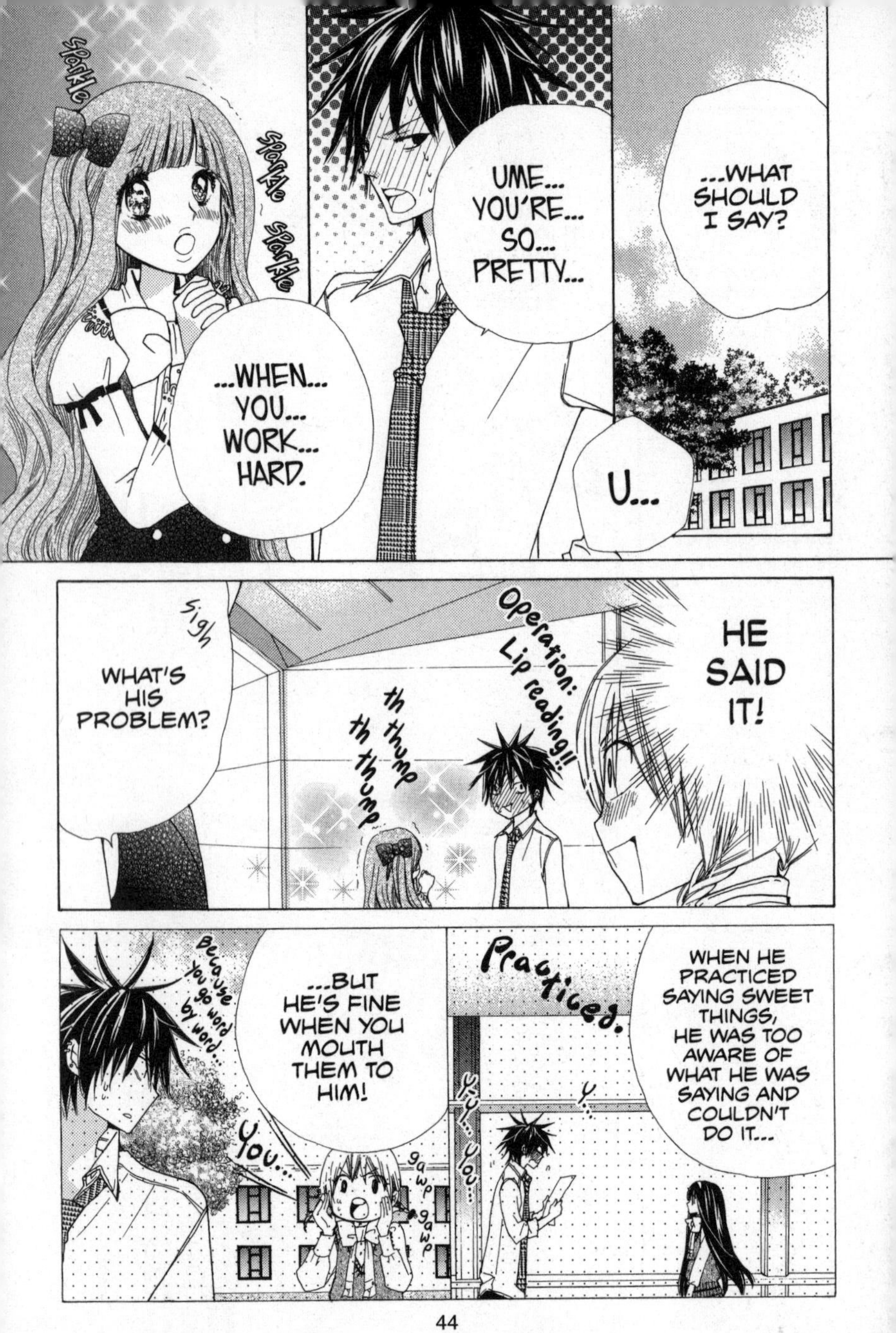

...WHAT SHOULD I SAY?
U...
UME... YOU'RE... SO... PRETTY...
Sparkle
Sparkle
Sparkle
...WHEN... YOU... WORK... HARD.
HE SAID IT!
Operation: Lip reading!!
th thump th thump
sigh
WHAT'S HIS PROBLEM?
WHEN HE PRACTICED SAYING SWEET THINGS, HE WAS TOO AWARE OF WHAT HE WAS SAYING AND COULDN'T DO IT...
Practiced.
Y...
Y-Y-Y... You...
...BUT HE'S FINE WHEN YOU MOUTH THEM TO HIM!
gawp gawp
You...
Because you go word by word...

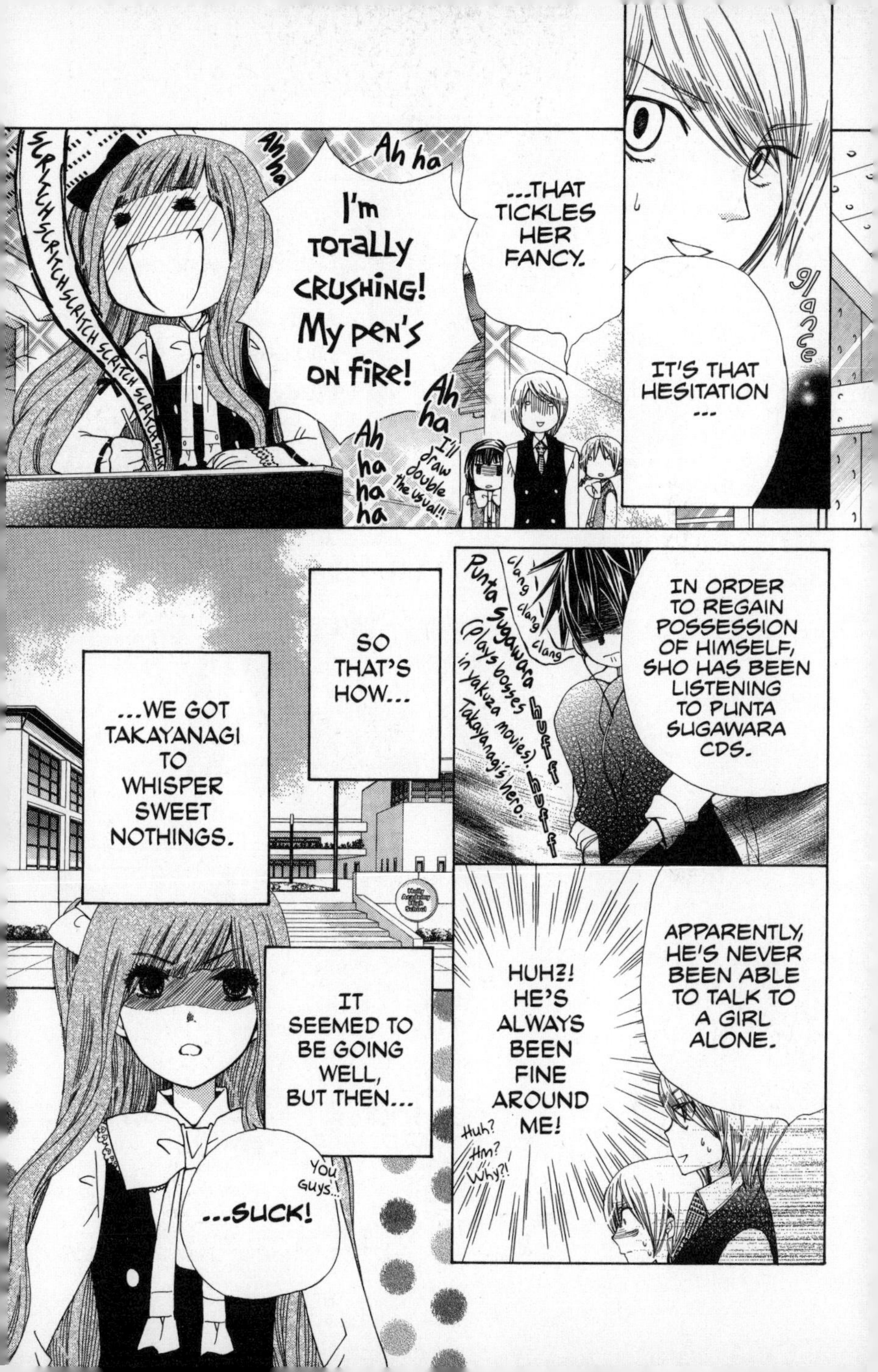
glance
IT'S THAT HESITATION...
...THAT TICKLES HER FANCY.
Ah ha
Ah ha
I'm totally crushing! My pen's on fire!
Ah ha
Ah ha ha ha
I'll draw double the usual!!
SCRITCH SCRITCH SCRITCH SCRITCH SCRITCH SCRITCH
clang clang clang
Punta Sugawara (plays bosses in yakuza movies). Takayanagi's hero.
huff huff
IN ORDER TO REGAIN POSSESSION OF HIMSELF, SHO HAS BEEN LISTENING TO PUNTA SUGAWARA CDS.
APPARENTLY, HE'S NEVER BEEN ABLE TO TALK TO A GIRL ALONE.
HUH?! HE'S ALWAYS BEEN FINE AROUND ME!
Huh?
Hm?
Why?!
SO THAT'S HOW...
...WE GOT TAKAYANAGI TO WHISPER SWEET NOTHINGS.
IT SEEMED TO BE GOING WELL, BUT THEN...
You guys...
...SUCK!

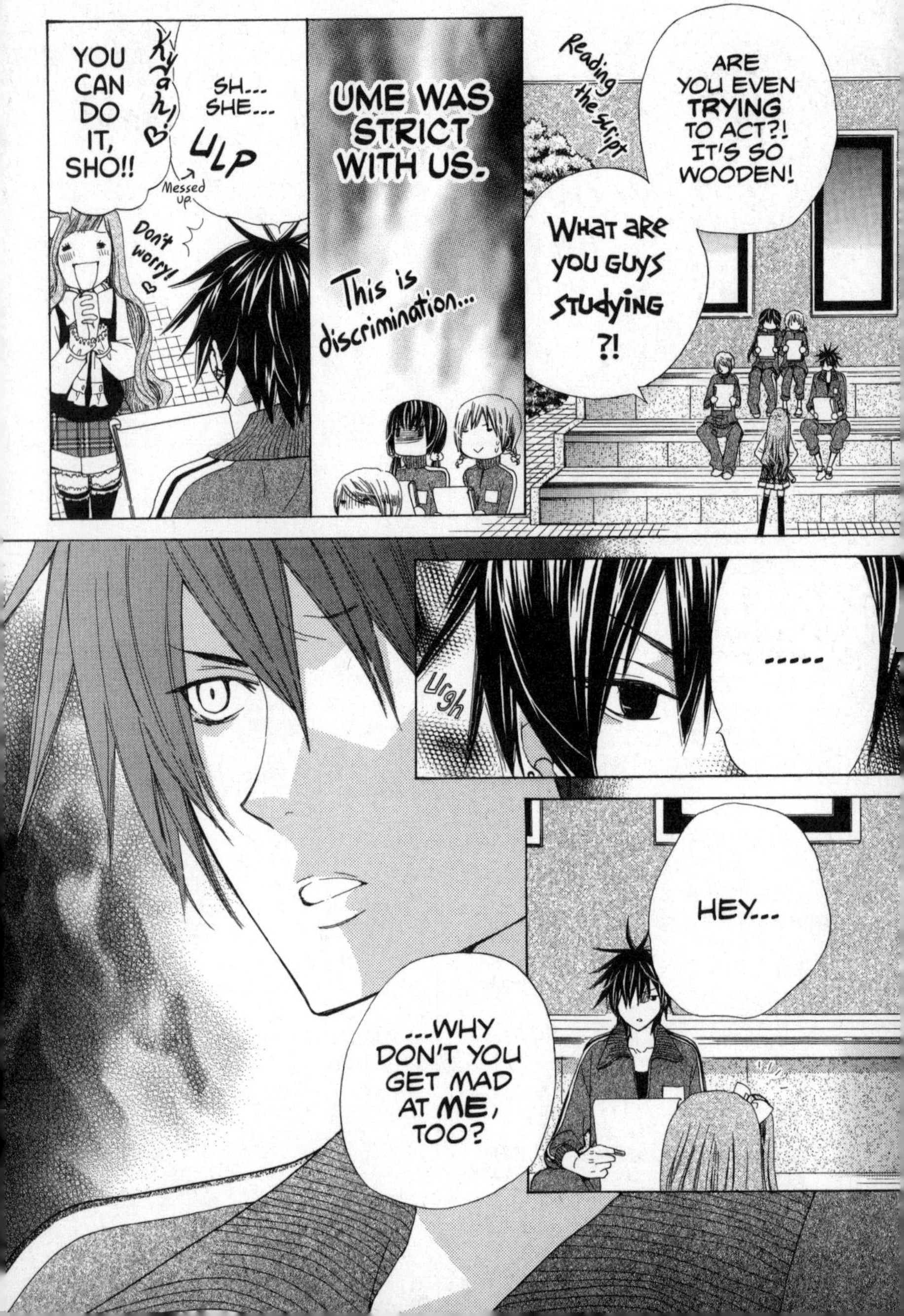
Reading the script
ARE YOU EVEN TRYING TO ACT?! IT'S SO WOODEN!
What are you guys studying ?!
UME WAS STRICT WITH US.
This is discrimination...
YOU CAN DO IT, SHO!!
Kyaah! ♥
SH... SHE...
ULP
Messed up
Don't worry! ♥
Urgh
.....
HEY...
...WHY DON'T YOU GET MAD AT ME, TOO?

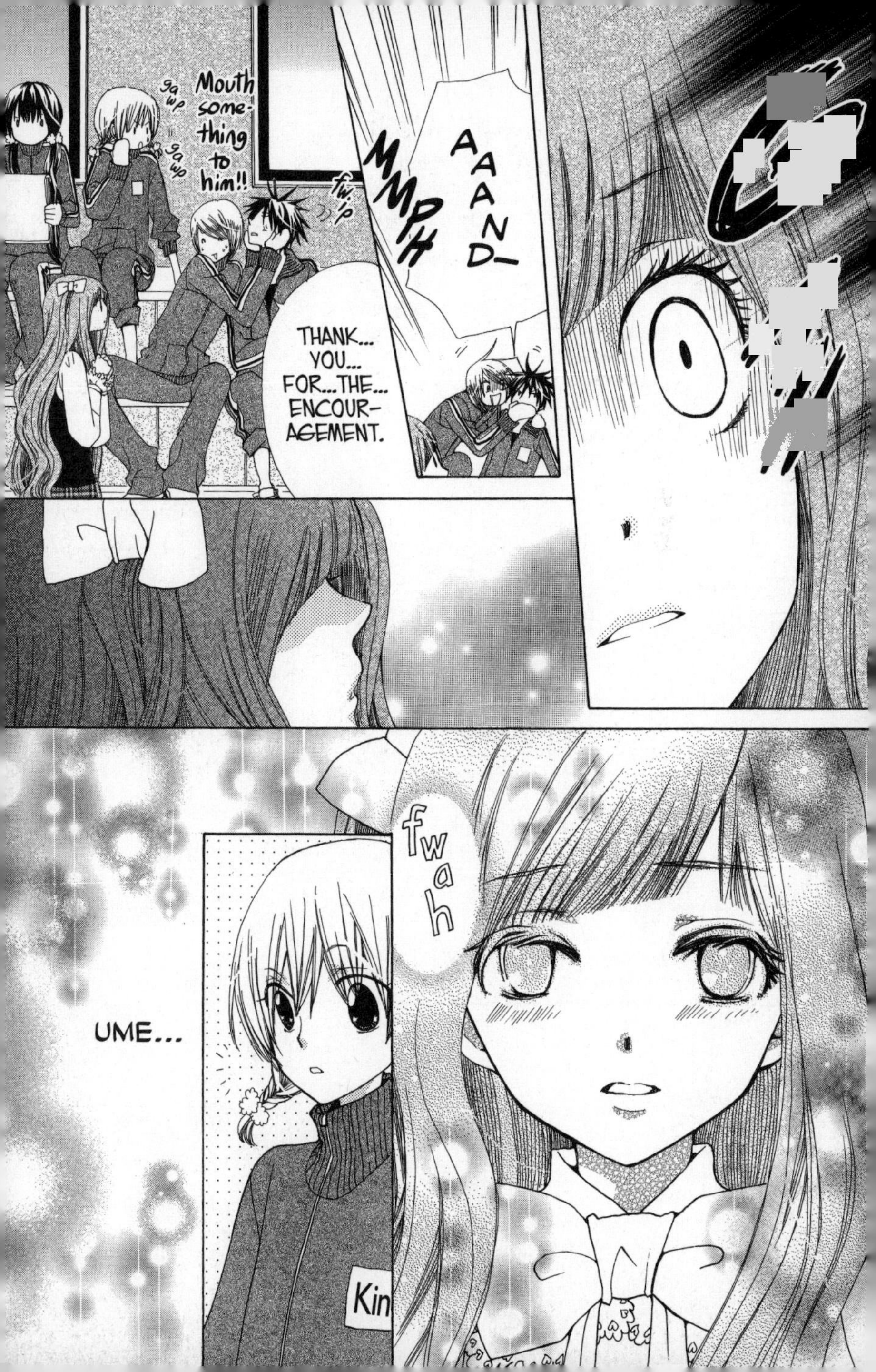

AAAND—
MMPH
fwip
Mouth some-thing to him!!
gawp
gawp
THANK... YOU... FOR... THE... ENCOUR-AGEMENT.
fwah
UME...
Kin

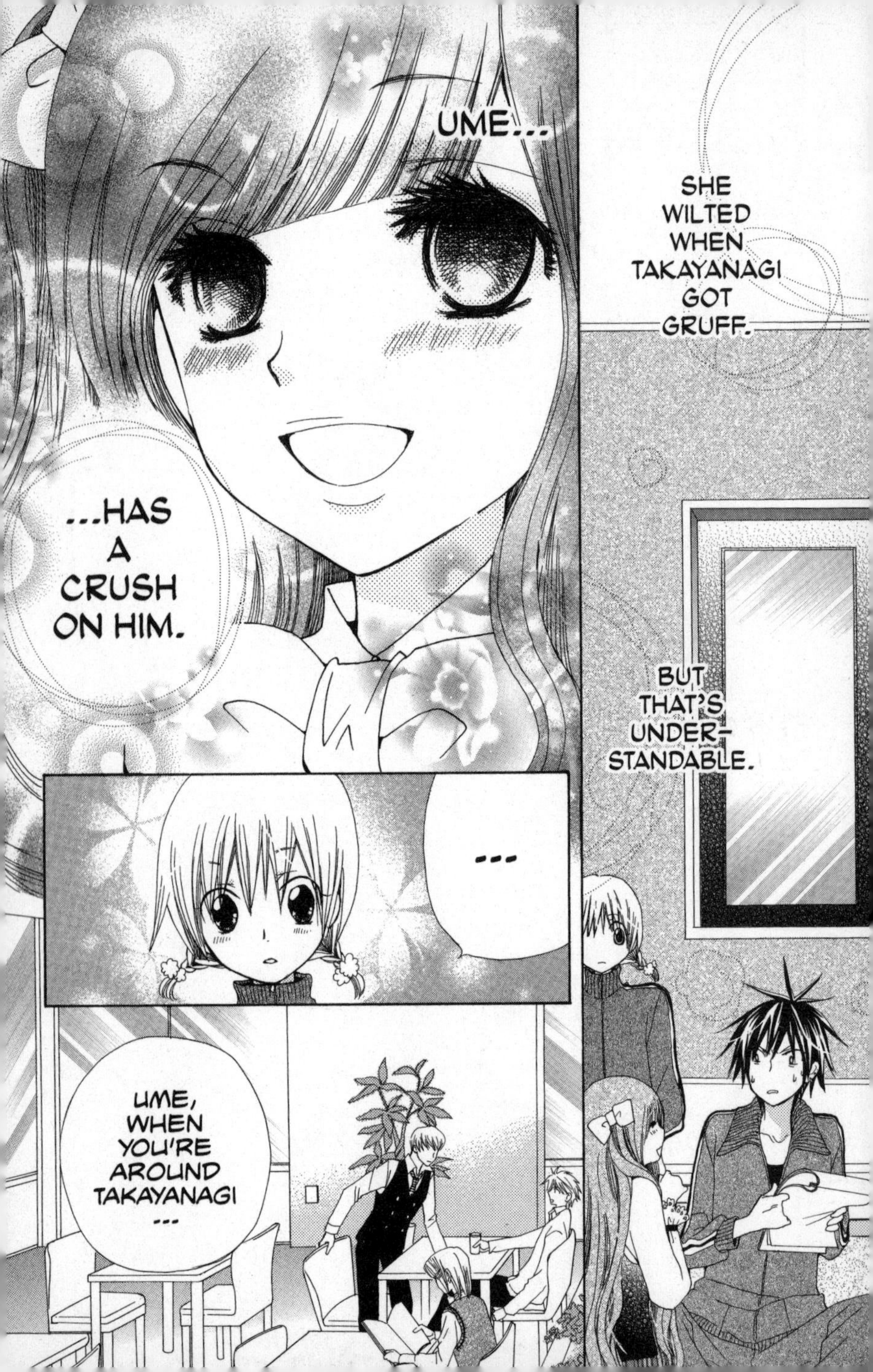
SHE WILTED WHEN TAKAYANAGI GOT GRUFF.
BUT THAT'S UNDER-STANDABLE.
UME...
...HAS A CRUSH ON HIM.
...
UME, WHEN YOU'RE AROUND TAKAYANAGI...

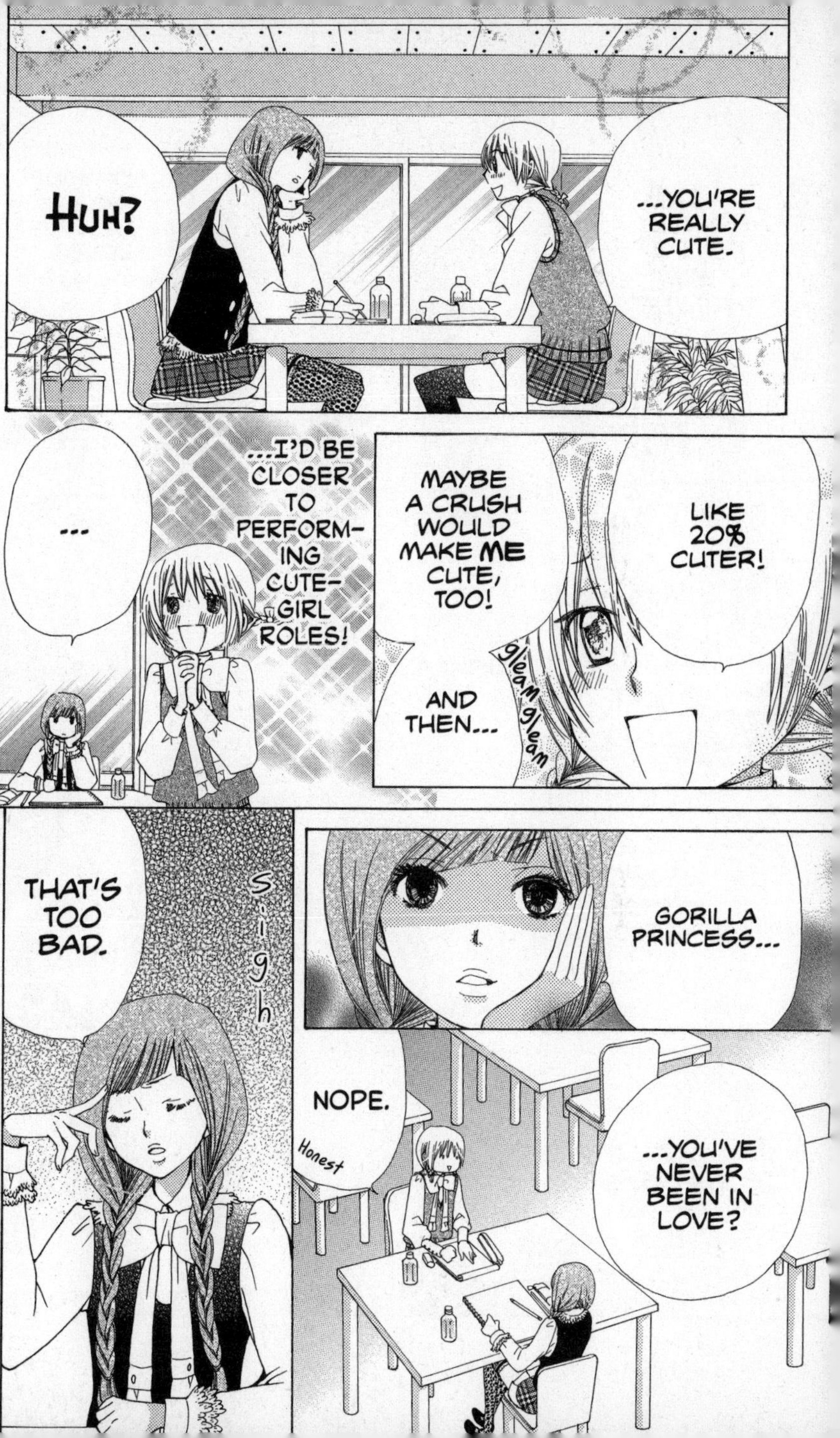
...YOU'RE REALLY CUTE.
HUH?
LIKE 20% CUTER!
MAYBE A CRUSH WOULD MAKE ME CUTE, TOO!
gleam gleam
AND THEN...
...I'D BE CLOSER TO PERFORMING-ING CUTE-GIRL ROLES!
...
GORILLA PRINCESS...
...YOU'VE NEVER BEEN IN LOVE?
NOPE.
Honest
Sigh
THAT'S TOO BAD.

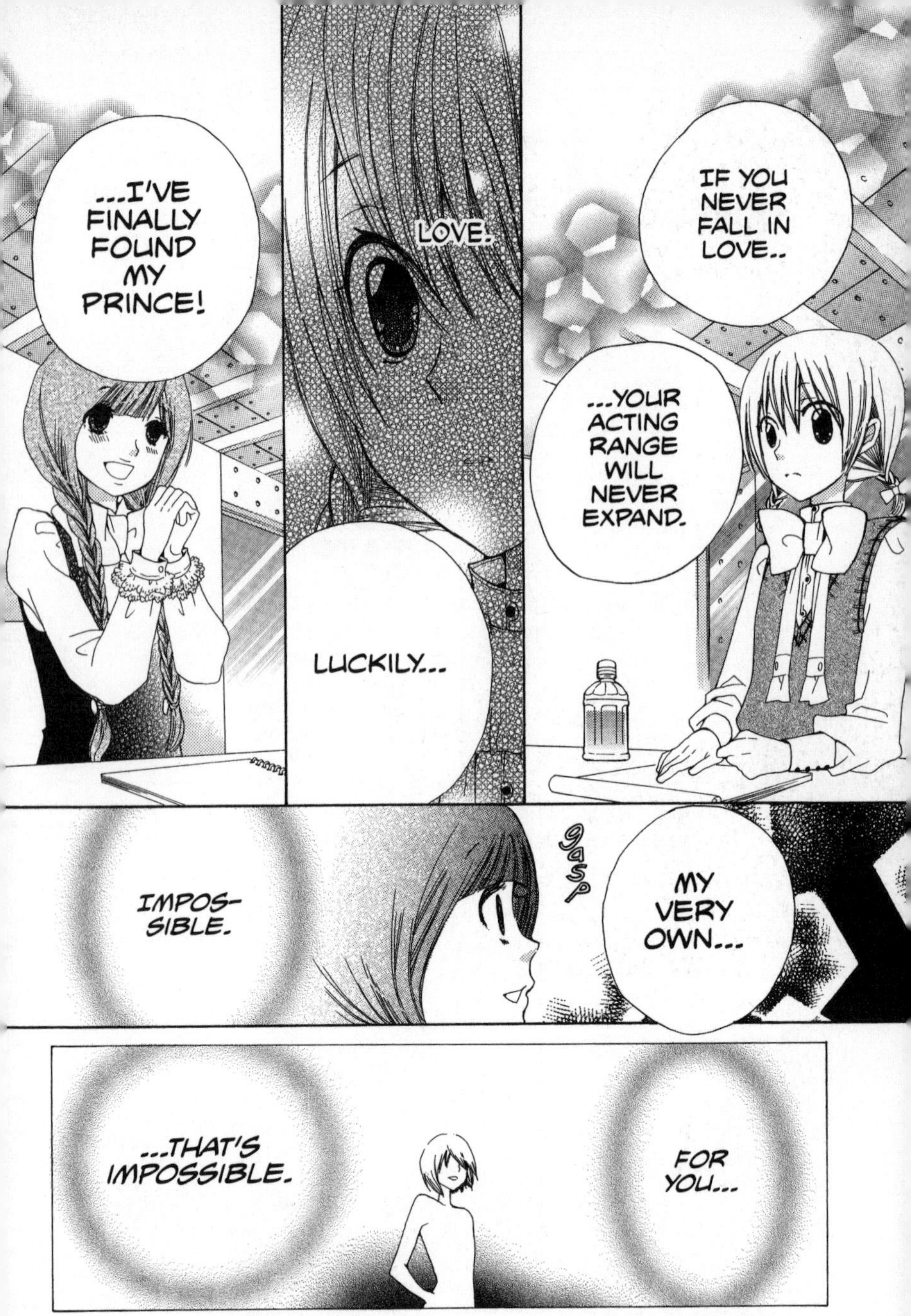
IF YOU NEVER FALL IN LOVE..
...YOUR ACTING RANGE WILL NEVER EXPAND.
LOVE.
LUCKILY...
...I'VE FINALLY FOUND MY PRINCE!
gasp
MY VERY OWN...
IMPOS-SIBLE.
FOR YOU...
...THAT'S IMPOSSIBLE.

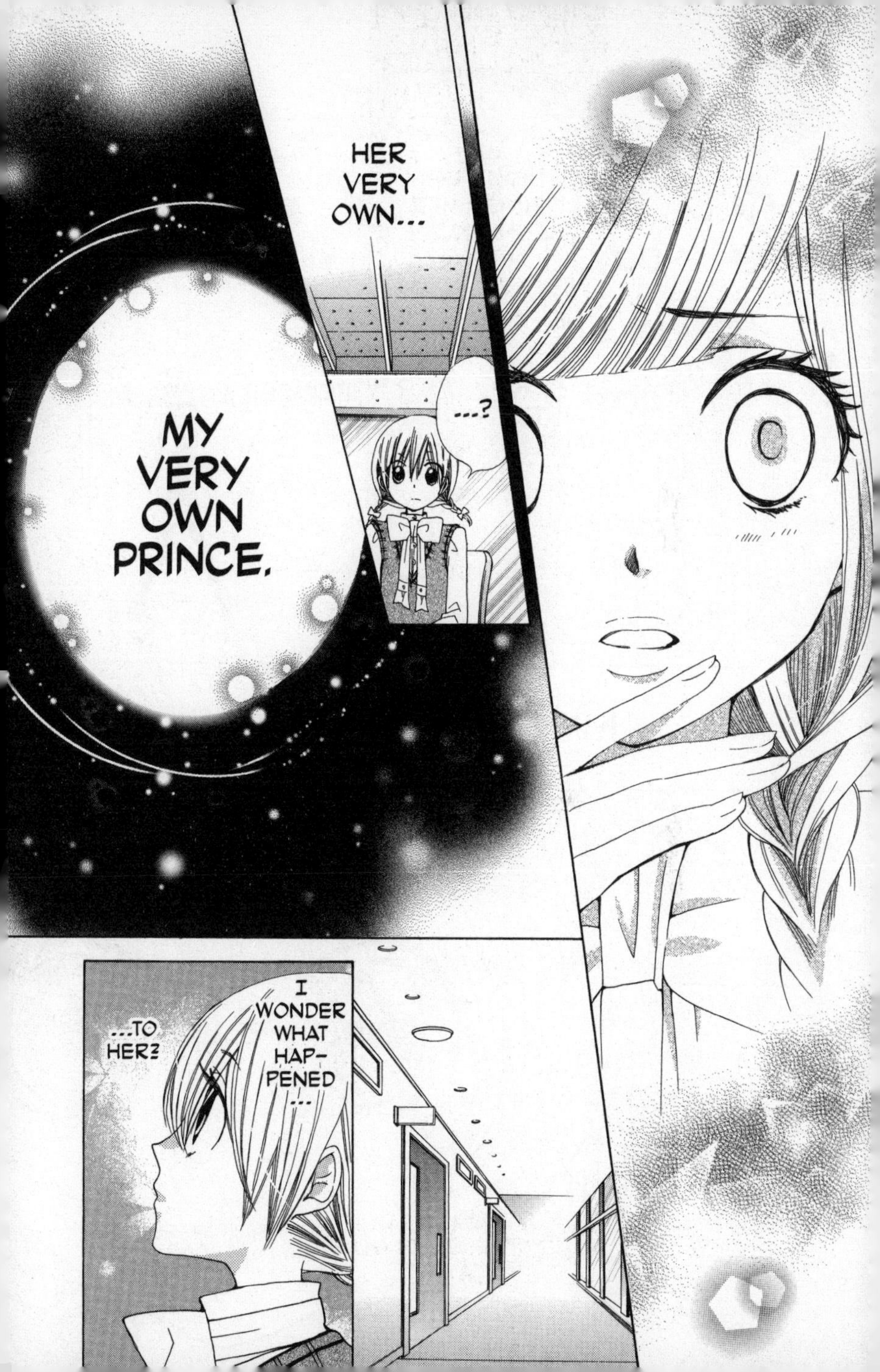
HER VERY OWN...
...?
MY VERY OWN PRINCE.
I WONDER WHAT HAPPENED...
...TO HER?

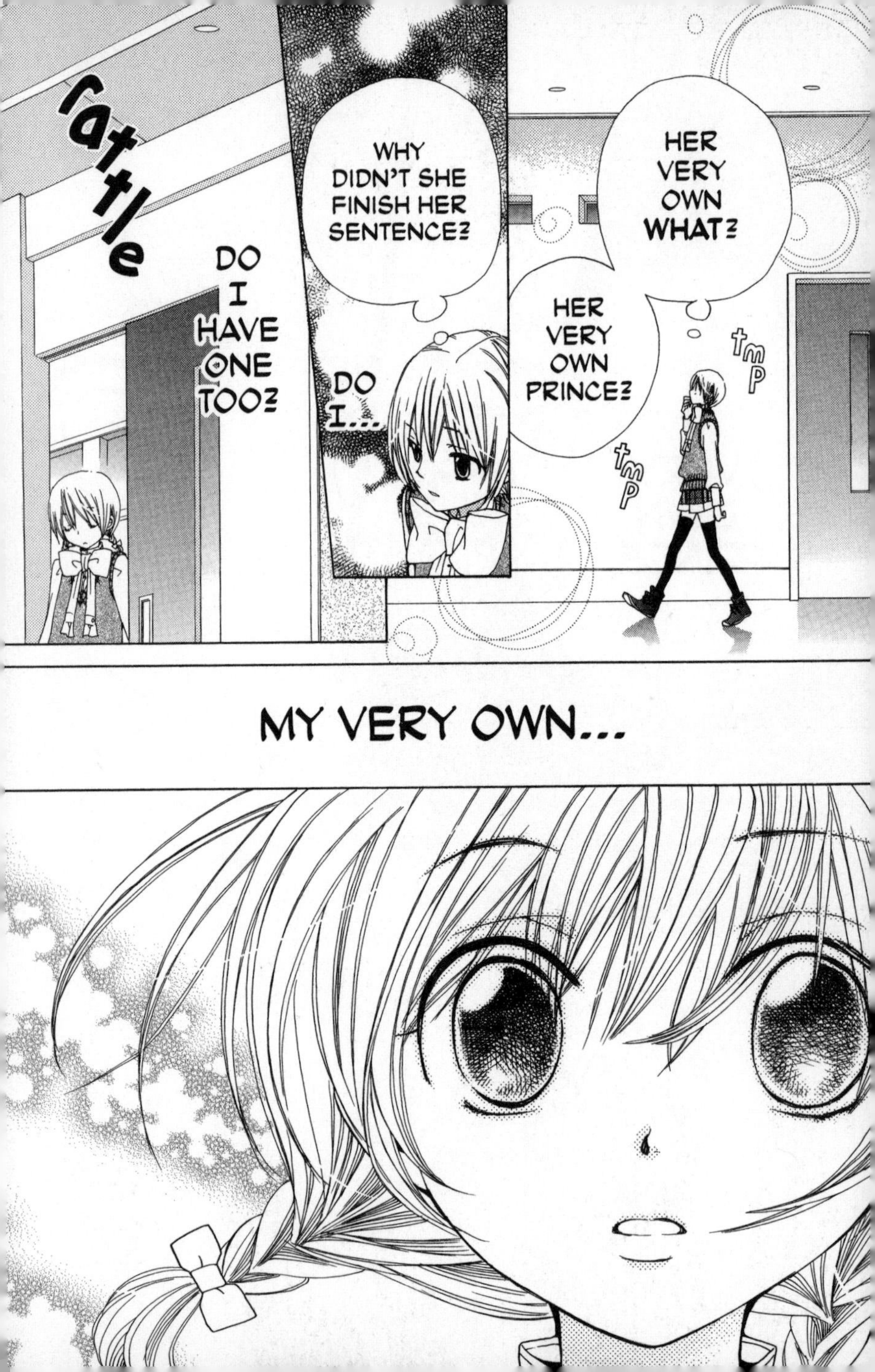
HER VERY OWN WHAT?
HER VERY OWN PRINCE?
tmp
tmp
WHY DIDN'T SHE FINISH HER SENTENCE?
DO I...
rattle
DO I HAVE ONE TOO?
MY VERY OWN...

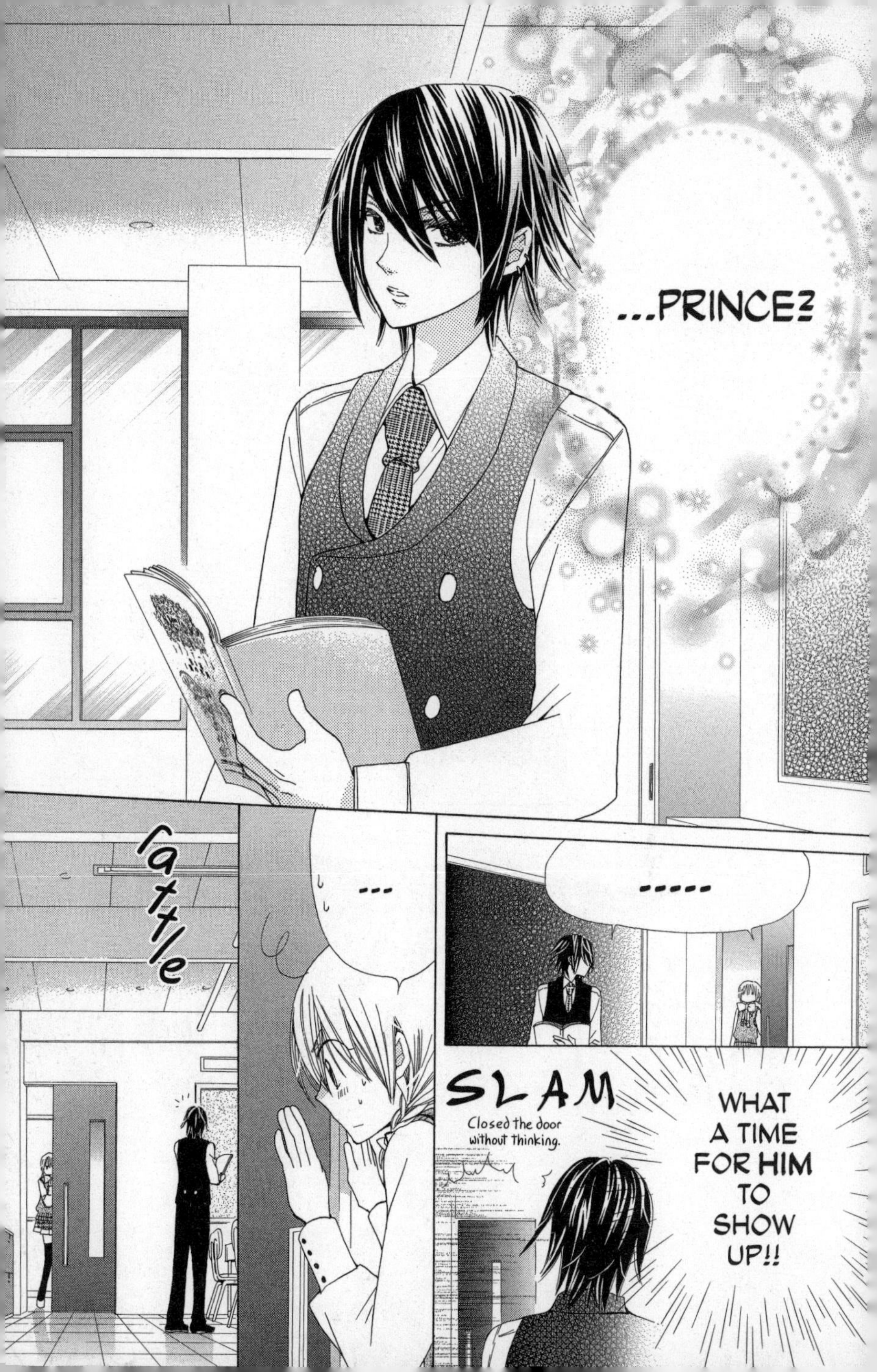
...PRINCE?
.....
WHAT A TIME FOR HIM TO SHOW UP!!
SLAM
Closed the door without thinking.
...
rattle

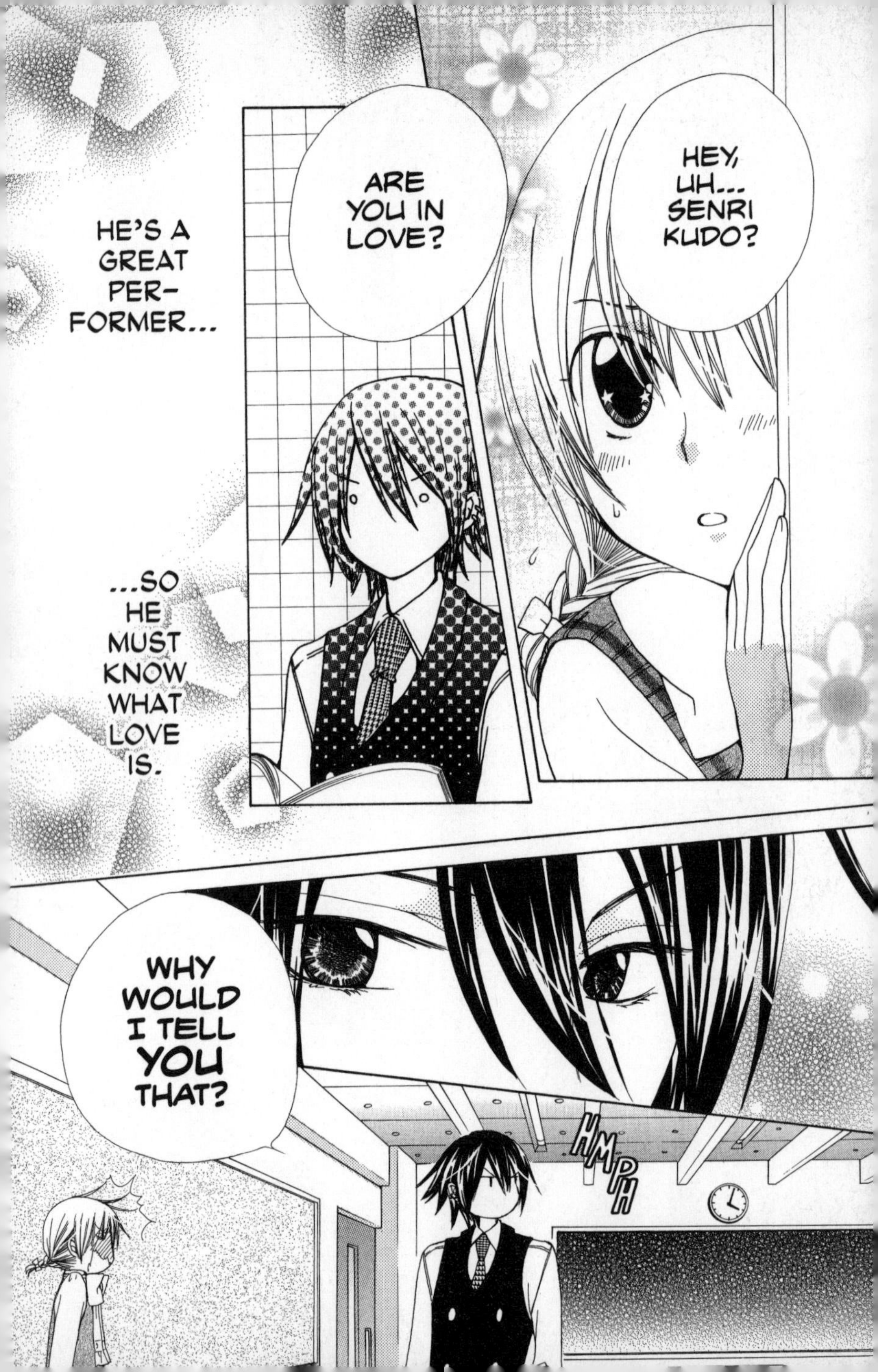
HEY, UH... SENRI KUDO?
ARE YOU IN LOVE?
HE'S A GREAT PER-FORMER...
...SO HE MUST KNOW WHAT LOVE IS.
WHY WOULD I TELL YOU THAT?
HMPH

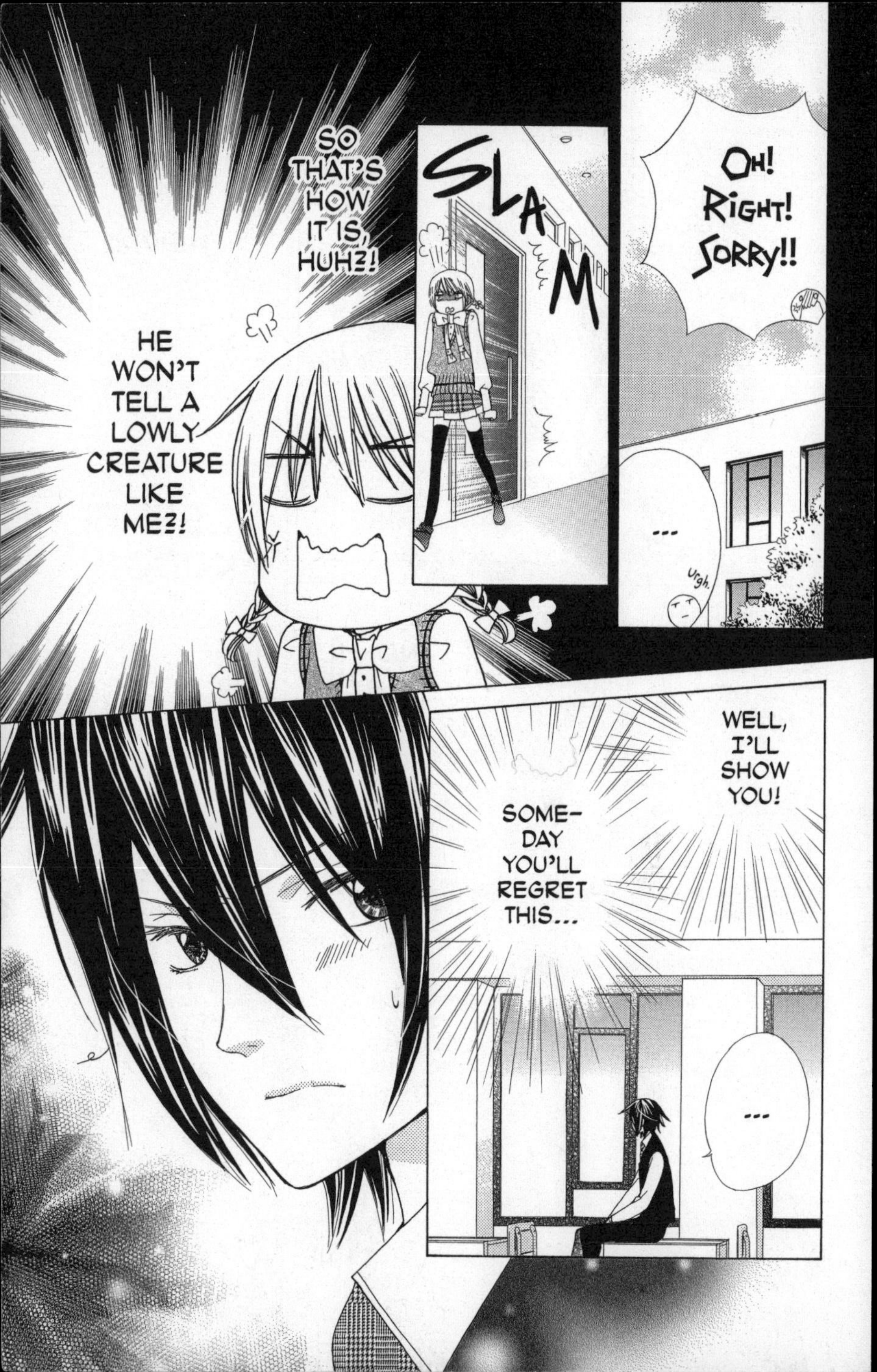

OH! RIGHT! SORRY!!
...
Urgh.
SLAM
SO THAT'S HOW IT IS, HUH?!
HE WON'T TELL A LOWLY CREATURE LIKE ME?!
WELL, I'LL SHOW YOU!
SOME-DAY YOU'LL REGRET THIS...
...

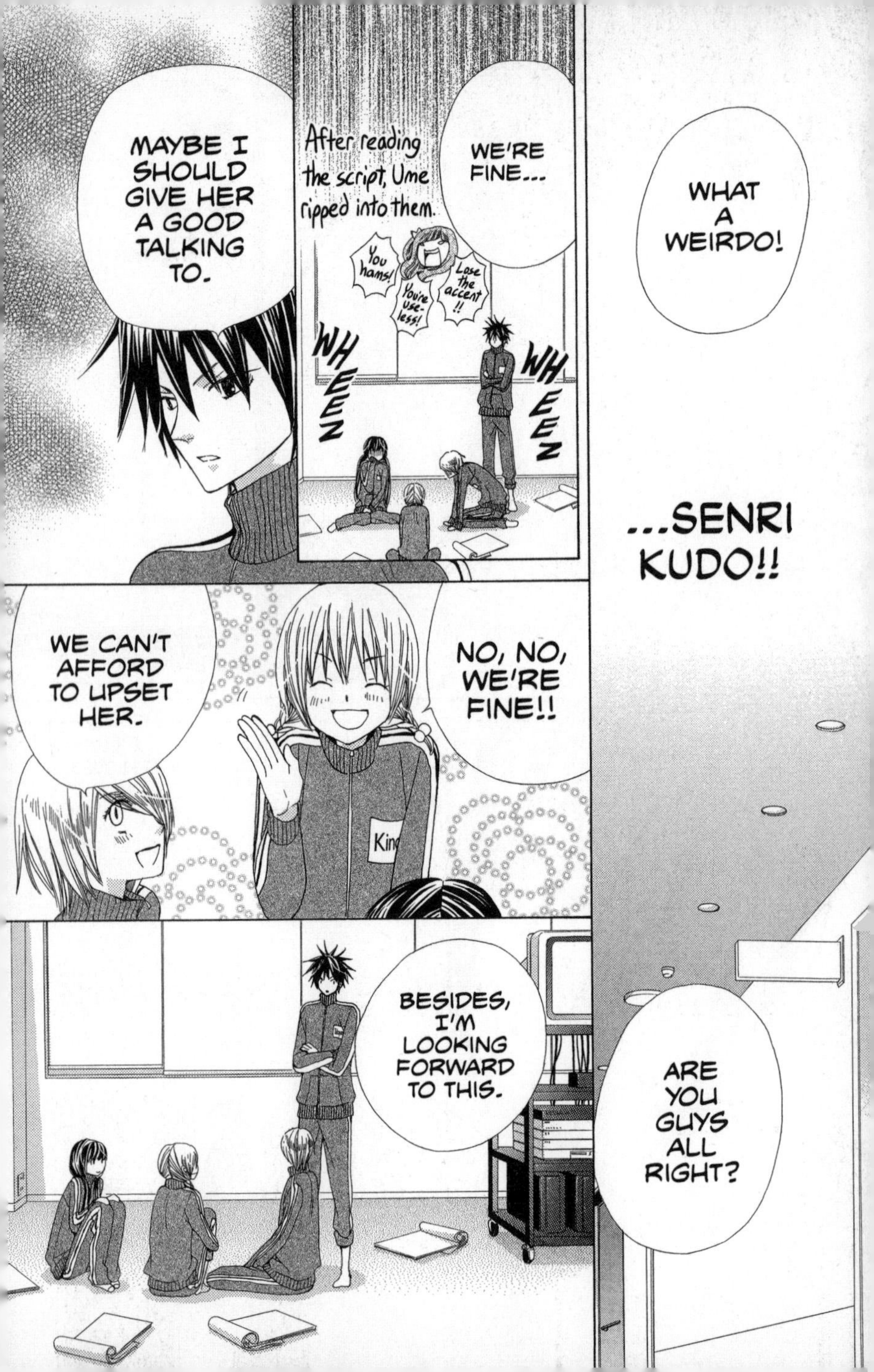
WHAT A WEIRDO!
...SENRI KUDO!!
ARE YOU GUYS ALL RIGHT?
WE'RE FINE...
After reading the script, Ume ripped into them.
Lose the accent!!
You're useless!
You hams!
WHEEZ
WHEEZ
MAYBE I SHOULD GIVE HER A GOOD TALKING TO.
NO, NO, WE'RE FINE!!
King
WE CAN'T AFFORD TO UPSET HER.
BESIDES, I'M LOOKING FORWARD TO THIS.

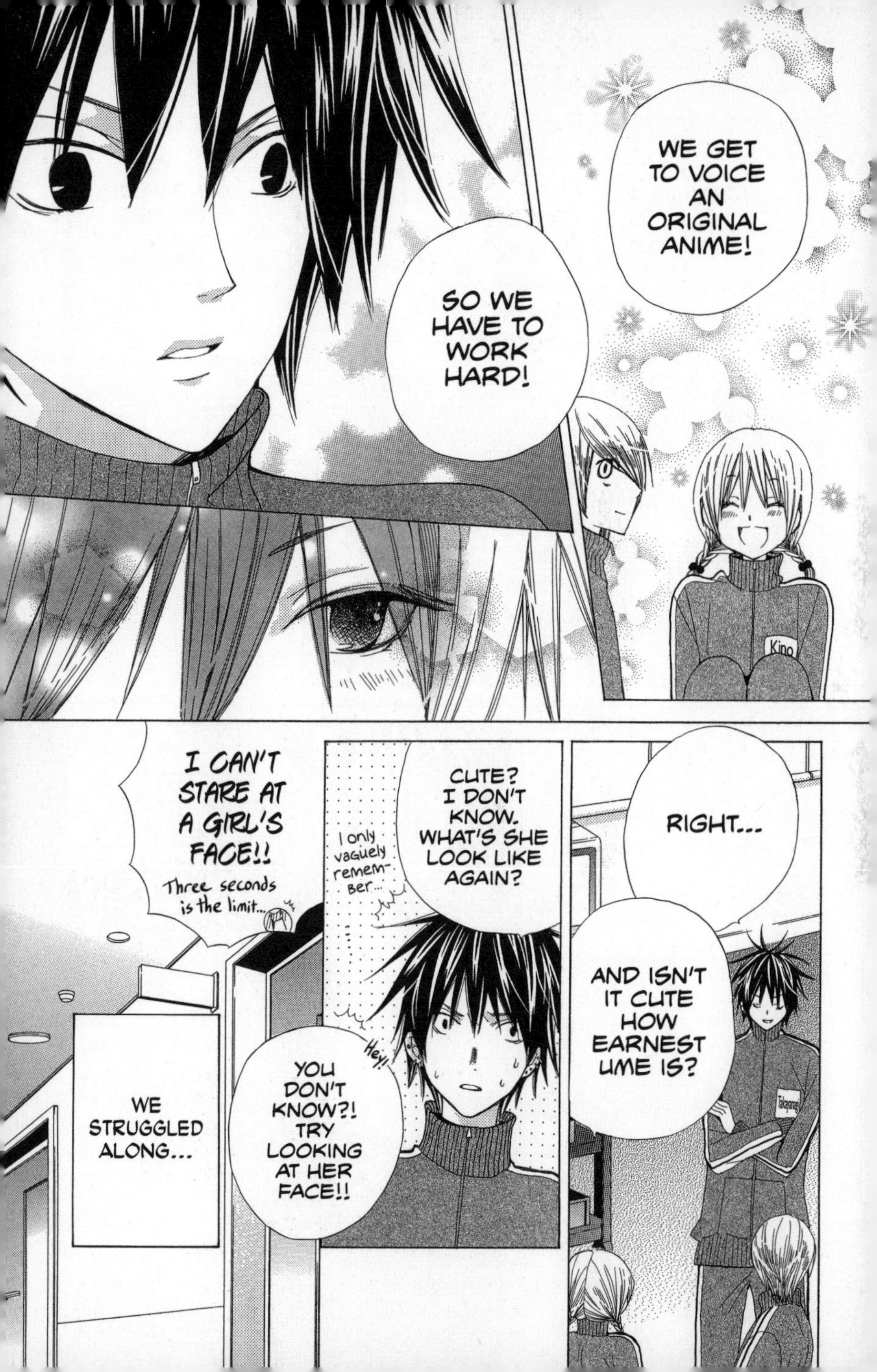
WE GET TO VOICE AN ORIGINAL ANIME!
SO WE HAVE TO WORK HARD!
Kino
RIGHT...
AND ISN'T IT CUTE HOW EARNEST UME IS?
CUTE? I DON'T KNOW. WHAT'S SHE LOOK LIKE AGAIN?
I only vaguely remember...
Hey!
YOU DON'T KNOW?! TRY LOOKING AT HER FACE!!
I CAN'T STARE AT A GIRL'S FACE!!
Three seconds is the limit...
WE STRUGGLED ALONG...

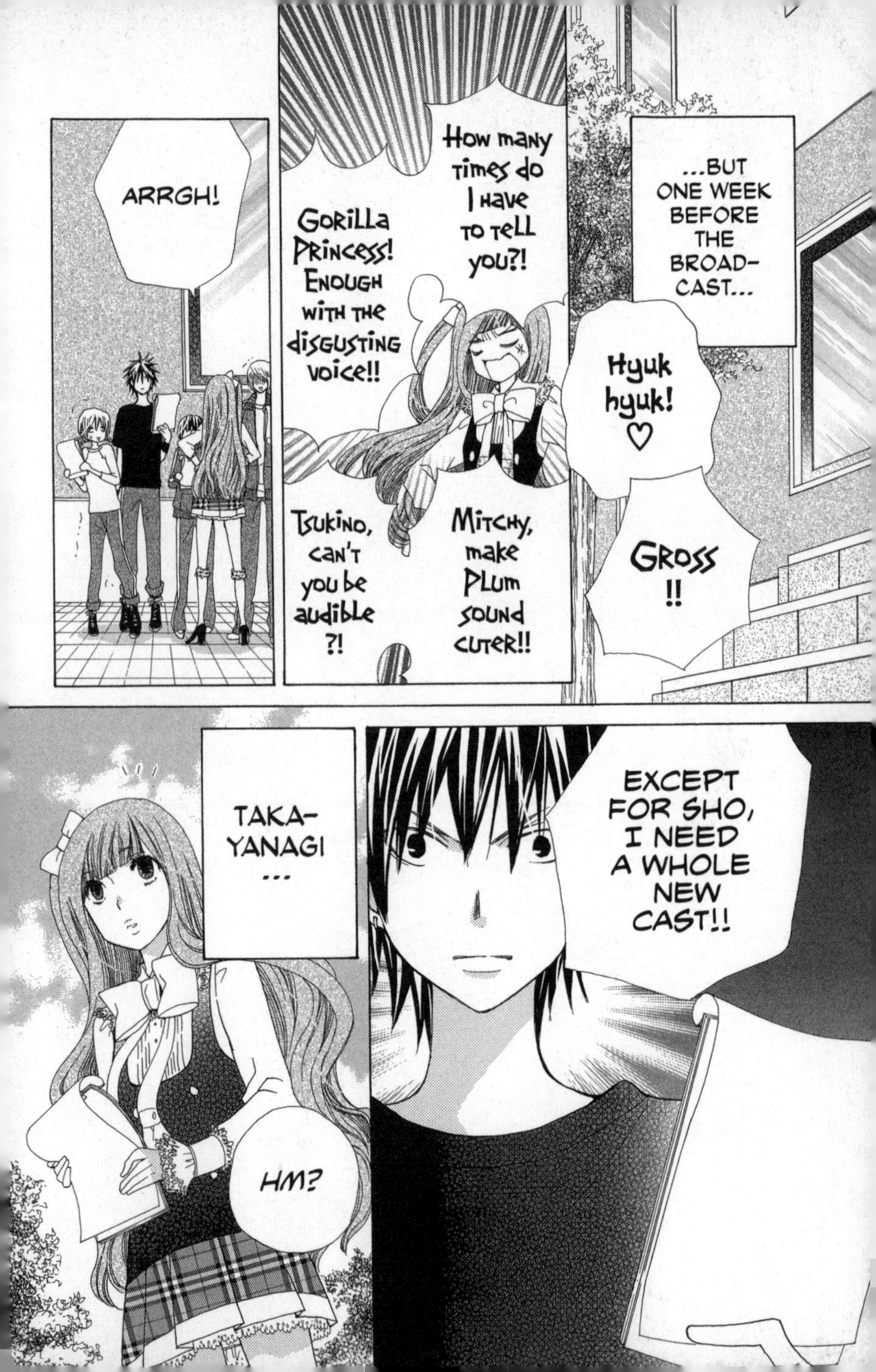
...BUT ONE WEEK BEFORE THE BROAD-CAST...
Hyuk hyuk! ♡
GROSS!!
How many times do I have to tell you?!
Gorilla Princess! Enough with the disgusting voice!!
Mitchy, make Plum sound cuter!!
Tsukino, can't you be audible?!
ARRGH!
EXCEPT FOR SHO, I NEED A WHOLE NEW CAST!!
TAKA-YANAGI ...
HM?

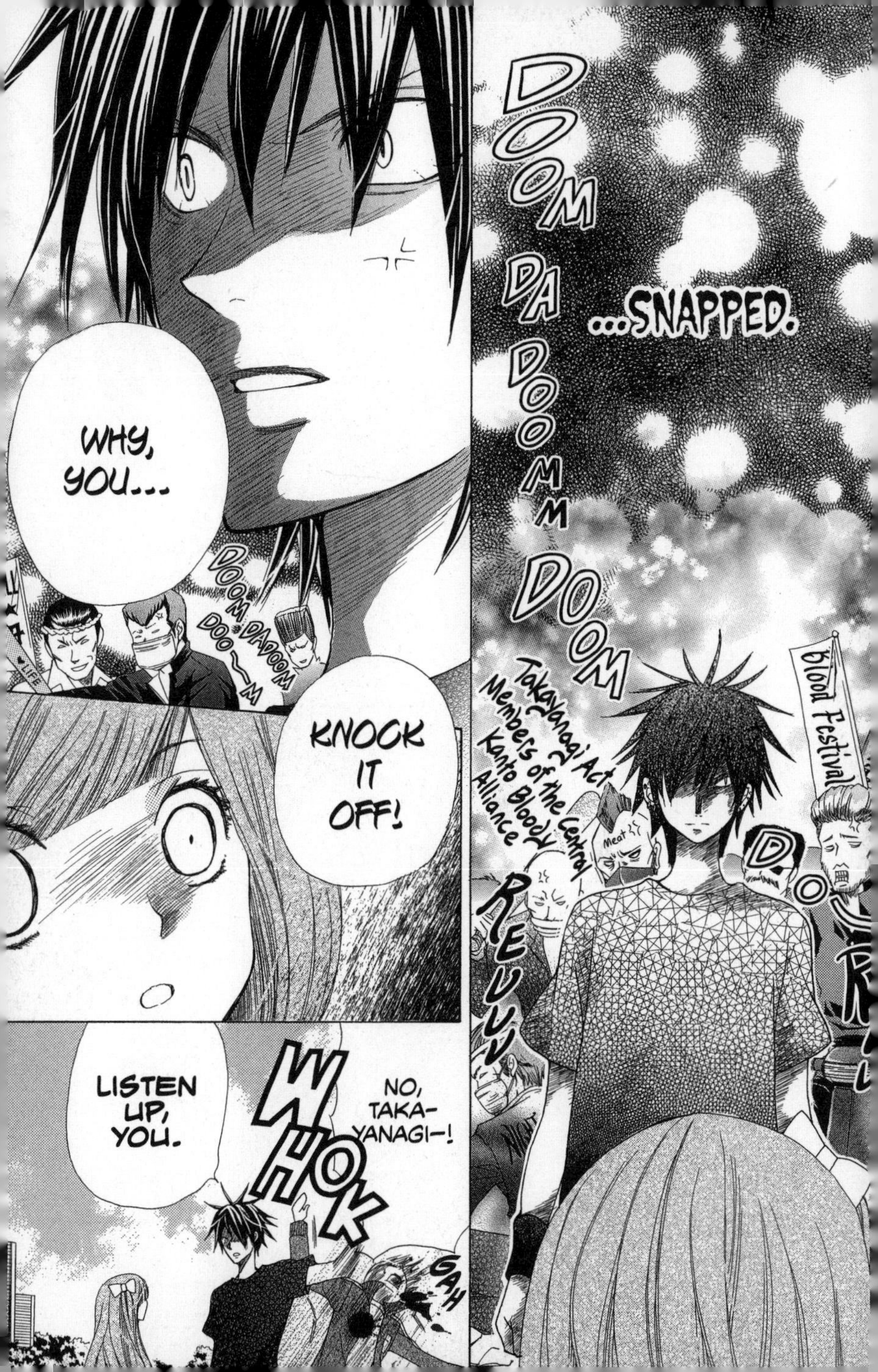
DOOOM DA DOOOMMM DOOOM
...SNAPPED.
Blood Festival
Takayanagi Act 2 Members of the Central Kanto Bloody Alliance
Meat
D.O
REVUUN
WHY, YOU...
DOOOM DADOOM DOO~M
KNOCK IT OFF!
LISTEN UP, YOU.
WHOK
NO, TAKA-YANAGI--!
GAH

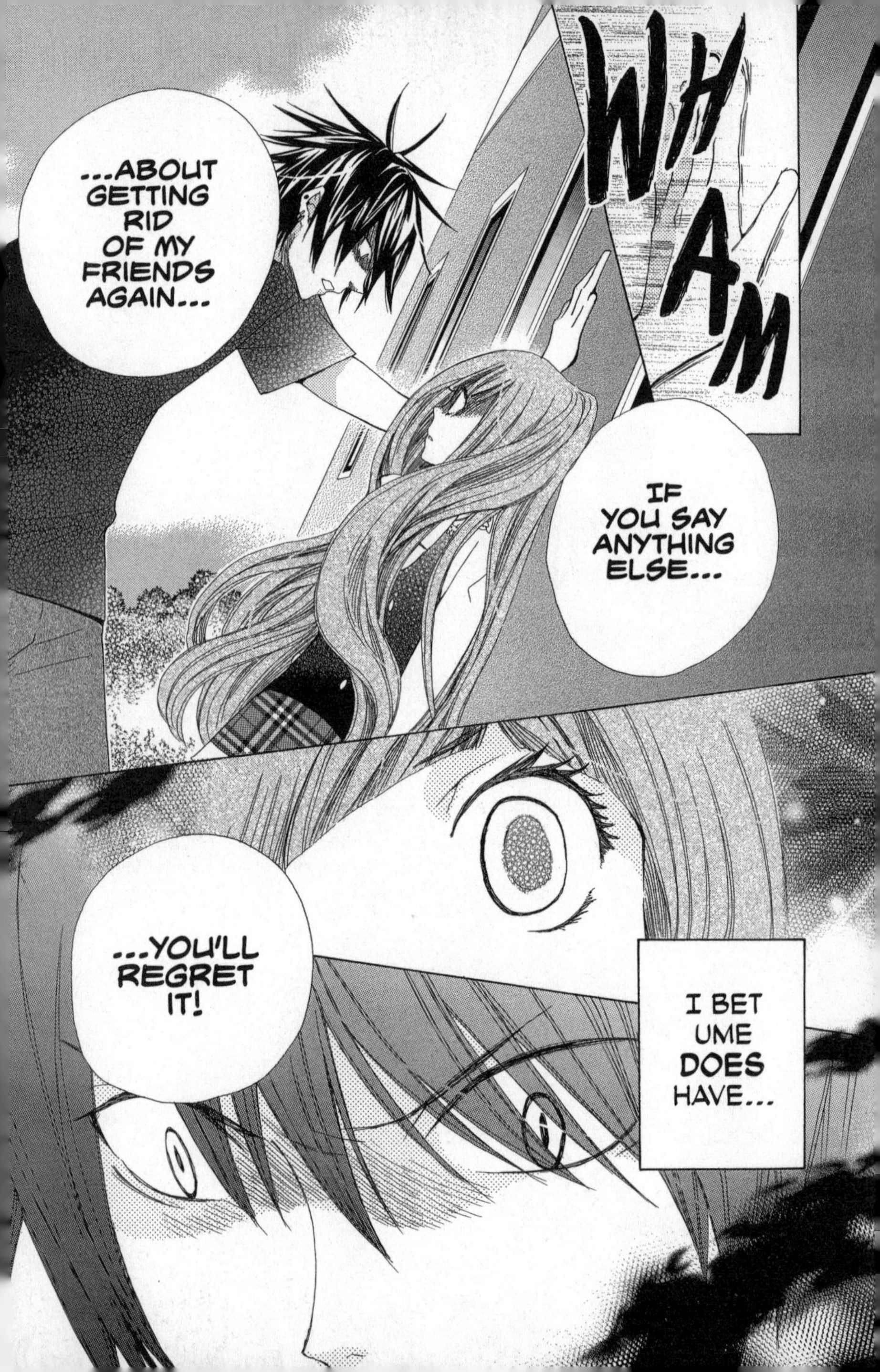
WHAM
IF YOU SAY ANYTHING ELSE...
...ABOUT GETTING RID OF MY FRIENDS AGAIN...
...YOU'LL REGRET IT!
I BET UME DOES HAVE...

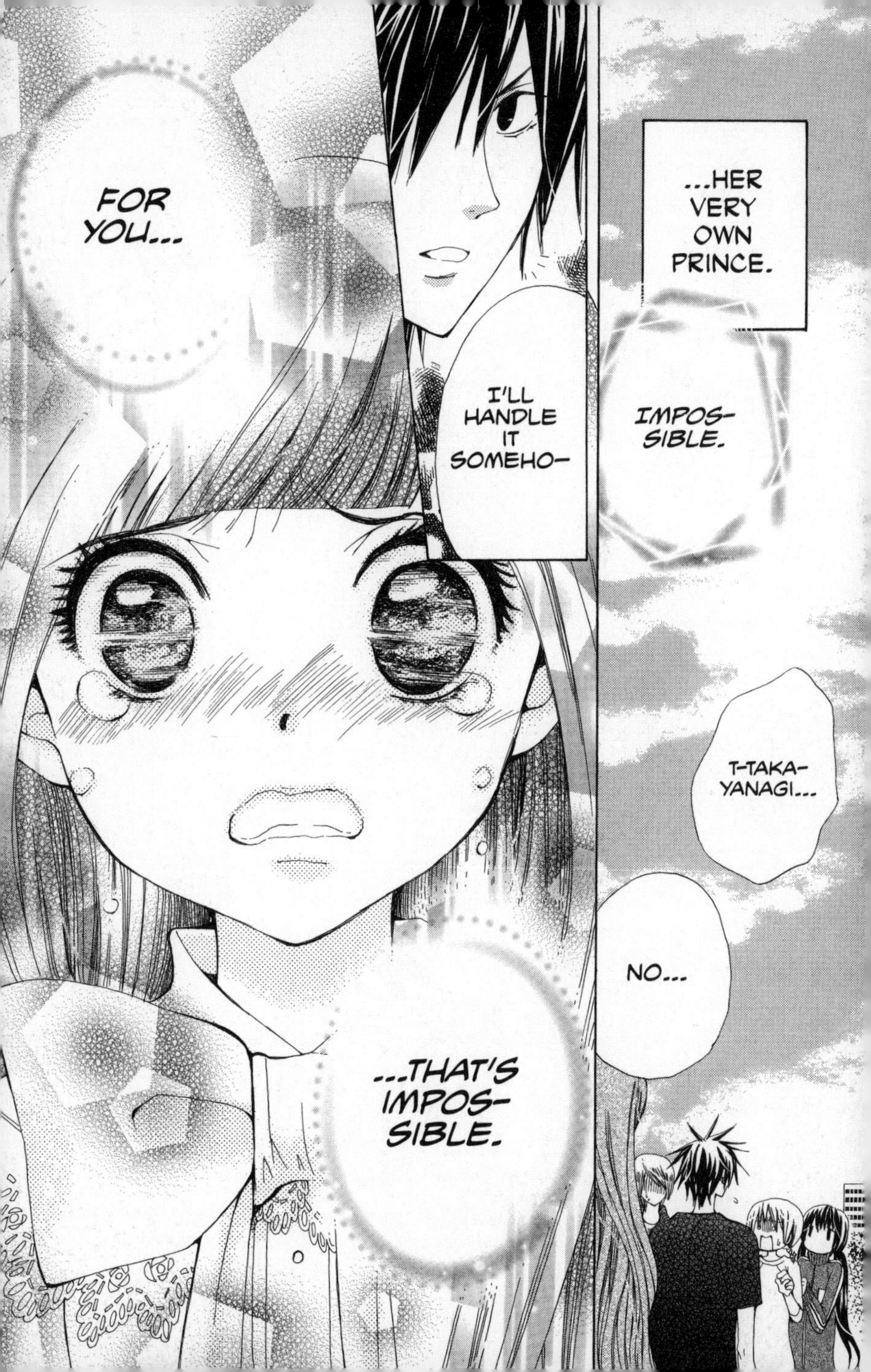
...HER VERY OWN PRINCE.
IMPOS-SIBLE.
T-TAKA-YANAGI...
NO...
FOR YOU...
I'LL HANDLE IT SOMEHO-
...THAT'S IMPOS-SIBLE.

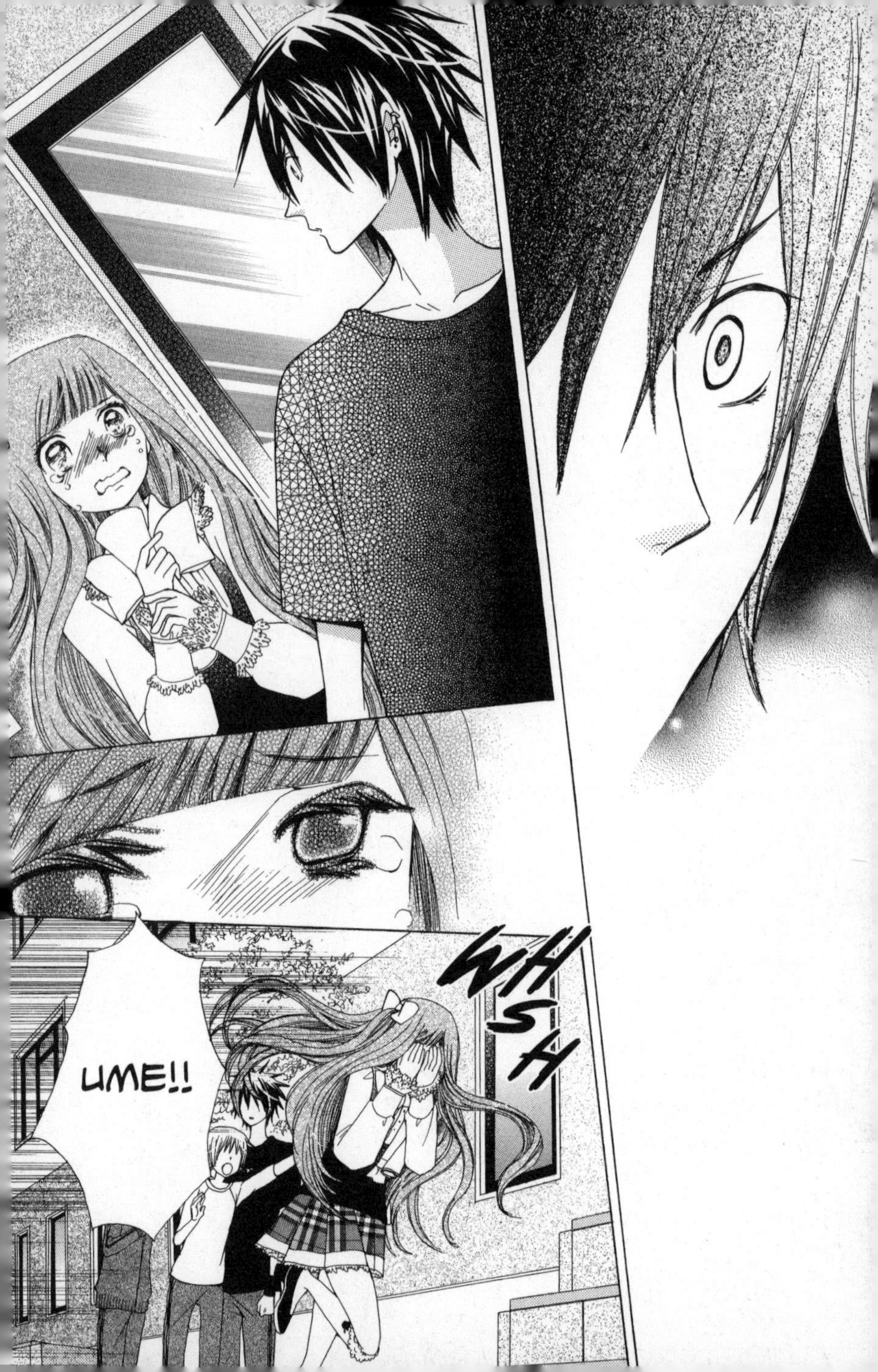
WHSH
UME!!

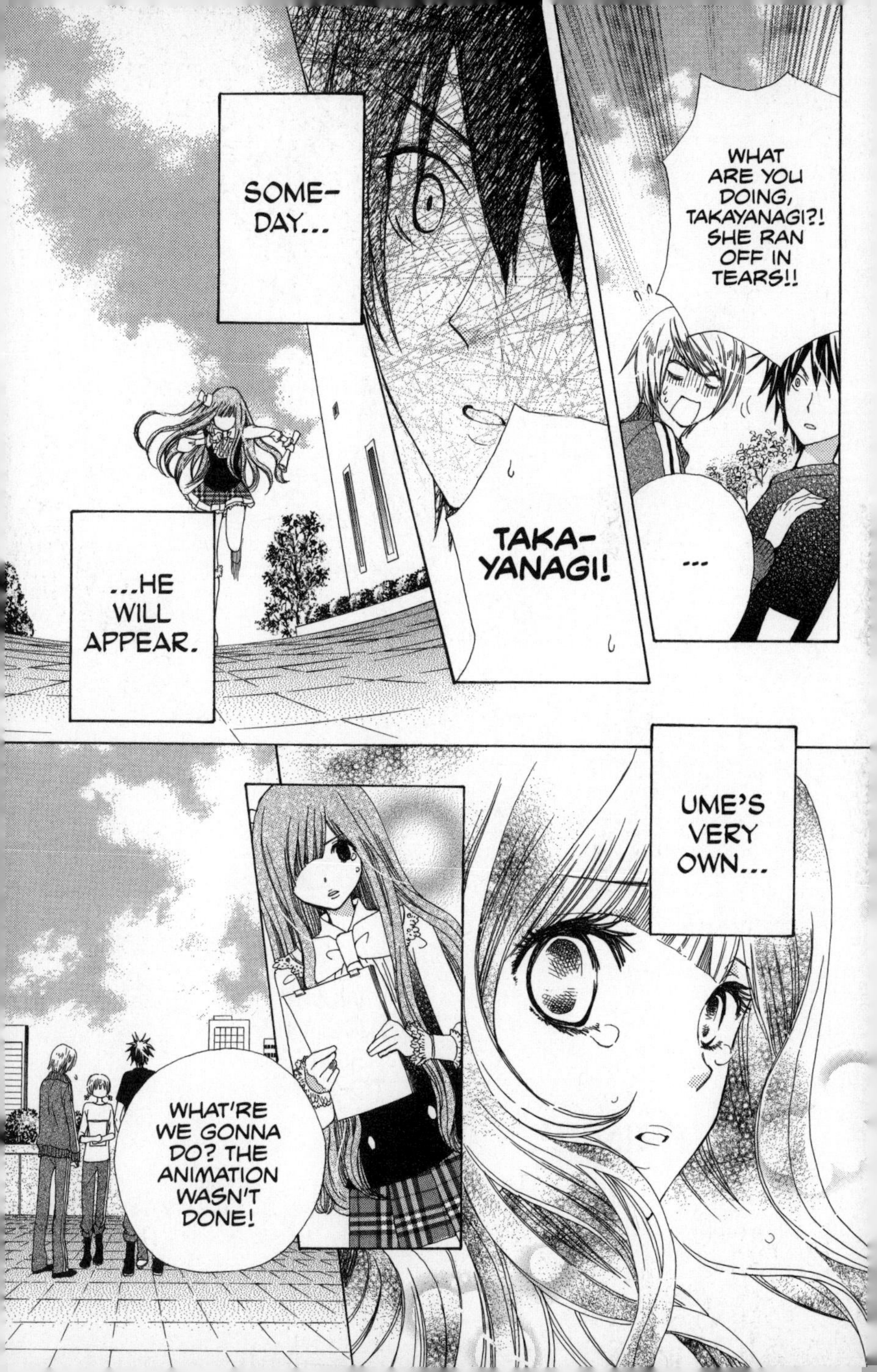
WHAT ARE YOU DOING, TAKAYANAGI?! SHE RAN OFF IN TEARS!!
...
TAKA-YANAGI!
SOME-DAY...
...HE WILL APPEAR.
UME'S VERY OWN...
WHAT'RE WE GONNA DO? THE ANIMATION WASN'T DONE!

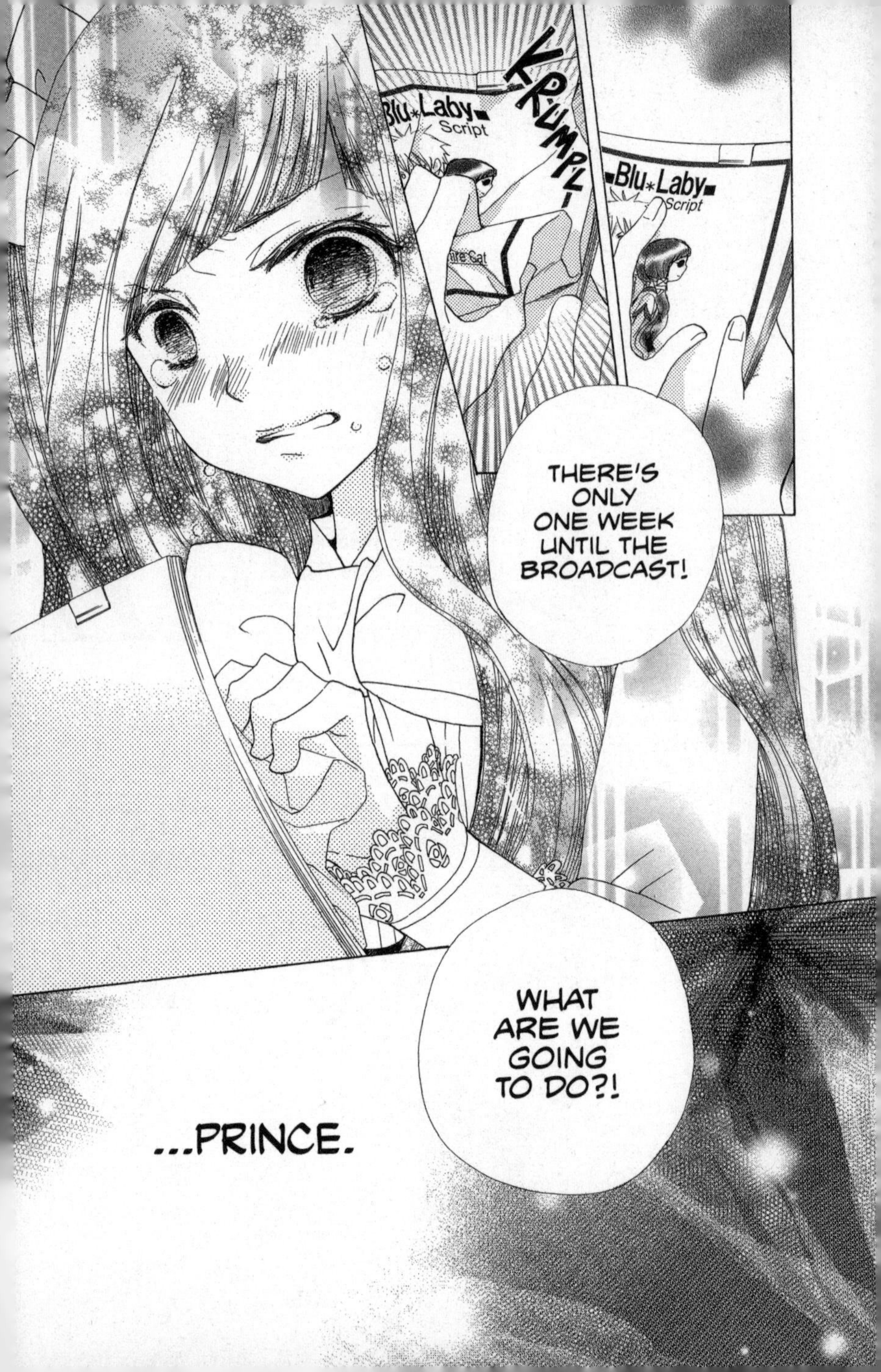
Blu*Laby Script
KRUMPL
Blu*Laby Script
THERE'S ONLY ONE WEEK UNTIL THE BROADCAST!
WHAT ARE WE GOING TO DO?!
...PRINCE.

Chapter 8

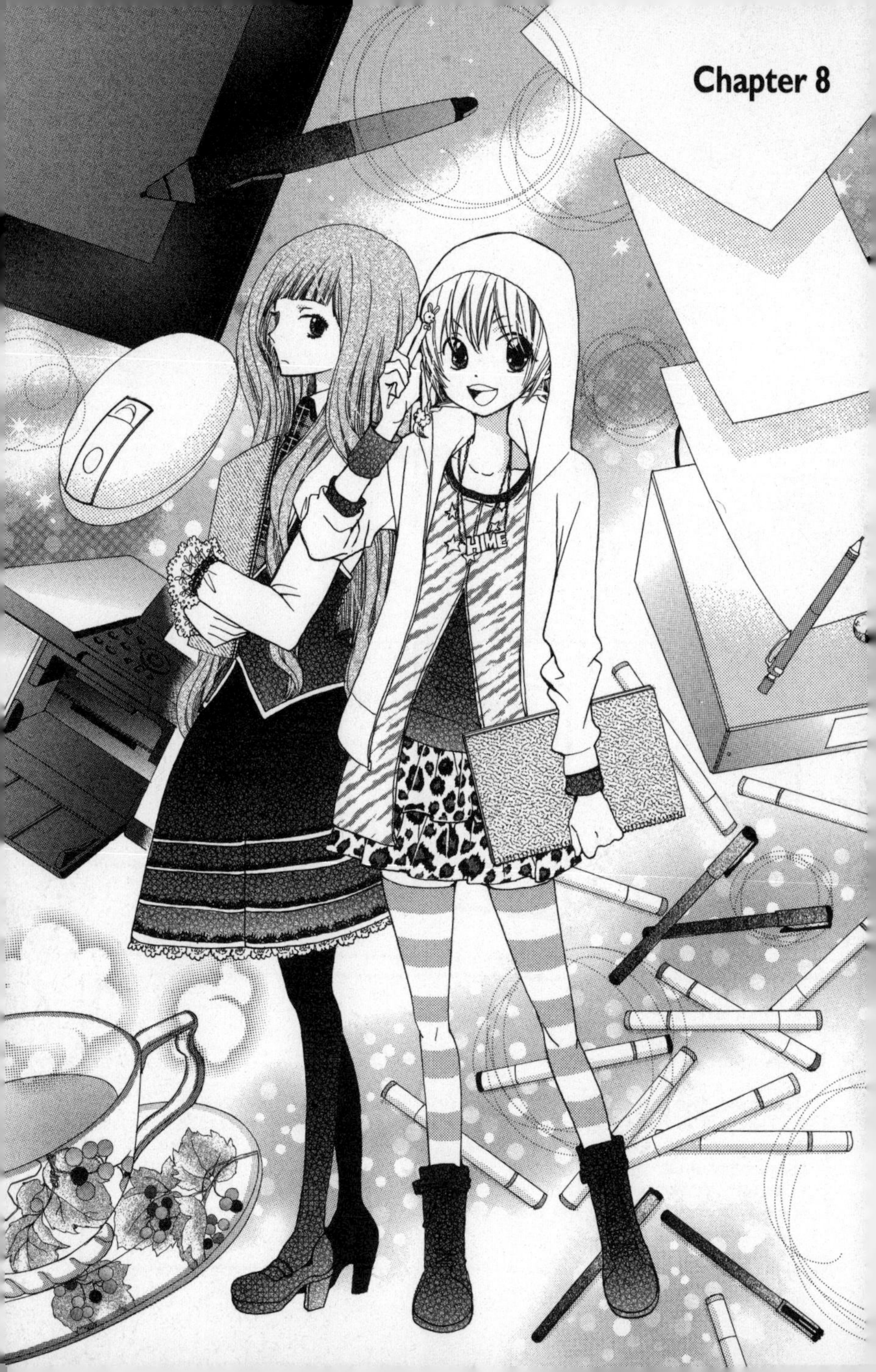
HIME

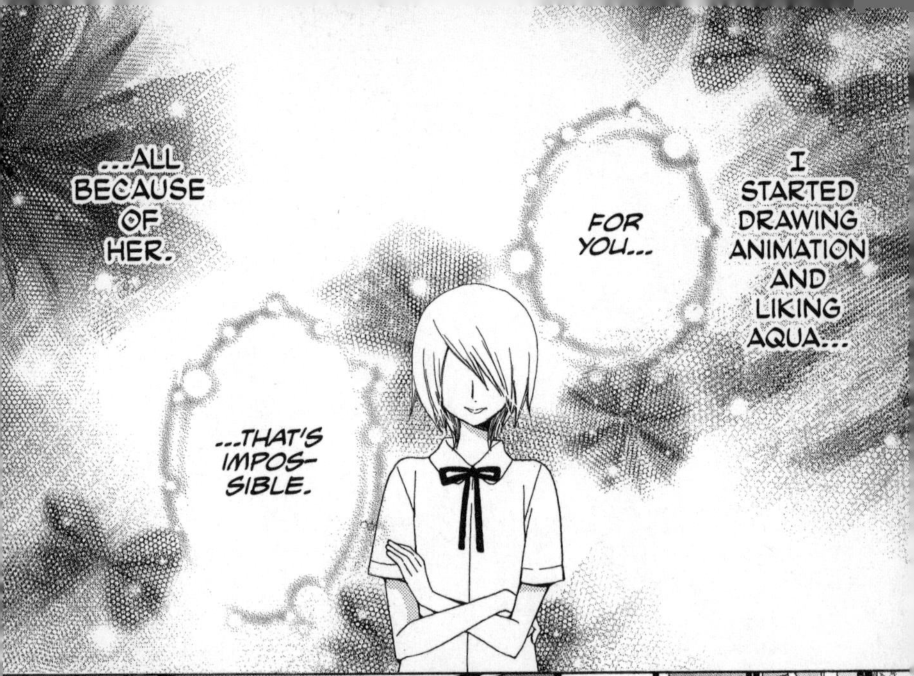
I STARTED DRAWING ANIMATION AND LIKING AQUA...
FOR YOU...
...ALL BECAUSE OF HER.
...THAT'S IMPOSSIBLE.

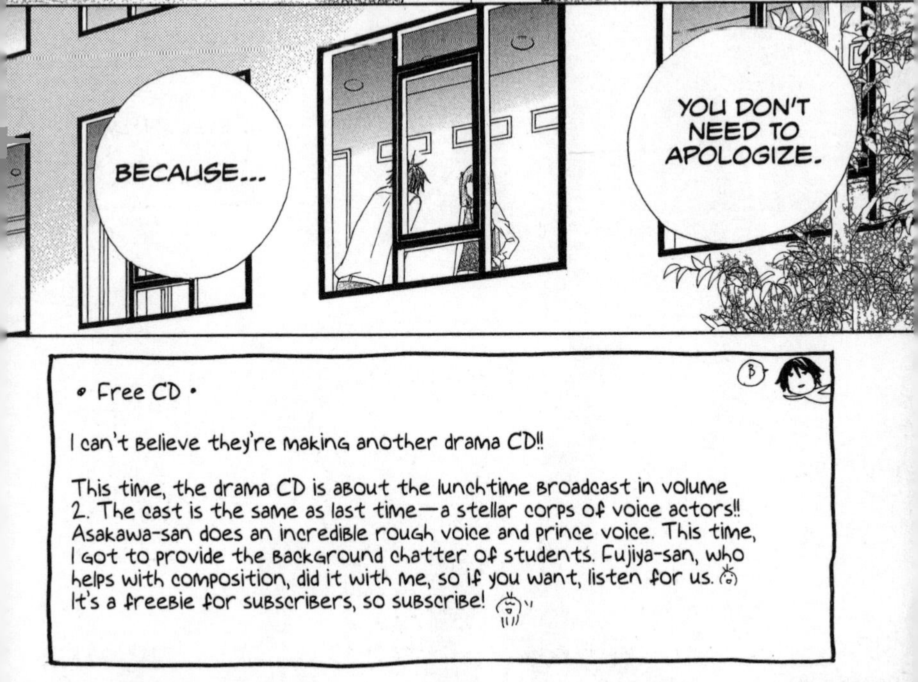
YOU DON'T NEED TO APOLOGIZE.
BECAUSE...

• Free CD •

I can't believe they're making another drama CD!!

This time, the drama CD is about the lunchtime broadcast in volume 2. The cast is the same as last time—a stellar corps of voice actors!! Asakawa-san does an incredible rough voice and prince voice. This time, I got to provide the background chatter of students. Fujiya-san, who helps with composition, did it with me, so if you want, listen for us. It's a freebie for subscribers, so subscribe!

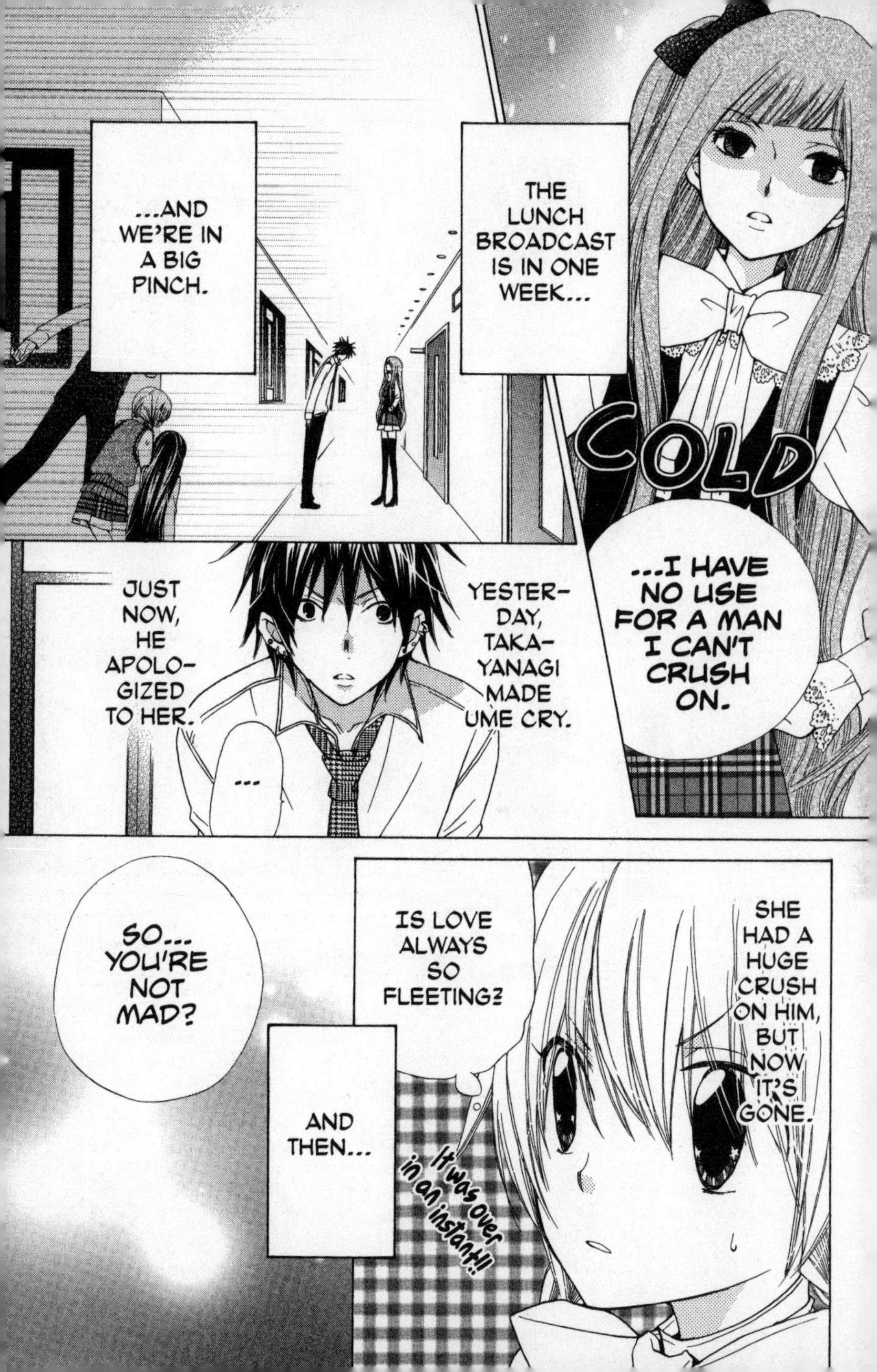
COLD
...I HAVE NO USE FOR A MAN I CAN'T CRUSH ON.
THE LUNCH BROADCAST IS IN ONE WEEK...
...AND WE'RE IN A BIG PINCH.
YESTERDAY, TAKAYANAGI MADE UME CRY.
JUST NOW, HE APOLOGIZED TO HER.
...
SHE HAD A HUGE CRUSH ON HIM, BUT NOW IT'S GONE.
IS LOVE ALWAYS SO FLEETING?
It was over in an instant!!
AND THEN...
SO... YOU'RE NOT MAD?

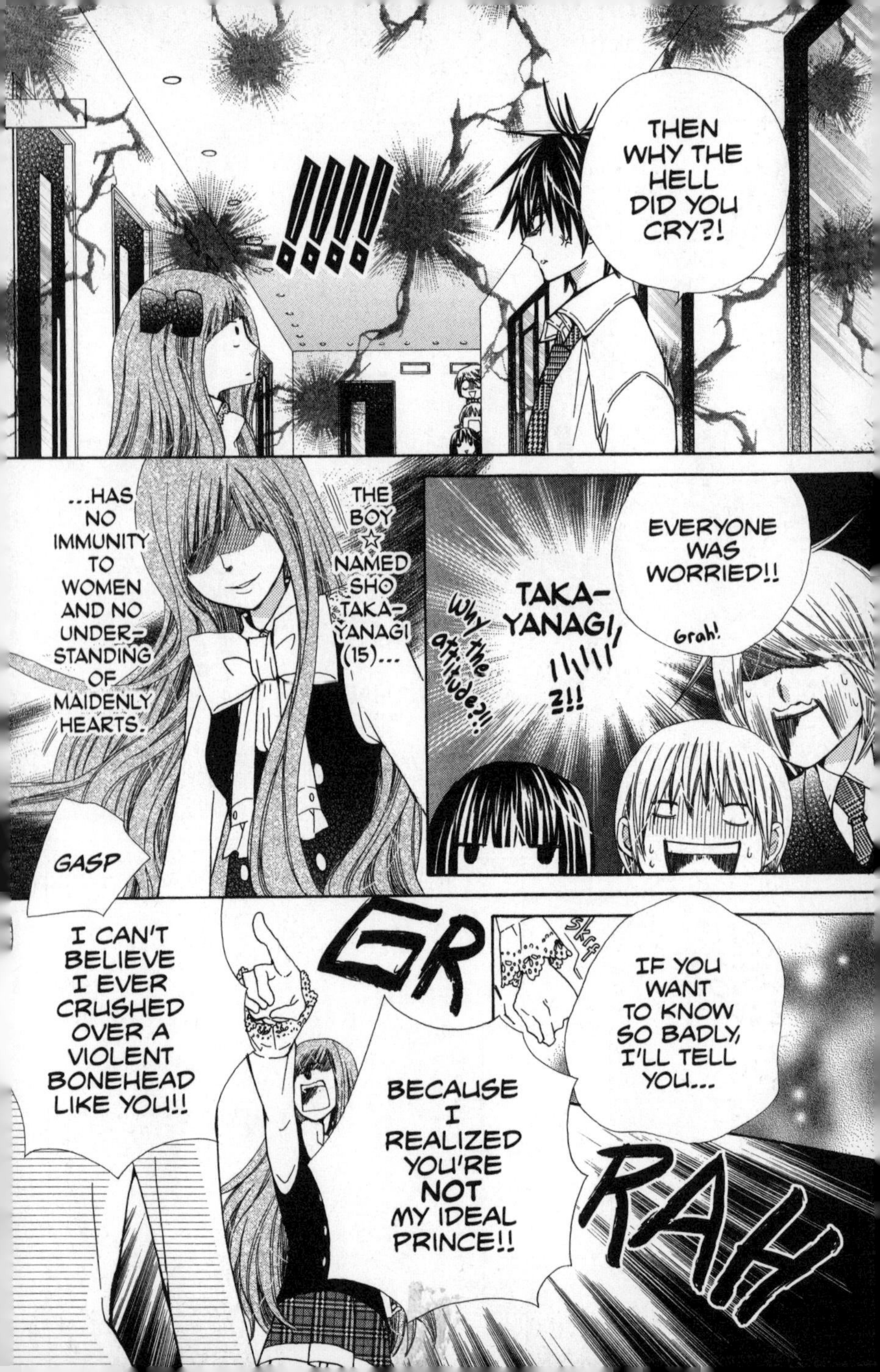
!!!!
THEN WHY THE HELL DID YOU CRY?!
EVERYONE WAS WORRIED!!
Grah!
TAKA-YANAGI!!!!!?!!
Why the attitude?!!
THE BOY☆NAMED SHO TAKA-YANAGI (15)...
...HAS NO IMMUNITY TO WOMEN AND NO UNDER-STANDING OF MAIDENLY HEARTS.
GASP
Skrf
IF YOU WANT TO KNOW SO BADLY, I'LL TELL YOU...
BECAUSE I REALIZED YOU'RE NOT MY IDEAL PRINCE!!
GR
RAH
I CAN'T BELIEVE I EVER CRUSHED OVER A VIOLENT BONEHEAD LIKE YOU!!

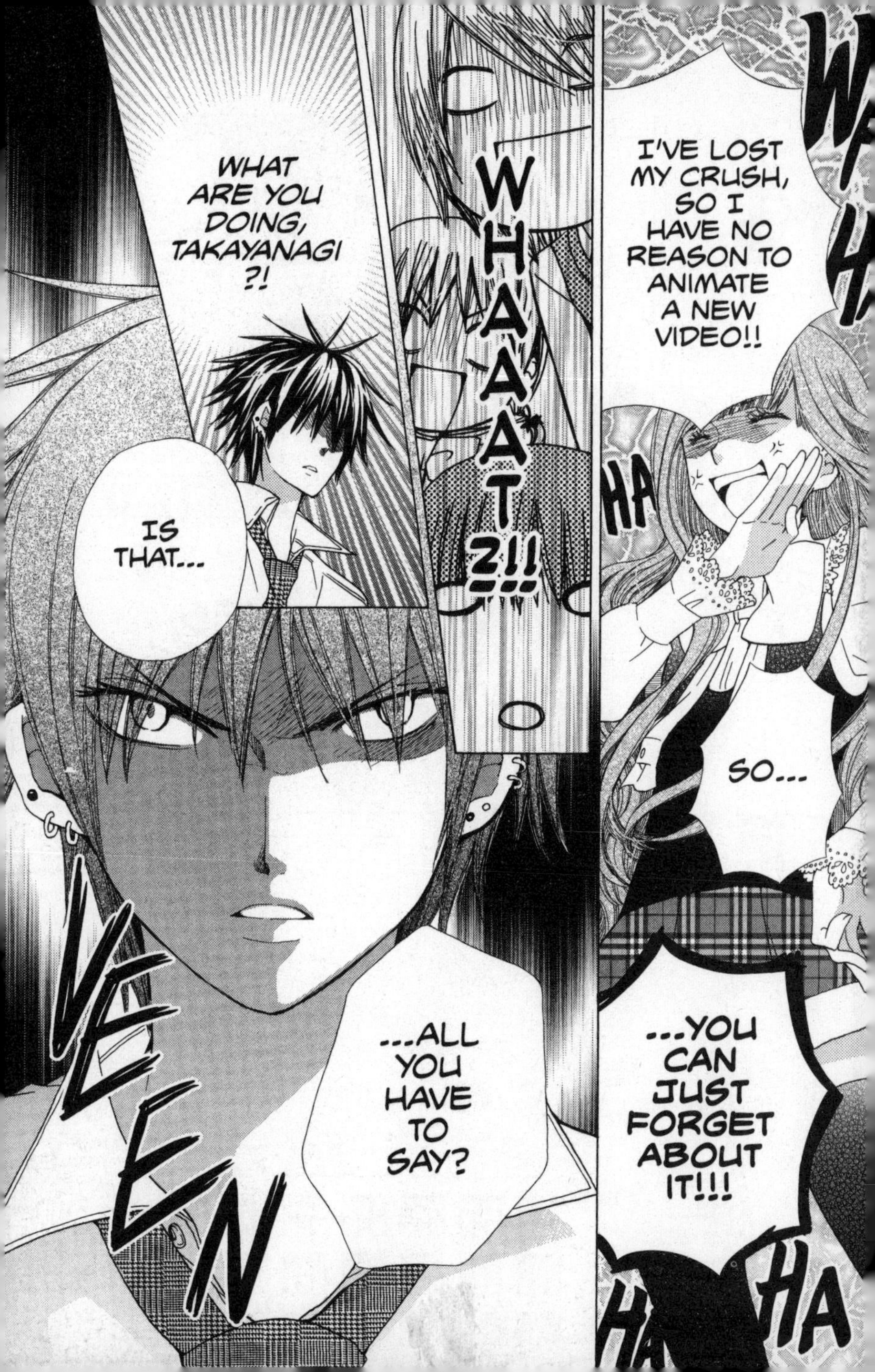
I'VE LOST MY CRUSH, SO I HAVE NO REASON TO ANIMATE A NEW VIDEO!!
HA
SO...
...YOU CAN JUST FORGET ABOUT IT!!!
HA HA HA
WHAAAT?!!
WHAT ARE YOU DOING, TAKAYANAGI?!
IS THAT...
...ALL YOU HAVE TO SAY?
VEEEN

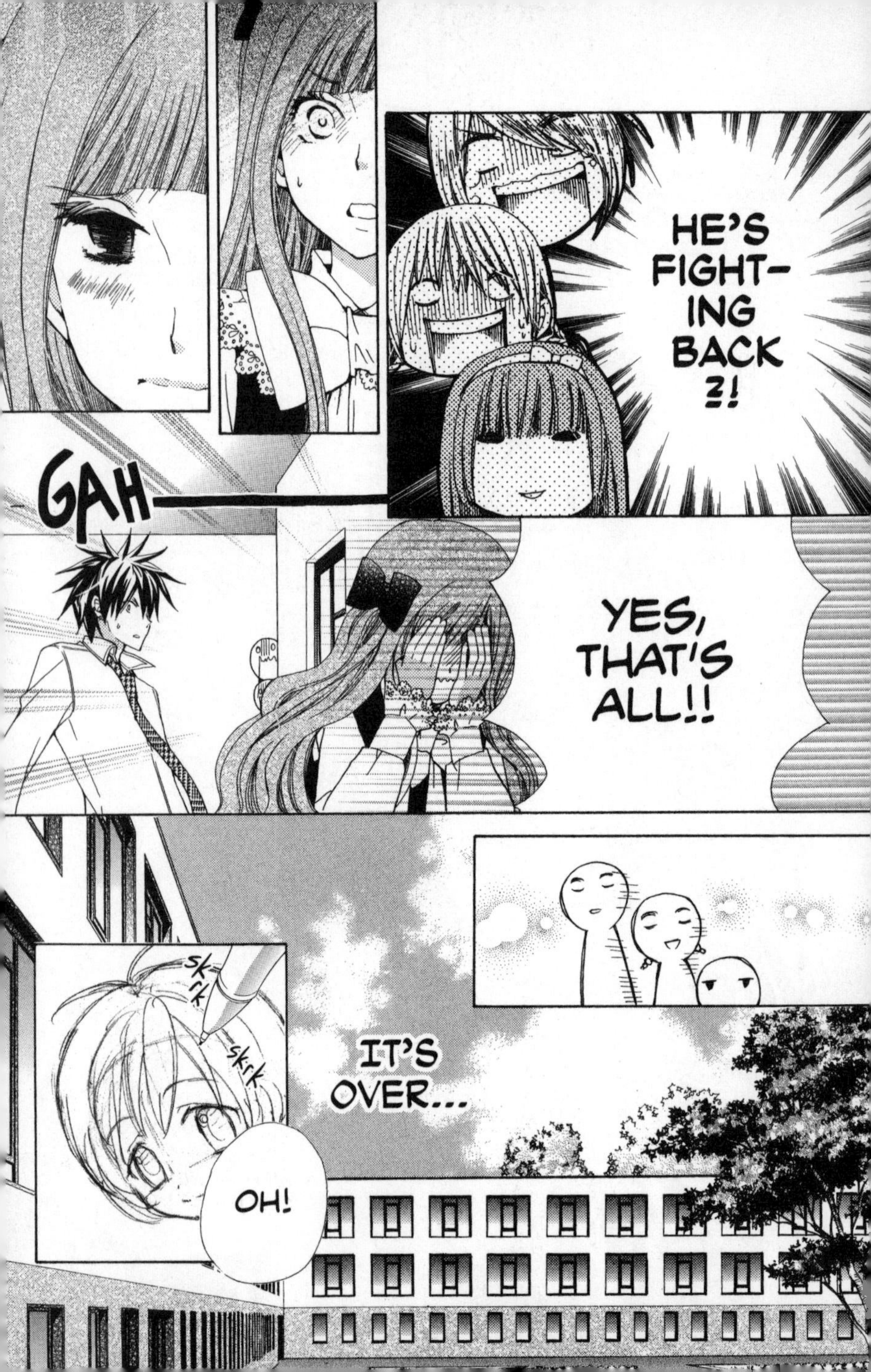
HE'S FIGHT-ING BACK ?!
GAH
YES, THAT'S ALL!!
IT'S OVER...
SKRK
SKRK
OH!

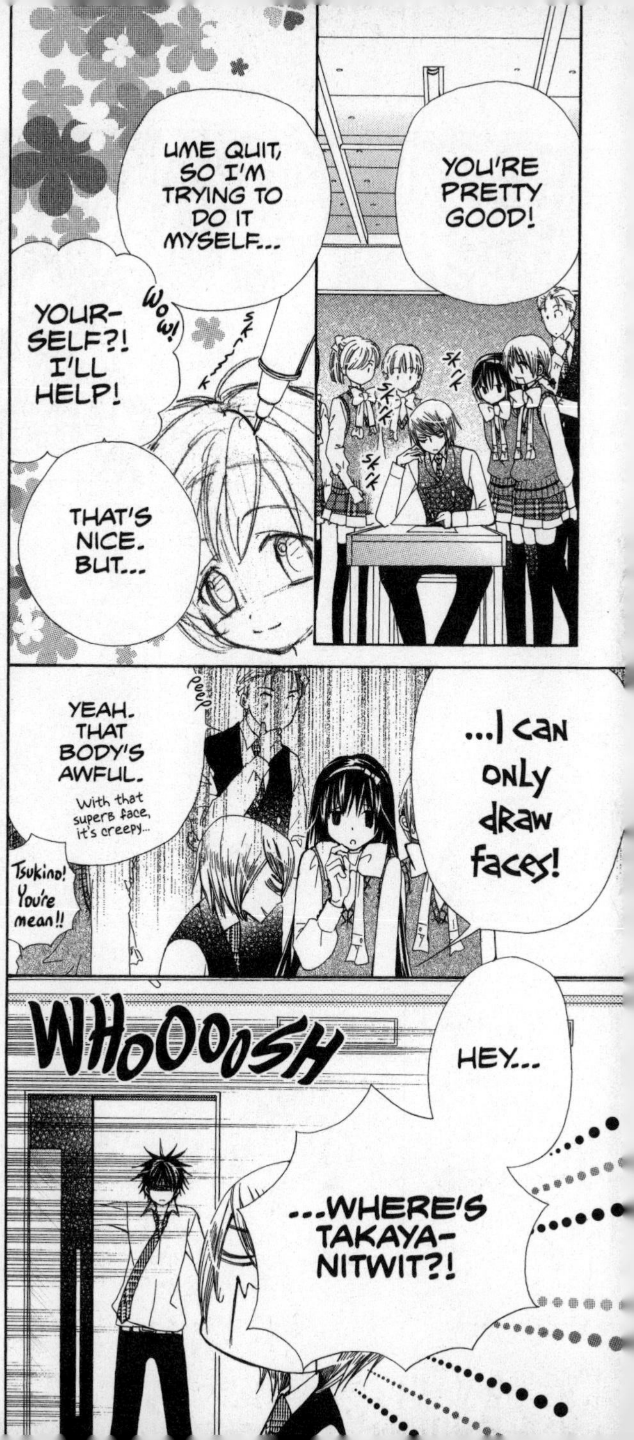
YOU'RE PRETTY GOOD!
SKRIK
SKRIK
SKRIK
SKRIK
UME QUIT, SO I'M TRYING TO DO IT MYSELF...
WOW!
YOURSELF?! I'LL HELP!
SKRIK
THAT'S NICE. BUT...
...I CAN ONLY DRAW FACES!
YEAH. THAT BODY'S AWFUL.
With that superb face, it's creepy...
PEER
Tsukino! You're mean!!
WHOOOOOSH
HEY...
...WHERE'S TAKAYA-NITWIT?!

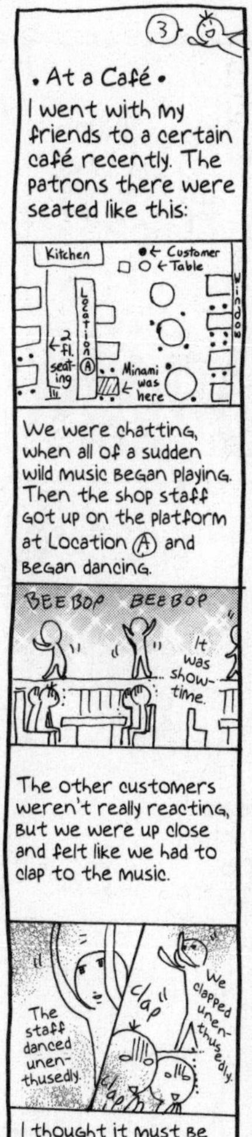
3
• At a Café •
I went with my friends to a certain café recently. The patrons there were seated like this:
Kitchen
● ← Customer
□ ○ ← Table
Window
Location Ⓐ
← 2 fl. seating
Minami was here
We were chatting, when all of a sudden wild music began playing. Then the shop staff got up on the platform at Location Ⓐ and began dancing.
BEEBOP BEEBOP
It was show-time.
The other customers weren't really reacting, but we were up close and felt like we had to clap to the music.
The staff danced unenthusedly.
We clapped unenthusedly.
clap
clap
I thought it must be some new kind of torture.
Roar!

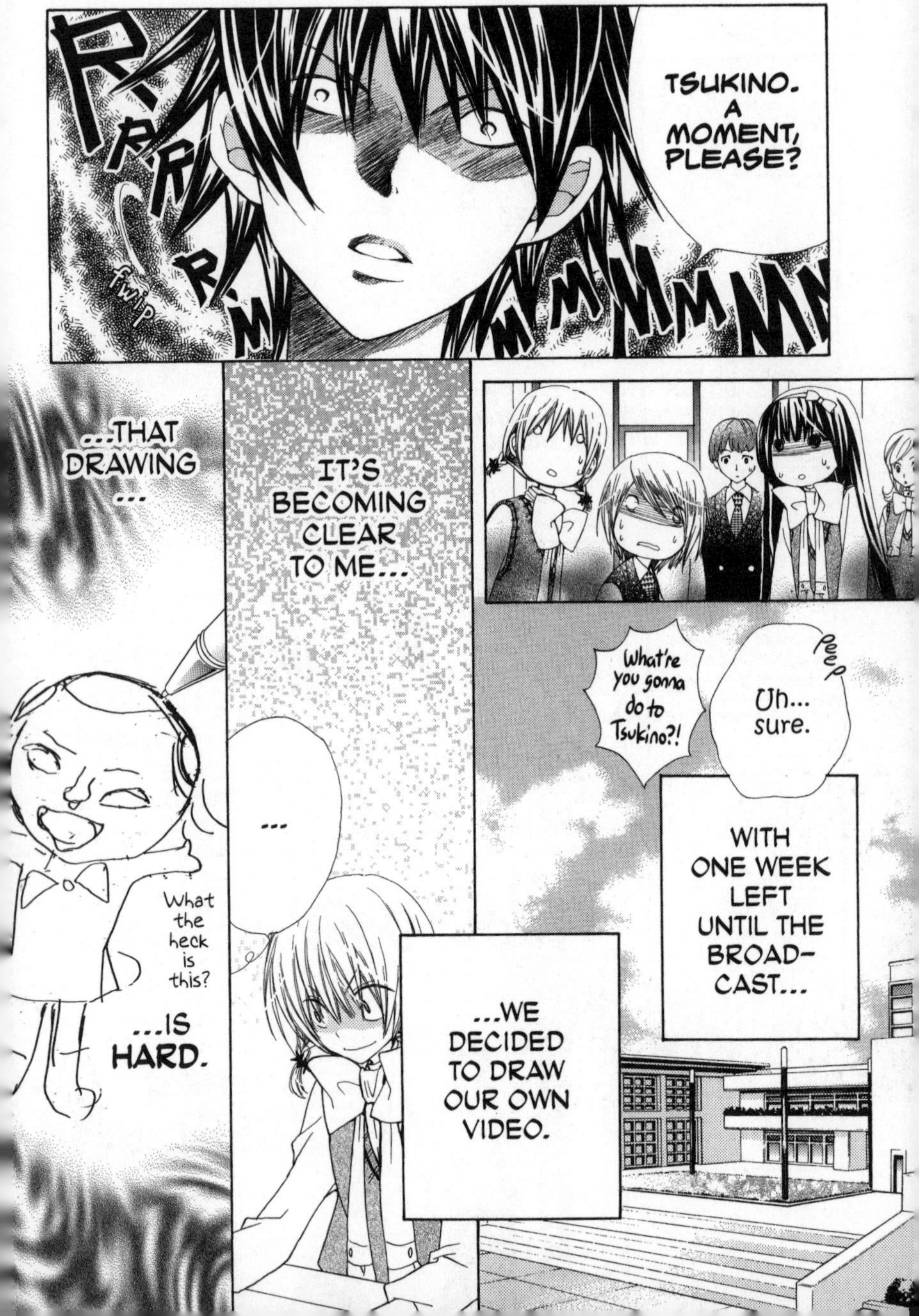
RRRRRM
fwip
MMMMMN
TSUKINO. A MOMENT, PLEASE?
What're you gonna do to Tsukino?!
Peep
Uh... sure.
WITH ONE WEEK LEFT UNTIL THE BROAD-CAST...
...WE DECIDED TO DRAW OUR OWN VIDEO.
IT'S BECOMING CLEAR TO ME...
...
...THAT DRAWING...
What the heck is this?
...IS HARD.

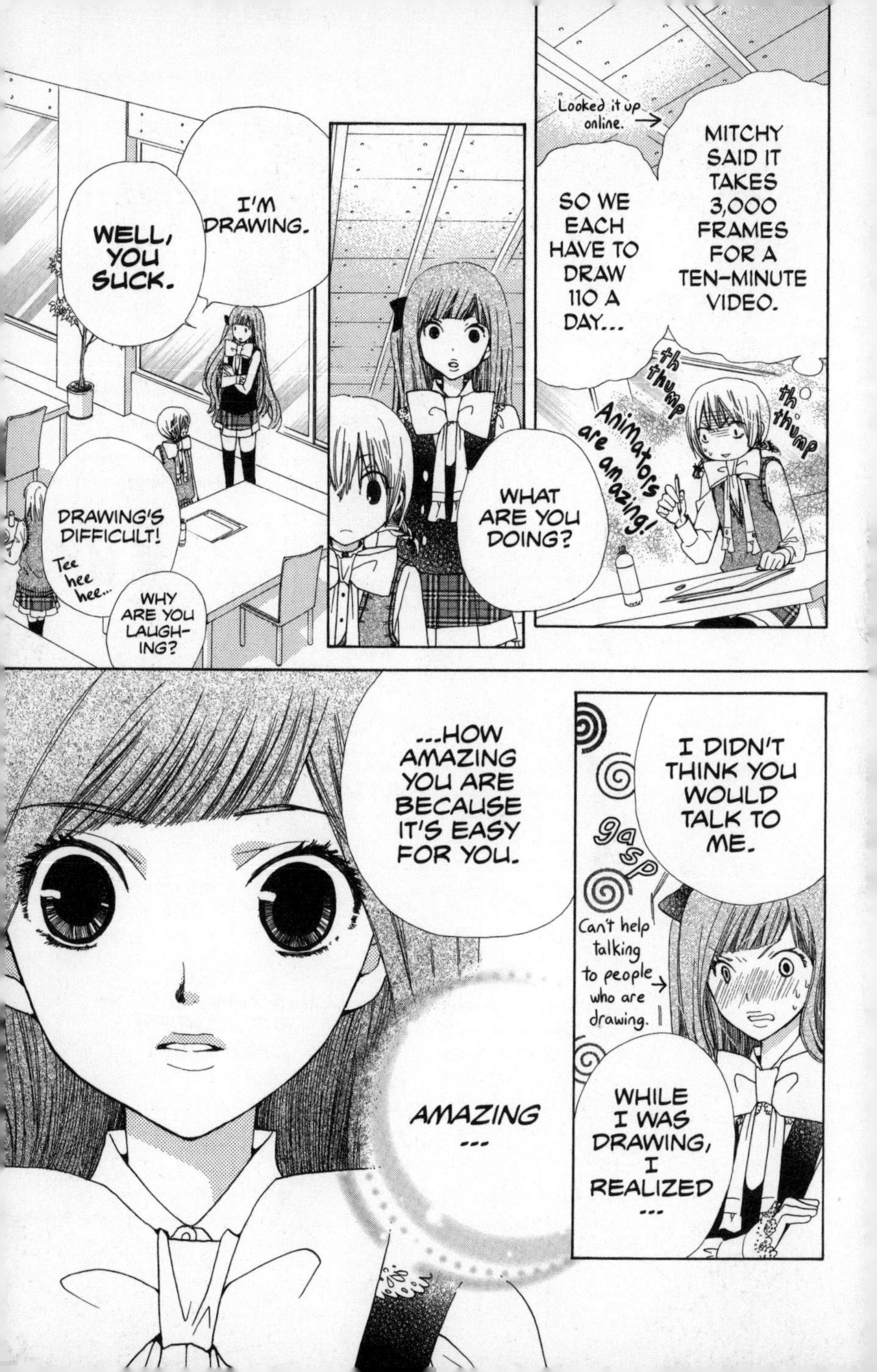

Looked it up online.
MITCHY SAID IT TAKES 3,000 FRAMES FOR A TEN-MINUTE VIDEO.
SO WE EACH HAVE TO DRAW 110 A DAY...
th thump
th thump
Animators are amazing!
WHAT ARE YOU DOING?
I'M DRAWING.
WELL, YOU SUCK.
DRAWING'S DIFFICULT!
Tee hee hee...
WHY ARE YOU LAUGHING?
I DIDN'T THINK YOU WOULD TALK TO ME.
gasp
Can't help talking to people who are drawing.
WHILE I WAS DRAWING, I REALIZED...
...HOW AMAZING YOU ARE BECAUSE IT'S EASY FOR YOU.
AMAZING...

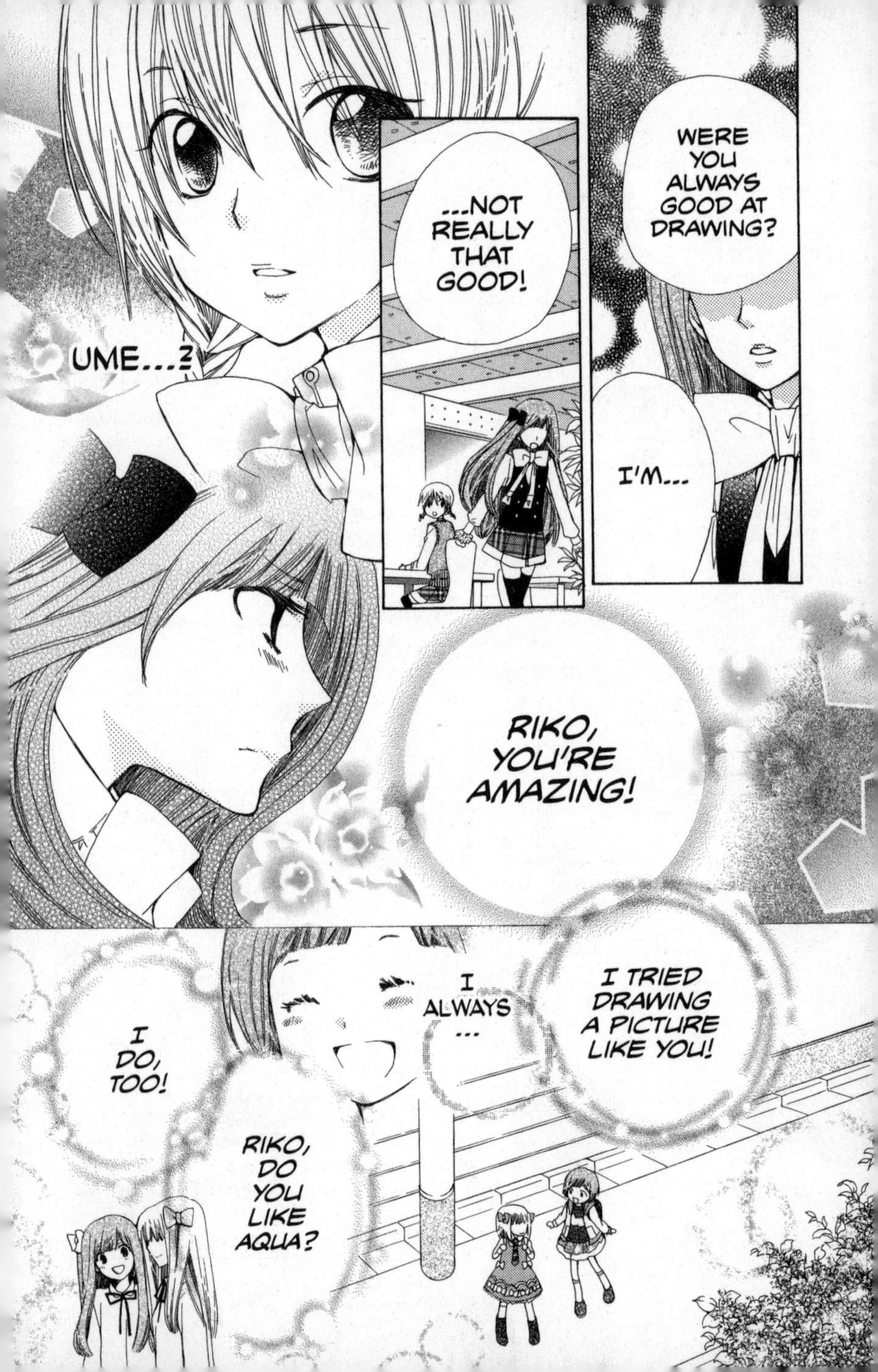
WERE YOU ALWAYS GOOD AT DRAWING?
I'M...
...NOT REALLY THAT GOOD!
UME...?
RIKO, YOU'RE AMAZING!
I TRIED DRAWING A PICTURE LIKE YOU!
I ALWAYS ...
I DO, TOO!
RIKO, DO YOU LIKE AQUA?

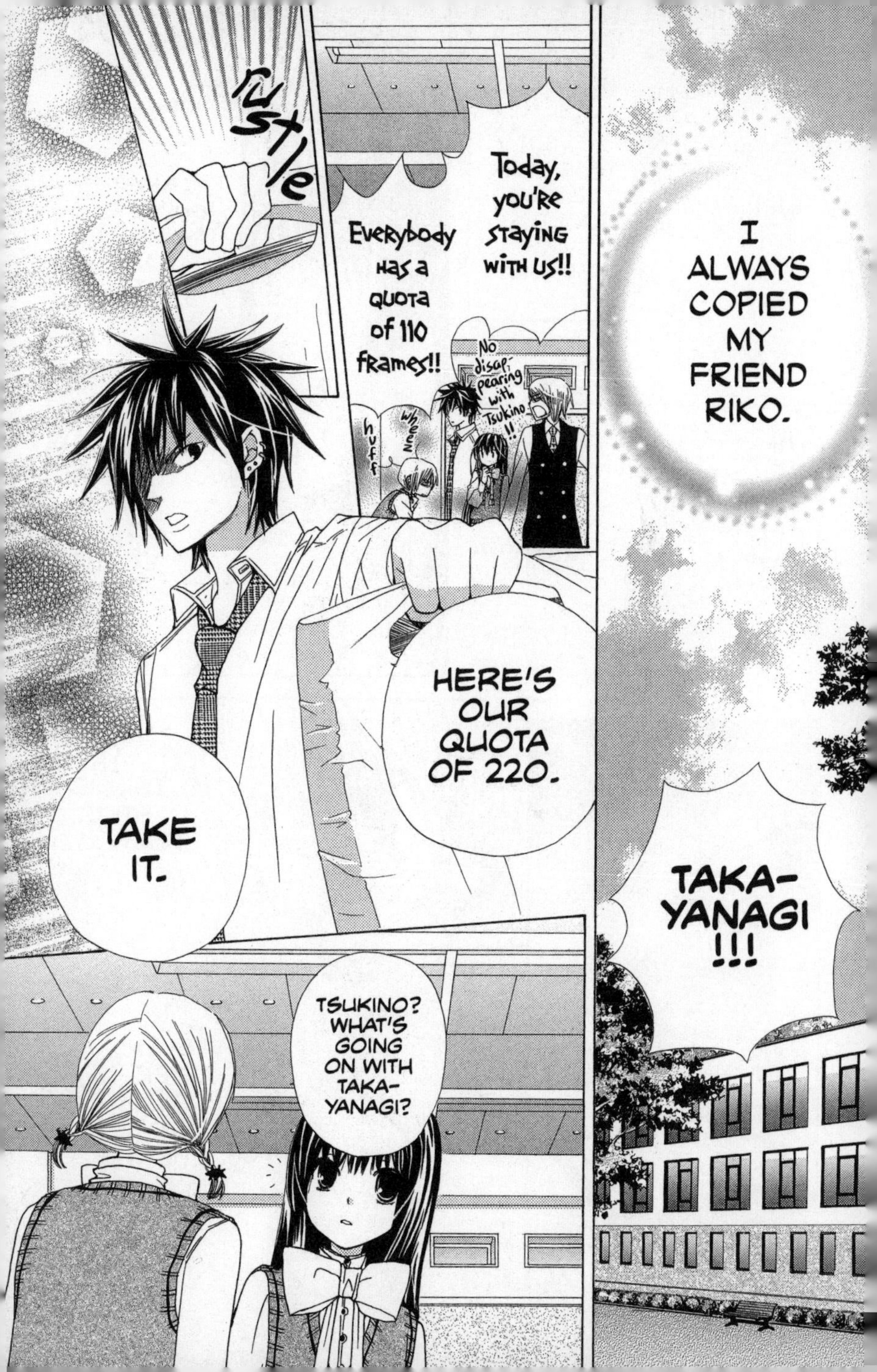
I ALWAYS COPIED MY FRIEND RIKO.
TAKA-YANAGI!!!
Today, you're staying with us!!
Everybody has a quota of 110 frames!!
No disap-pearing with Tsukino!!
wheeze
huff
rustle
HERE'S OUR QUOTA OF 220.
TAKE IT.
TSUKINO? WHAT'S GOING ON WITH TAKA-YANAGI?

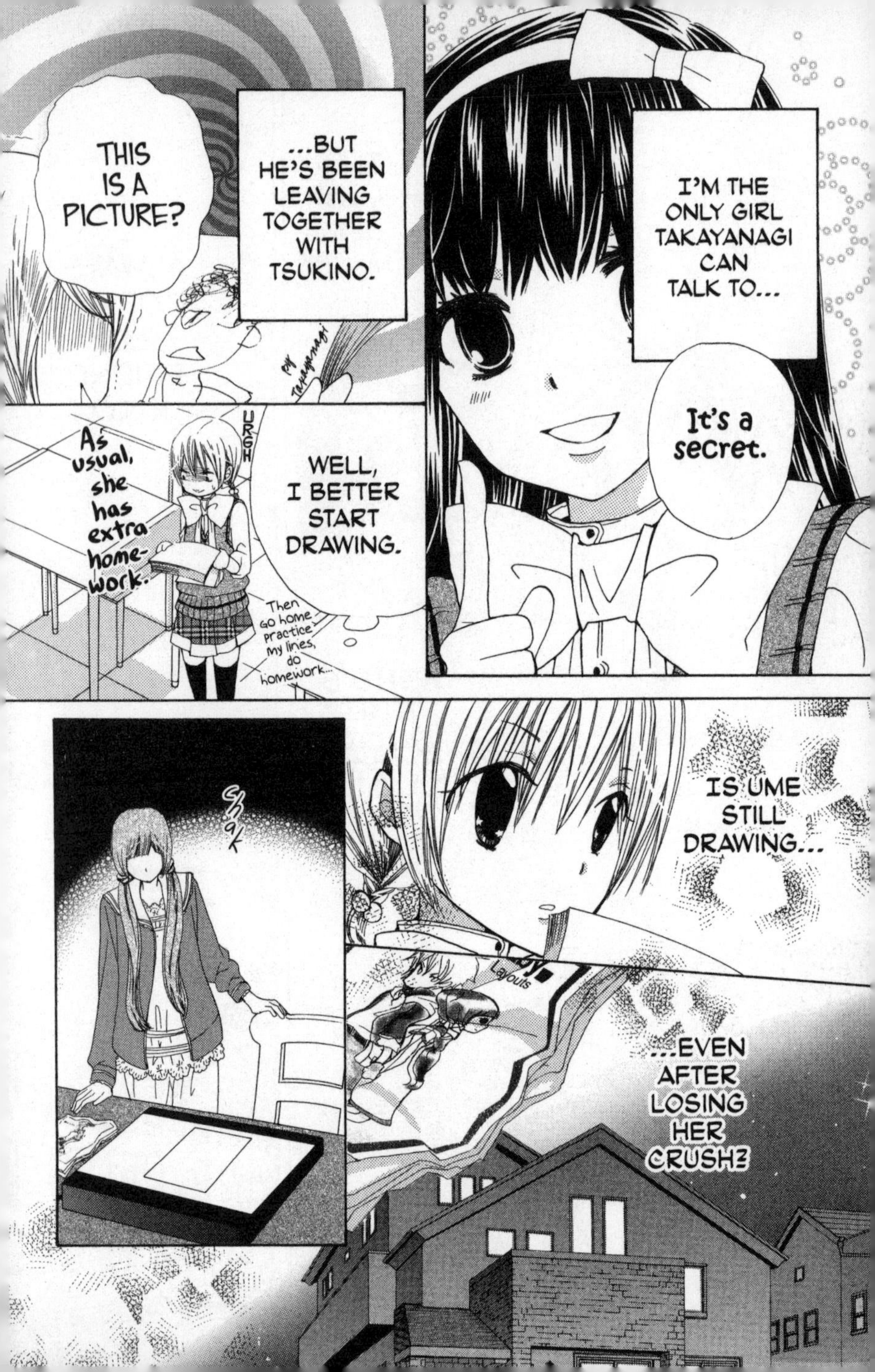
I'M THE ONLY GIRL TAKAYANAGI CAN TALK TO...
It's a secret.
...BUT HE'S BEEN LEAVING TOGETHER WITH TSUKINO.
THIS IS A PICTURE?
by Takayanagi
URGH
WELL, I BETTER START DRAWING.
As usual, she has extra home-work.
Then go home practice my lines, do homework...
IS UME STILL DRAWING...
Layouts
...EVEN AFTER LOSING HER CRUSH?
Shak

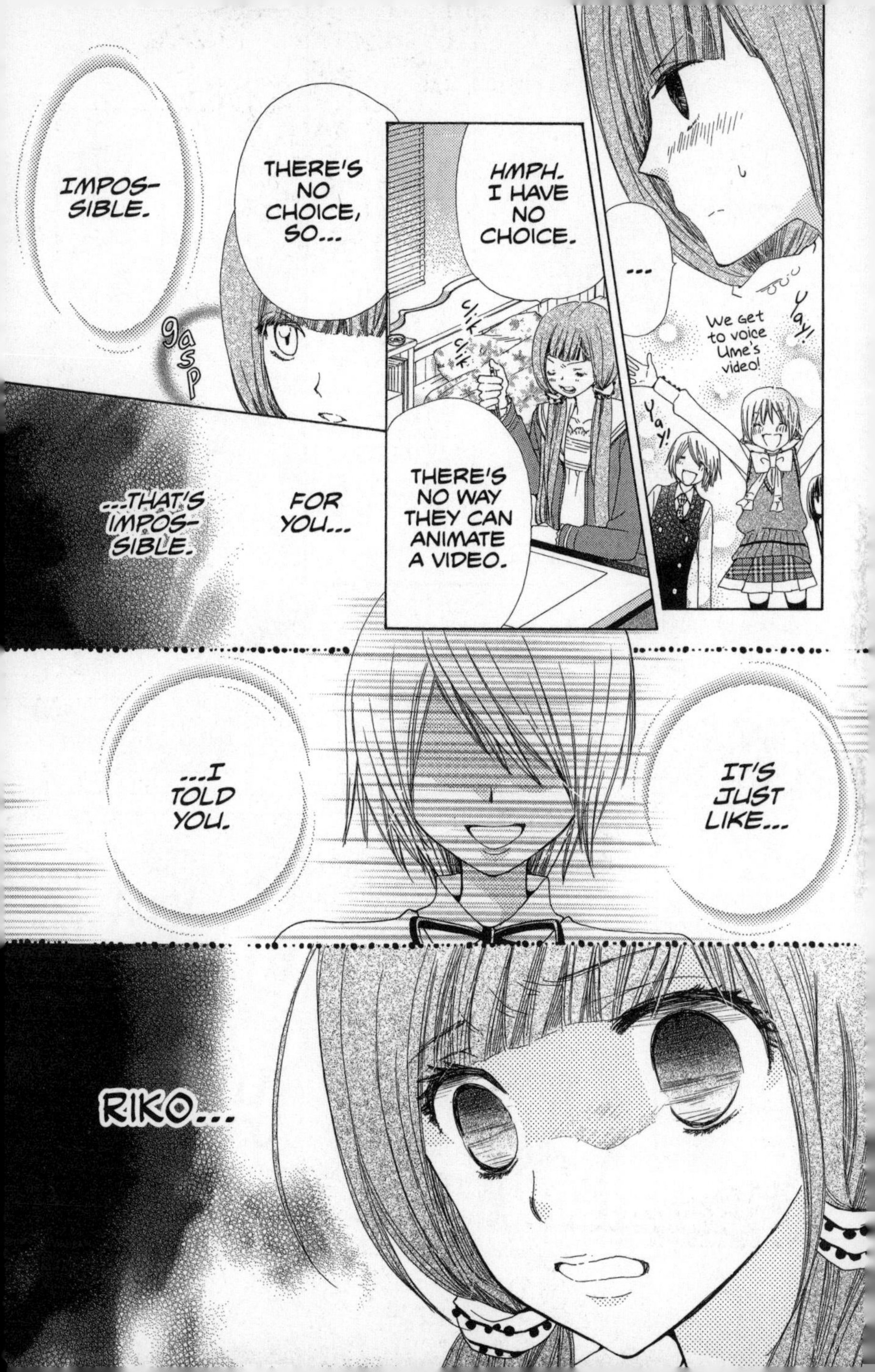
...
Yay!
We get to voice Ume's video!
Yay!
HMPH. I HAVE NO CHOICE.
clik clik
THERE'S NO WAY THEY CAN ANIMATE A VIDEO.
THERE'S NO CHOICE, SO...
IMPOS-SIBLE.
gasp
FOR YOU...
...THAT'S IMPOS-SIBLE.
IT'S JUST LIKE...
...I TOLD YOU.
RIKO...

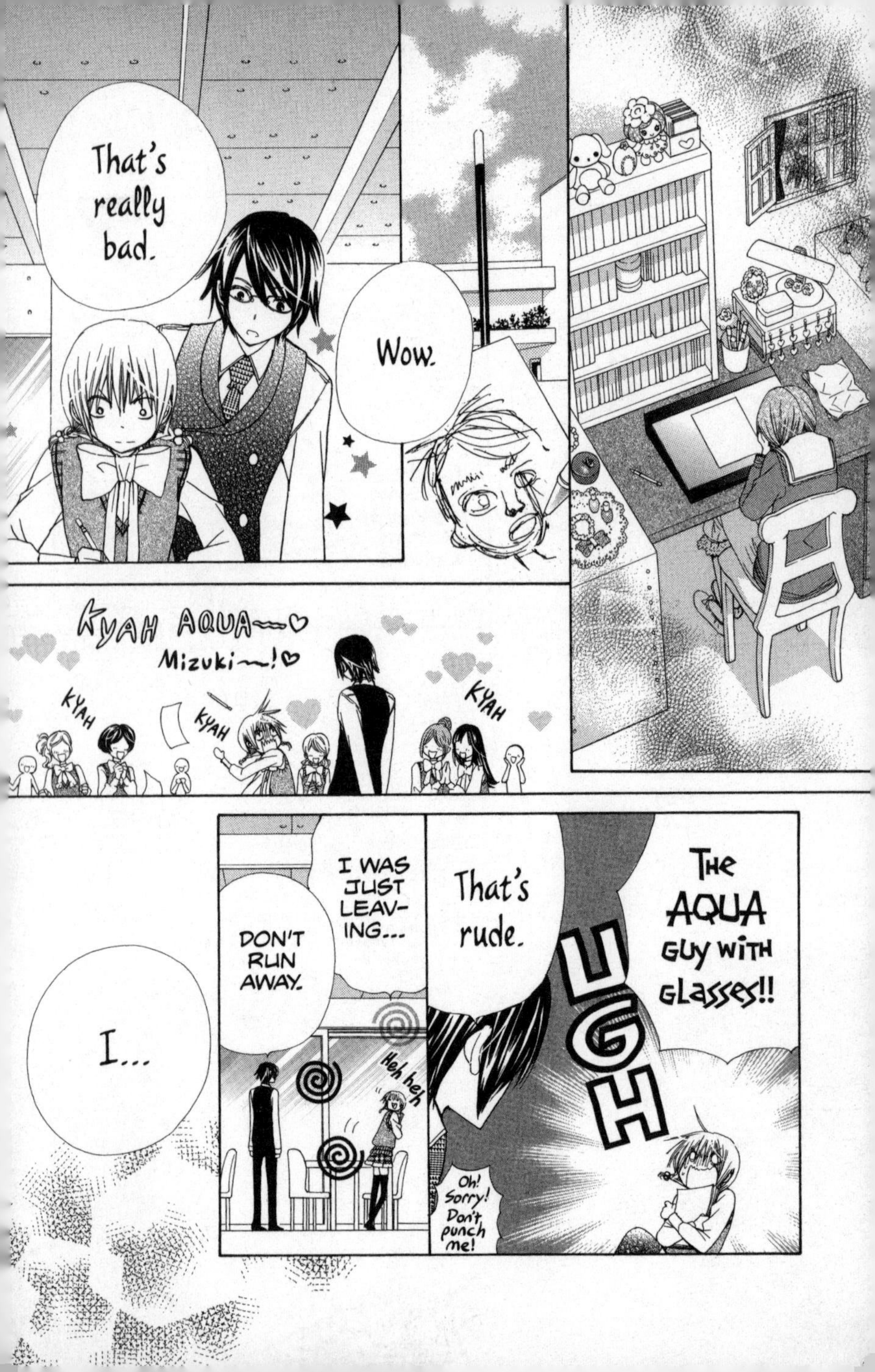
Wow.
That's really bad.
KYAH AQUA~♡
Mizuki~!♡
KYAH
KYAH
KYAH
THE AQUA GUY WITH GLASSES!!
That's rude.
UGH
Oh! Sorry! Don't punch me!
I WAS JUST LEAVING...
DON'T RUN AWAY.
Heh heh
I...

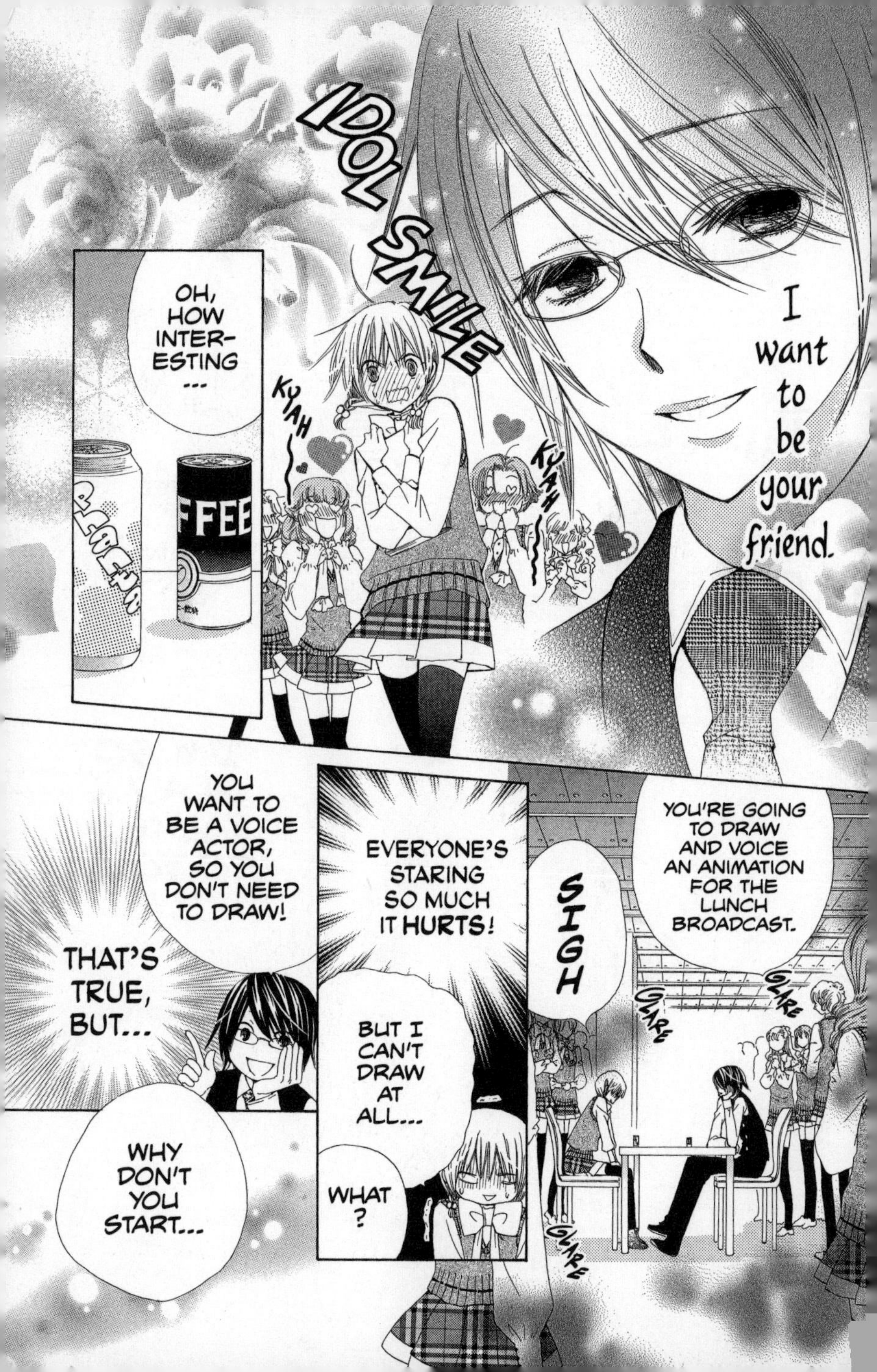
I want to be your friend.
IDOL SMILE
KYAH
KYAH
OH, HOW INTER-ESTING ---
FFEE
YOU'RE GOING TO DRAW AND VOICE AN ANIMATION FOR THE LUNCH BROADCAST.
SIGH
GLARE
GLARE
GLARE
EVERYONE'S STARING SO MUCH IT HURTS!
BUT I CAN'T DRAW AT ALL...
WHAT?
YOU WANT TO BE A VOICE ACTOR, SO YOU DON'T NEED TO DRAW!
THAT'S TRUE, BUT...
WHY DON'T YOU START...

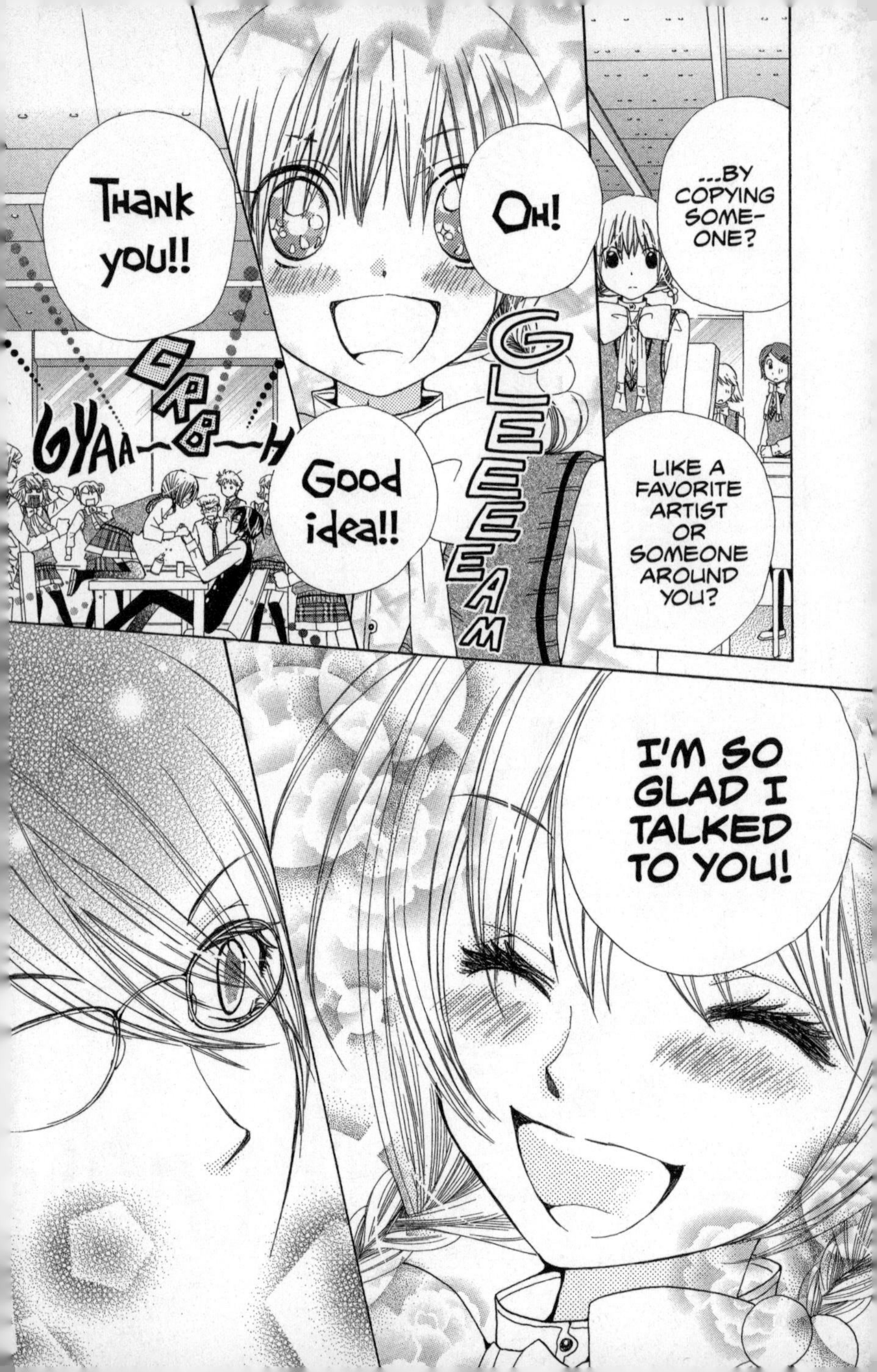
...BY COPYING SOME-ONE?
LIKE A FAVORITE ARTIST OR SOMEONE AROUND YOU?
OH!
GLEEEEAM
Good idea!!
Thank you!!
GRB
GYAA~~H
I'M SO GLAD I TALKED TO YOU!

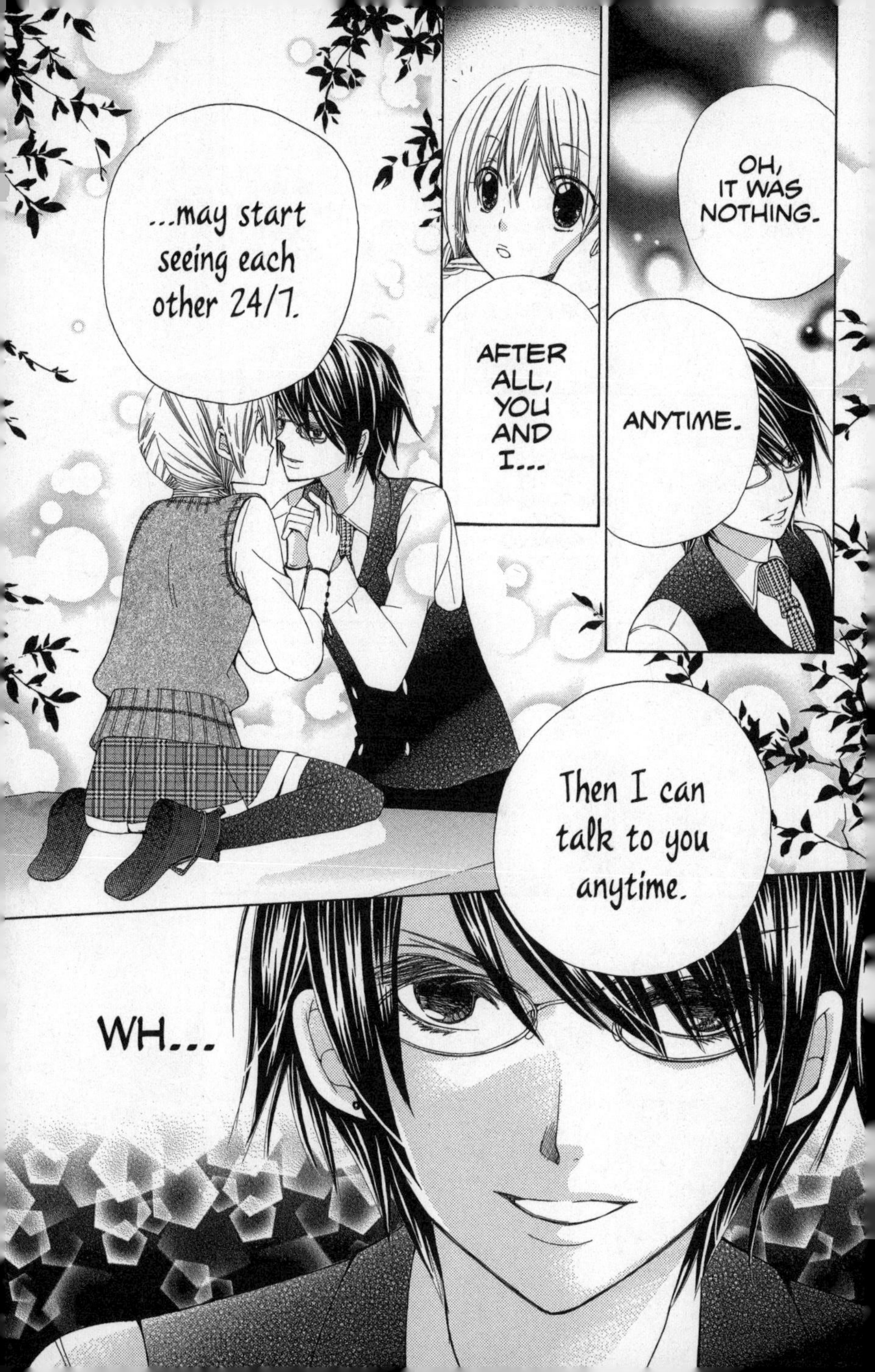
OH, IT WAS NOTHING.
ANYTIME.
AFTER ALL, YOU AND I...
...may start seeing each other 24/7.
Then I can talk to you anytime.
WH...

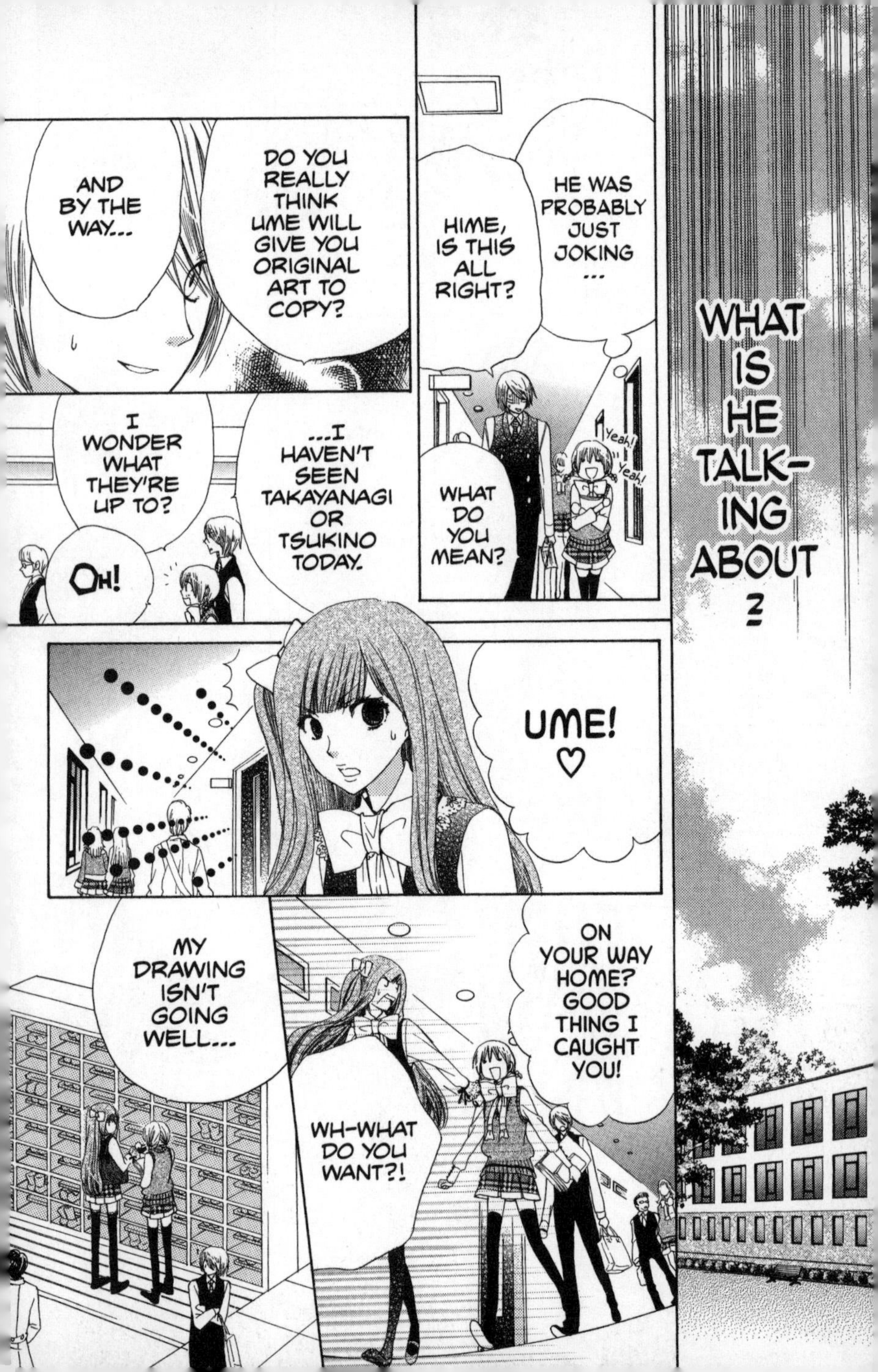
WHAT IS HE TALKING ABOUT?
HE WAS PROBABLY JUST JOKING...
HIME, IS THIS ALL RIGHT?
Yeah!
Yeah!
WHAT DO YOU MEAN?
DO YOU REALLY THINK UME WILL GIVE YOU ORIGINAL ART TO COPY?
AND BY THE WAY...
...I HAVEN'T SEEN TAKAYANAGI OR TSUKINO TODAY.
I WONDER WHAT THEY'RE UP TO?
OH!
UME! ♡
ON YOUR WAY HOME? GOOD THING I CAUGHT YOU!
WH-WHAT DO YOU WANT?!
MY DRAWING ISN'T GOING WELL...

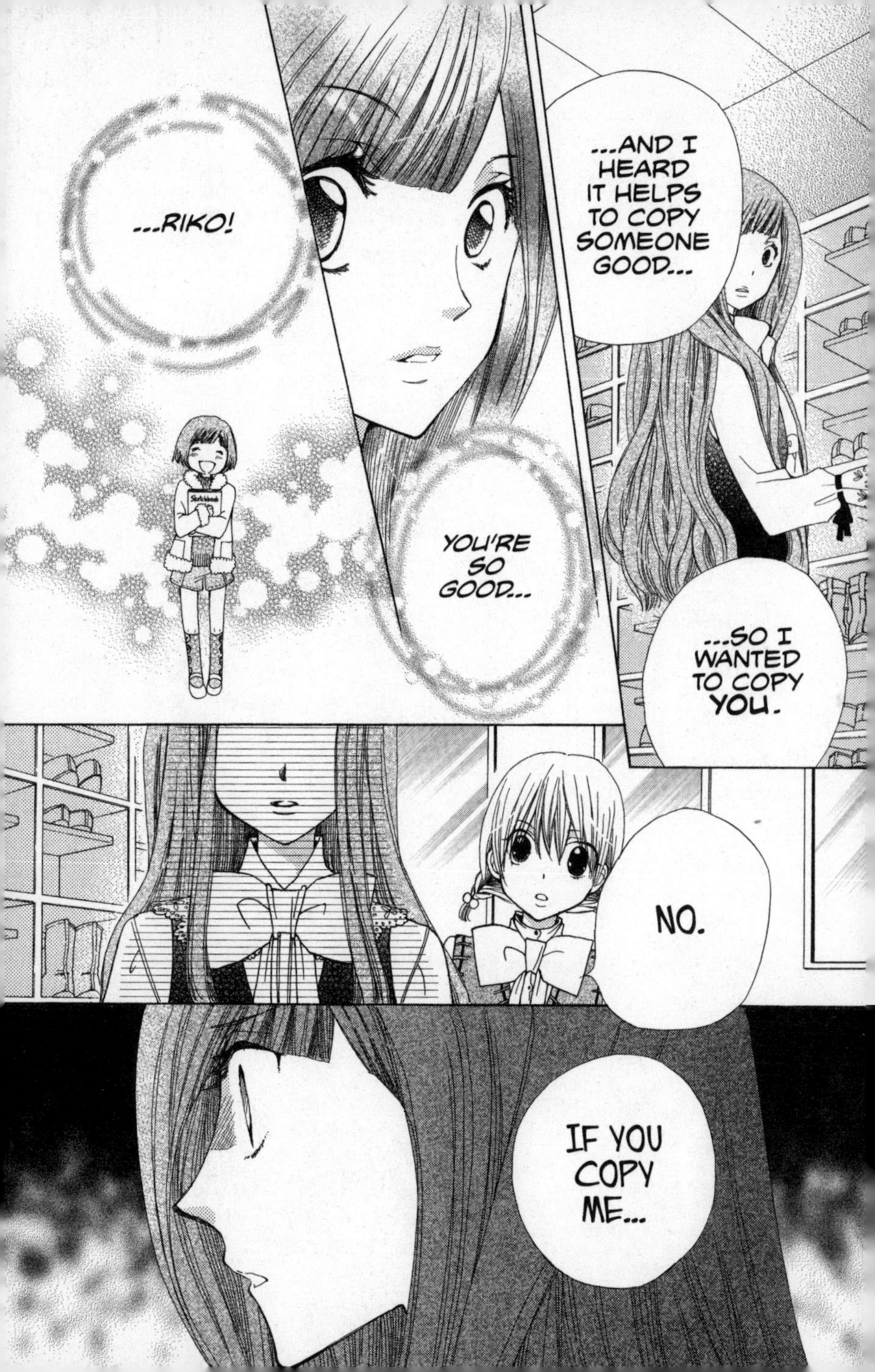
...AND I HEARD IT HELPS TO COPY SOMEONE GOOD...
...SO I WANTED TO COPY YOU.
YOU'RE SO GOOD...
...RIKO!
Sketchbook
NO.
IF YOU COPY ME...

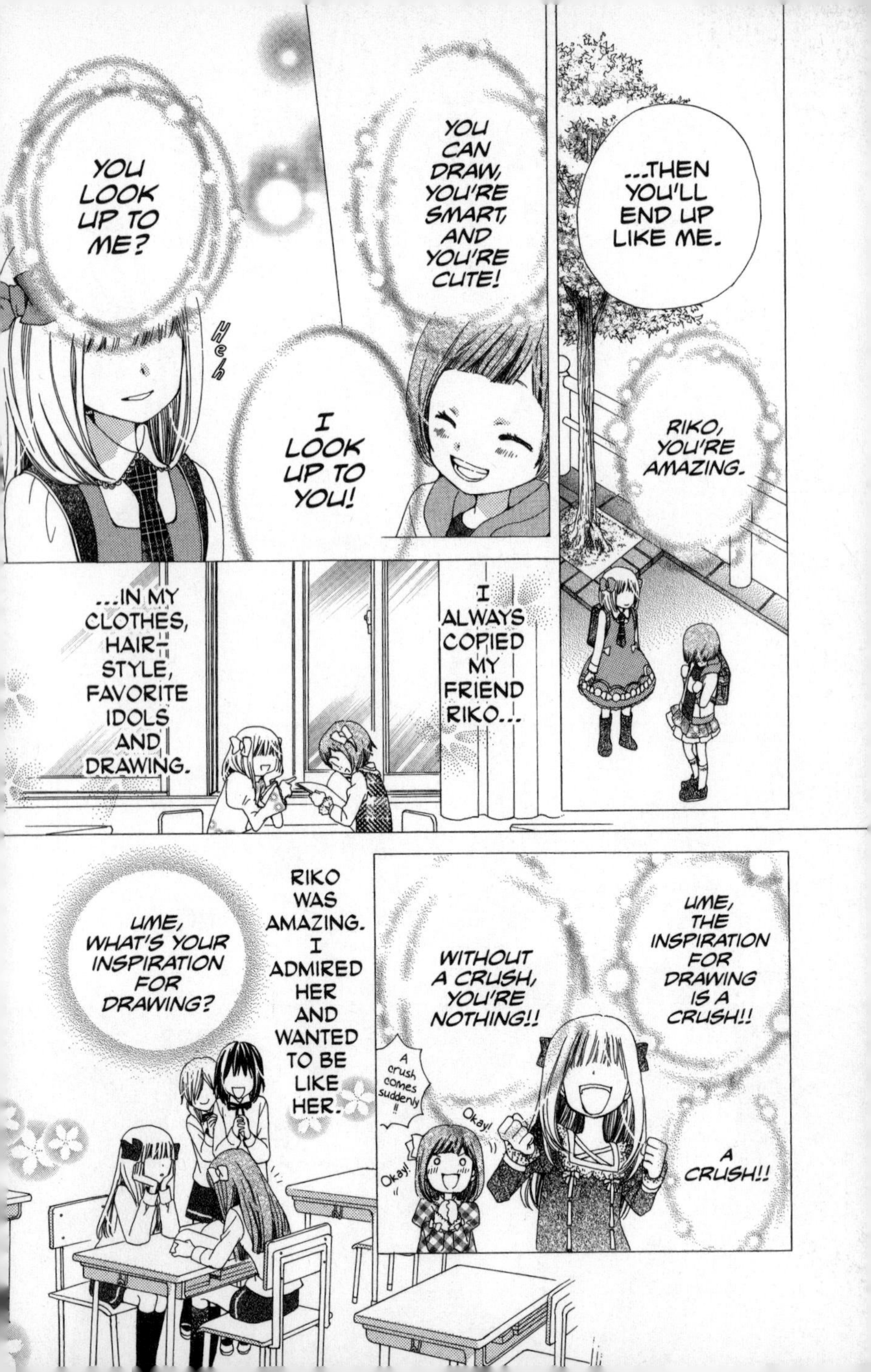
...THEN YOU'LL END UP LIKE ME.
RIKO, YOU'RE AMAZING.
YOU CAN DRAW, YOU'RE SMART, AND YOU'RE CUTE!
I LOOK UP TO YOU!
YOU LOOK UP TO ME?
Heh
I ALWAYS COPIED MY FRIEND RIKO...
...IN MY CLOTHES, HAIR-STYLE, FAVORITE IDOLS AND DRAWING.
UME, THE INSPIRATION FOR DRAWING IS A CRUSH!!
WITHOUT A CRUSH, YOU'RE NOTHING!!
A CRUSH!!
Okay!
A crush comes suddenly!!
Okay!
RIKO WAS AMAZING. I ADMIRED HER AND WANTED TO BE LIKE HER.
UME, WHAT'S YOUR INSPIRATION FOR DRAWING?

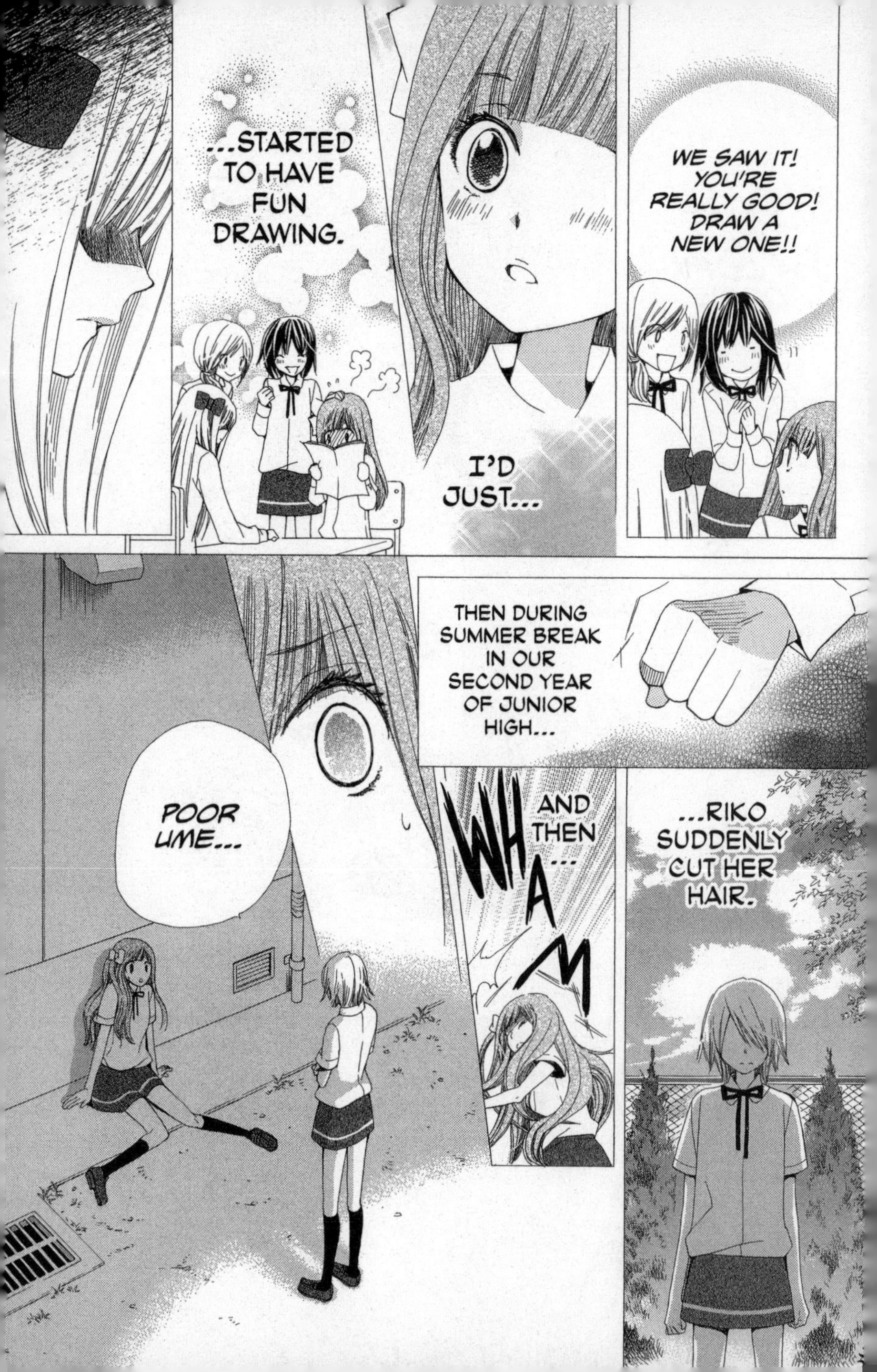
WE SAW IT! YOU'RE REALLY GOOD! DRAW A NEW ONE!!
I'D JUST...
...STARTED TO HAVE FUN DRAWING.
THEN DURING SUMMER BREAK IN OUR SECOND YEAR OF JUNIOR HIGH...
...RIKO SUDDENLY CUT HER HAIR.
AND THEN...
WHAM
POOR UME...

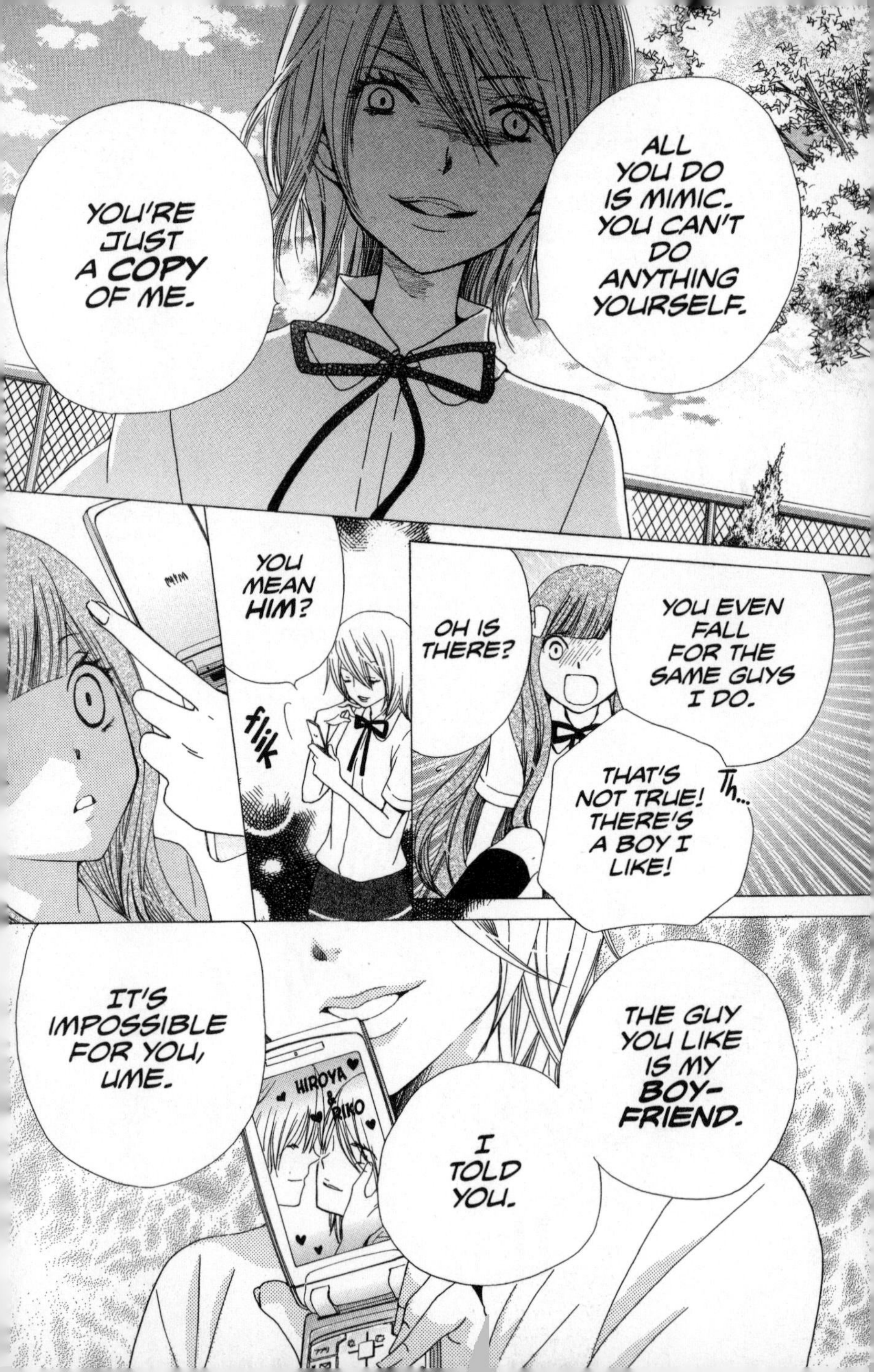
ALL YOU DO IS MIMIC. YOU CAN'T DO ANYTHING YOURSELF.
YOU'RE JUST A COPY OF ME.
YOU EVEN FALL FOR THE SAME GUYS I DO.
THAT'S NOT TRUE! THERE'S A BOY I LIKE!
Th...
OH IS THERE?
YOU MEAN HIM?
flik
THE GUY YOU LIKE IS MY BOY-FRIEND.
I TOLD YOU.
HIROYA & RIKO
IT'S IMPOSSIBLE FOR YOU, UME.

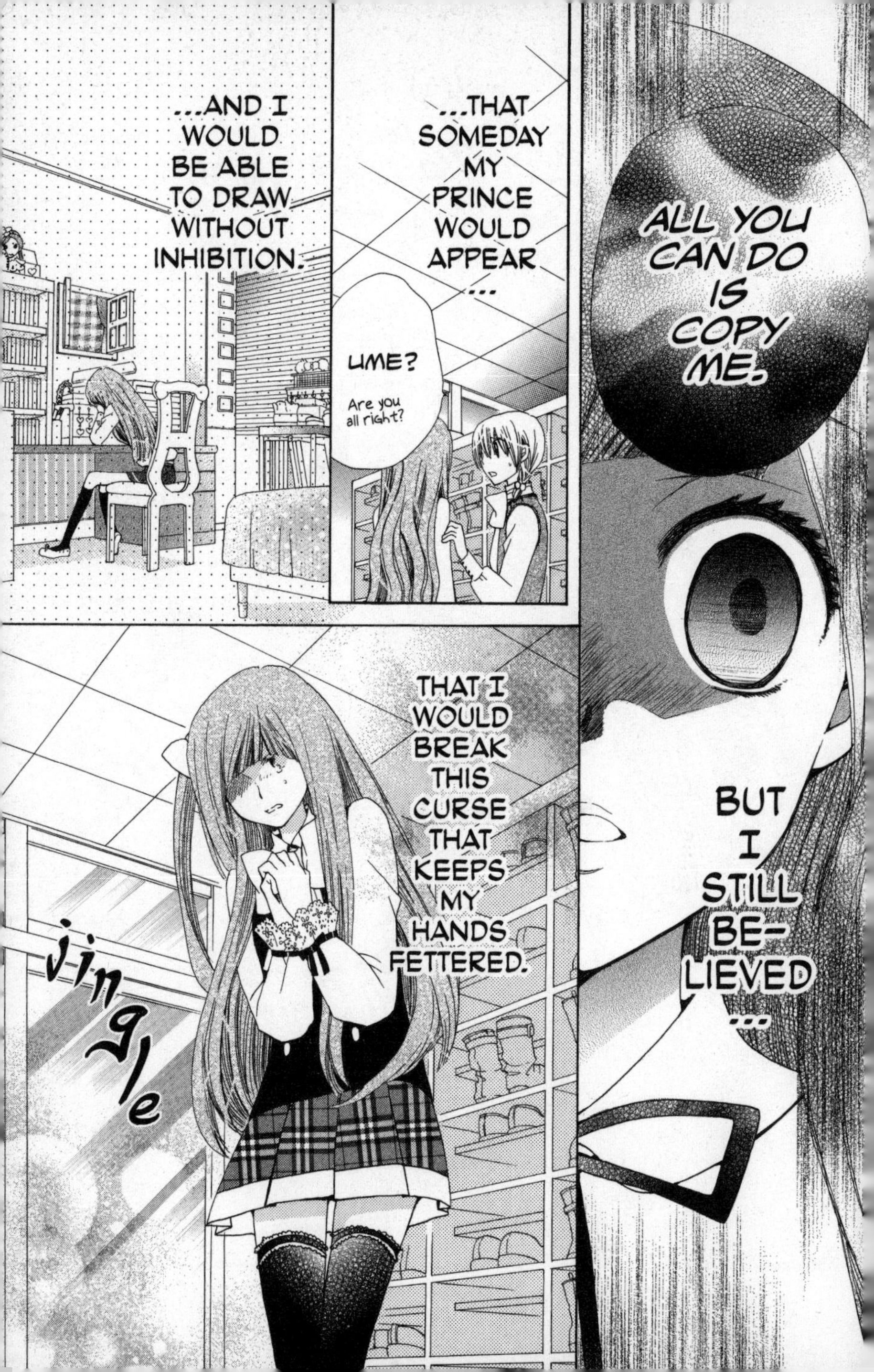
ALL YOU CAN DO IS COPY ME.
BUT I STILL BE-LIEVED...
...THAT SOMEDAY MY PRINCE WOULD APPEAR...
UME?
Are you all right?
...AND I WOULD BE ABLE TO DRAW WITHOUT INHIBITION.
THAT I WOULD BREAK THIS CURSE THAT KEEPS MY HANDS FETTERED.
jingle

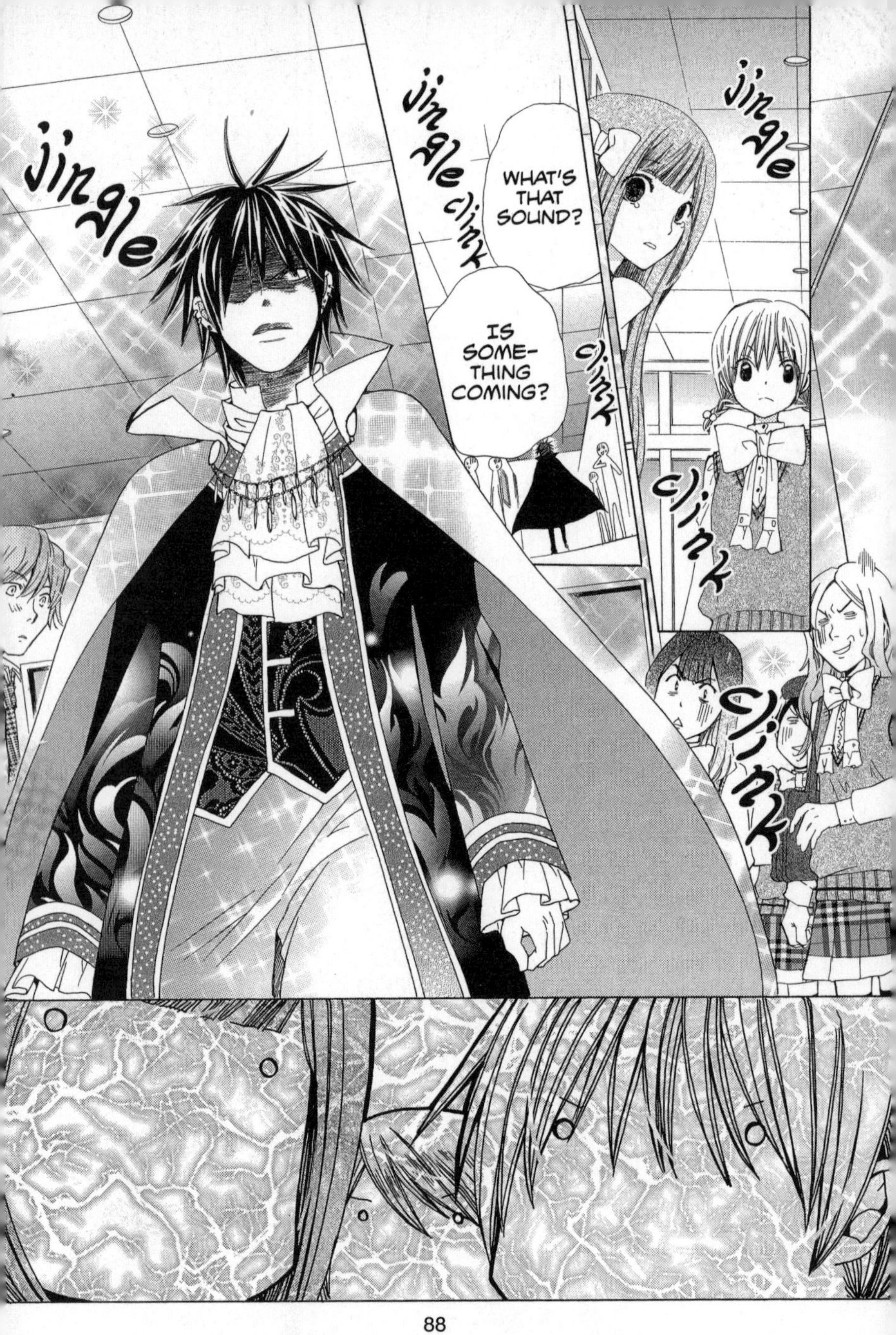
jingle
jingle clink
WHAT'S THAT SOUND?
IS SOME-THING COMING?
clink
clink
clink
jingle

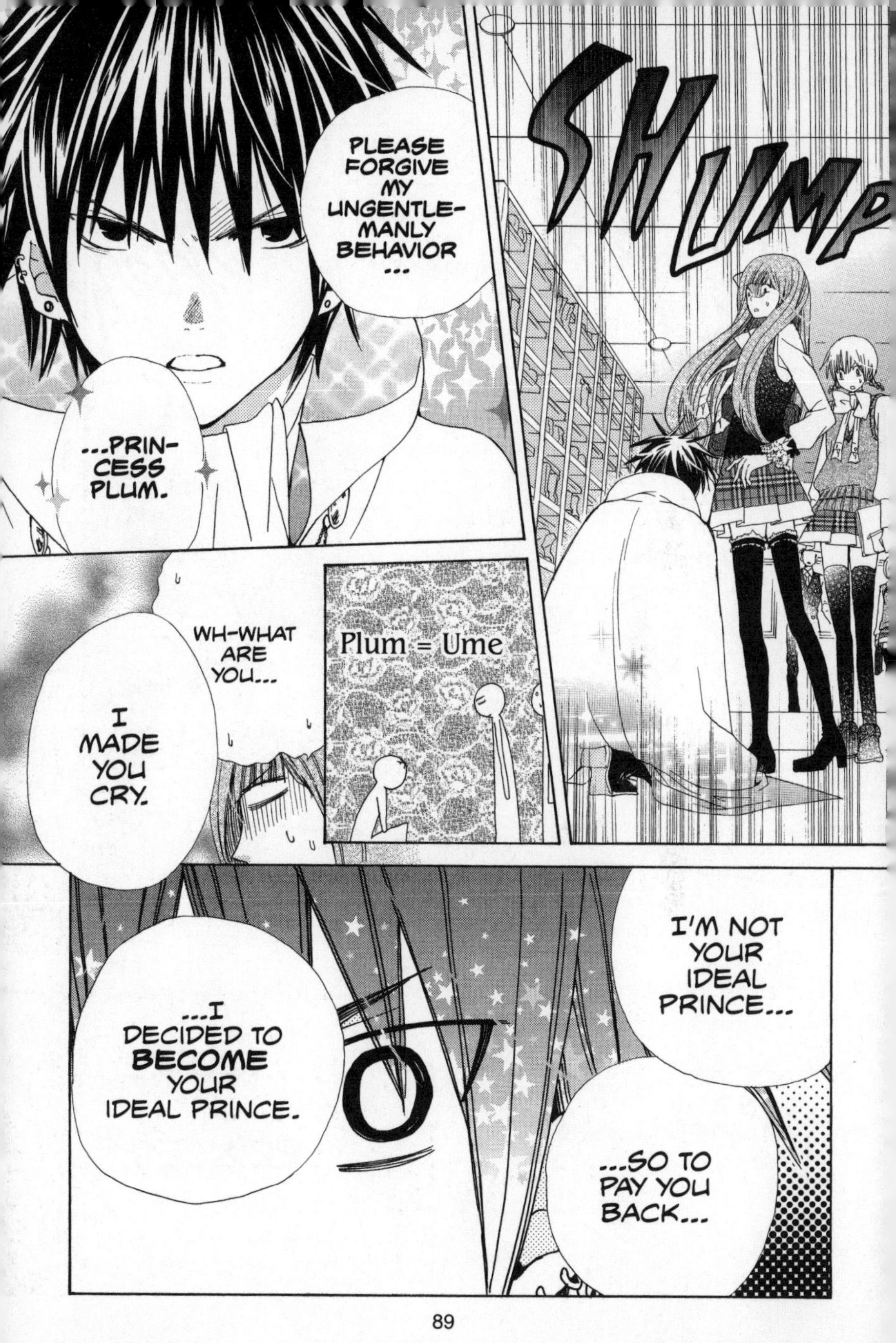
SHUMP
PLEASE FORGIVE MY UNGENTLE-MANLY BEHAVIOR...
...PRINCESS PLUM.
Plum = Ume
WH-WHAT ARE YOU...
I MADE YOU CRY.
I'M NOT YOUR IDEAL PRINCE...
...SO TO PAY YOU BACK...
...I DECIDED TO BECOME YOUR IDEAL PRINCE.

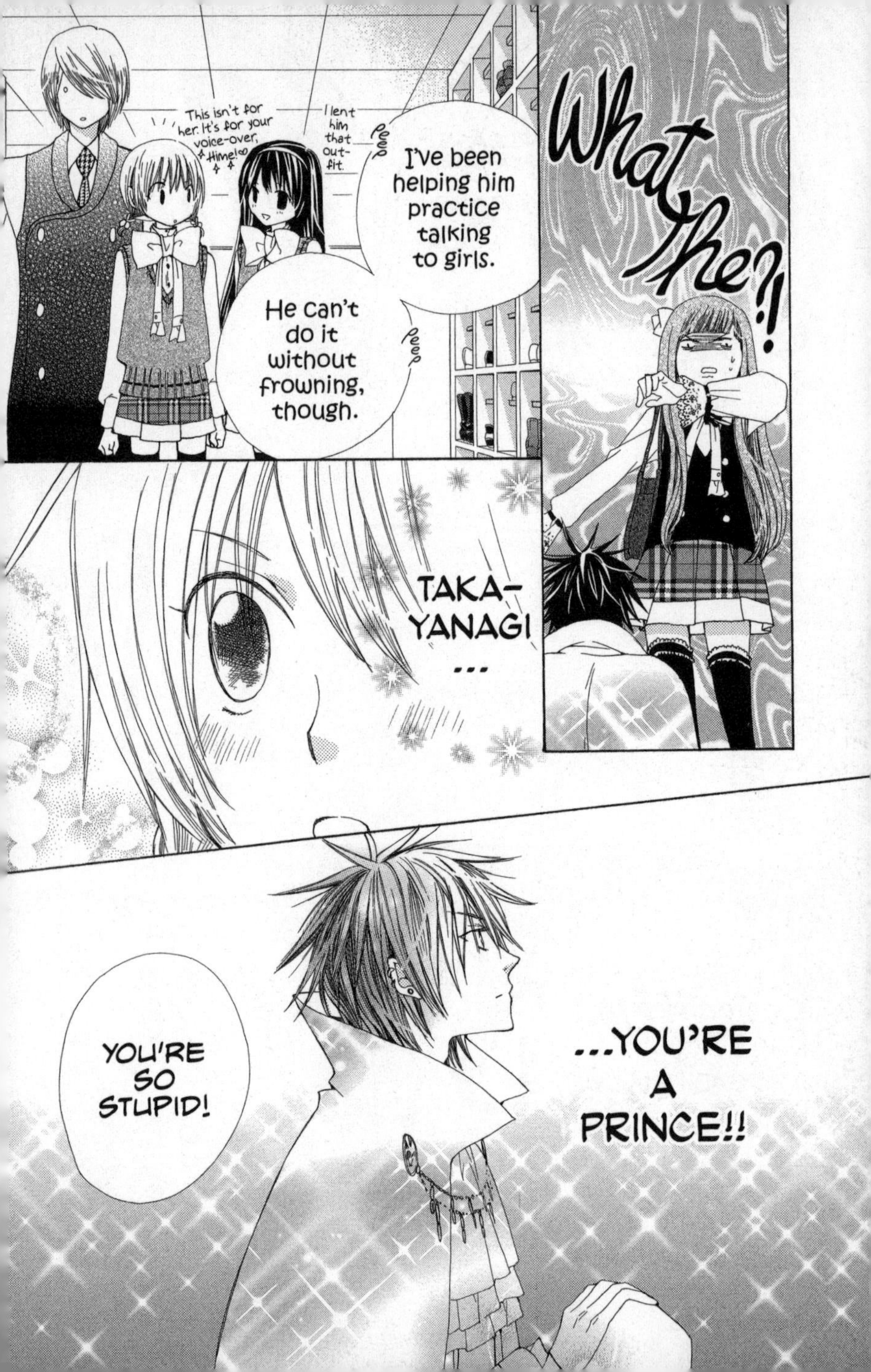
What the?!
peep
I've been helping him practice talking to girls.
peep
He can't do it without frowning, though.
I lent him that out-fit.
This isn't for her. It's for your voice-over, Hime!♡
TAKA-YANAGI...
...YOU'RE A PRINCE!!
YOU'RE SO STUPID!

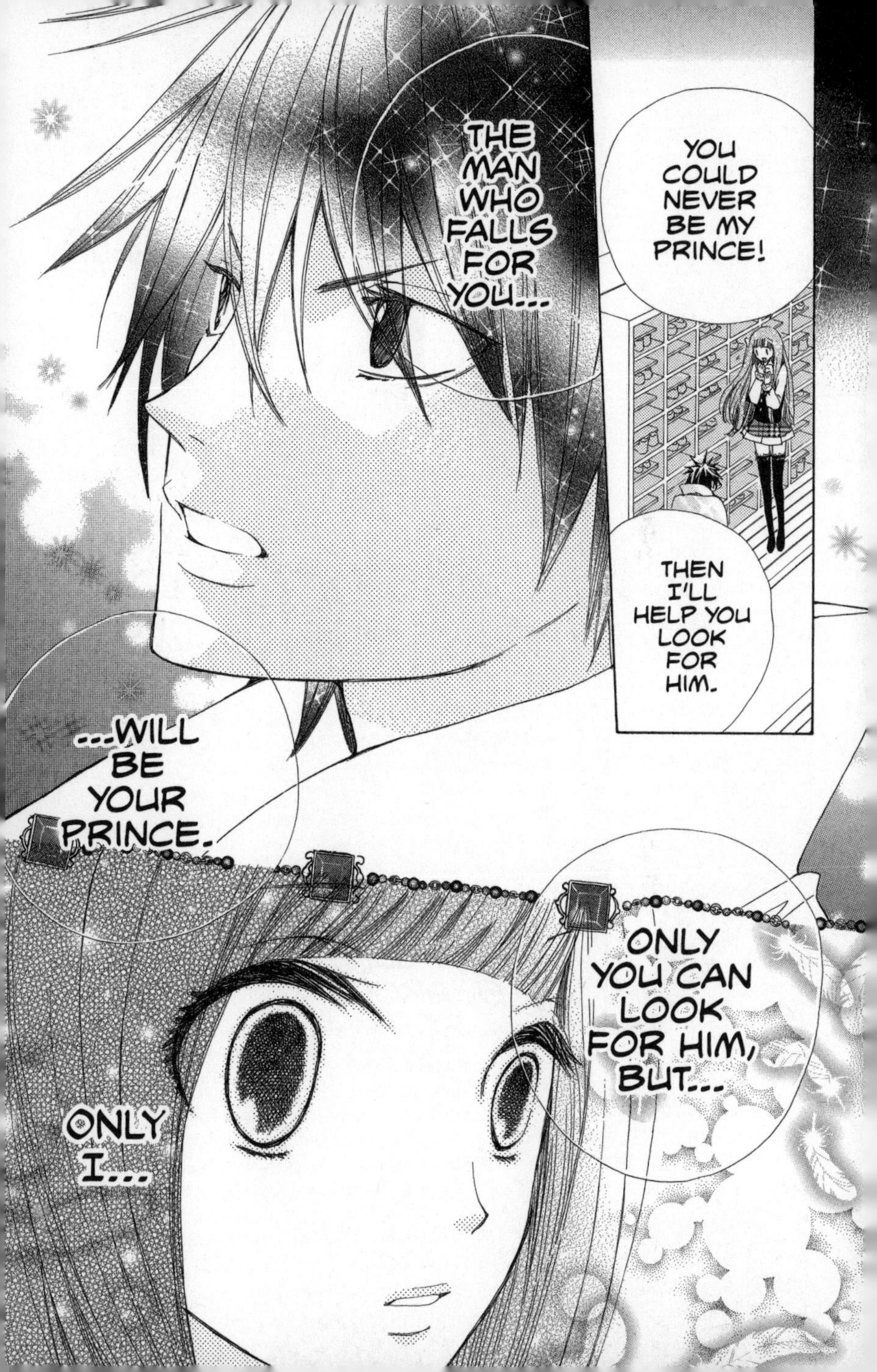
YOU COULD NEVER BE MY PRINCE!
THEN I'LL HELP YOU LOOK FOR HIM.
THE MAN WHO FALLS FOR YOU...
...WILL BE YOUR PRINCE.
ONLY YOU CAN LOOK FOR HIM, BUT...
ONLY I...

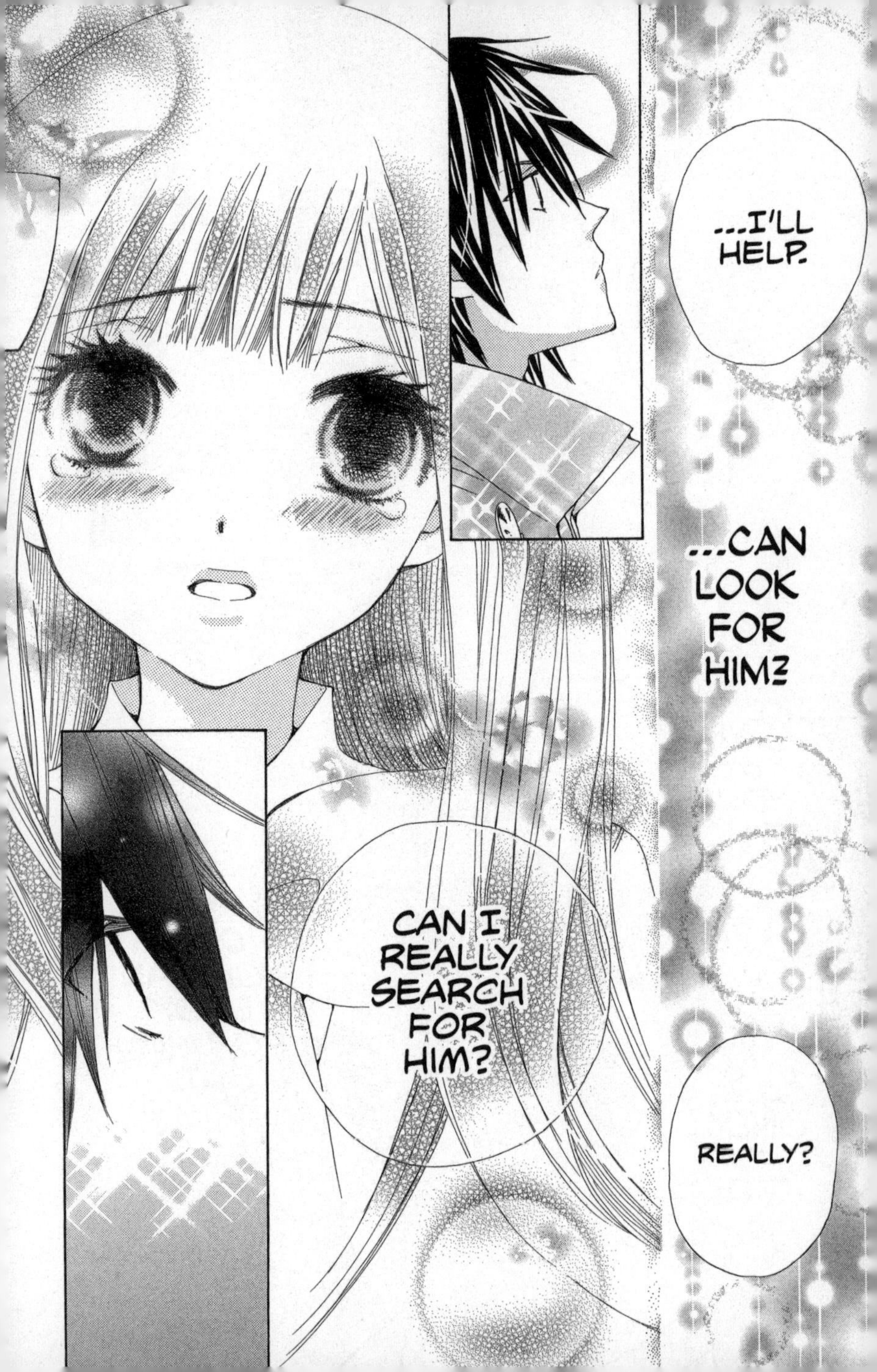
...I'LL HELP.
...CAN LOOK FOR HIM?
REALLY?
CAN I REALLY SEARCH FOR HIM?

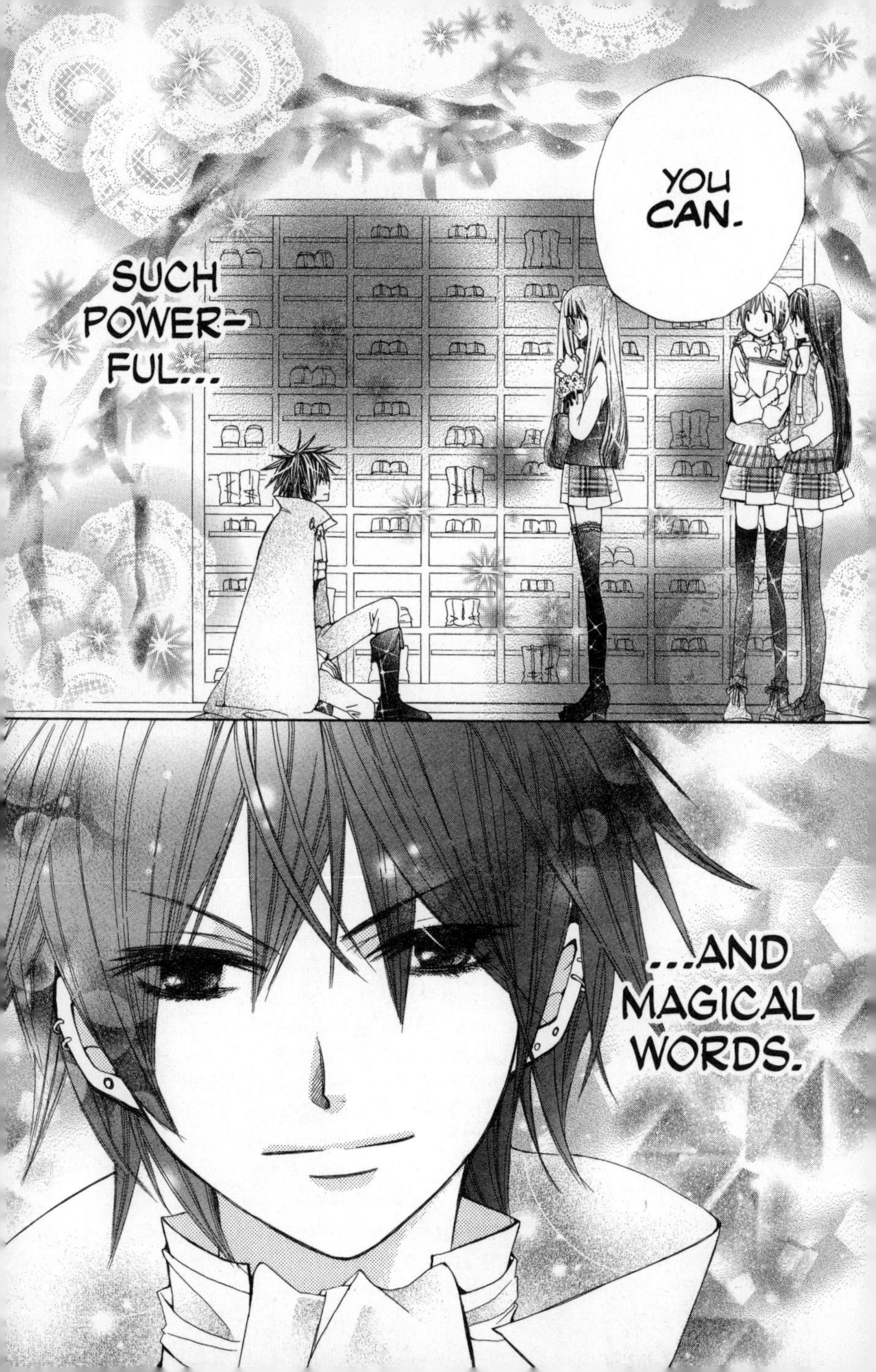
YOU CAN.
SUCH POWER-FUL...
...AND MAGICAL WORDS.

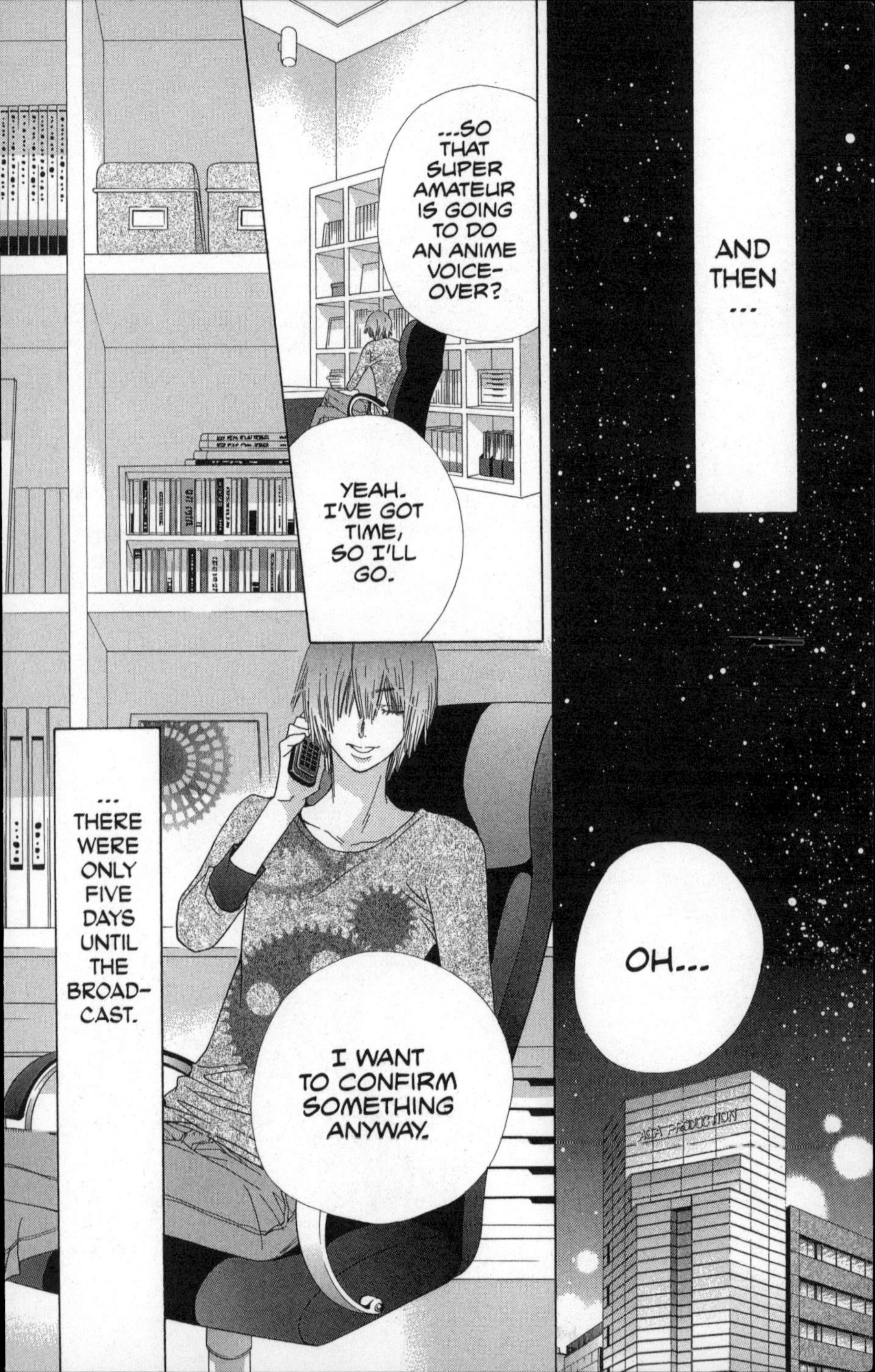
AND THEN ...
OH...
...SO THAT SUPER AMATEUR IS GOING TO DO AN ANIME VOICE-OVER?
YEAH. I'VE GOT TIME, SO I'LL GO.
I WANT TO CONFIRM SOMETHING ANYWAY.
... THERE WERE ONLY FIVE DAYS UNTIL THE BROAD-CAST.

VOICE OVER!

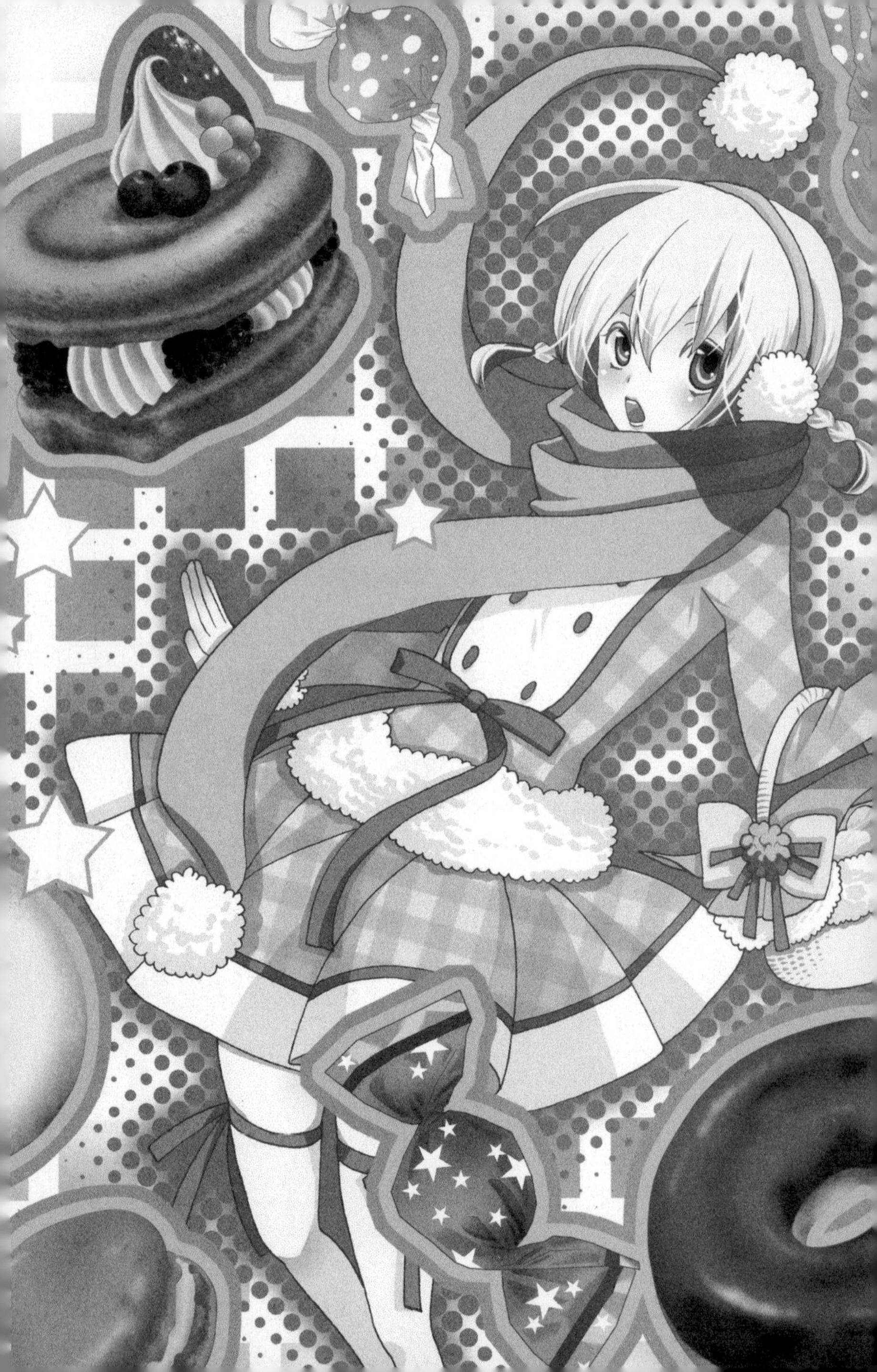

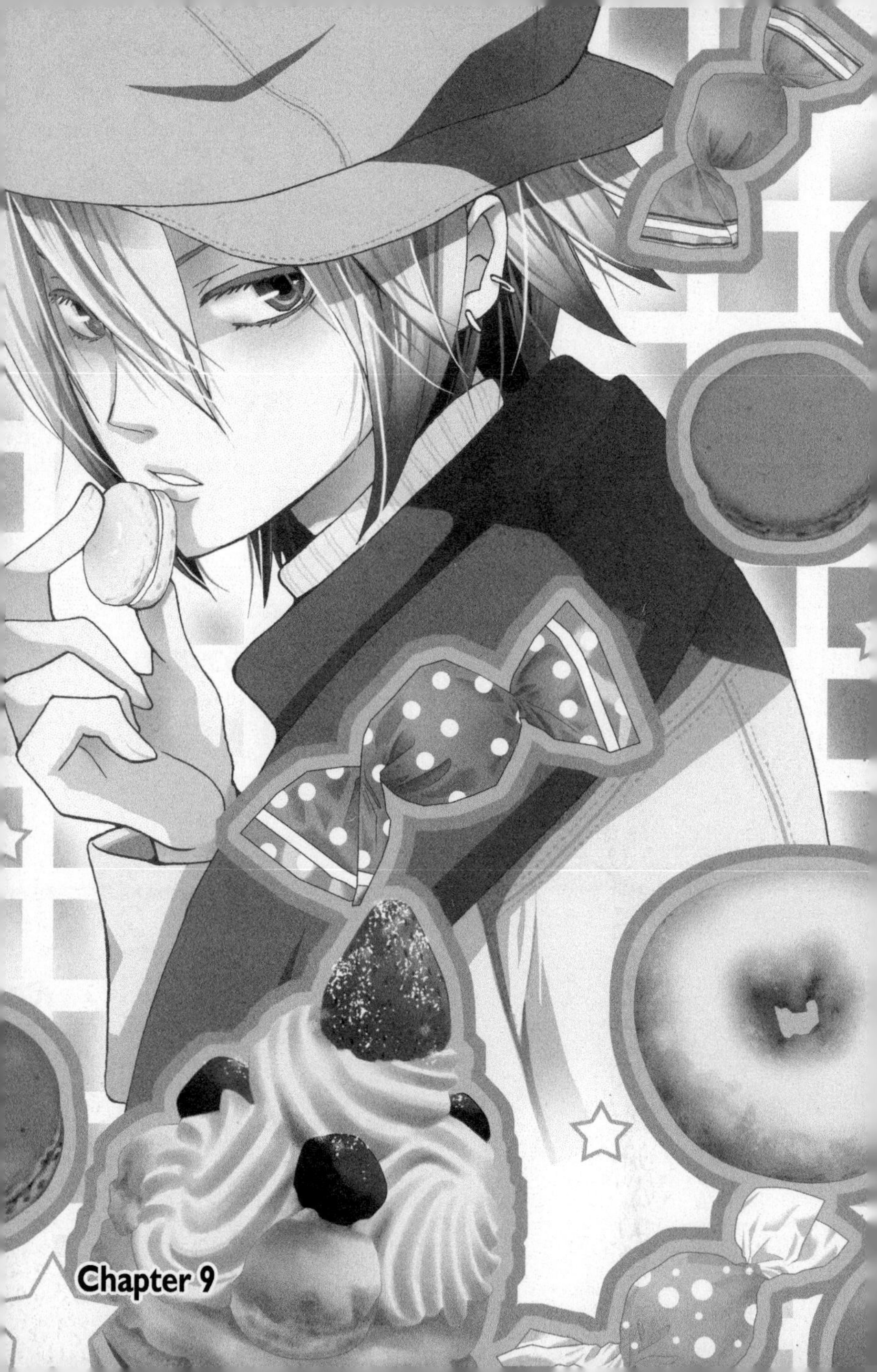
Chapter 9

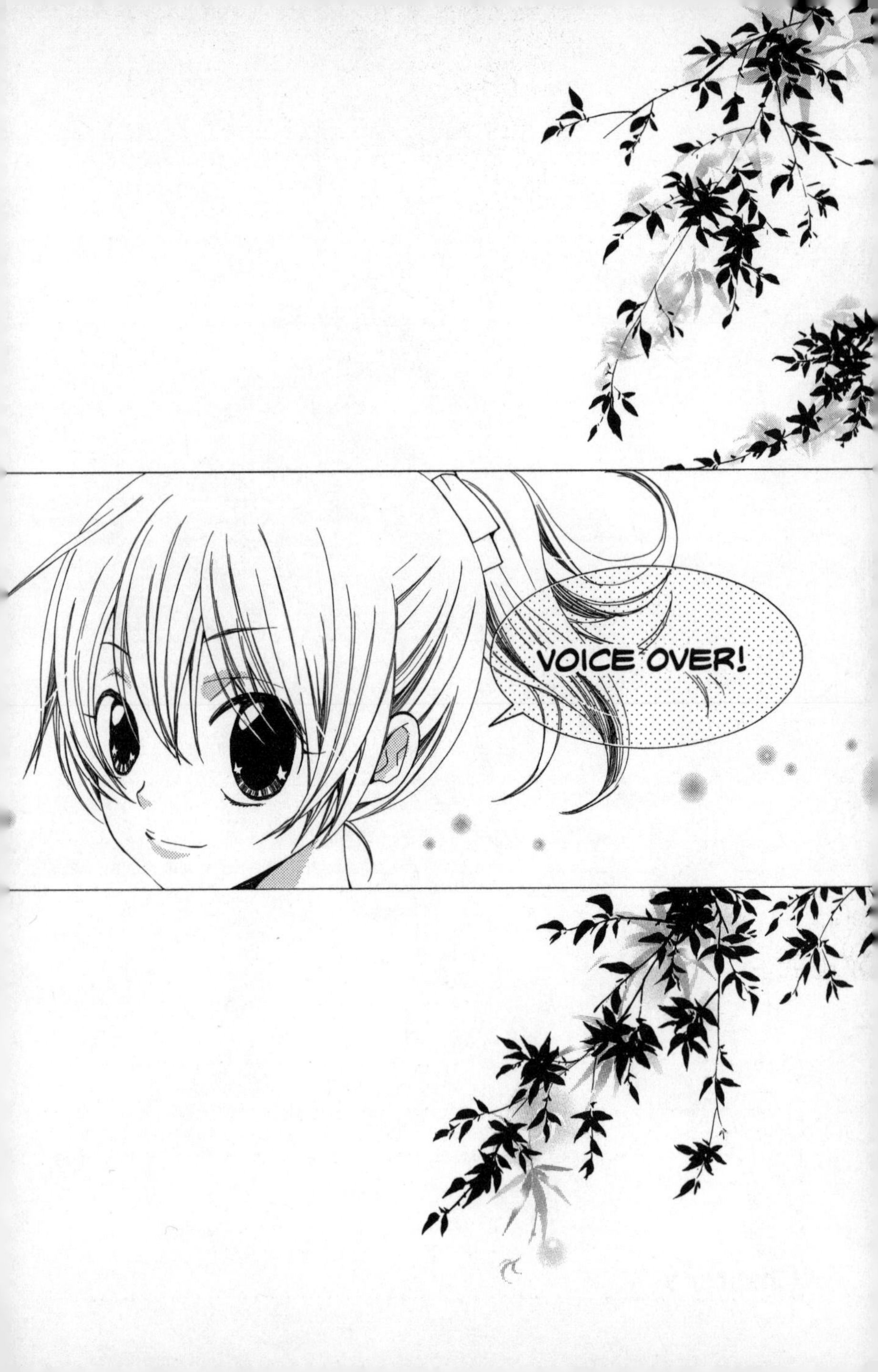
VOICE OVER!

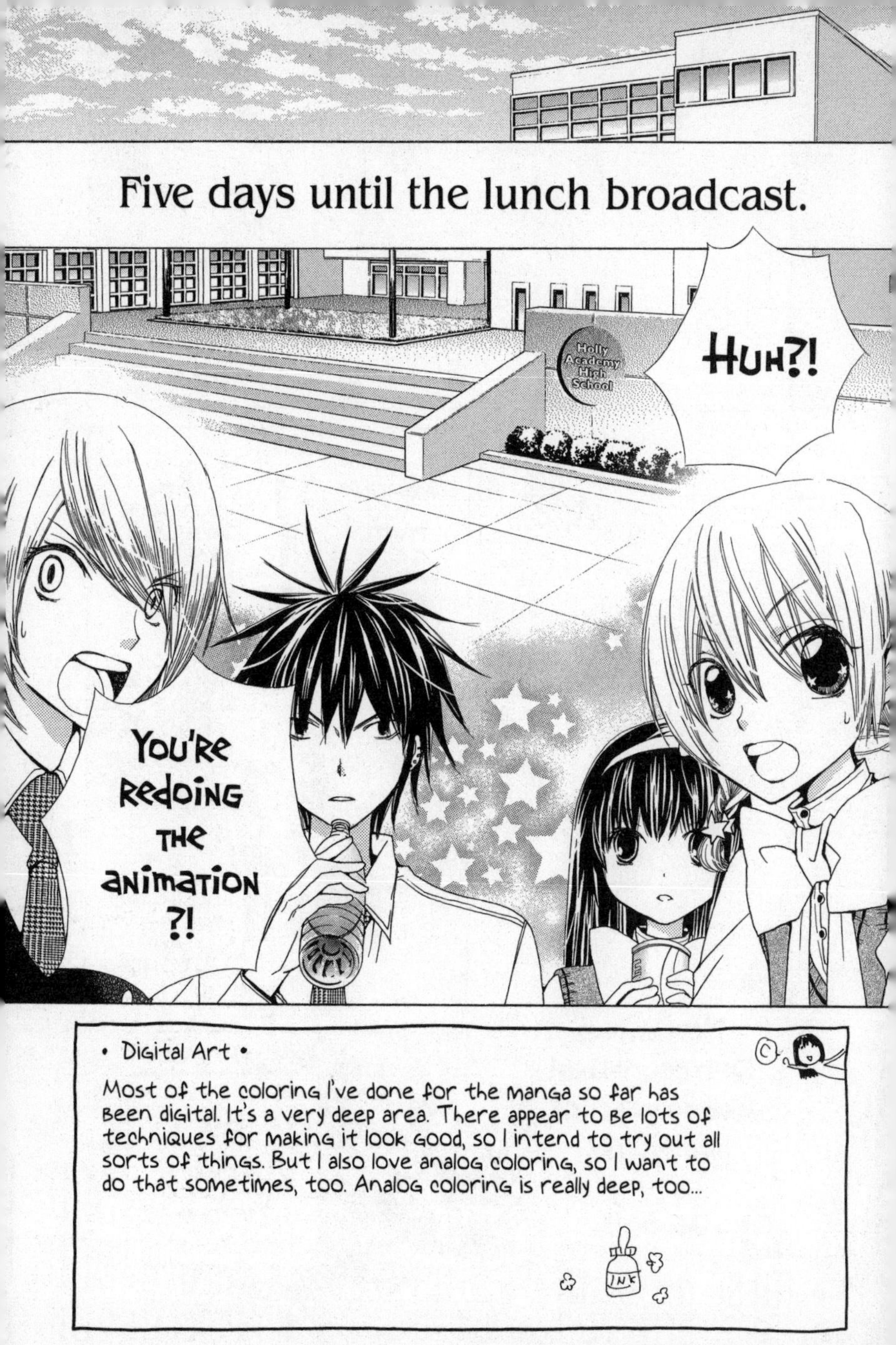
Five days until the lunch broadcast.
Holly Academy High School
HUH?!
YOU'RE REDOING THE ANIMATION ?!

• Digital Art •

Most of the coloring I've done for the manga so far has been digital. It's a very deep area. There appear to be lots of techniques for making it look good, so I intend to try out all sorts of things. But I also love analog coloring, so I want to do that sometimes, too. Analog coloring is really deep, too...

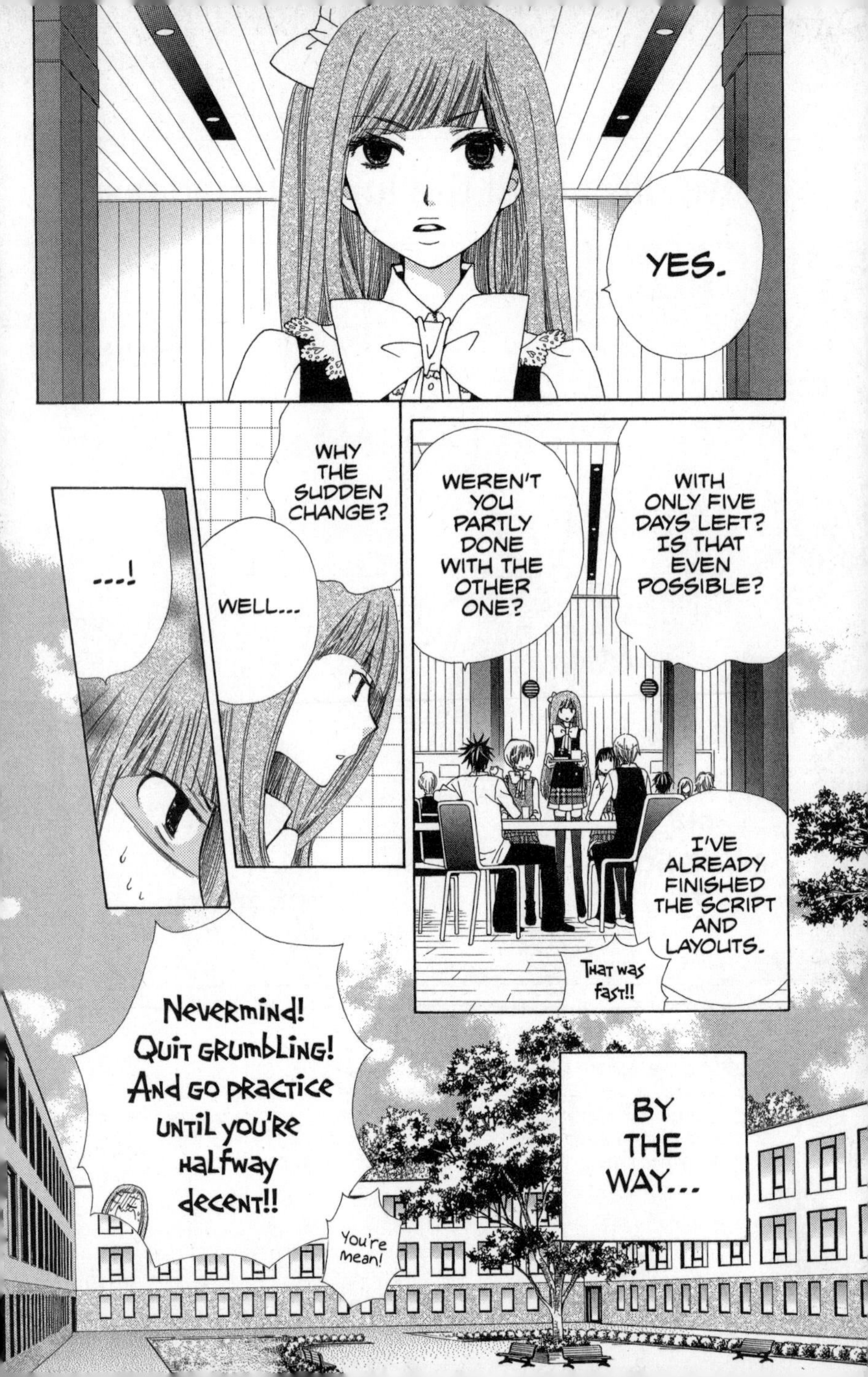
YES.
WITH ONLY FIVE DAYS LEFT? IS THAT EVEN POSSIBLE?
WEREN'T YOU PARTLY DONE WITH THE OTHER ONE?
I'VE ALREADY FINISHED THE SCRIPT AND LAYOUTS.
That was fast!!
WHY THE SUDDEN CHANGE?
WELL...
...!
BY THE WAY...
Nevermind! Quit grumbling! And go practice until you're halfway decent!!
You're mean!

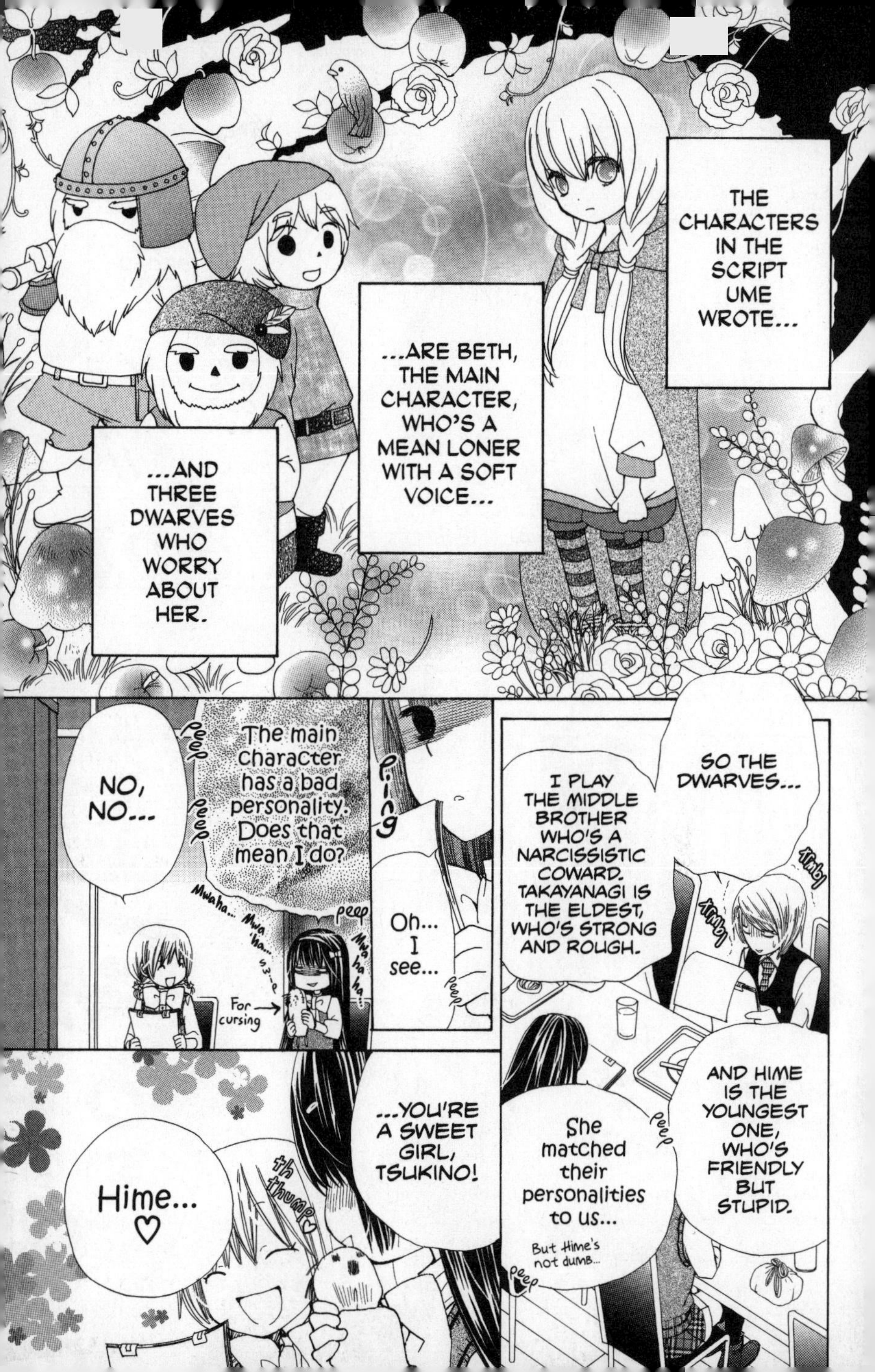
THE CHARACTERS IN THE SCRIPT UME WROTE...
...ARE BETH, THE MAIN CHARACTER, WHO'S A MEAN LONER WITH A SOFT VOICE...
...AND THREE DWARVES WHO WORRY ABOUT HER.
SO THE DWARVES...
I PLAY THE MIDDLE BROTHER WHO'S A NARCISSISTIC COWARD. TAKAYANAGI IS THE ELDEST, WHO'S STRONG AND ROUGH.
thmp
thmp
Ping
Oh... I see...
peep
NO, NO...
peep
peep
The main character has a bad personality. Does that mean I do?
Mwaha...
Mwa ha...
peep
Mwa ha ha...
For cursing
AND HIME IS THE YOUNGEST ONE, WHO'S FRIENDLY BUT STUPID.
peep
She matched their personalities to us...
But Hime's not dumb...
peep
...YOU'RE A SWEET GIRL, TSUKINO!
Hime... ♡
th thump

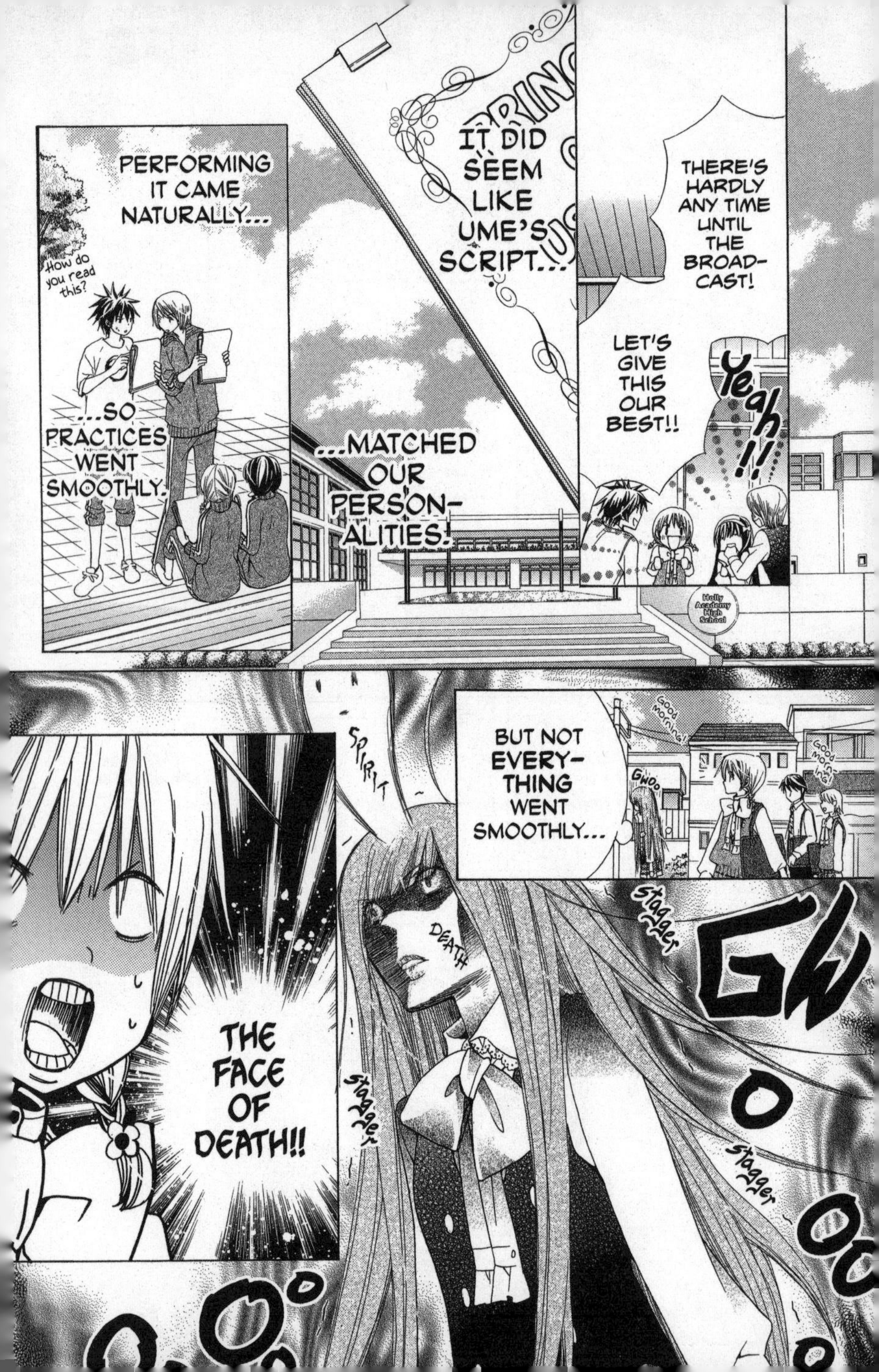
THERE'S HARDLY ANY TIME UNTIL THE BROAD-CAST!
LET'S GIVE THIS OUR BEST!!
Yeah!!
Holly Academy High School
IT DID SEEM LIKE UME'S SCRIPT...
...MATCHED OUR PERSON-ALITIES.
PERFORMING IT CAME NATURALLY...
How do you read this?
...SO PRACTICES WENT SMOOTHLY.
BUT NOT EVERY-THING WENT SMOOTHLY...
Good morning!
Good morn-ing!
Gwoo
GWOOOO
stagger
stagger
SPIRIT
DEATH
stagger
THE FACE OF DEATH!!
OOO

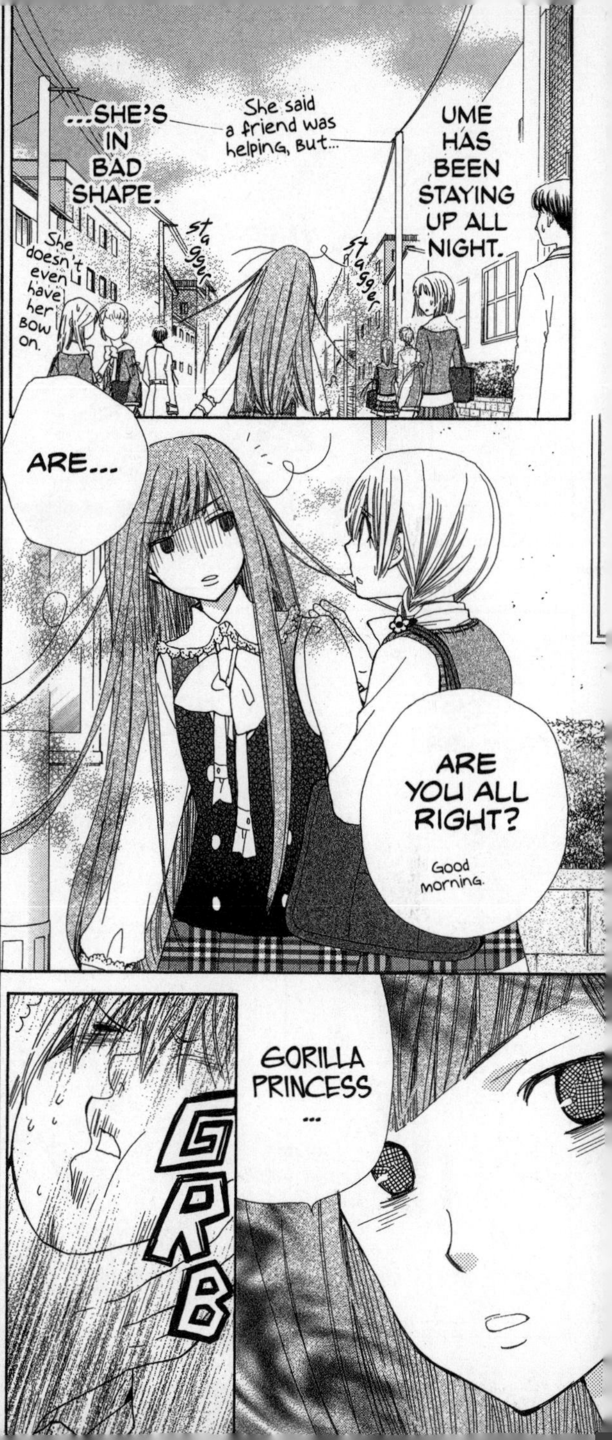
UME HAS BEEN STAYING UP ALL NIGHT.
She said a friend was helping, but...
...SHE'S IN BAD SHAPE.
stagger
stagger
She doesn't even have her bow on.
Good morning.
ARE YOU ALL RIGHT?
ARE...
GORILLA PRINCESS...
GRB
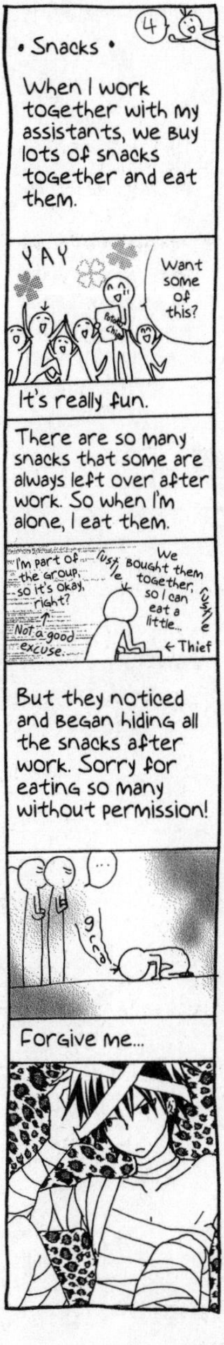
4
• Snacks •
When I work together with my assistants, we buy lots of snacks together and eat them.
YAY
Want some of this?
Potato Chips
It's really fun.
There are so many snacks that some are always left over after work. So when I'm alone, I eat them.
I'm part of the group, so it's okay, right?
Not a good excuse.
rustle
We bought them together, so I can eat a little...
rustle
← Thief
But they noticed and began hiding all the snacks after work. Sorry for eating so many without permission!
...
grab
Forgive me...

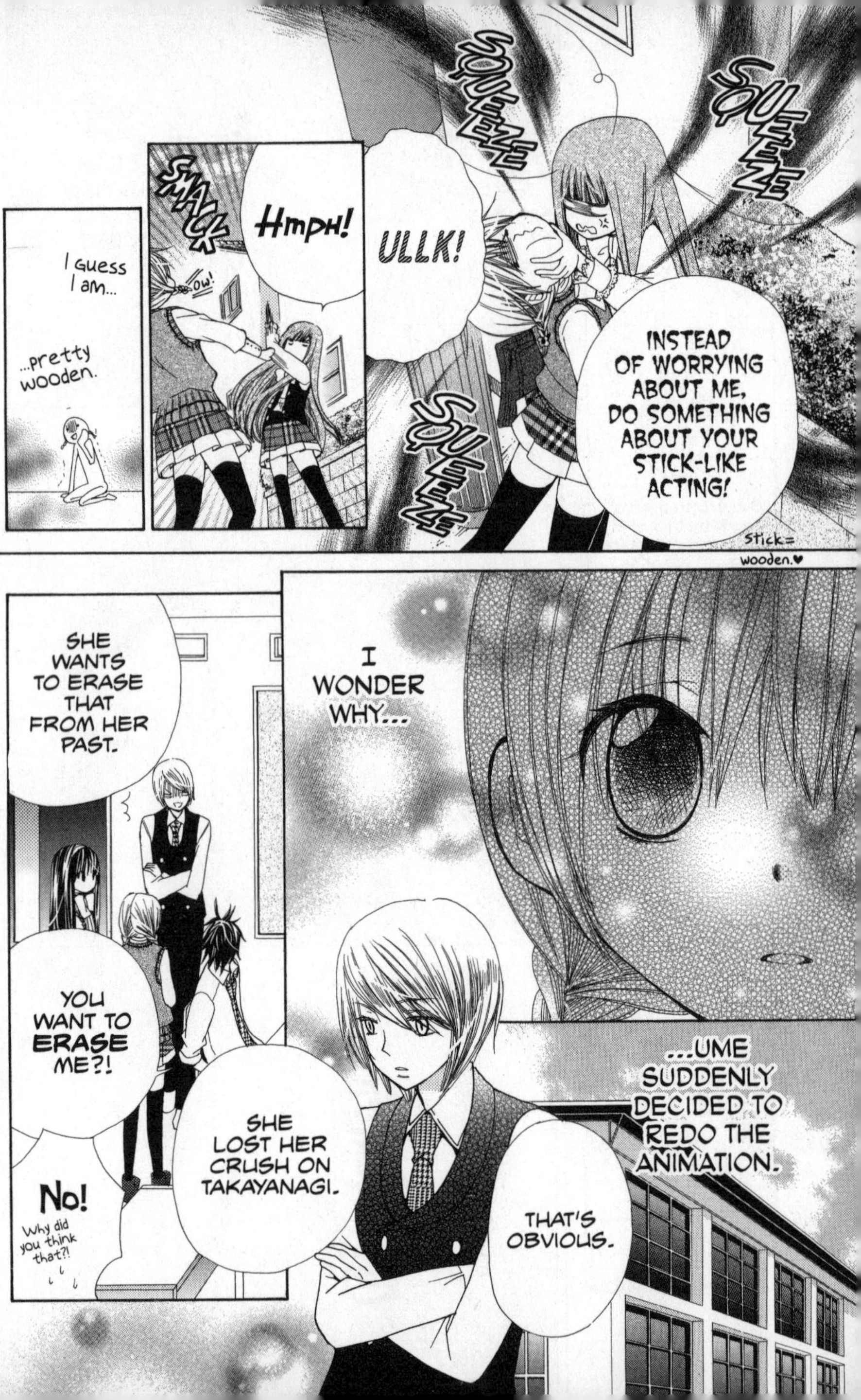
SQUEEZE
SQUEEZE
ULLK!
INSTEAD OF WORRYING ABOUT ME, DO SOMETHING ABOUT YOUR STICK-LIKE ACTING!
SQUEEZE
Stick= wooden.♥
SMACK
OW!
Hmph!
I guess I am...
...pretty wooden.
I WONDER WHY...
...UME SUDDENLY DECIDED TO REDO THE ANIMATION.
THAT'S OBVIOUS.
SHE LOST HER CRUSH ON TAKAYANAGI.
SHE WANTS TO ERASE THAT FROM HER PAST.
YOU WANT TO ERASE ME?!
No!
Why did you think that?!

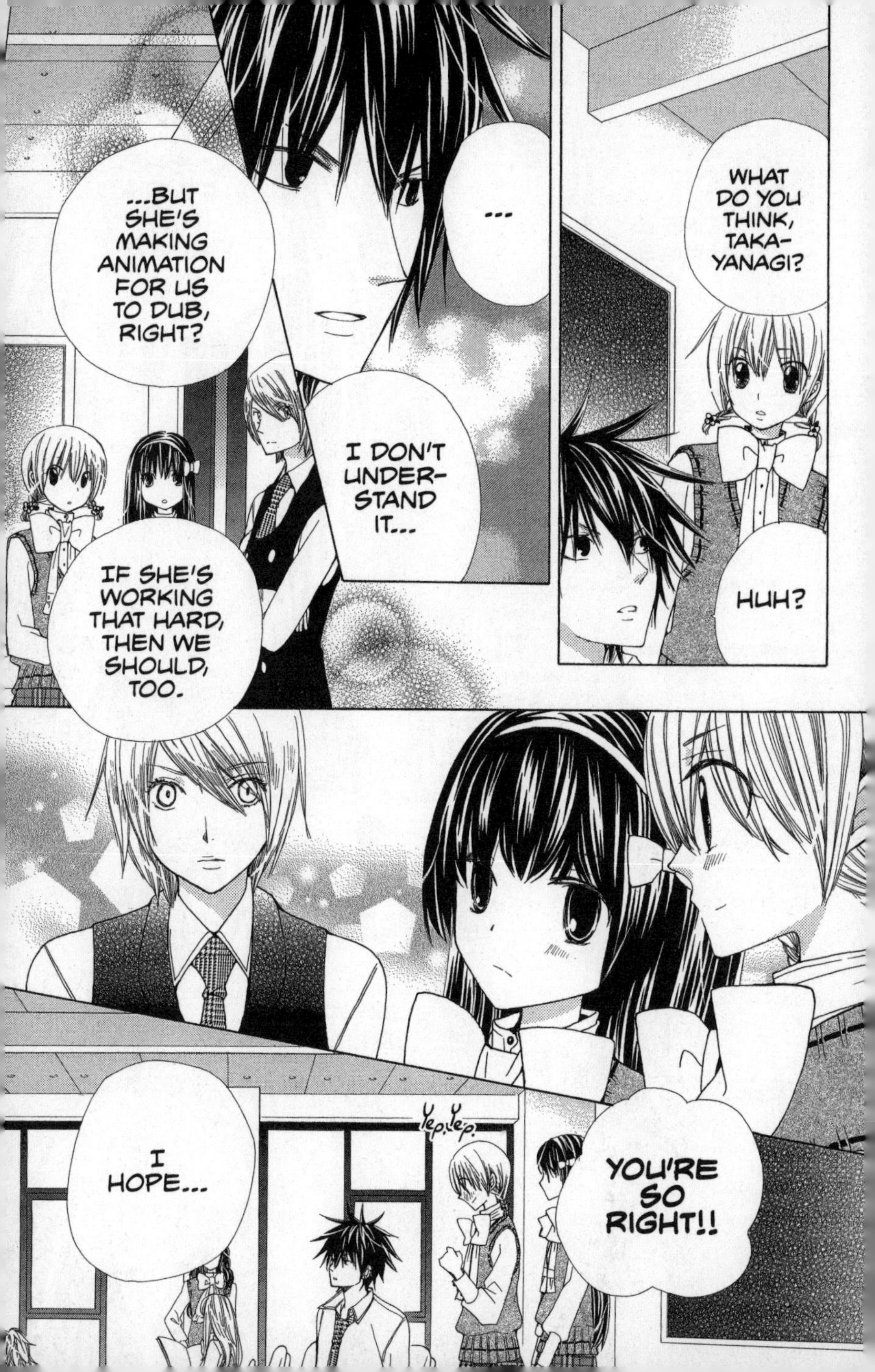

WHAT DO YOU THINK, TAKA-YANAGI?
HUH?
...
I DON'T UNDER-STAND IT...
...BUT SHE'S MAKING ANIMATION FOR US TO DUB, RIGHT?
IF SHE'S WORKING THAT HARD, THEN WE SHOULD, TOO.
YOU'RE SO RIGHT!!
Yep. Yep.
I HOPE...

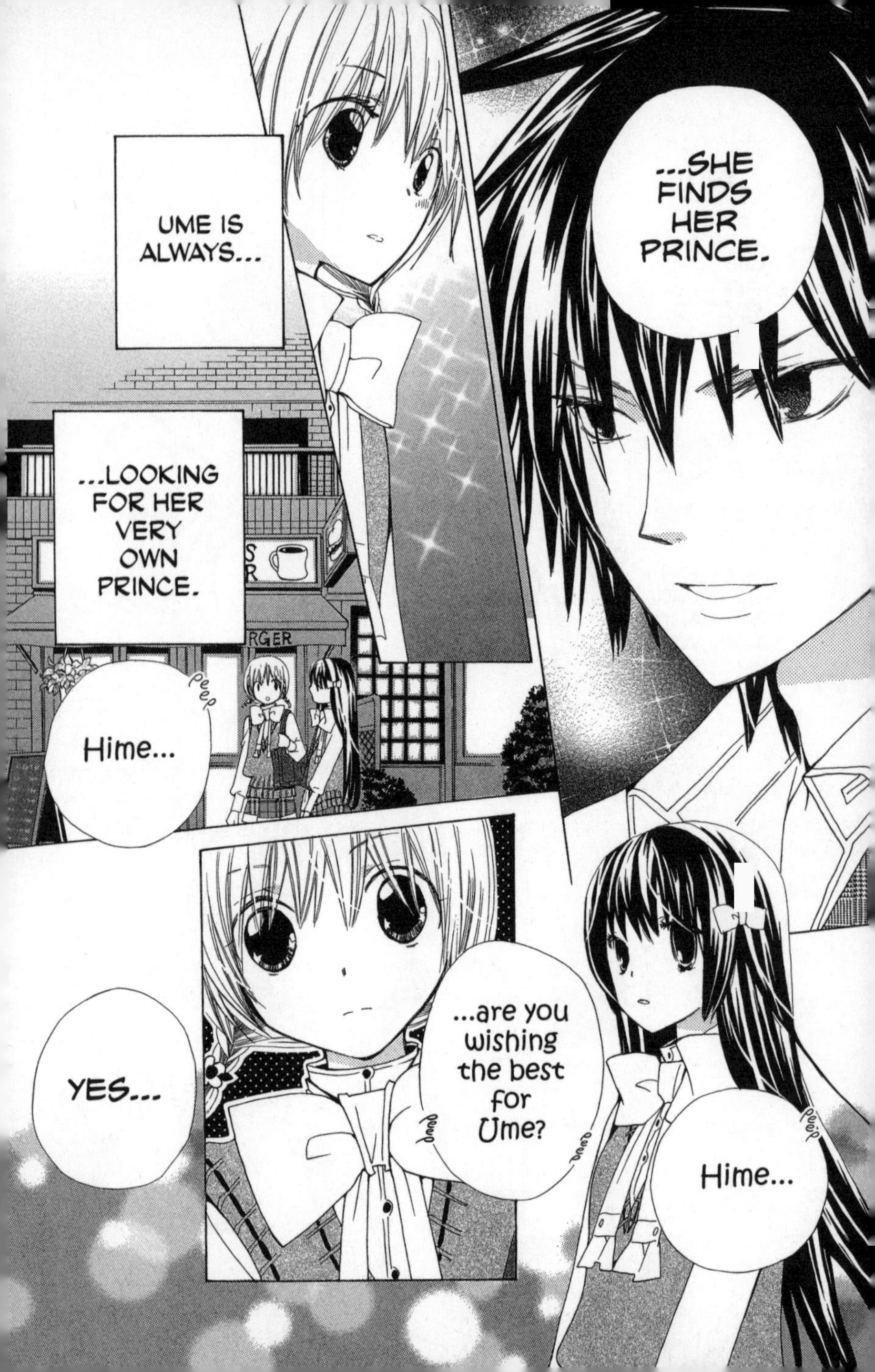
...SHE FINDS HER PRINCE.
UME IS ALWAYS...
...LOOKING FOR HER VERY OWN PRINCE.
peep
Hime...
peep
Hime...
peep
peep
...are you wishing the best for Ume?
YES...

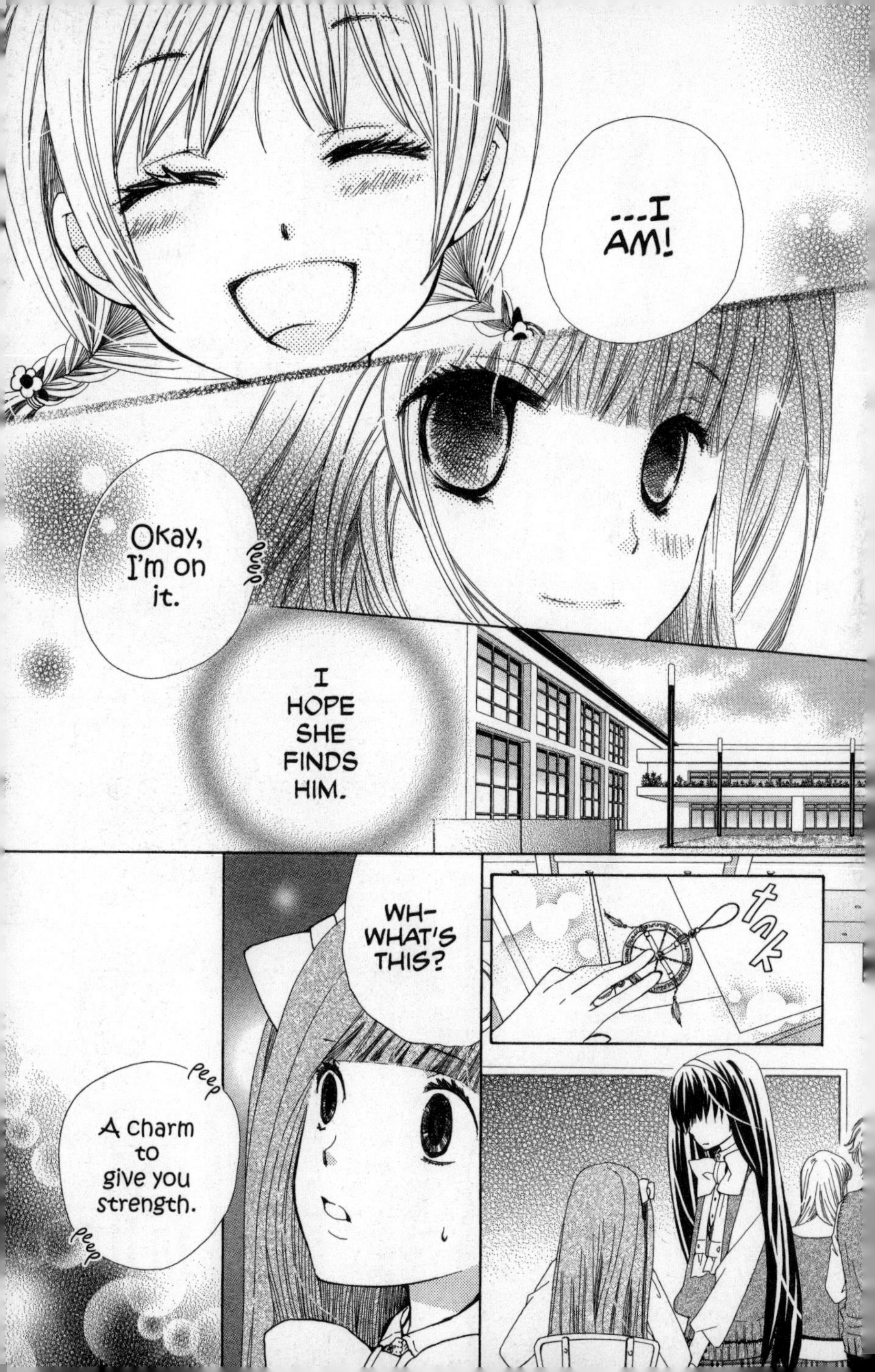
...I AM!
Okay, I'm on it.
peep
I HOPE SHE FINDS HIM.
tak
WH-WHAT'S THIS?
peep
A charm to give you strength.
peep

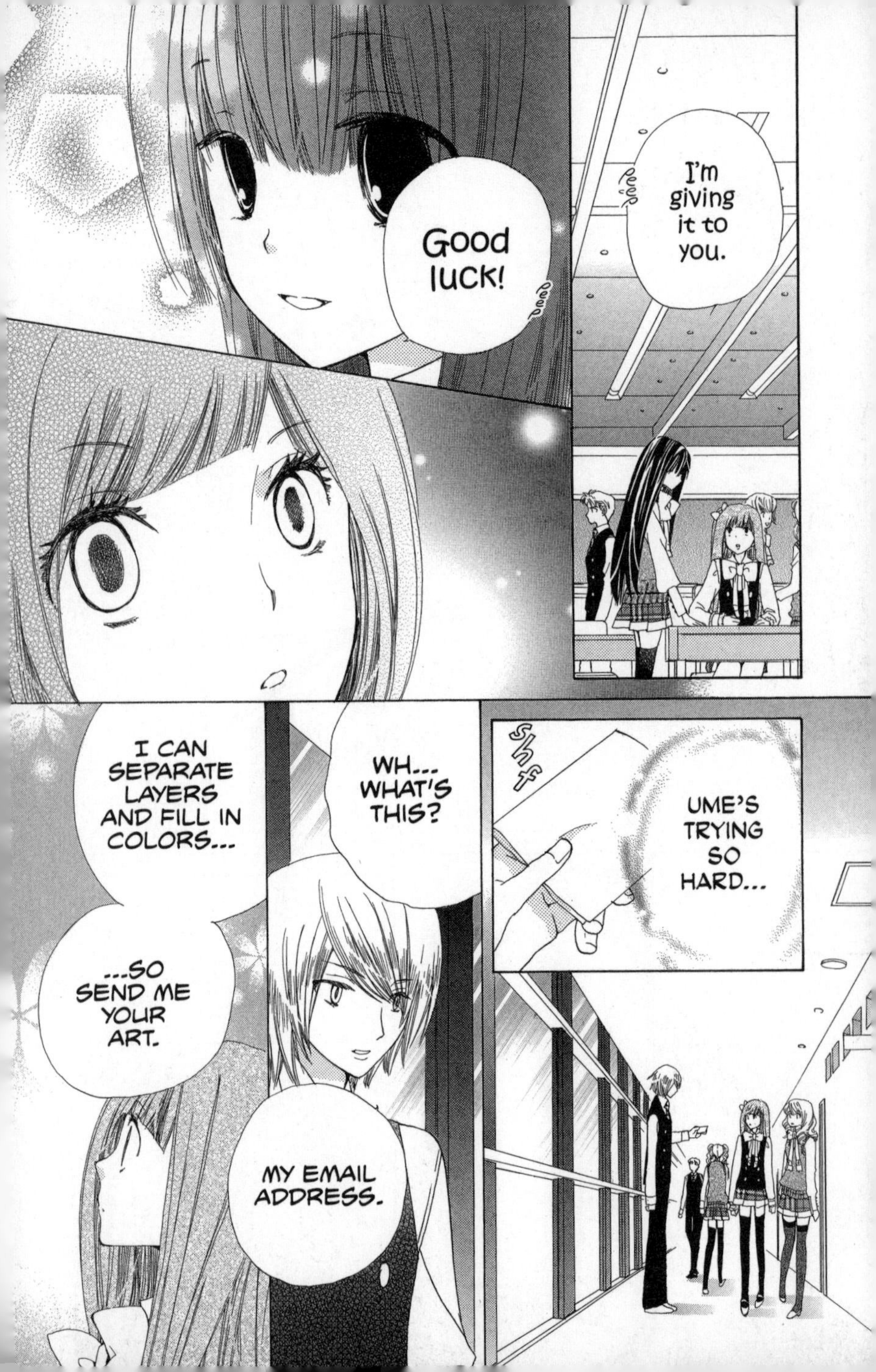

peep
I'm giving it to you.
Good luck!
peep
shf
UME'S TRYING SO HARD...
WH... WHAT'S THIS?
MY EMAIL ADDRESS.
I CAN SEPARATE LAYERS AND FILL IN COLORS...
...SO SEND ME YOUR ART.

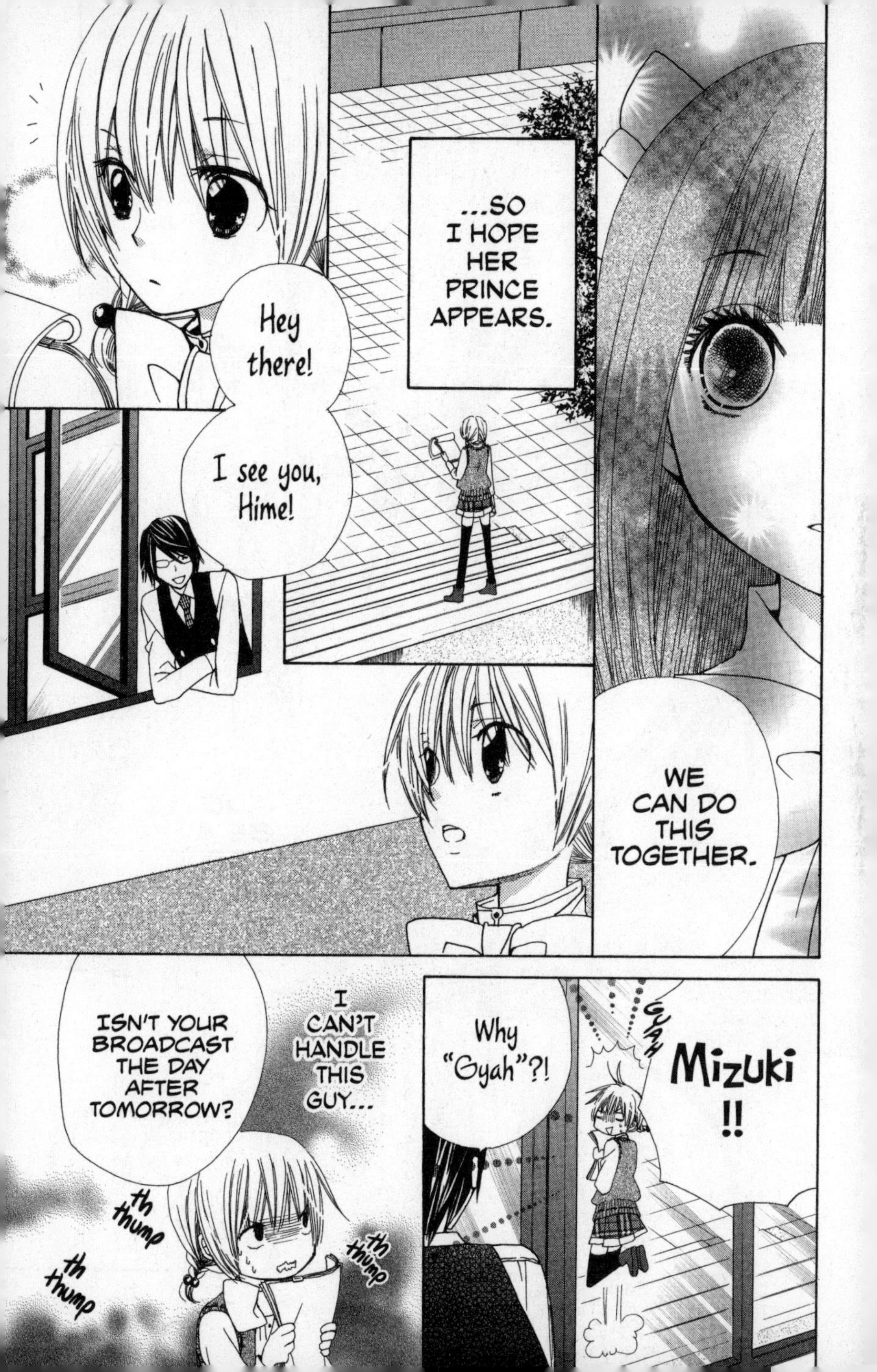
WE CAN DO THIS TOGETHER.
...SO I HOPE HER PRINCE APPEARS.
Hey there!
I see you, Hime!
Mizuki !!
GYAH
Why "Gyah"?!
I CAN'T HANDLE THIS GUY...
ISN'T YOUR BROADCAST THE DAY AFTER TOMORROW?
th thump
th thump
th thump

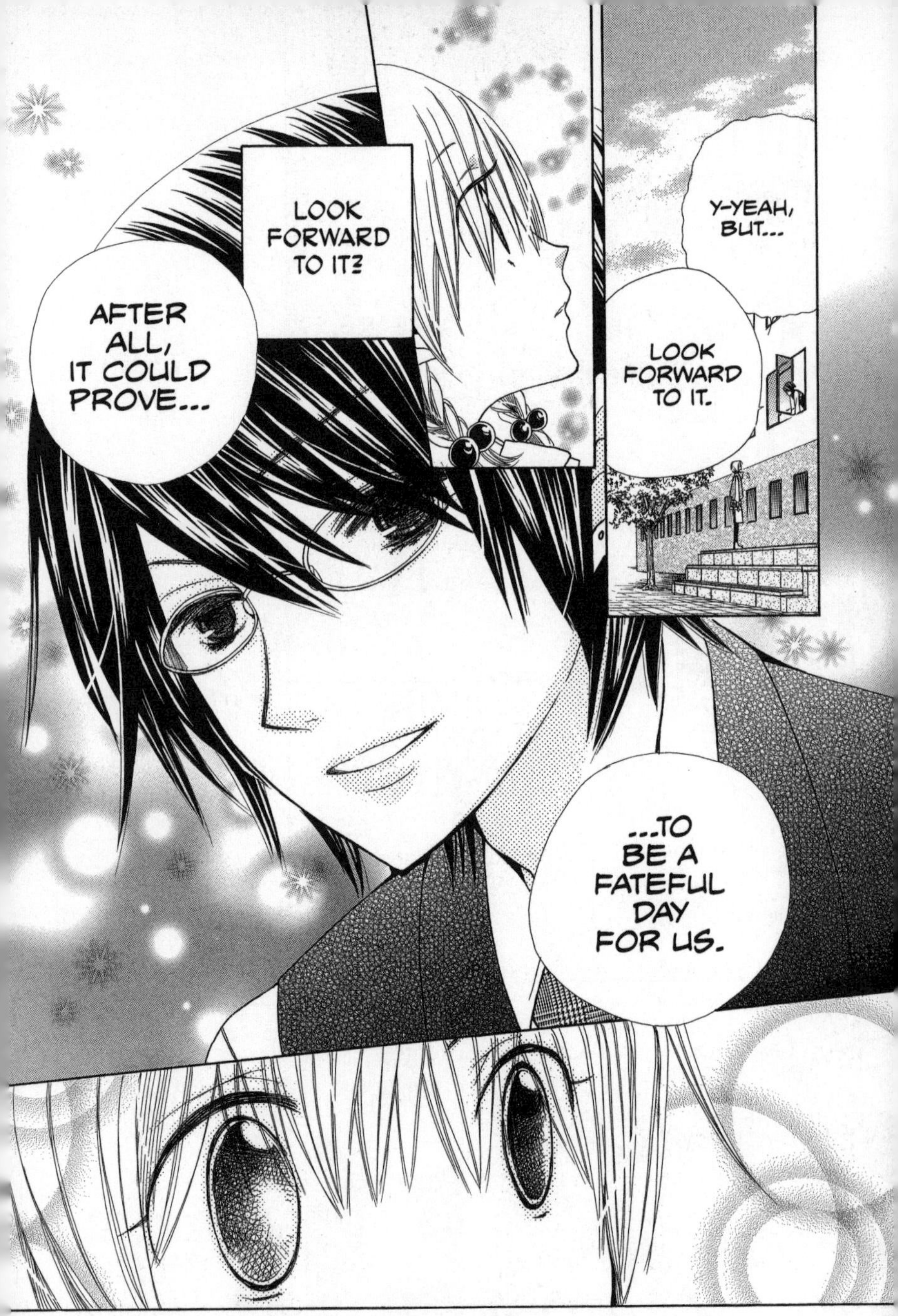
Y-YEAH, BUT...
LOOK FORWARD TO IT.
LOOK FORWARD TO IT?
AFTER ALL, IT COULD PROVE...
...TO BE A FATEFUL DAY FOR US.

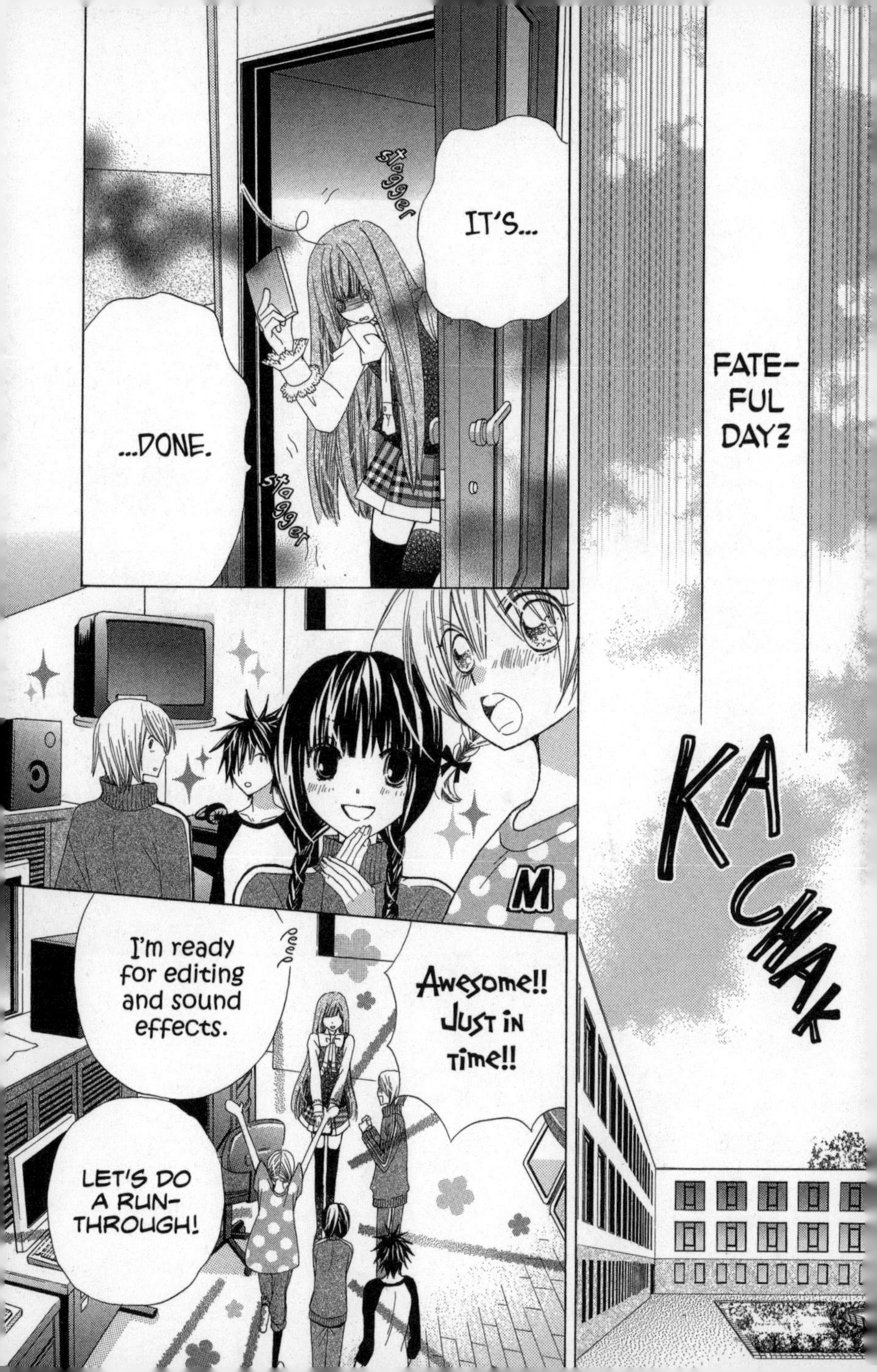
FATE-
FUL
DAY?
KA CHAK
stagger
IT'S...
stagger
...DONE.
M
I'm ready for editing and sound effects.
Awesome!! Just in time!!
LET'S DO A RUN-THROUGH!

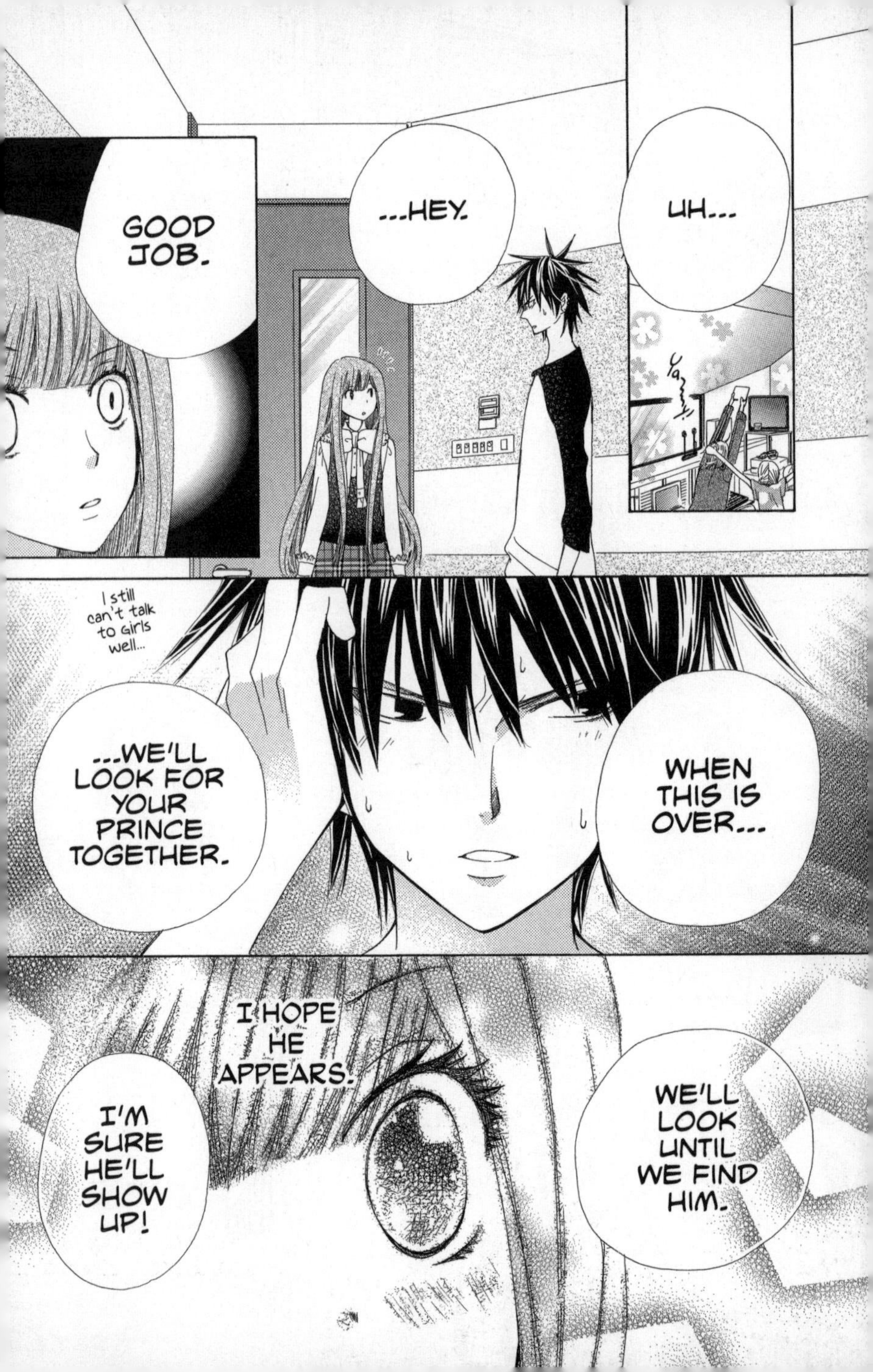
UH...
...HEY.
GOOD JOB.
WHEN THIS IS OVER...
...WE'LL LOOK FOR YOUR PRINCE TOGETHER.
I still can't talk to girls well...
WE'LL LOOK UNTIL WE FIND HIM.
I HOPE HE APPEARS.
I'M SURE HE'LL SHOW UP!

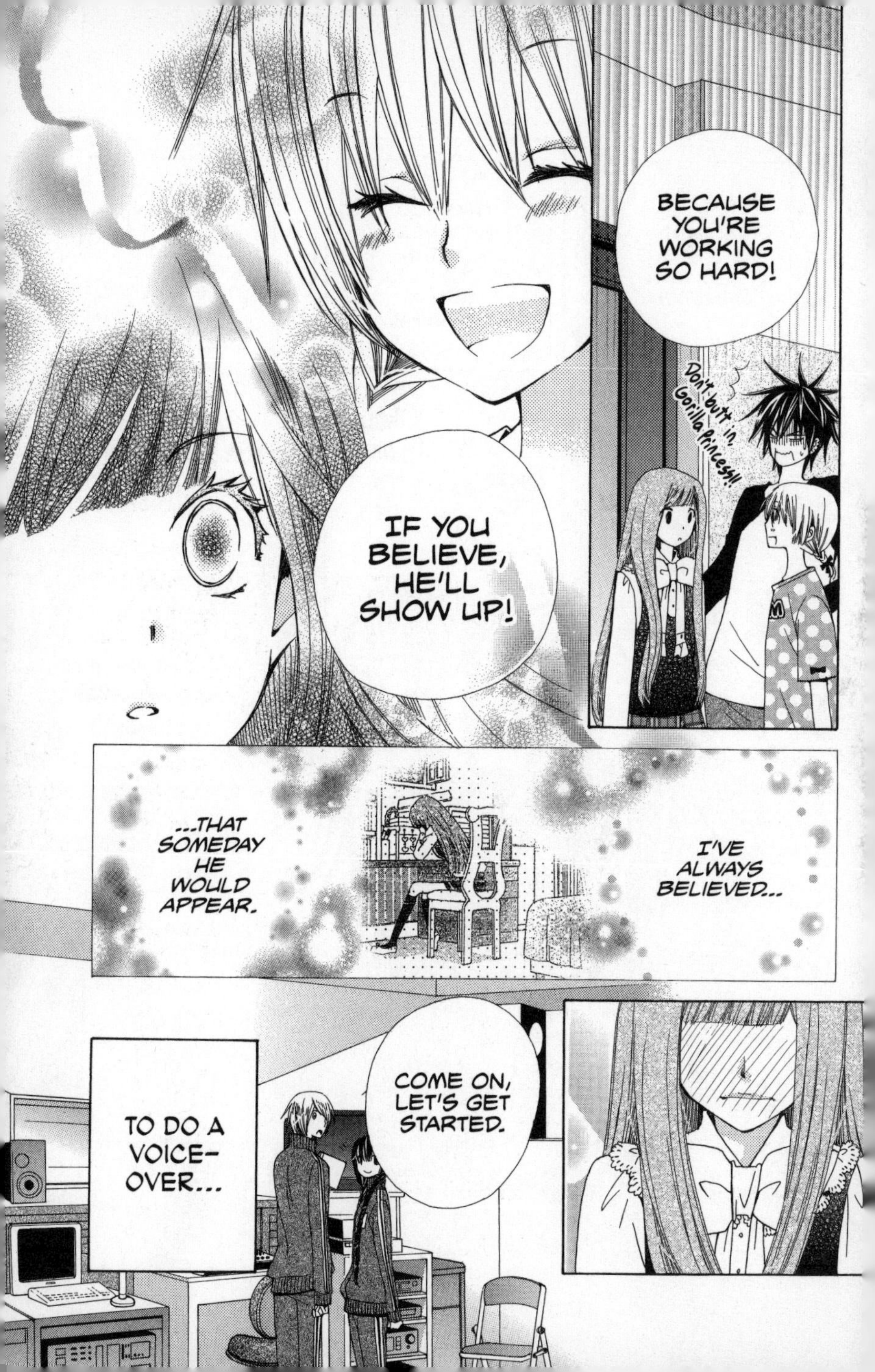
BECAUSE YOU'RE WORKING SO HARD!
Don't butt in, Gorilla Princess!!
IF YOU BELIEVE, HE'LL SHOW UP!
I'VE ALWAYS BELIEVED...
...THAT SOMEDAY HE WOULD APPEAR.
COME ON, LET'S GET STARTED.
TO DO A VOICE-OVER...

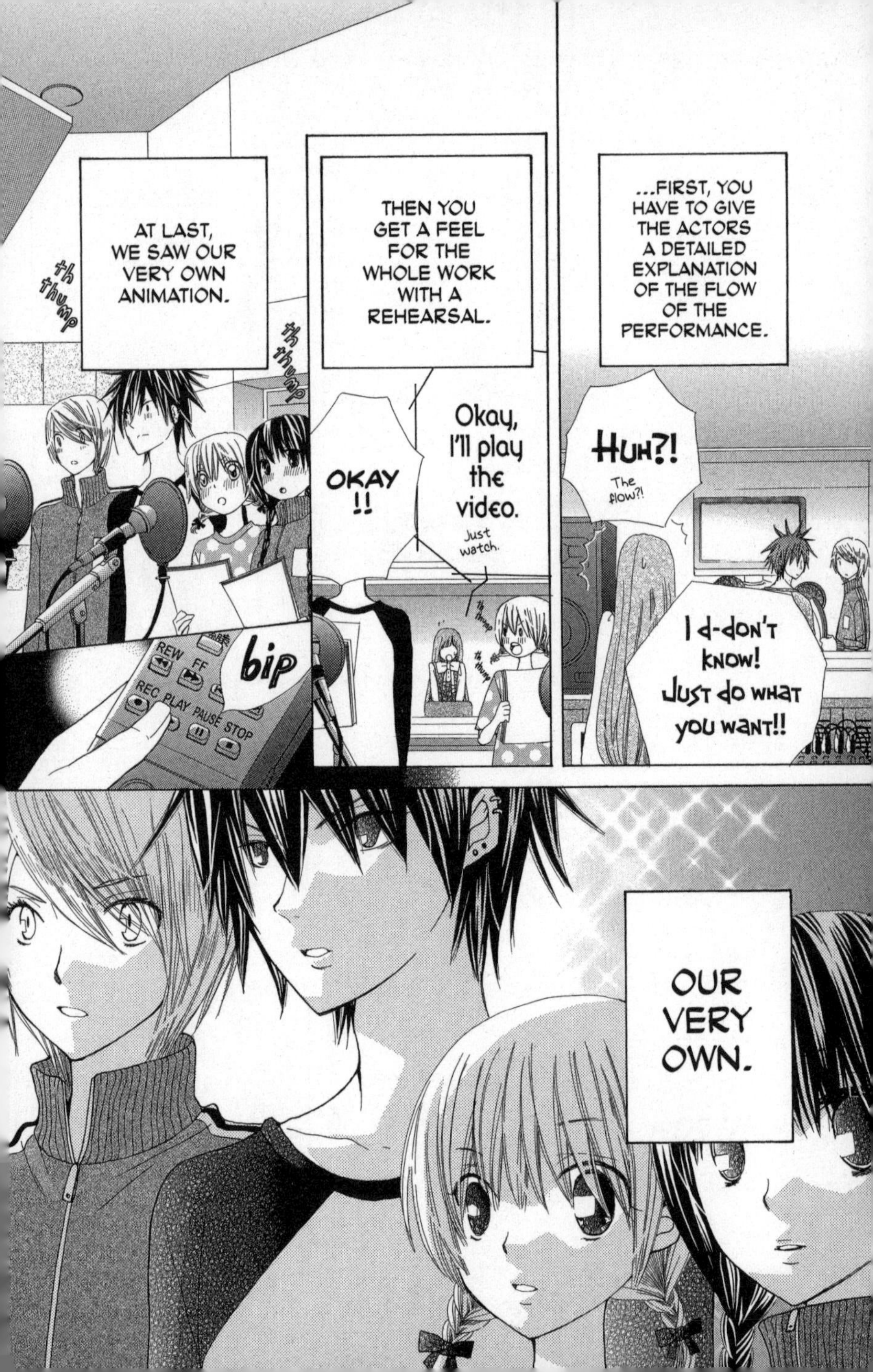
...FIRST, YOU HAVE TO GIVE THE ACTORS A DETAILED EXPLANATION OF THE FLOW OF THE PERFORMANCE.
HUH?!
The flow?!
I d-don't know! Just do what you want!!
THEN YOU GET A FEEL FOR THE WHOLE WORK WITH A REHEARSAL.
Okay, I'll play the video.
Just watch.
OKAY !!
AT LAST, WE SAW OUR VERY OWN ANIMATION.
th thump
th thump
bip
REW FF
REC PLAY PAUSE STOP
OUR VERY OWN.

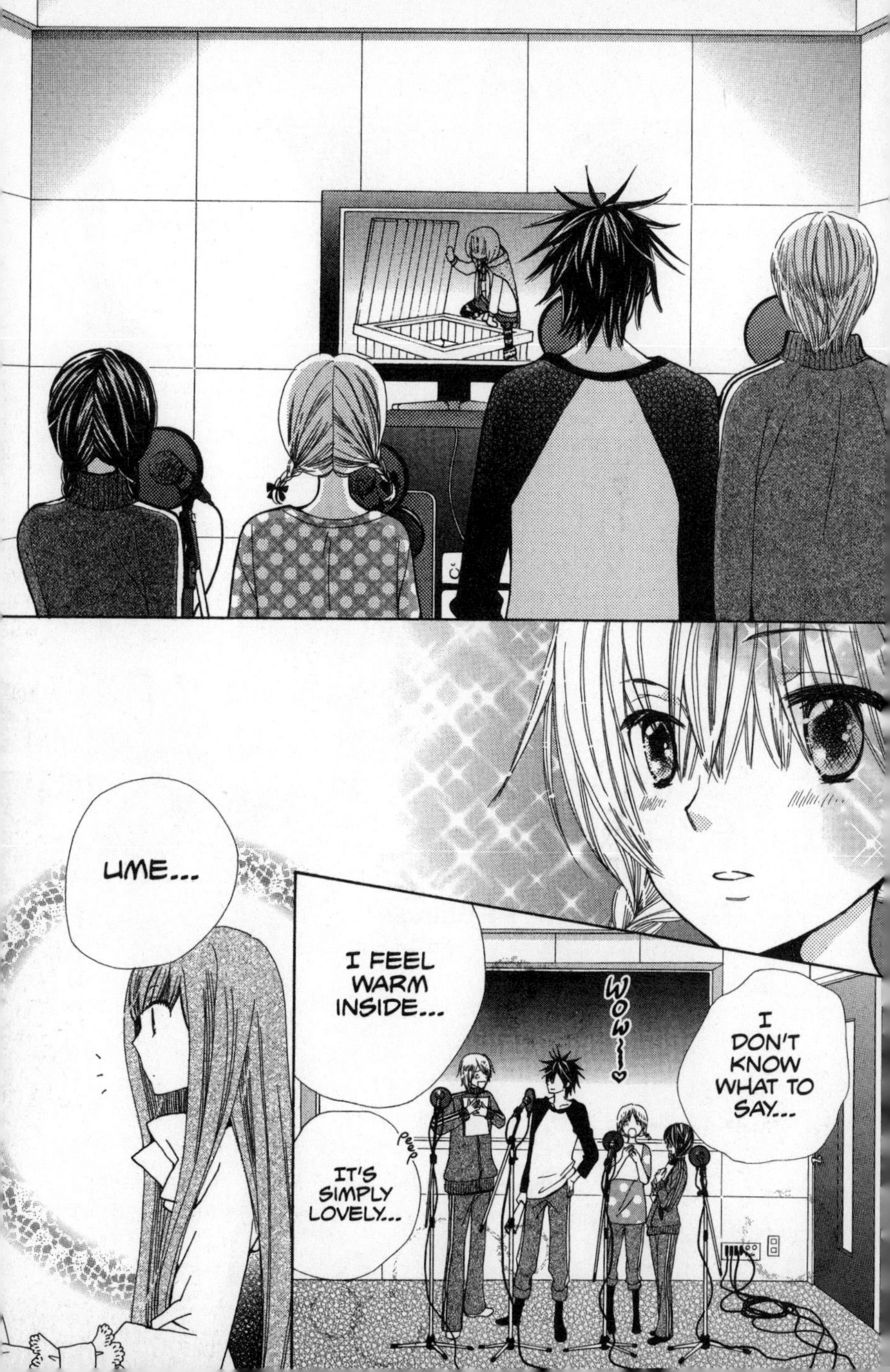
I DON'T KNOW WHAT TO SAY...
WOW~♥
I FEEL WARM INSIDE...
PEEP
IT'S SIMPLY LOVELY...
UME...

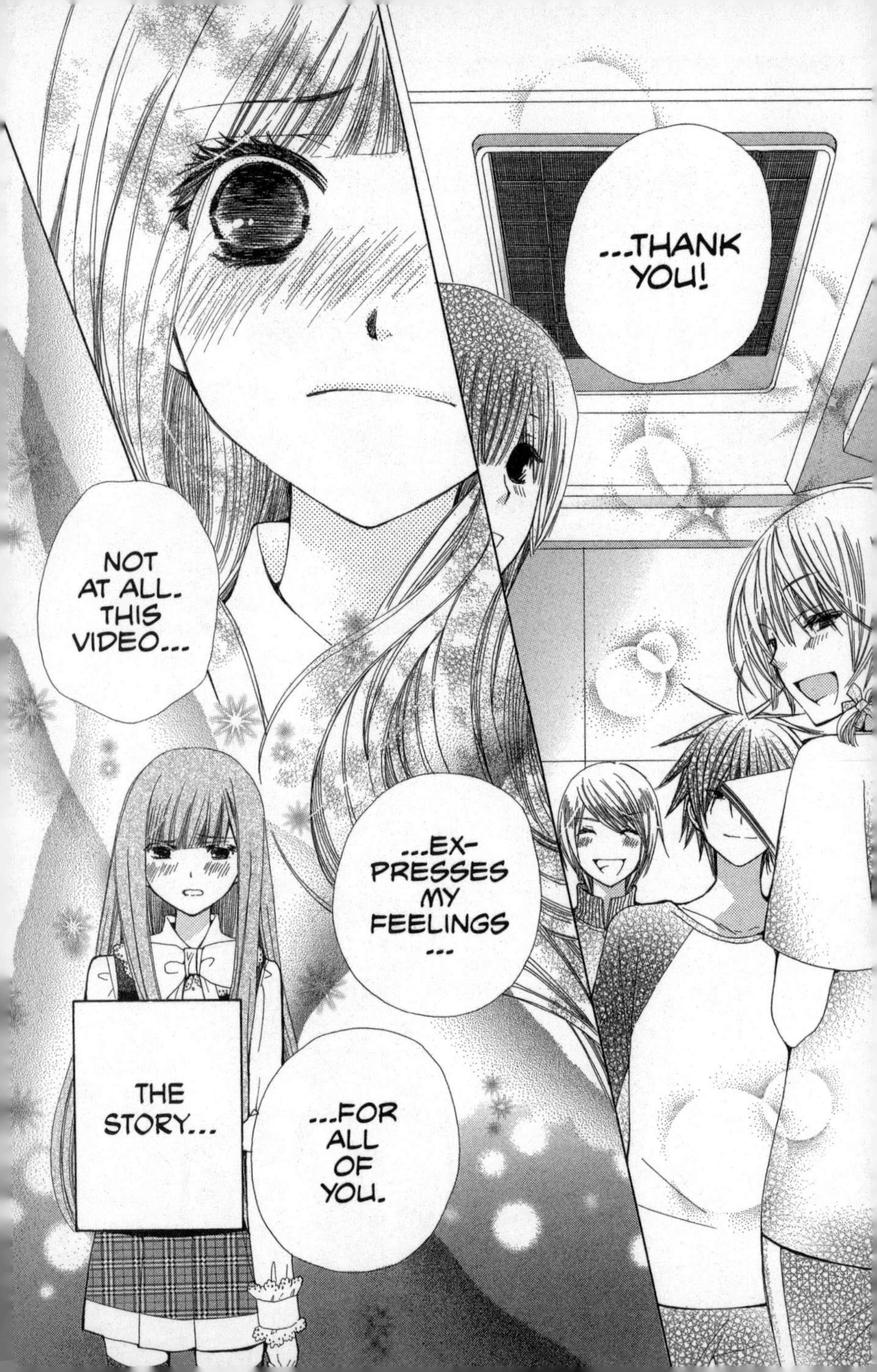
...THANK YOU!
NOT AT ALL. THIS VIDEO...
...EX-PRESSES MY FEELINGS ...
...FOR ALL OF YOU.
THE STORY...

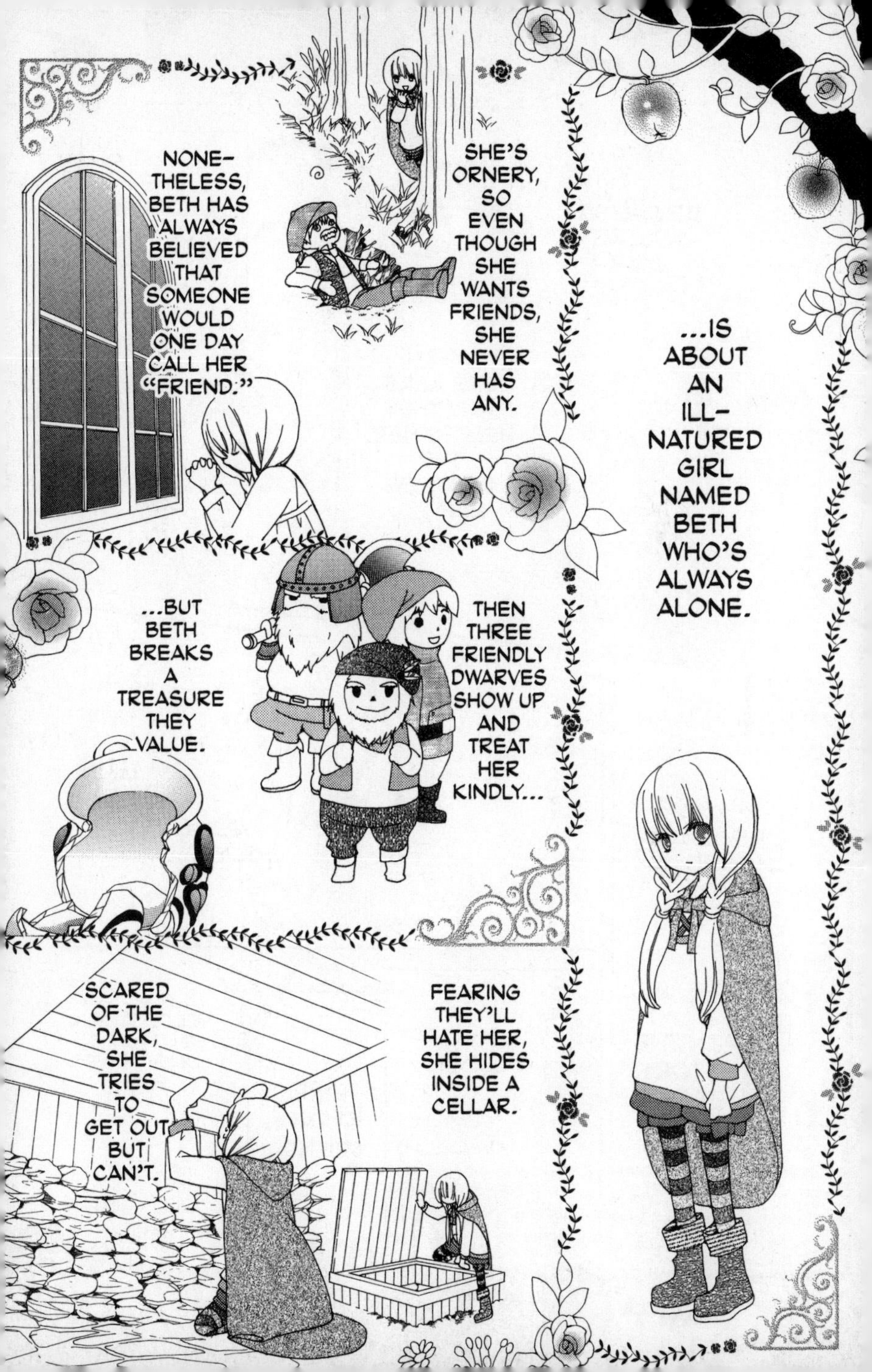
...IS ABOUT AN ILL-NATURED GIRL NAMED BETH WHO'S ALWAYS ALONE.
SHE'S ORNERY, SO EVEN THOUGH SHE WANTS FRIENDS, SHE NEVER HAS ANY.
NONE-THELESS, BETH HAS ALWAYS BELIEVED THAT SOMEONE WOULD ONE DAY CALL HER "FRIEND."
THEN THREE FRIENDLY DWARVES SHOW UP AND TREAT HER KINDLY...
...BUT BETH BREAKS A TREASURE THEY VALUE.
FEARING THEY'LL HATE HER, SHE HIDES INSIDE A CELLAR.
SCARED OF THE DARK, SHE TRIES TO GET OUT BUT CAN'T.

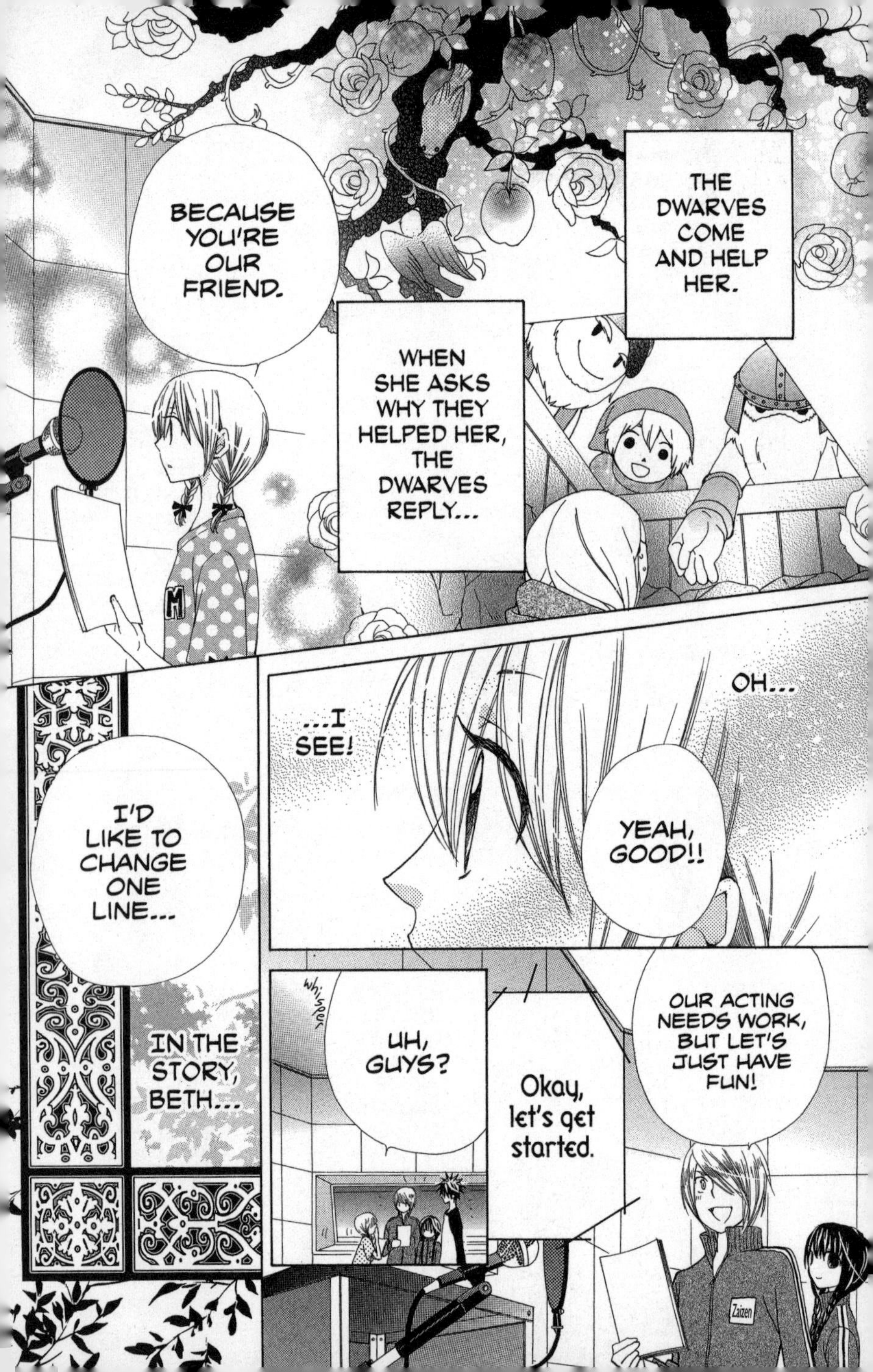
THE DWARVES COME AND HELP HER.
WHEN SHE ASKS WHY THEY HELPED HER, THE DWARVES REPLY...
BECAUSE YOU'RE OUR FRIEND.
OH...
...I SEE!
YEAH, GOOD!!
OUR ACTING NEEDS WORK, BUT LET'S JUST HAVE FUN!
Okay, let's get started.
UH, GUYS?
whisper
Zaizen
I'D LIKE TO CHANGE ONE LINE...
IN THE STORY, BETH...

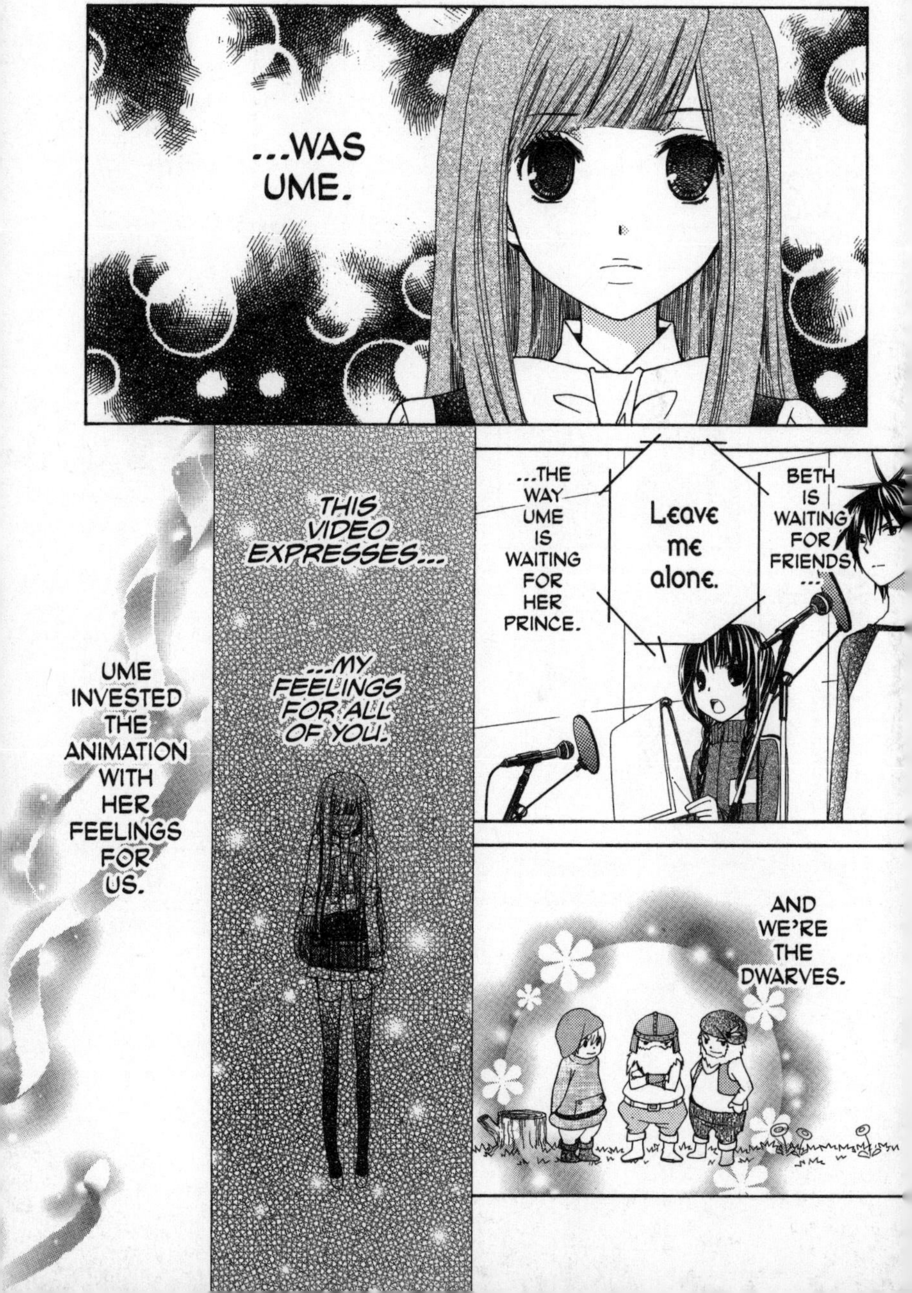
...WAS UME.
BETH IS WAITING FOR FRIENDS...
Leave me alone.
...THE WAY UME IS WAITING FOR HER PRINCE.
AND WE'RE THE DWARVES.
THIS VIDEO EXPRESSES...
...MY FEELINGS FOR ALL OF YOU.
UME INVESTED THE ANIMATION WITH HER FEELINGS FOR US.

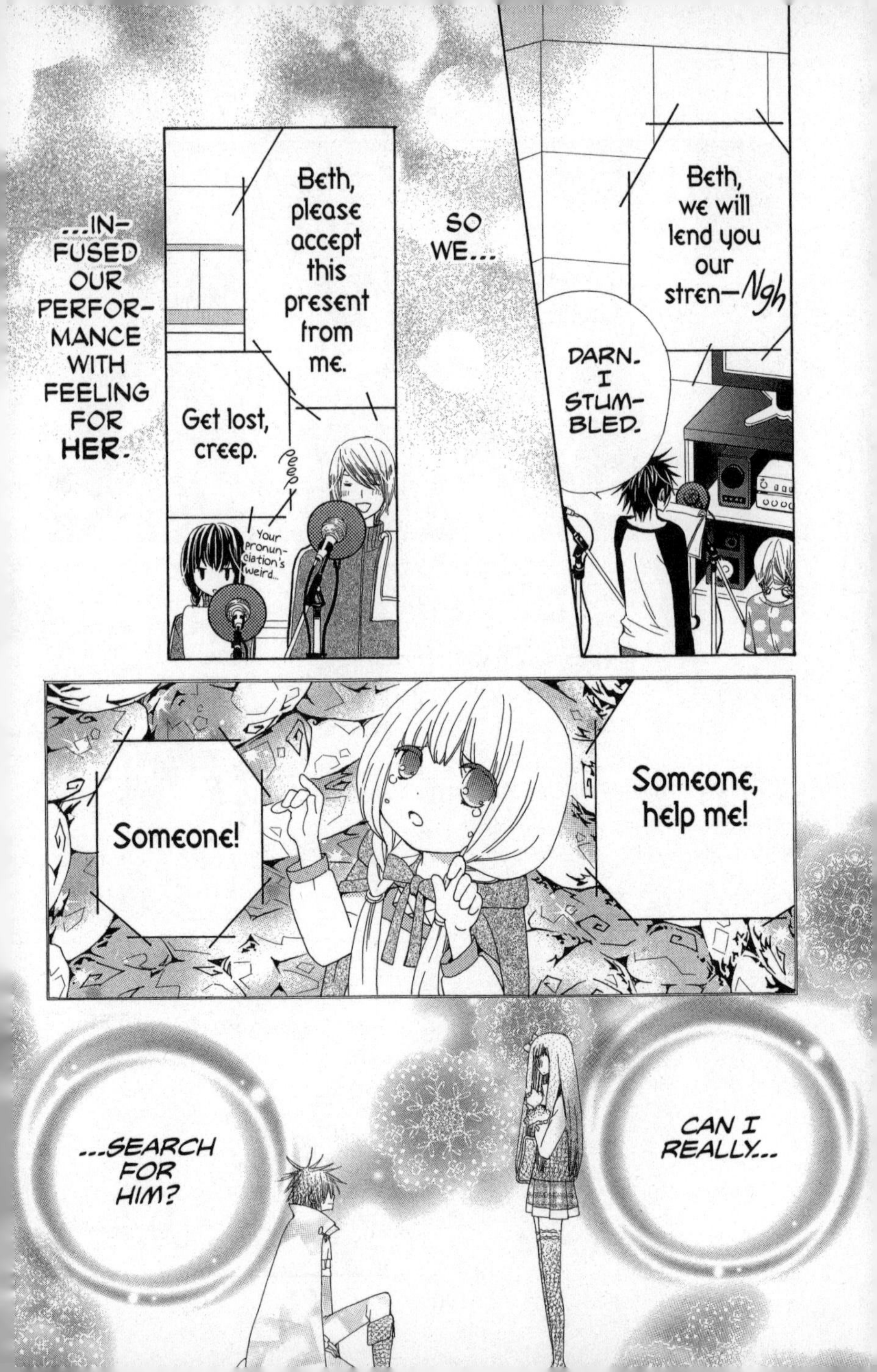
Beth, we will lend you our stren—Ngh
DARN. I STUMBLED.
SO WE...
Beth, please accept this present from me.
Get lost, creep.
PEEP
Your pronunciation's weird...
...IN-FUSED OUR PERFORMANCE WITH FEELING FOR HER.
Someone, help me!
Someone!
CAN I REALLY...
...SEARCH FOR HIM?

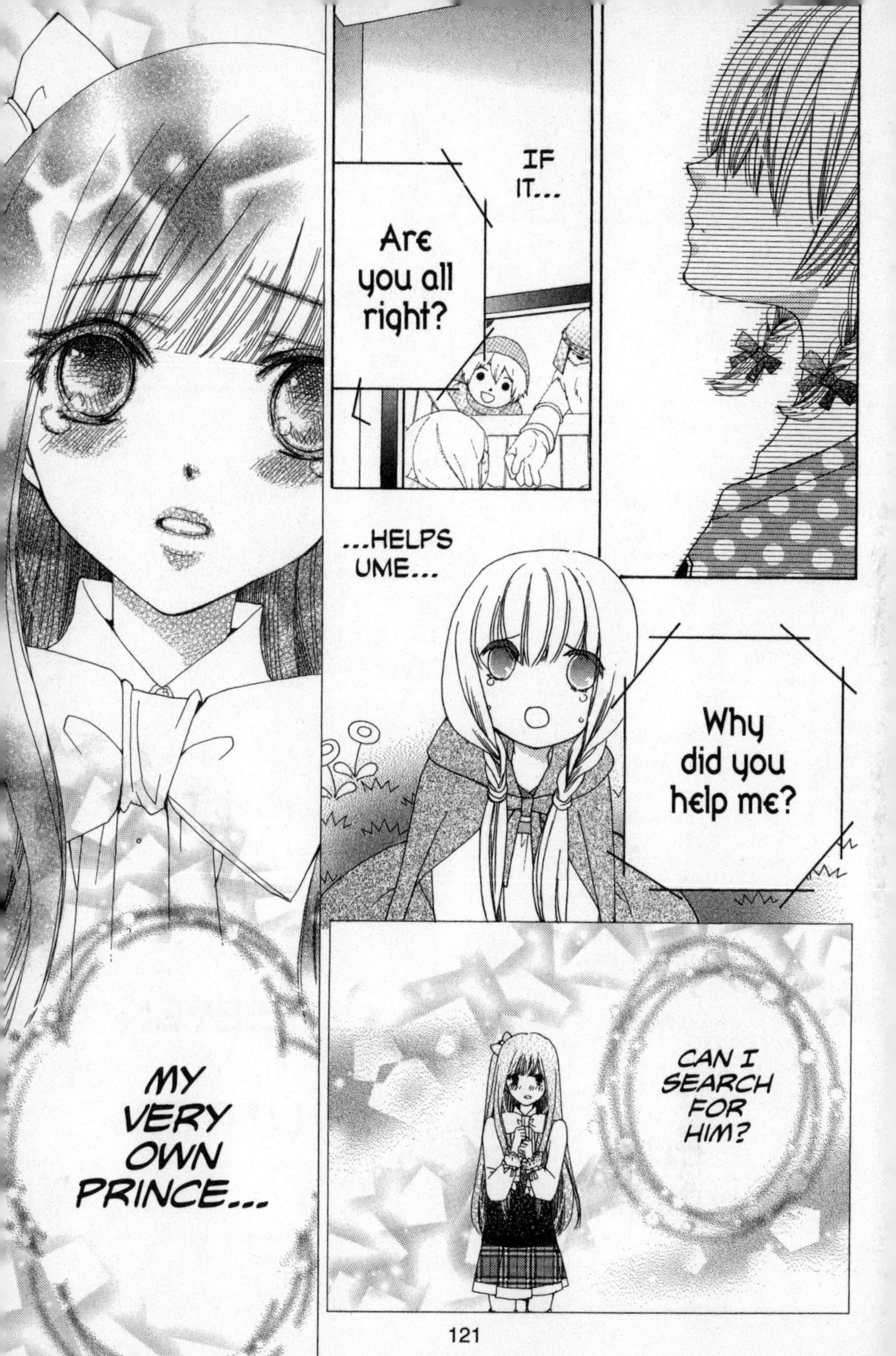
IF IT...
Are you all right?
...HELPS UME...
Why did you help me?
CAN I SEARCH FOR HIM?
MY VERY OWN PRINCE...

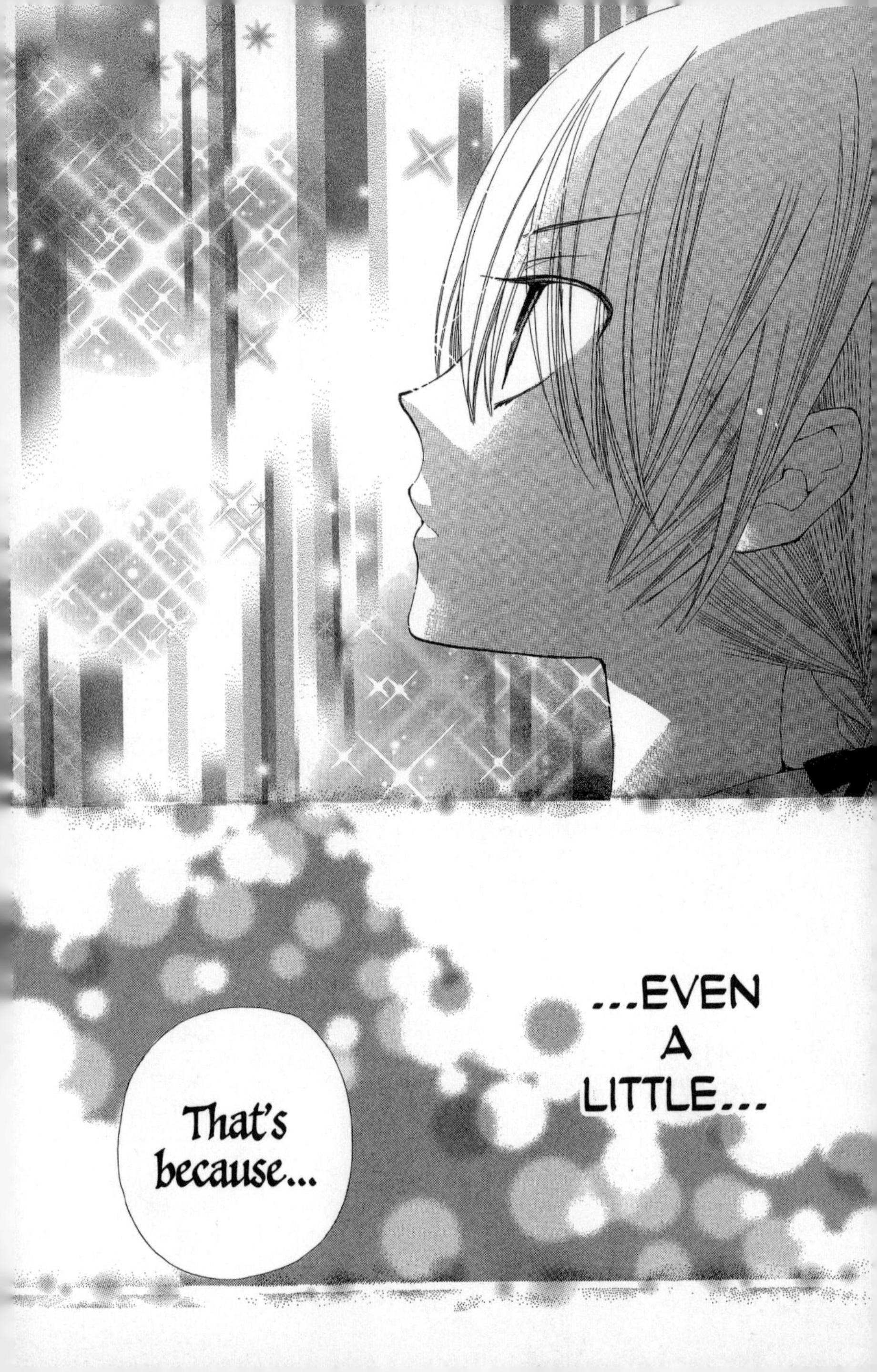
...EVEN A LITTLE...
That's because...

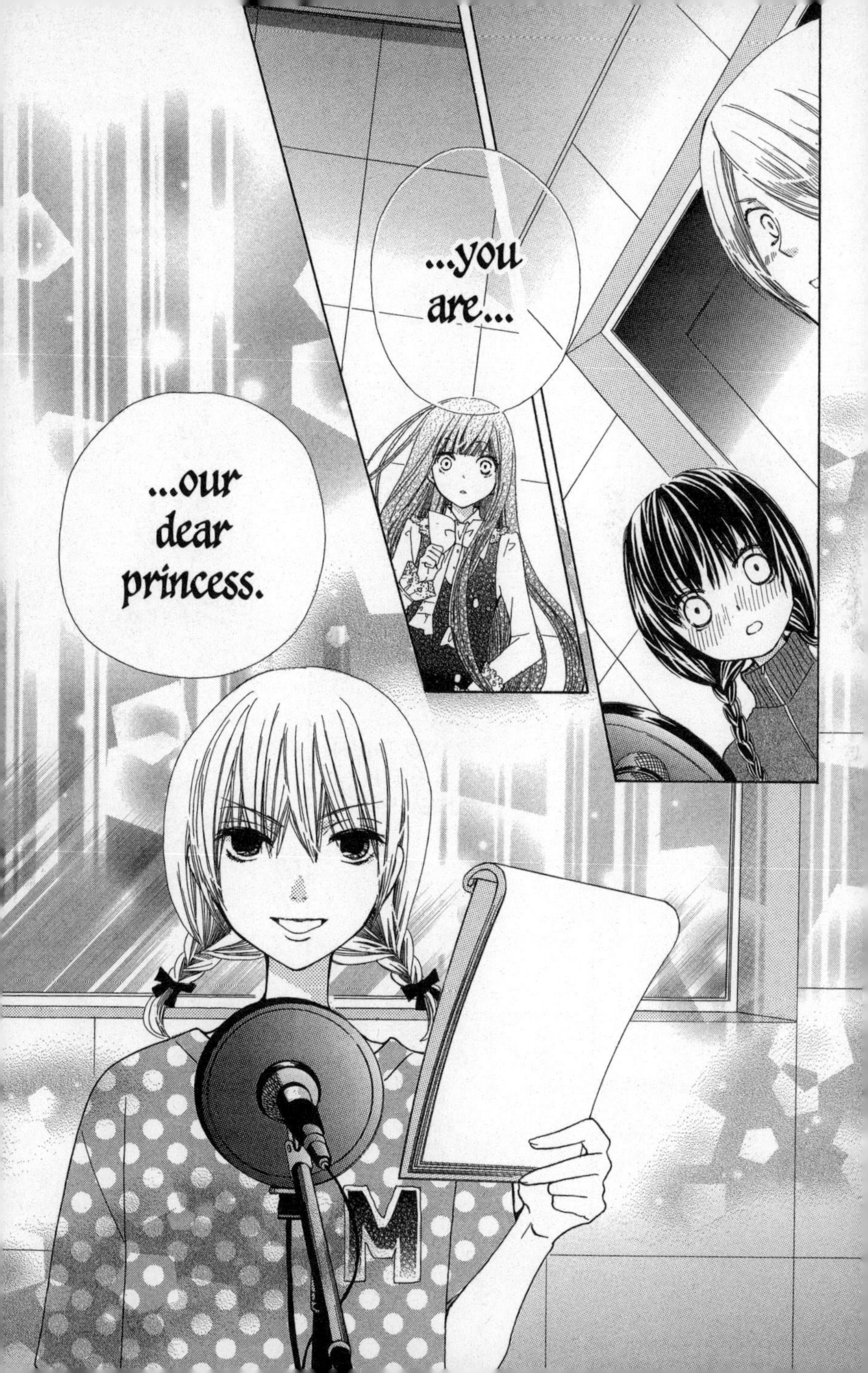
...you are...
...our dear princess.

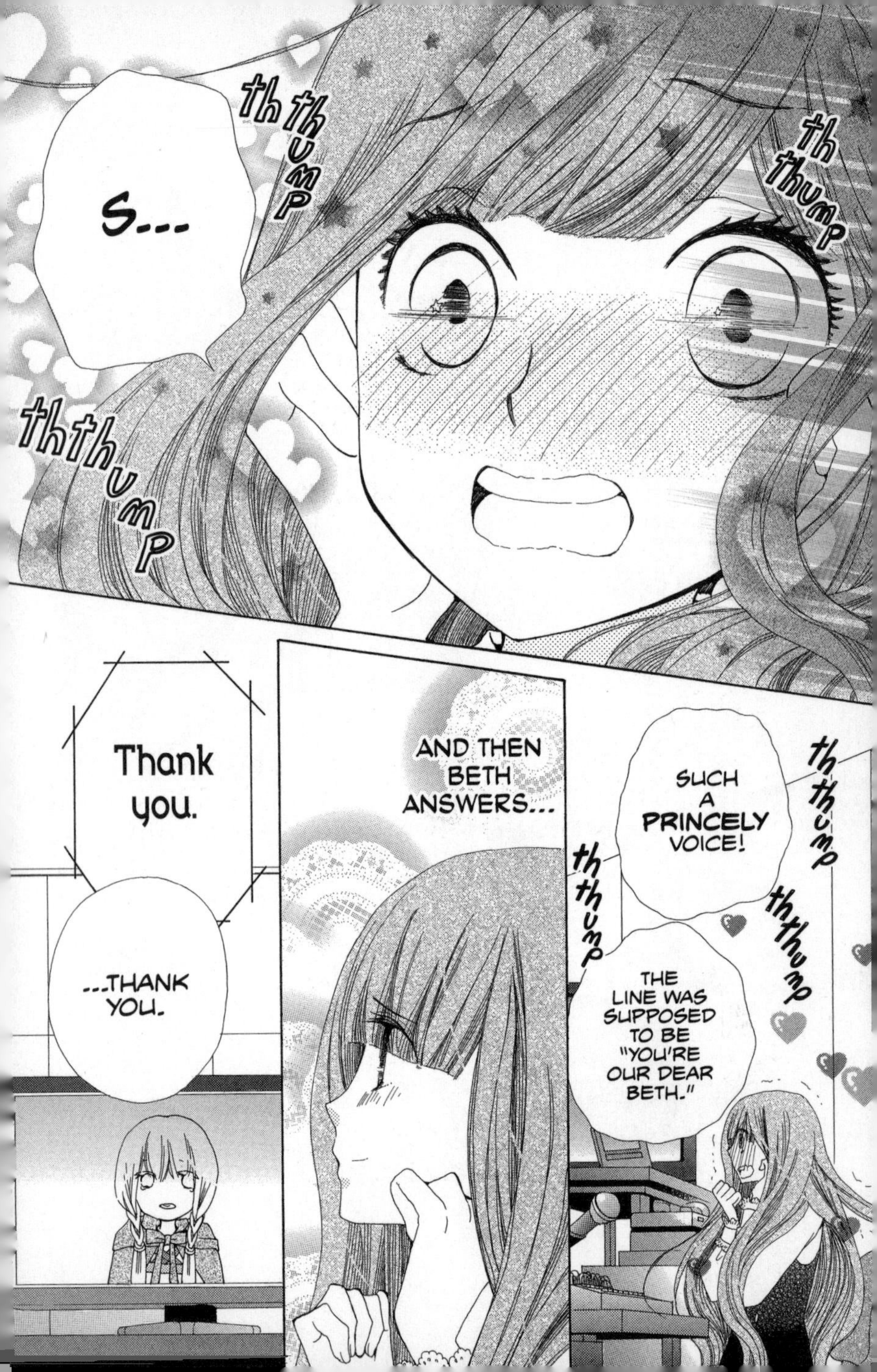
th thump
th thump
S...
thththump
th thump
SUCH A PRINCELY VOICE!
th thump
th thump
THE LINE WAS SUPPOSED TO BE "YOU'RE OUR DEAR BETH."
AND THEN BETH ANSWERS...
Thank you.
...THANK YOU.

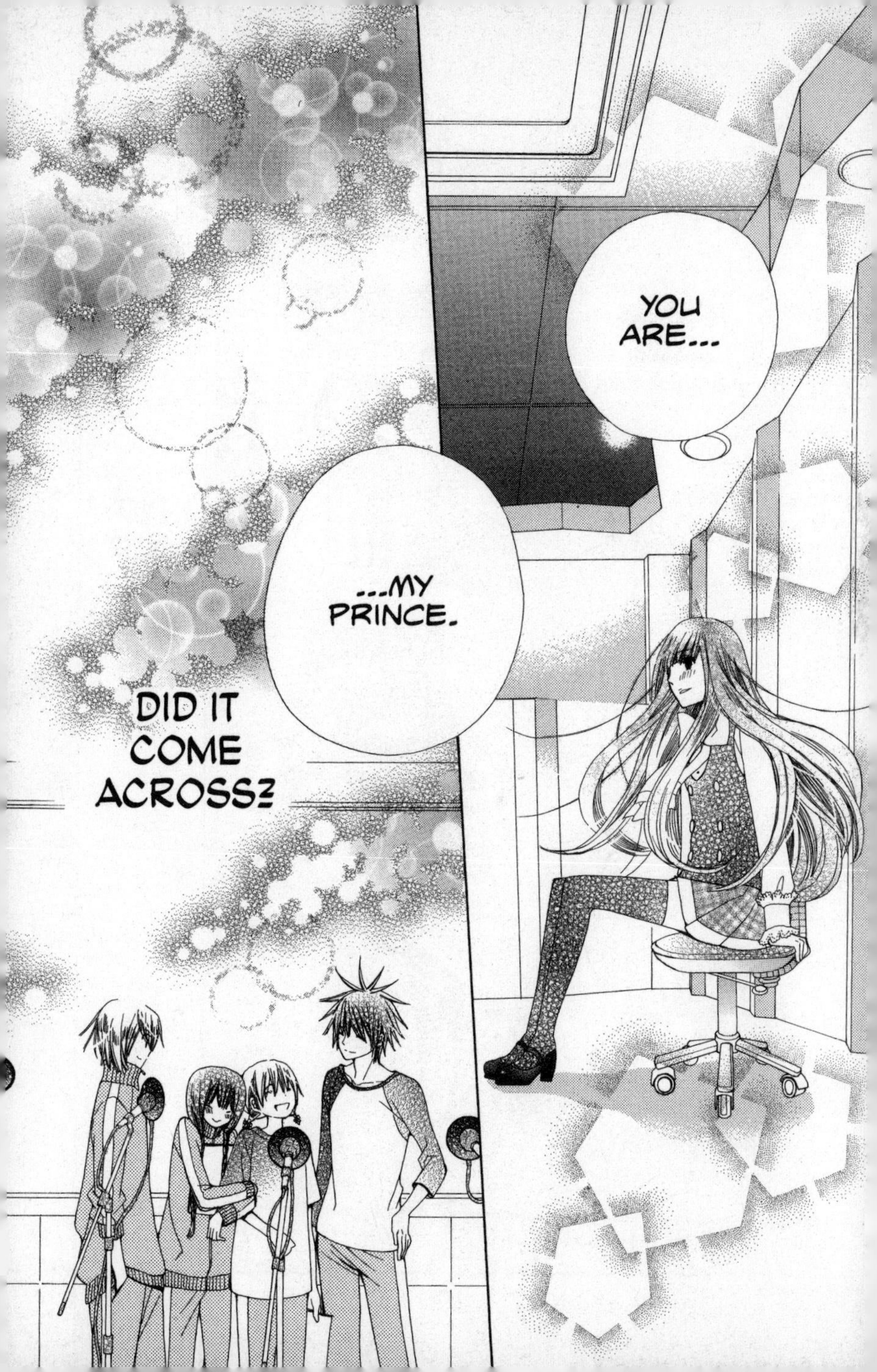
YOU ARE...
...MY PRINCE.
DID IT COME ACROSS?

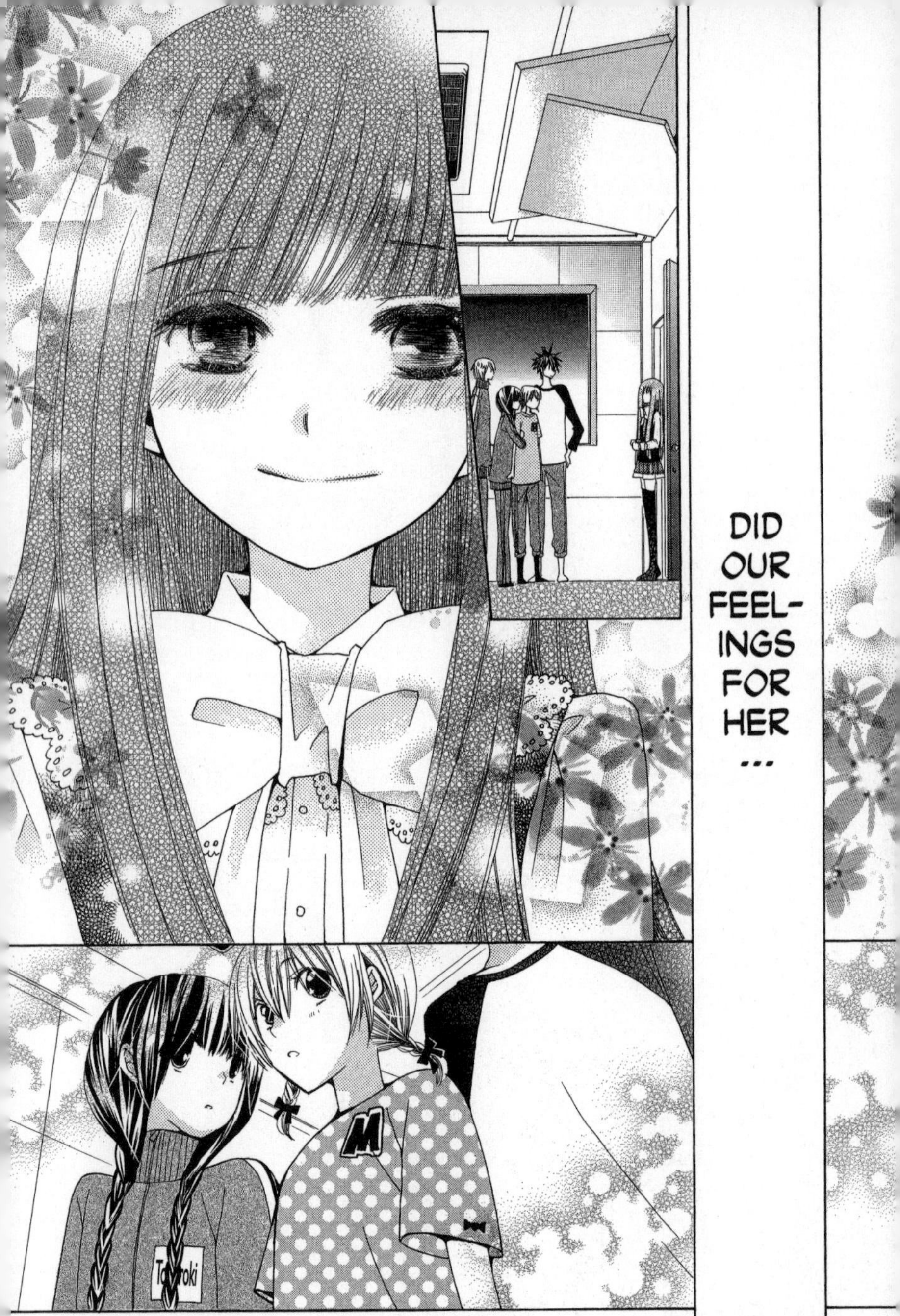
DID OUR FEEL- INGS FOR HER ...

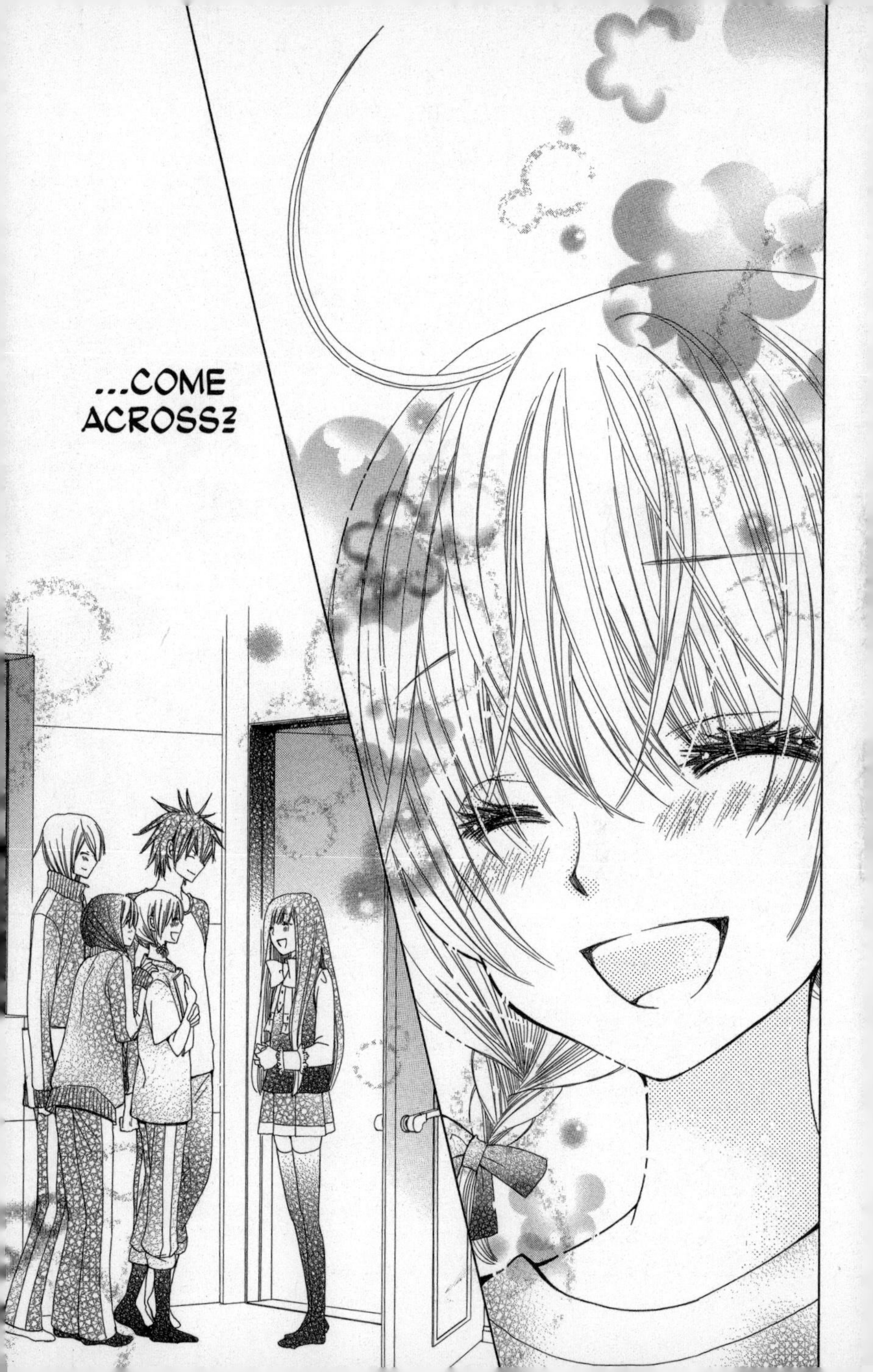
...COME ACROSS?

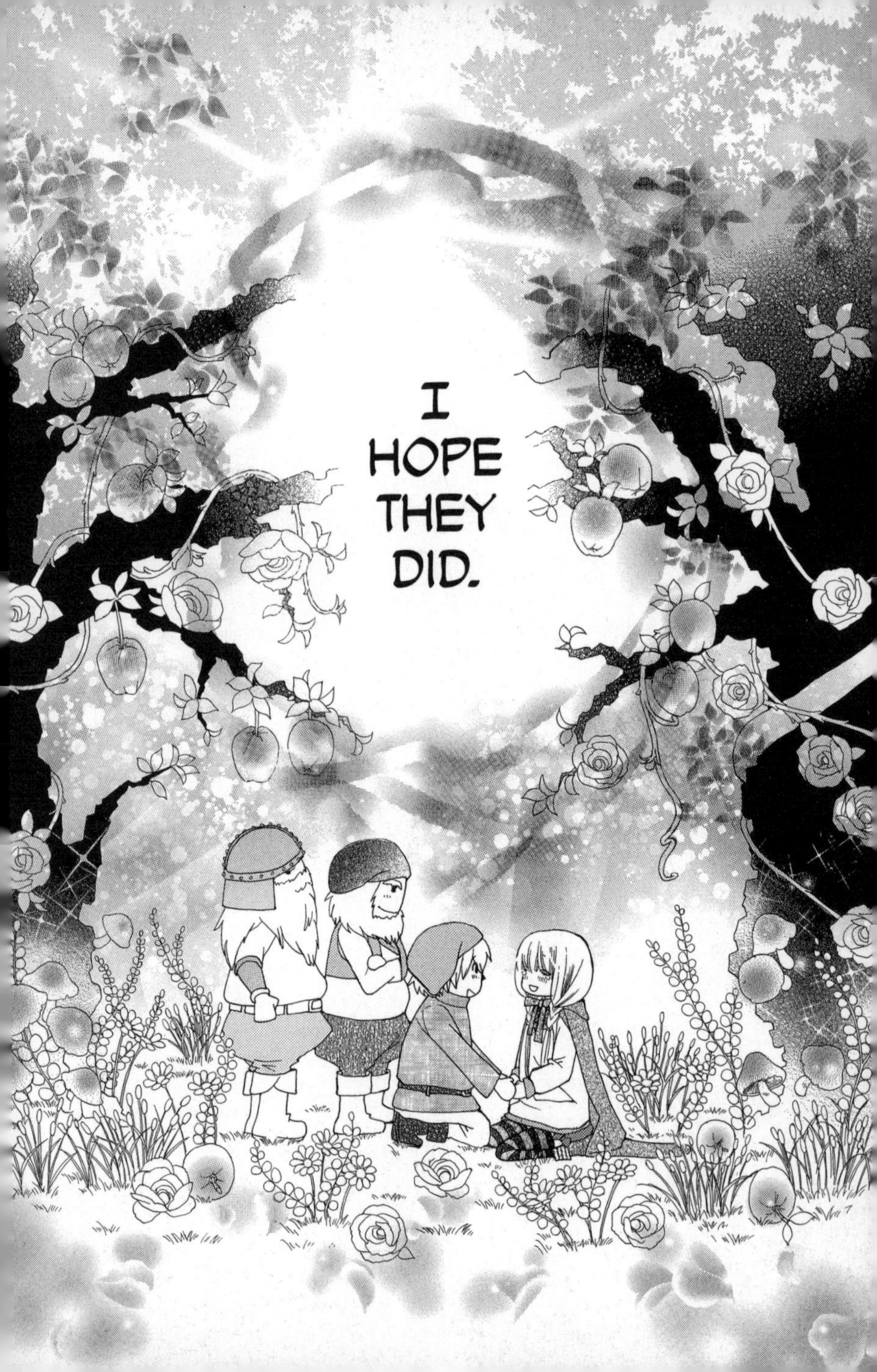
I HOPE THEY DID.

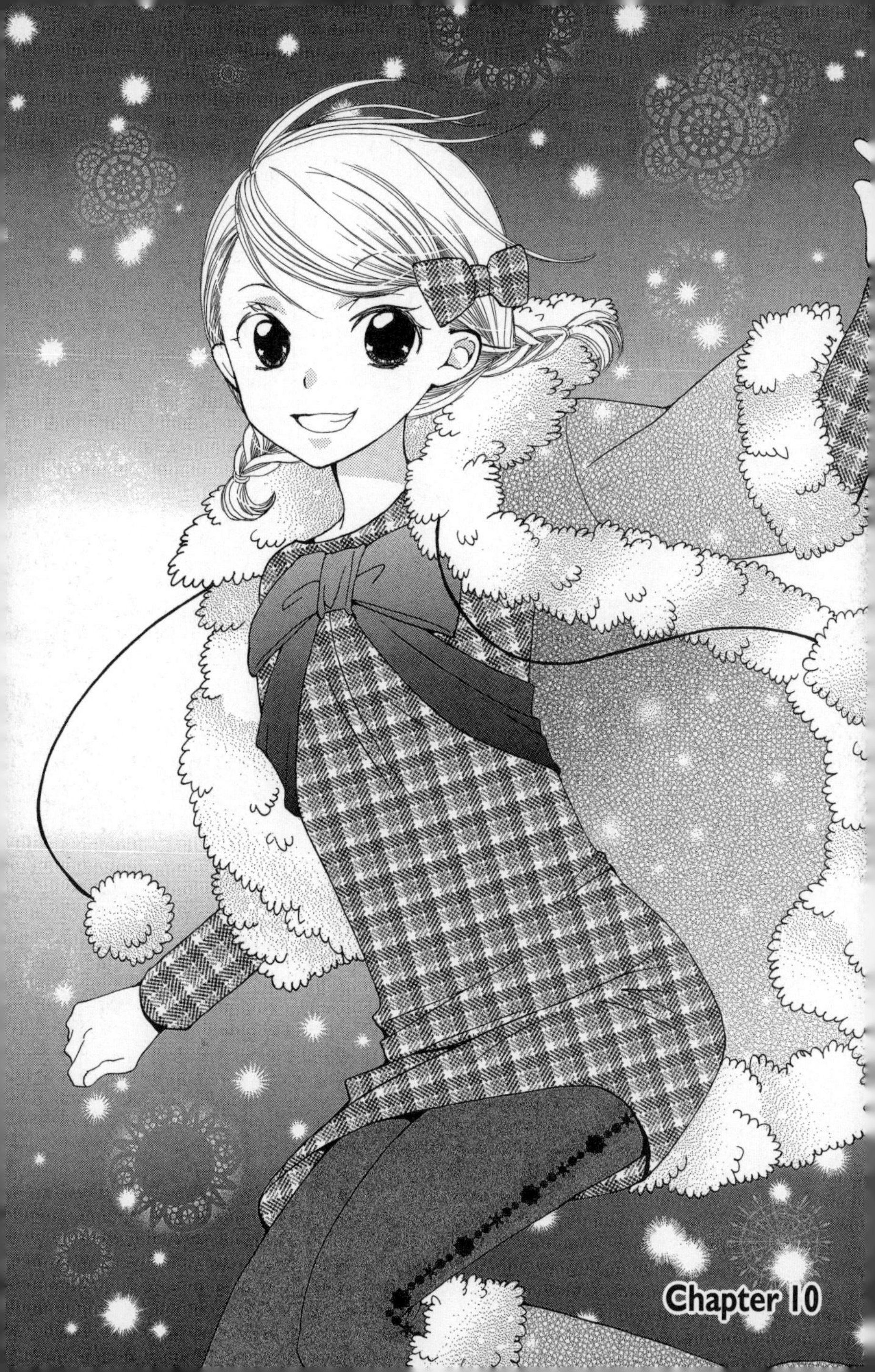
Chapter 10

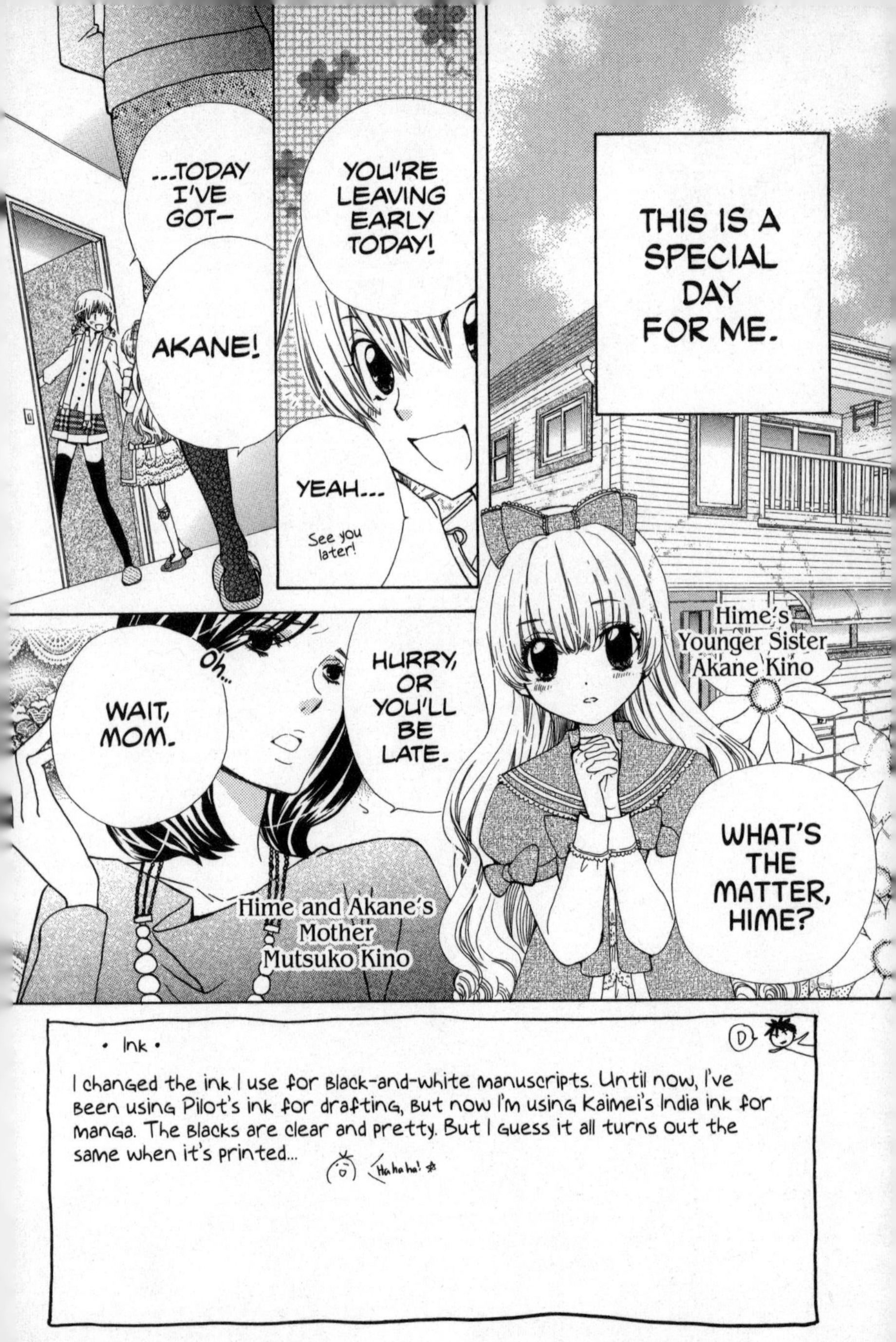
THIS IS A SPECIAL DAY FOR ME.
YOU'RE LEAVING EARLY TODAY!
YEAH...
See you later!
...TODAY I'VE GOT—
AKANE!
Hime's Younger Sister Akane Kino
WHAT'S THE MATTER, HIME?
HURRY, OR YOU'LL BE LATE.
Oh...
WAIT, MOM.
Hime and Akane's Mother Mutsuko Kino

• Ink •

I changed the ink I use for black-and-white manuscripts. Until now, I've been using Pilot's ink for drafting, but now I'm using Kaimei's India ink for manga. The blacks are clear and pretty. But I guess it all turns out the same when it's printed... Hahaha!

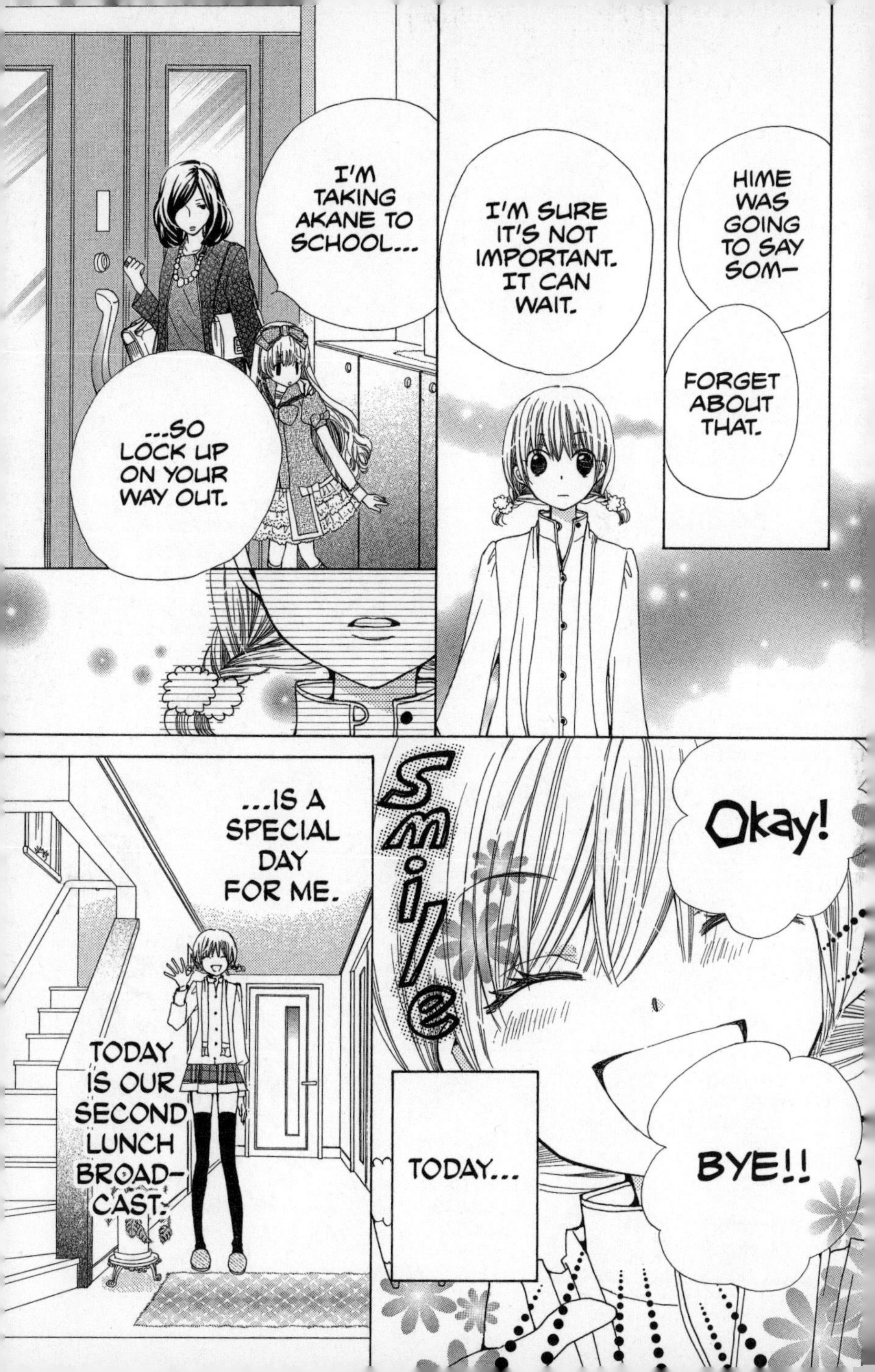
HIME WAS GOING TO SAY SOM—
FORGET ABOUT THAT.
I'M SURE IT'S NOT IMPORTANT. IT CAN WAIT.
I'M TAKING AKANE TO SCHOOL...
...SO LOCK UP ON YOUR WAY OUT.
Okay!
Smile
BYE!!
TODAY...
...IS A SPECIAL DAY FOR ME.
TODAY IS OUR SECOND LUNCH BROADCAST.

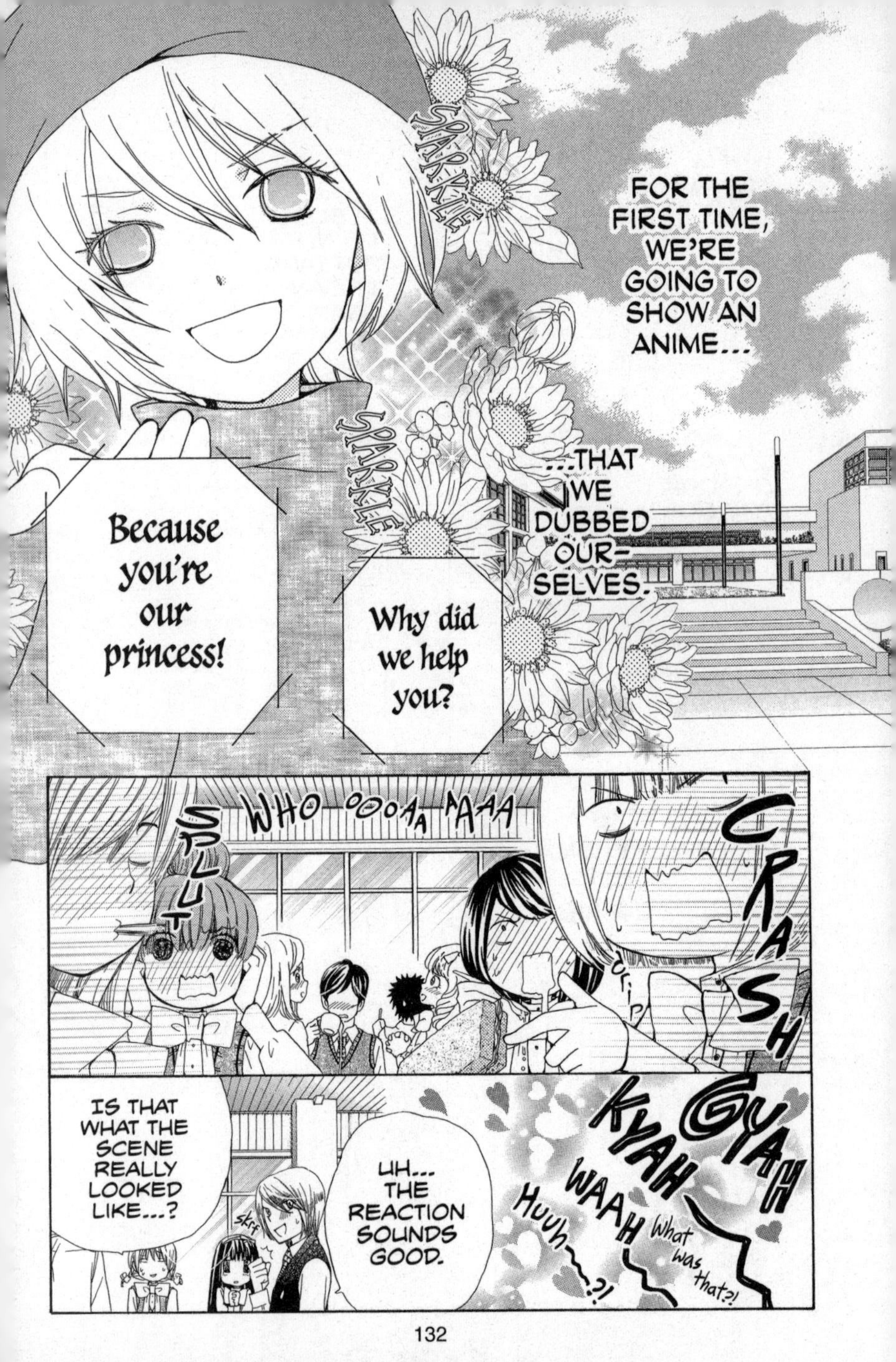
FOR THE FIRST TIME, WE'RE GOING TO SHOW AN ANIME...
...THAT WE DUBBED OUR-SELVES.
SPARKLE
SPARKLE
Why did we help you?
Because you're our princess!
CRASH
drip
WHOOOOAAAAA
SPLUT
GYAAH
KYAH
WAAH
What was that?!
Huuh~~?!
UH... THE REACTION SOUNDS GOOD.
skrf
IS THAT WHAT THE SCENE REALLY LOOKED LIKE...?

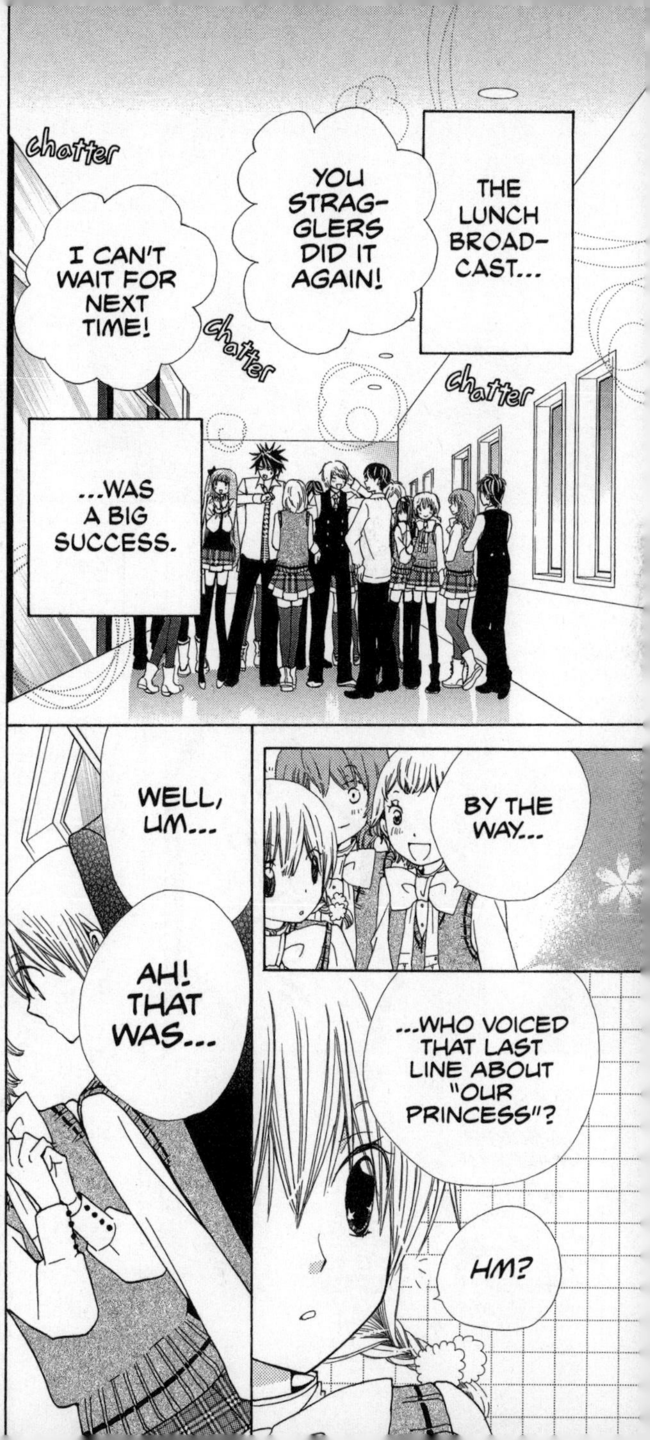
THE LUNCH BROAD-CAST...
YOU STRAG-GLERS DID IT AGAIN!
chatter
I CAN'T WAIT FOR NEXT TIME!
chatter
chatter
...WAS A BIG SUCCESS.
BY THE WAY...
...WHO VOICED THAT LAST LINE ABOUT "OUR PRINCESS"?
HM?
WELL, UM...
AH! THAT WAS...

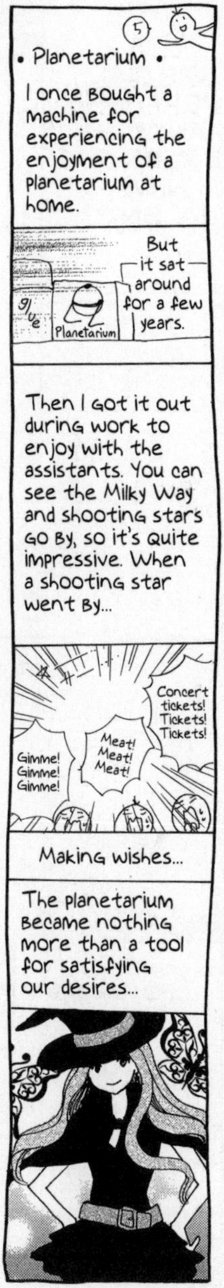
5
• Planetarium •
I once bought a machine for experiencing the enjoyment of a planetarium at home.
But it sat around for a few years.
glue
Planetarium
Then I got it out during work to enjoy with the assistants. You can see the Milky Way and shooting stars go by, so it's quite impressive. When a shooting star went by...
Concert tickets! Tickets! Tickets!
Meat! Meat! Meat!
Gimme! Gimme! Gimme!
Making wishes...
The planetarium became nothing more than a tool for satisfying our desires...

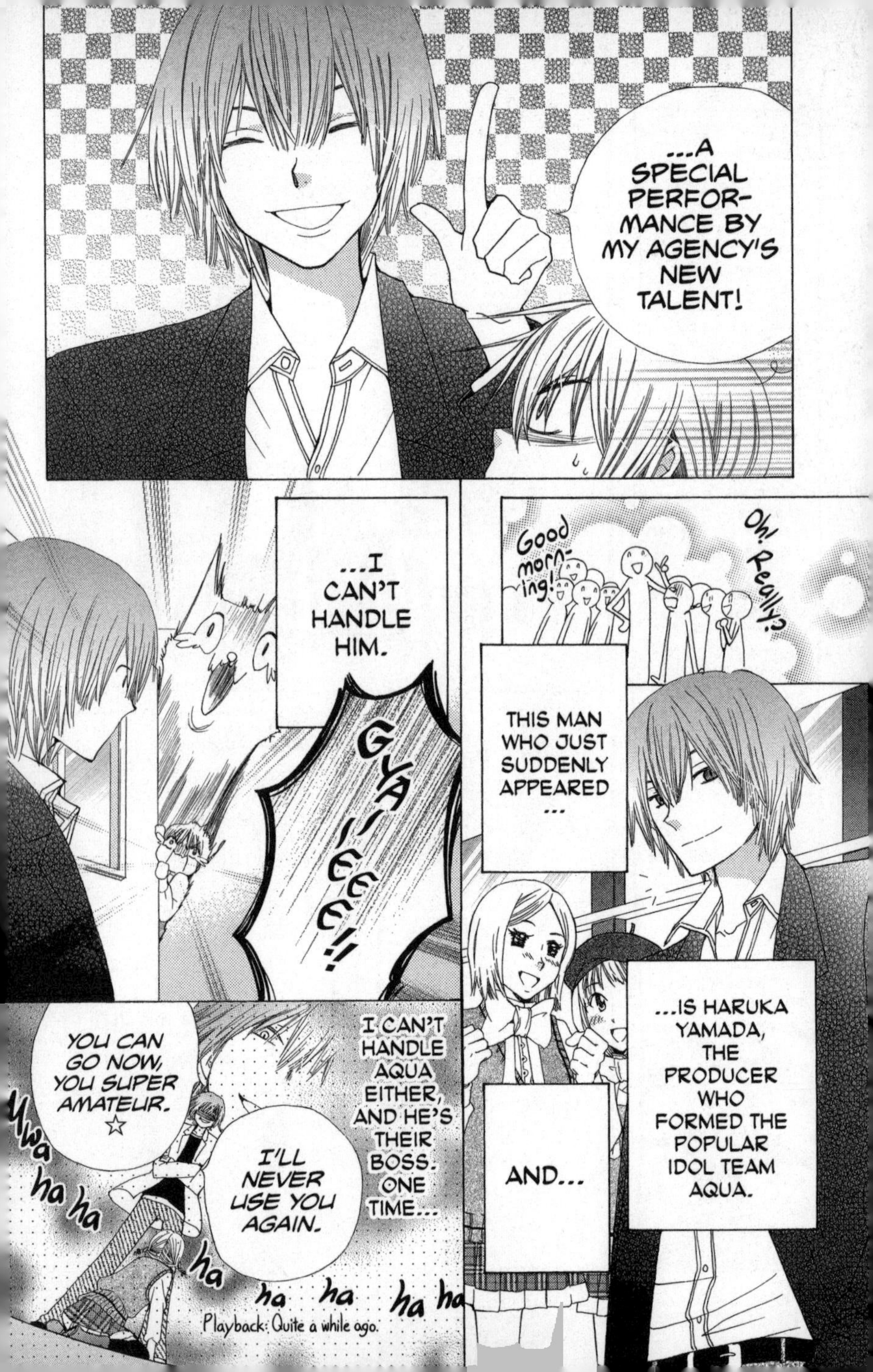
...A SPECIAL PERFORMANCE BY MY AGENCY'S NEW TALENT!
Oh! Really?
Good morning!
THIS MAN WHO JUST SUDDENLY APPEARED...
...IS HARUKA YAMADA, THE PRODUCER WHO FORMED THE POPULAR IDOL TEAM AQUA.
AND...
...I CAN'T HANDLE HIM.
GYAIIEEE!!
I CAN'T HANDLE AQUA EITHER, AND HE'S THEIR BOSS. ONE TIME...
YOU CAN GO NOW, YOU SUPER AMATEUR. ☆
I'LL NEVER USE YOU AGAIN.
Mwa ha ha ha ha ha ha ha ha
Playback: Quite a while ago.

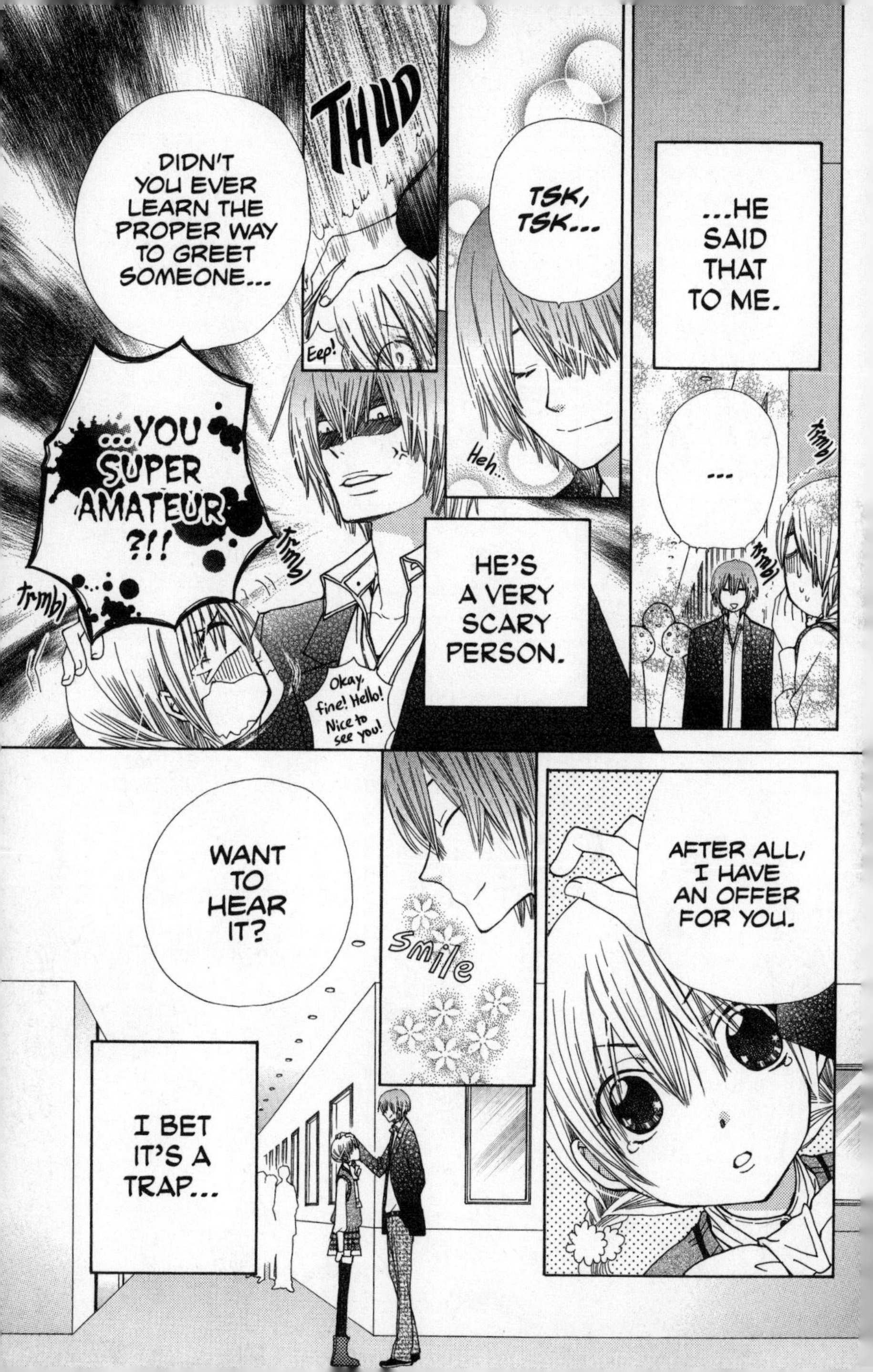
...HE SAID THAT TO ME.
...
trmbl
trmbl
TSK, TSK...
Heh...
THUD
Eep!
DIDN'T YOU EVER LEARN THE PROPER WAY TO GREET SOMEONE...
...YOU SUPER AMATEUR?!!
trmbl
trmbl
Okay, fine! Hello! Nice to see you!
HE'S A VERY SCARY PERSON.
AFTER ALL, I HAVE AN OFFER FOR YOU.
smile
WANT TO HEAR IT?
I BET IT'S A TRAP...

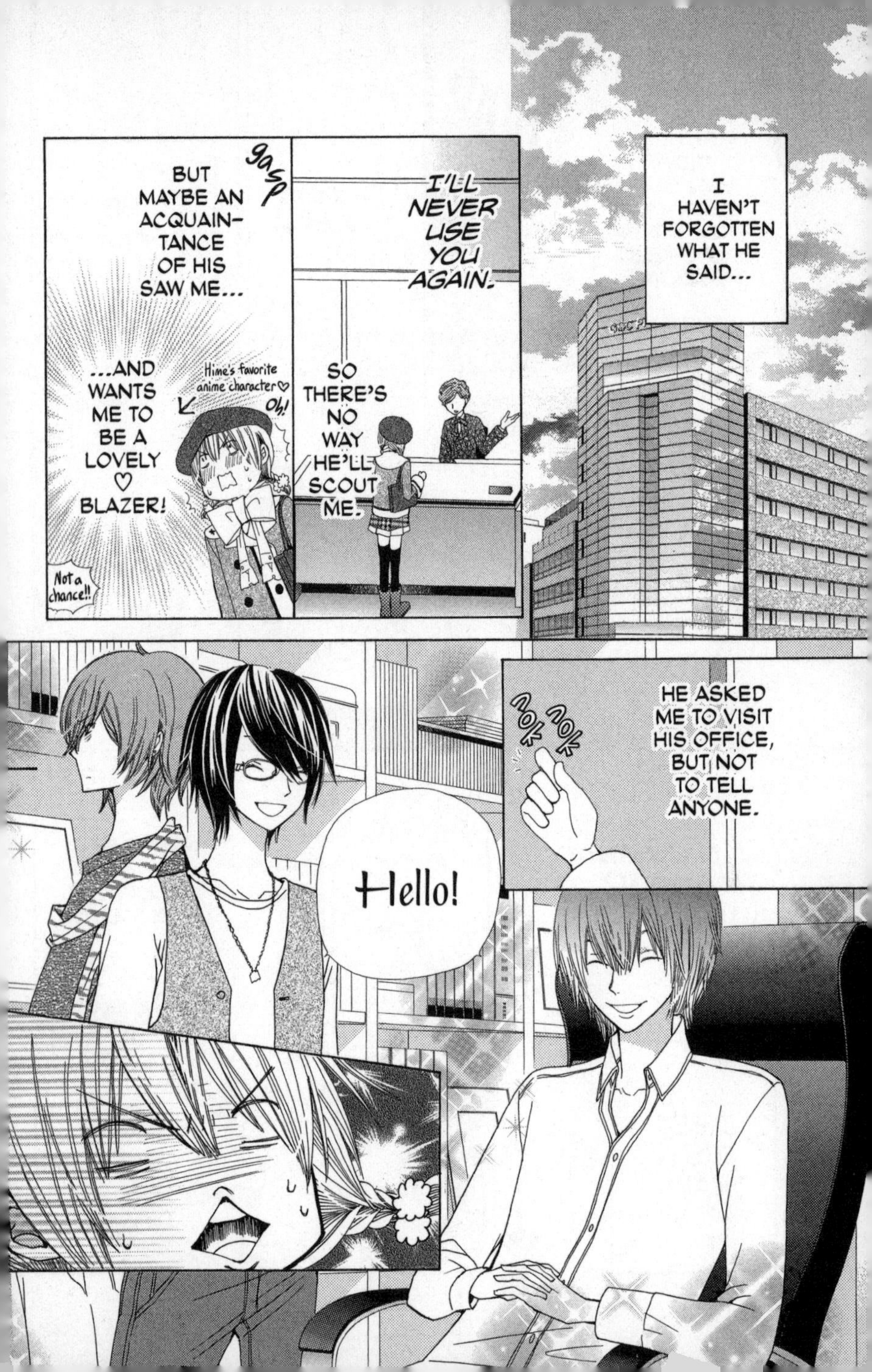
I HAVEN'T FORGOTTEN WHAT HE SAID...
I'LL NEVER USE YOU AGAIN.
SO THERE'S NO WAY HE'LL SCOUT ME.
gasp
BUT MAYBE AN ACQUAIN-TANCE OF HIS SAW ME...
...AND WANTS ME TO BE A LOVELY ♡ BLAZER!
Hime's favorite anime character♡
Oh!
Not a chance!!
HE ASKED ME TO VISIT HIS OFFICE, BUT NOT TO TELL ANYONE.
Hello!

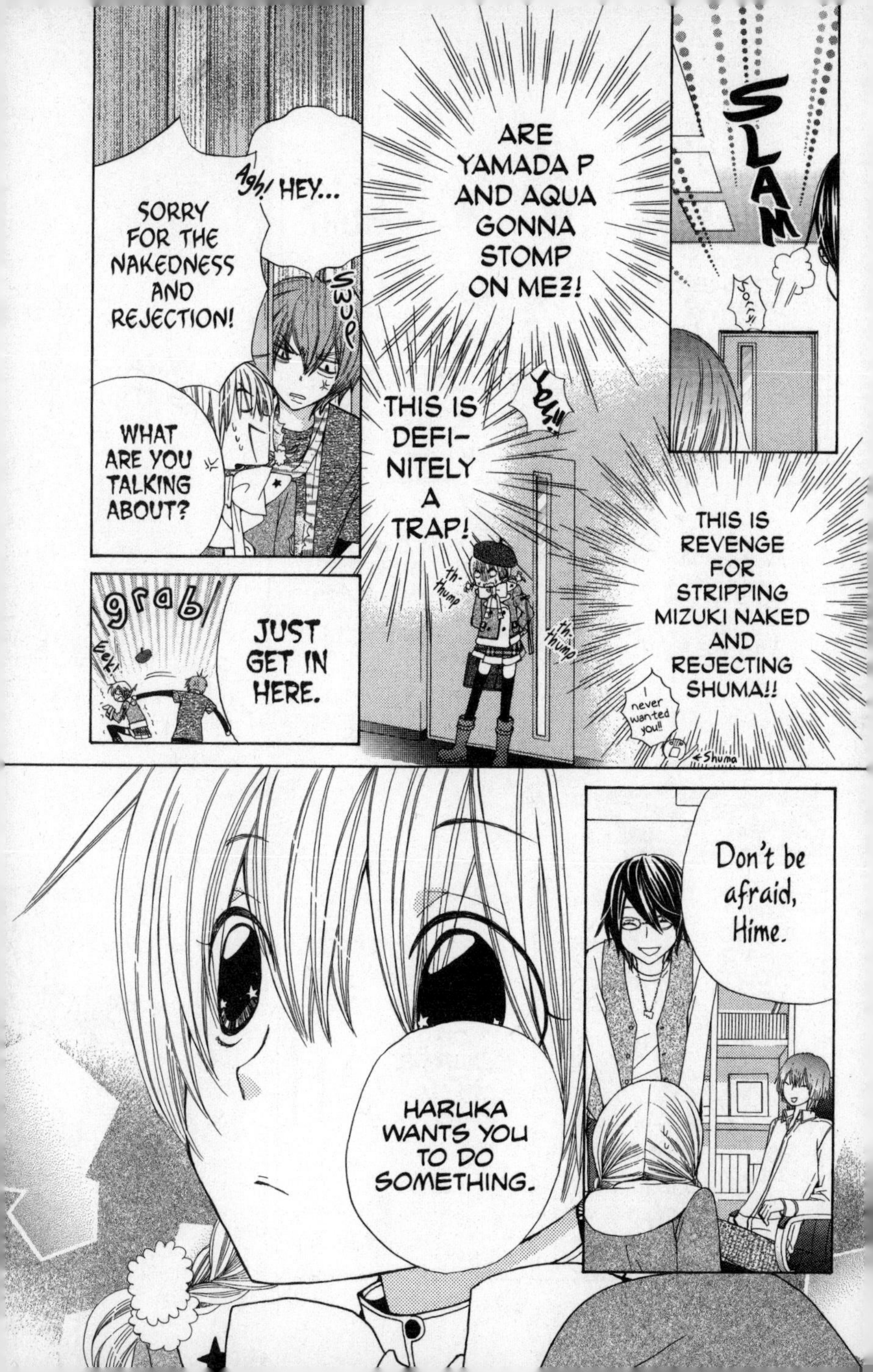
SLAM
sorry!
ARE YAMADA P AND AQUA GONNA STOMP ON ME?!
THIS IS REVENGE FOR STRIPPING MIZUKI NAKED AND REJECTING SHUMA!!
I never wanted you!!
←Shuma
THIS IS DEFINITELY A TRAP!
th-thump
th-thump
Agh! HEY...
SORRY FOR THE NAKEDNESS AND REJECTION!
swup
WHAT ARE YOU TALKING ABOUT?
JUST GET IN HERE.
grab
Eek!
Don't be afraid, Hime.
HARUKA WANTS YOU TO DO SOMETHING.

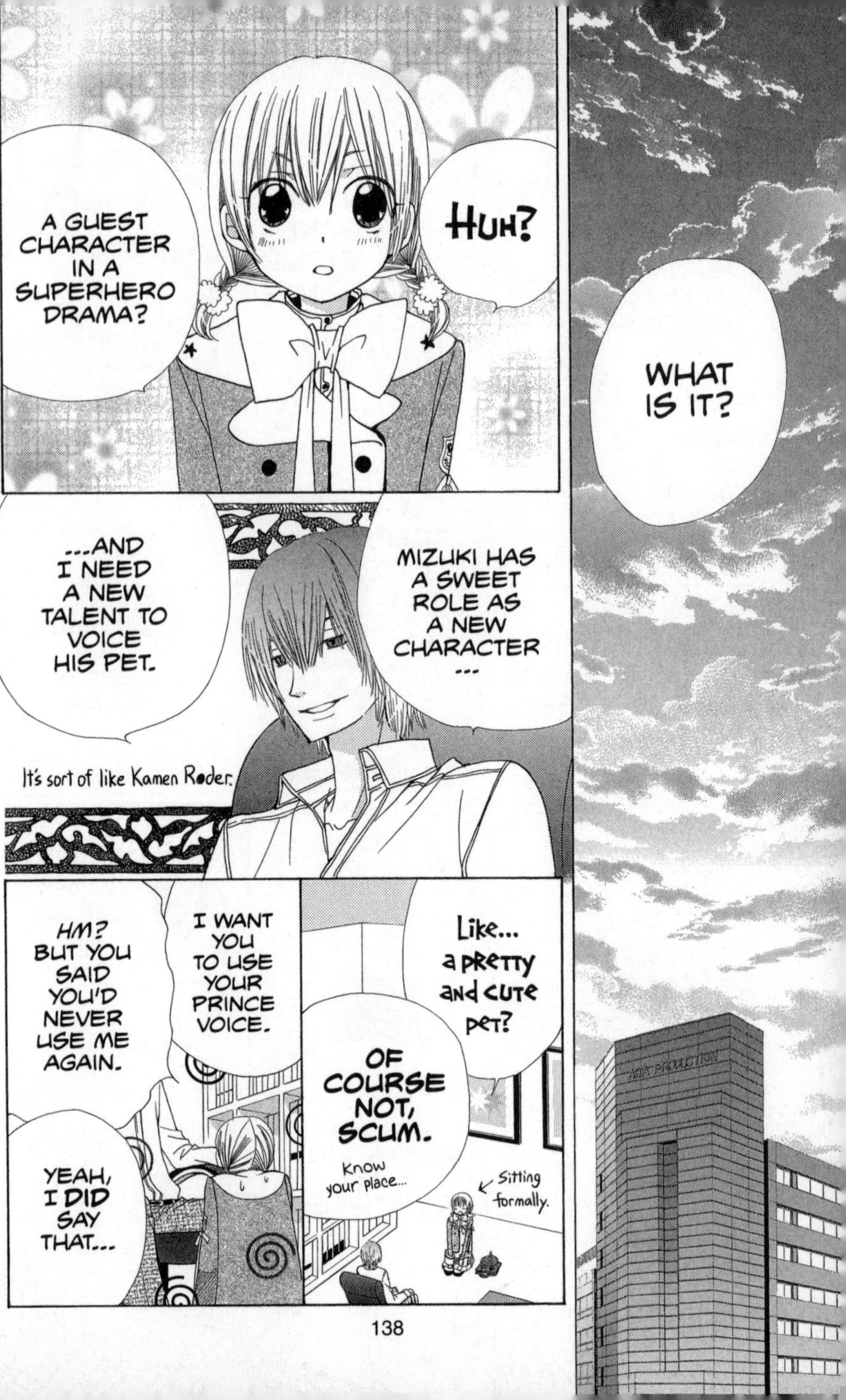
WHAT IS IT?
HUH?
A GUEST CHARACTER IN A SUPERHERO DRAMA?
MIZUKI HAS A SWEET ROLE AS A NEW CHARACTER...
...AND I NEED A NEW TALENT TO VOICE HIS PET.
It's sort of like Kamen Roder.
Like... a pretty and cute pet?
OF COURSE NOT, SCUM.
Know your place...
Sitting formally.
I WANT YOU TO USE YOUR PRINCE VOICE.
HM? BUT YOU SAID YOU'D NEVER USE ME AGAIN.
YEAH, I DID SAY THAT...

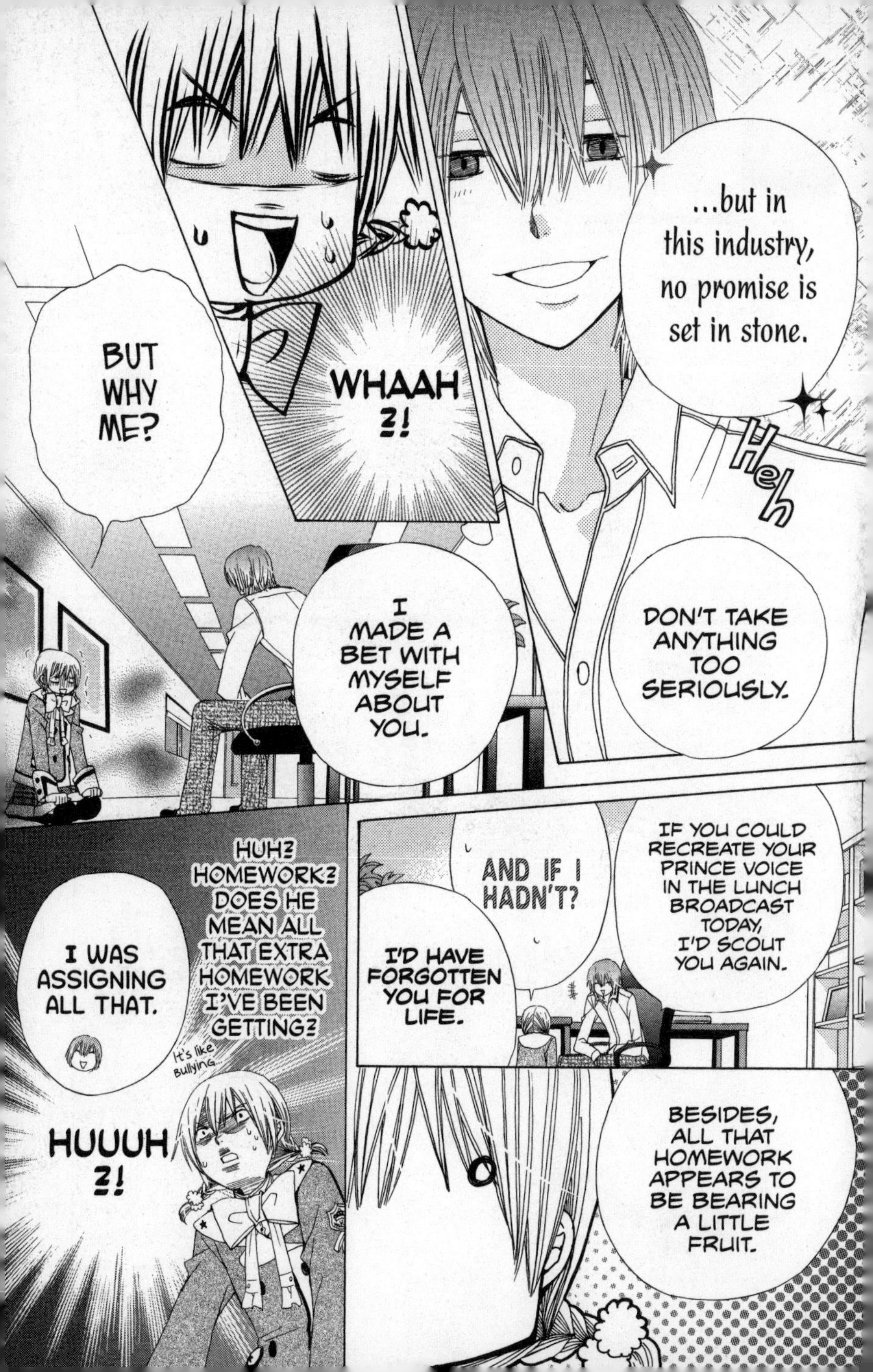
...but in this industry, no promise is set in stone.
Heh
DON'T TAKE ANYTHING TOO SERIOUSLY.
WHAAH ?!
BUT WHY ME?
I MADE A BET WITH MYSELF ABOUT YOU.
IF YOU COULD RECREATE YOUR PRINCE VOICE IN THE LUNCH BROADCAST TODAY, I'D SCOUT YOU AGAIN.
AND IF I HADN'T?
I'D HAVE FORGOTTEN YOU FOR LIFE.
BESIDES, ALL THAT HOMEWORK APPEARS TO BE BEARING A LITTLE FRUIT.
HUH? HOMEWORK? DOES HE MEAN ALL THAT EXTRA HOMEWORK I'VE BEEN GETTING?
I WAS ASSIGNING ALL THAT.
It's like Bullying...
HUUUH ?!

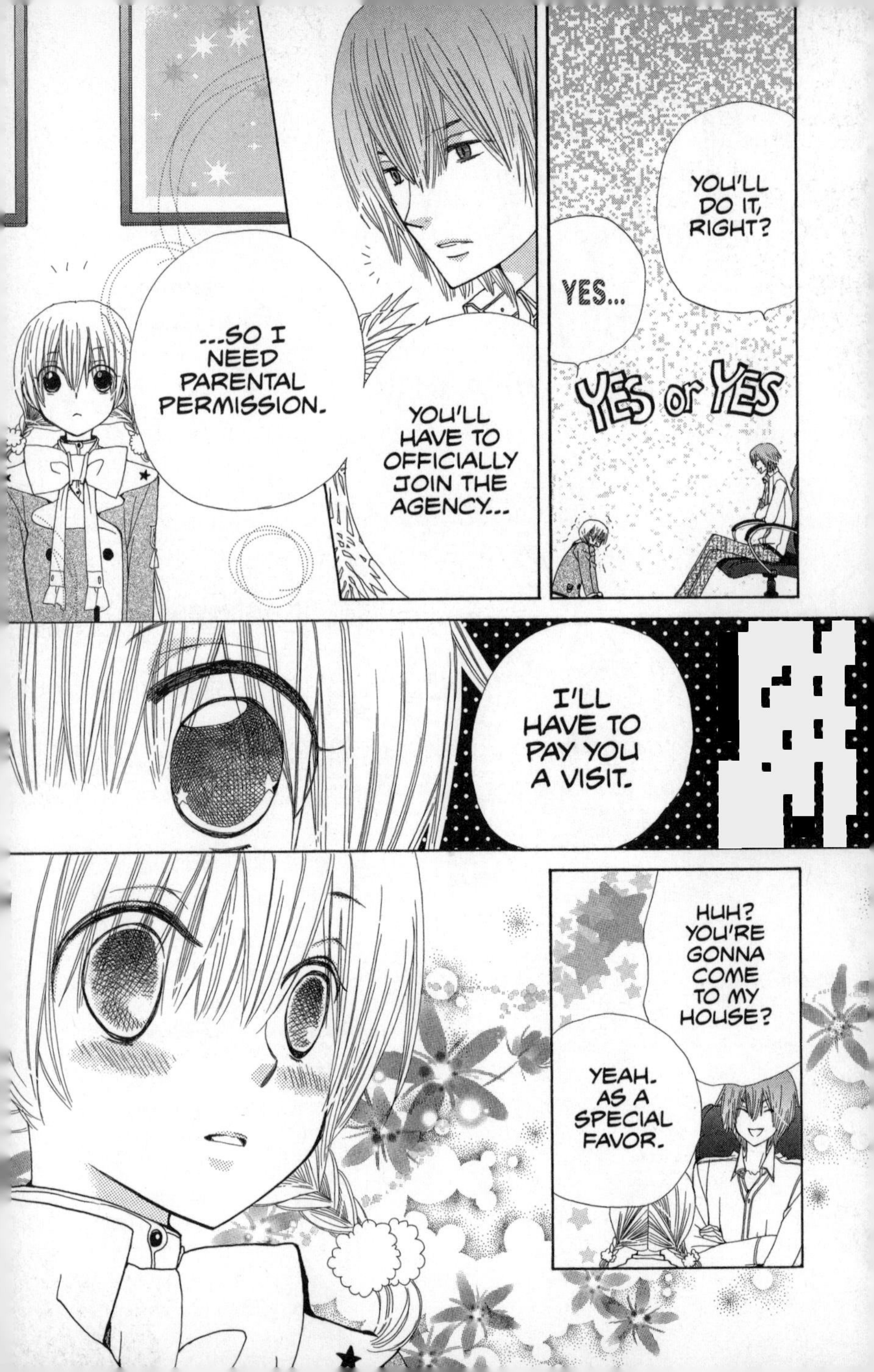
YOU'LL DO IT, RIGHT?
YES...
YES or YES
YOU'LL HAVE TO OFFICIALLY JOIN THE AGENCY...
...SO I NEED PARENTAL PERMISSION.
I'LL HAVE TO PAY YOU A VISIT.
HUH? YOU'RE GONNA COME TO MY HOUSE?
YEAH. AS A SPECIAL FAVOR.

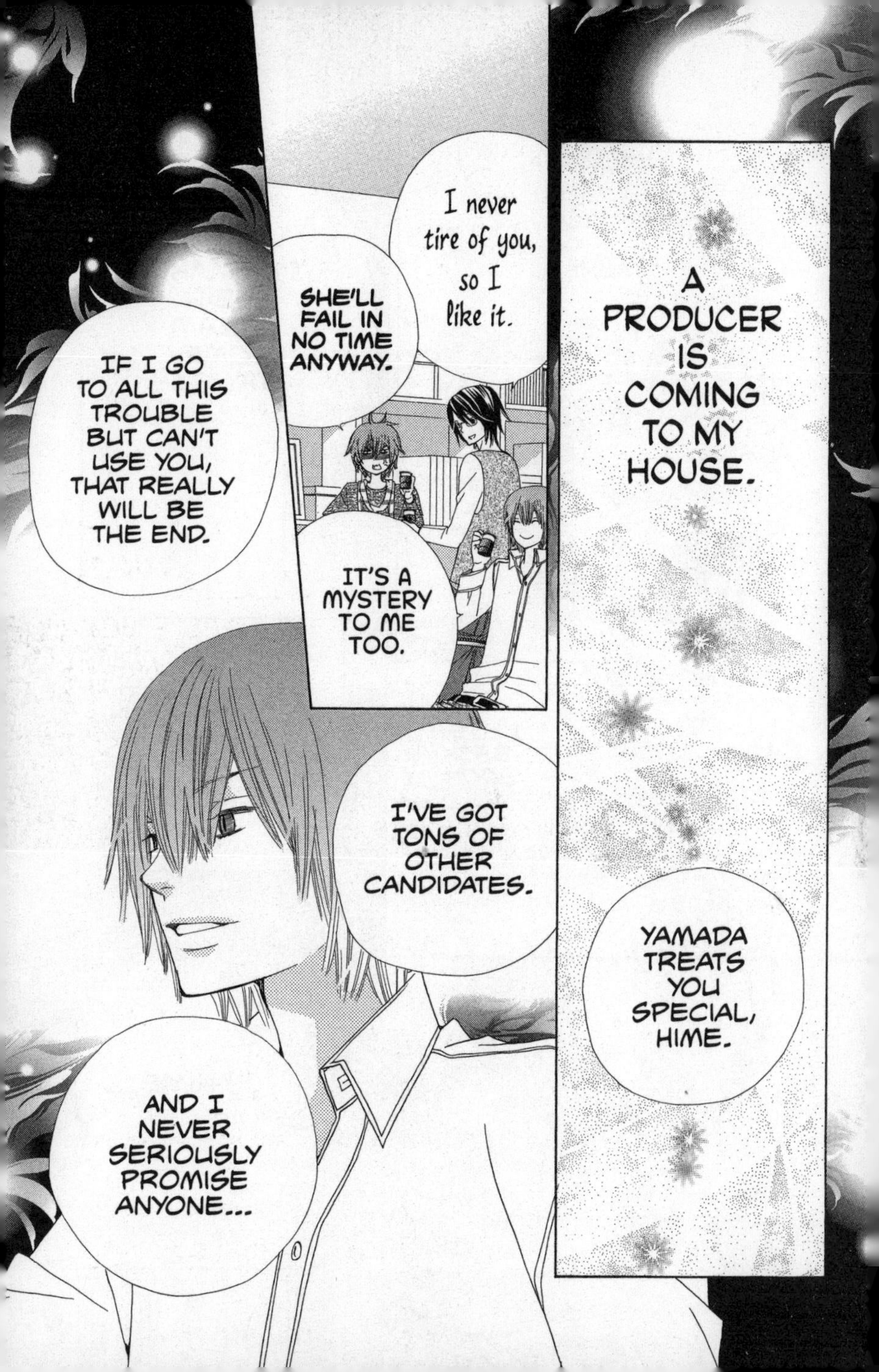
A PRODUCER IS COMING TO MY HOUSE.
YAMADA TREATS YOU SPECIAL, HIME.
I never tire of you, so I like it.
SHE'LL FAIL IN NO TIME ANYWAY.
IT'S A MYSTERY TO ME TOO.
IF I GO TO ALL THIS TROUBLE BUT CAN'T USE YOU, THAT REALLY WILL BE THE END.
I'VE GOT TONS OF OTHER CANDIDATES.
AND I NEVER SERIOUSLY PROMISE ANYONE...

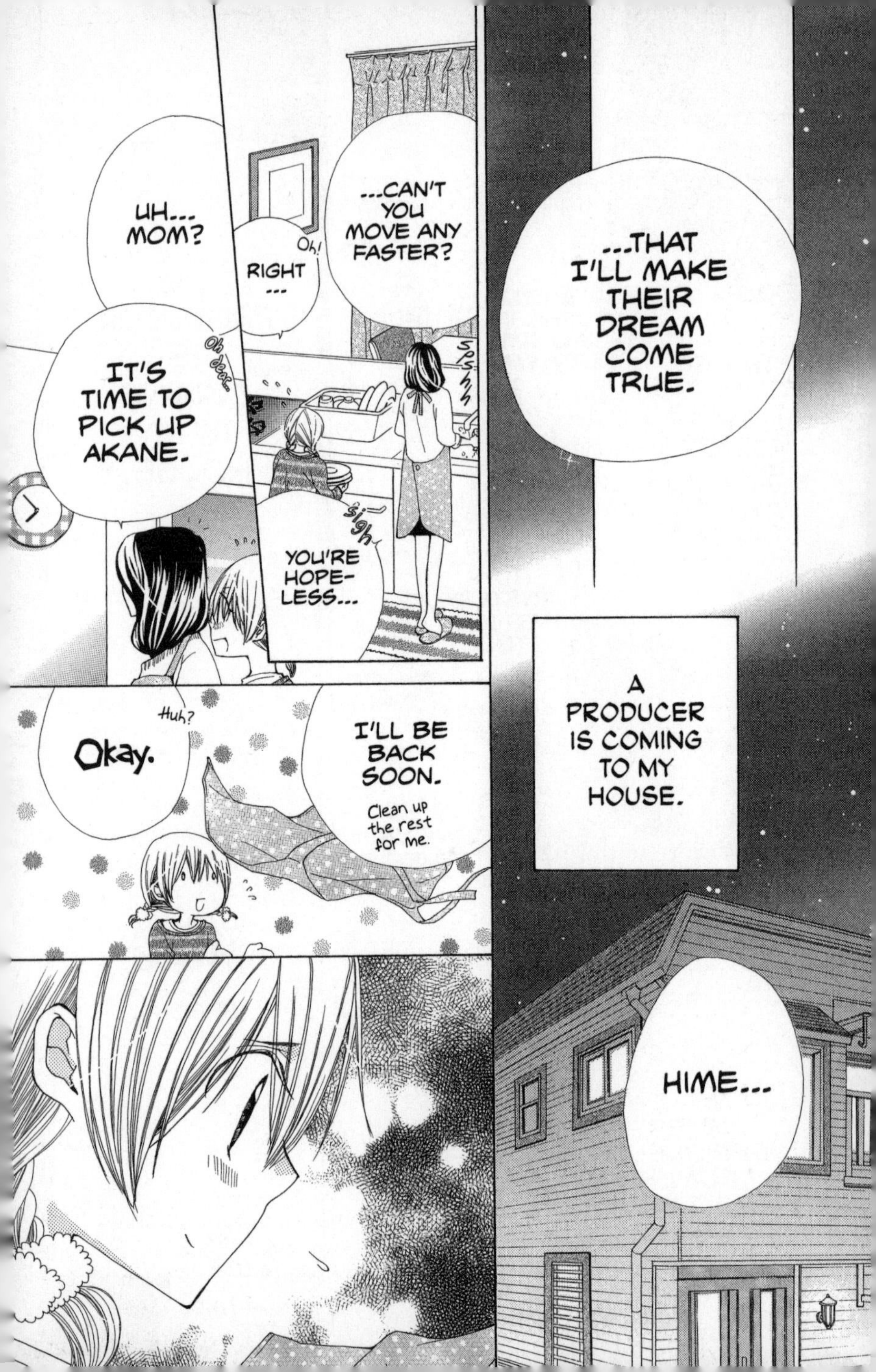
...THAT I'LL MAKE THEIR DREAM COME TRUE.
A PRODUCER IS COMING TO MY HOUSE.
HIME...
...CAN'T YOU MOVE ANY FASTER?
SPSHH
Oh!
RIGHT...
sigh
YOU'RE HOPE-LESS...
UH... MOM?
Oh dear...
IT'S TIME TO PICK UP AKANE.
I'LL BE BACK SOON.
Clean up the rest for me.
Huh?
Okay.

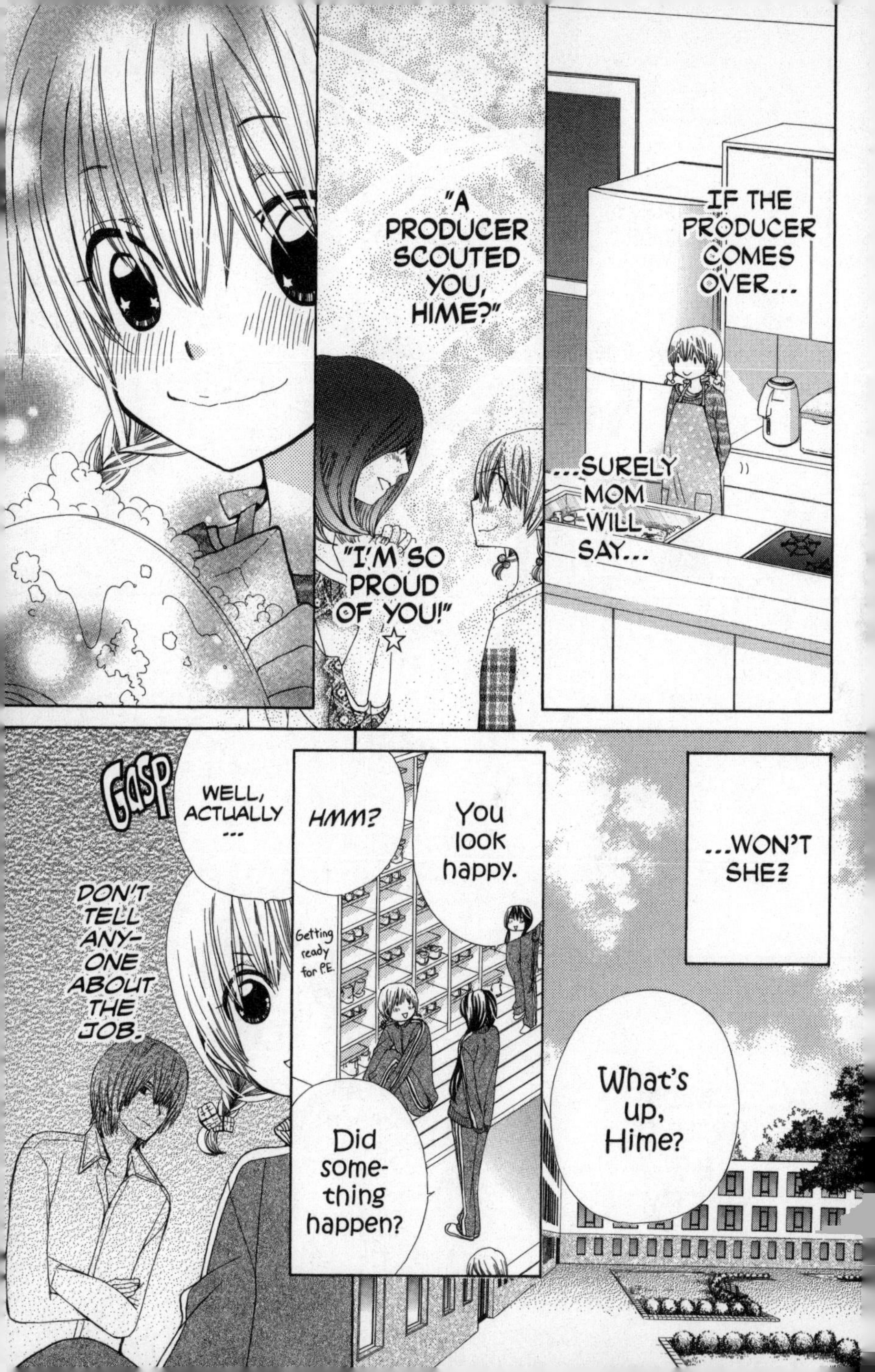
IF THE PRODUCER COMES OVER...
...SURELY MOM WILL SAY...
"A PRODUCER SCOUTED YOU, HIME?"
"I'M SO PROUD OF YOU!" ☆
...WON'T SHE?
What's up, Hime?
You look happy.
HMM?
Did something happen?
Getting ready for P.E.
WELL, ACTUALLY...
GASP
DON'T TELL ANYONE ABOUT THE JOB.

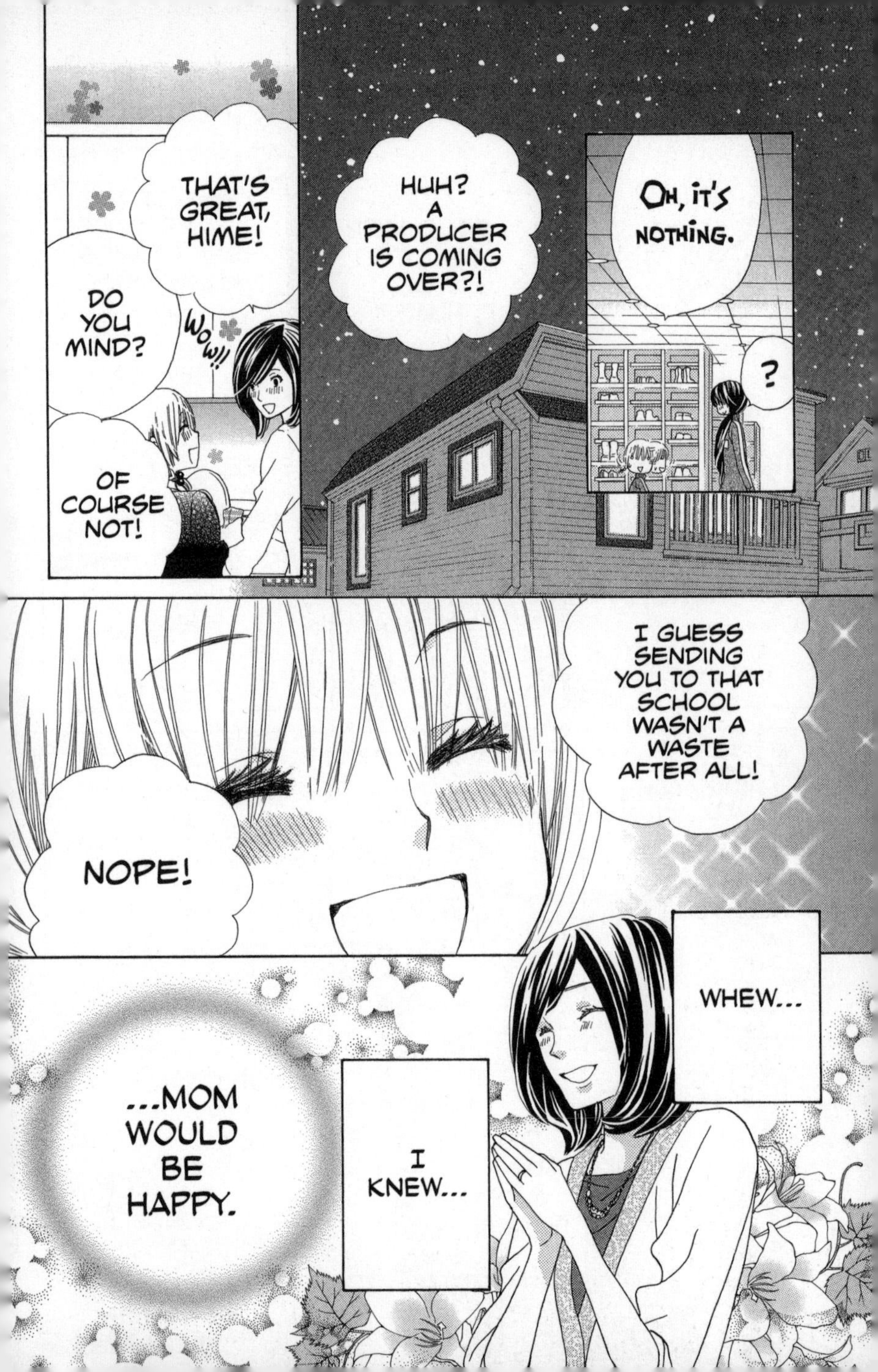

OH, IT'S NOTHING.
?
HUH? A PRODUCER IS COMING OVER?!
THAT'S GREAT, HIME!
WOW!!
DO YOU MIND?
OF COURSE NOT!
I GUESS SENDING YOU TO THAT SCHOOL WASN'T A WASTE AFTER ALL!
NOPE!
WHEW...
I KNEW...
...MOM WOULD BE HAPPY.

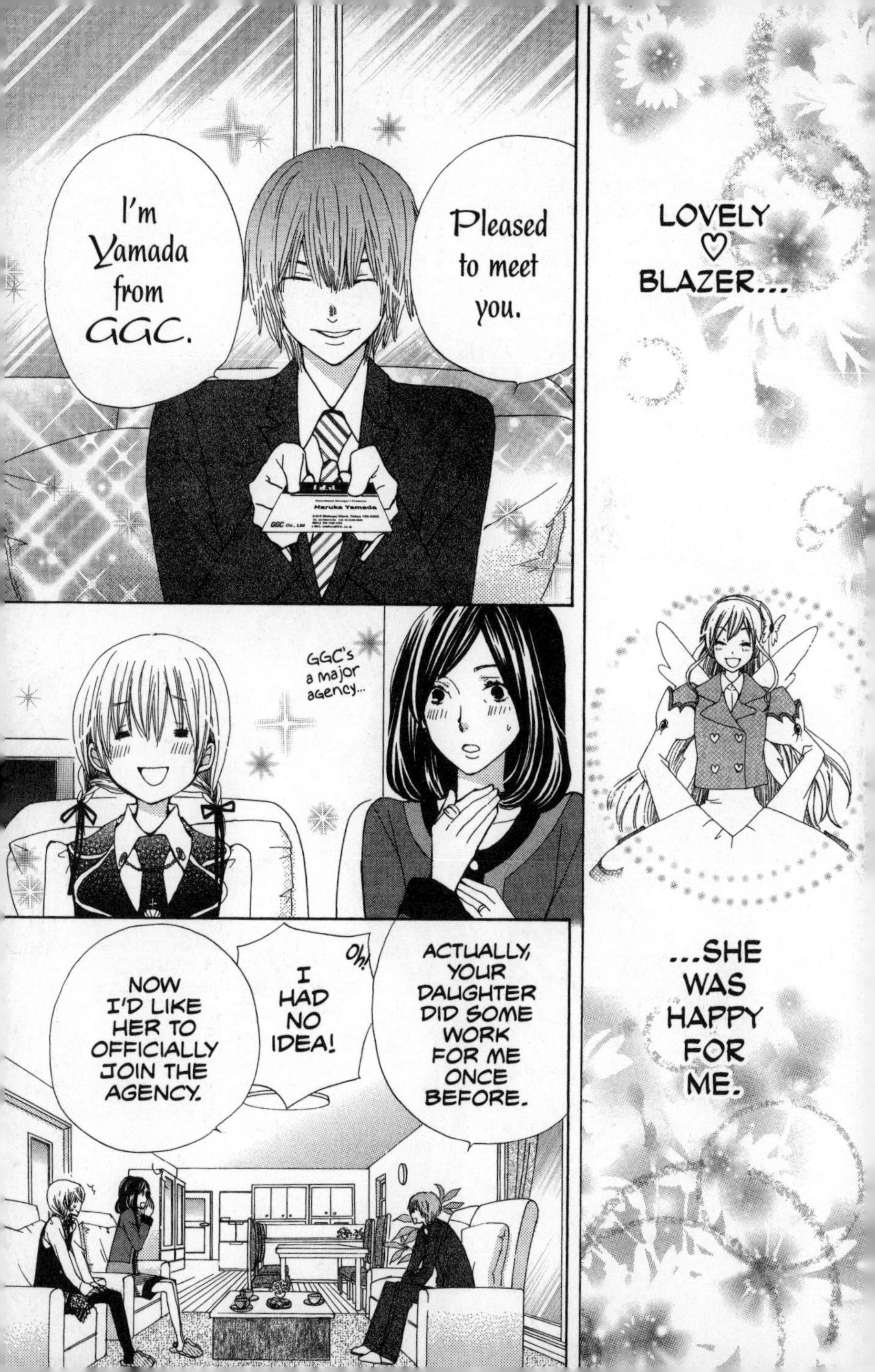
LOVELY ♡ BLAZER...
...SHE WAS HAPPY FOR ME.
Pleased to meet you.
I'm Yamada from GGC.
Haruka Yamada
GGC Co., Ltd
GGC's a major agency...
ACTUALLY, YOUR DAUGHTER DID SOME WORK FOR ME ONCE BEFORE.
Oh!
I HAD NO IDEA!
NOW I'D LIKE HER TO OFFICIALLY JOIN THE AGENCY.

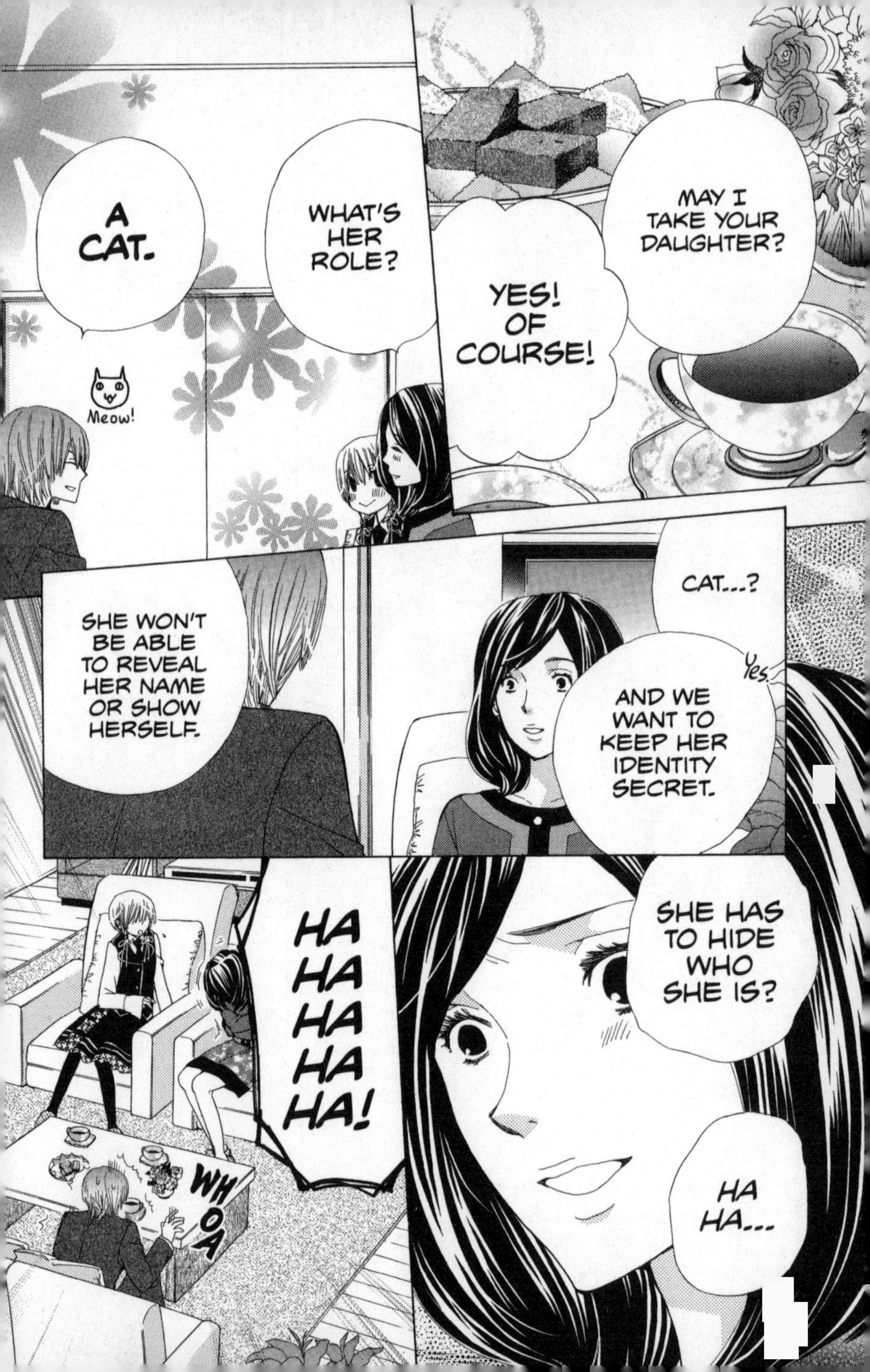
MAY I TAKE YOUR DAUGHTER?
YES! OF COURSE!
WHAT'S HER ROLE?
A CAT.
Meow!
CAT...?
Yes.
AND WE WANT TO KEEP HER IDENTITY SECRET.
SHE WON'T BE ABLE TO REVEAL HER NAME OR SHOW HERSELF.
SHE HAS TO HIDE WHO SHE IS?
HA HA...
HA HA HA HA HA HA!
WHOA

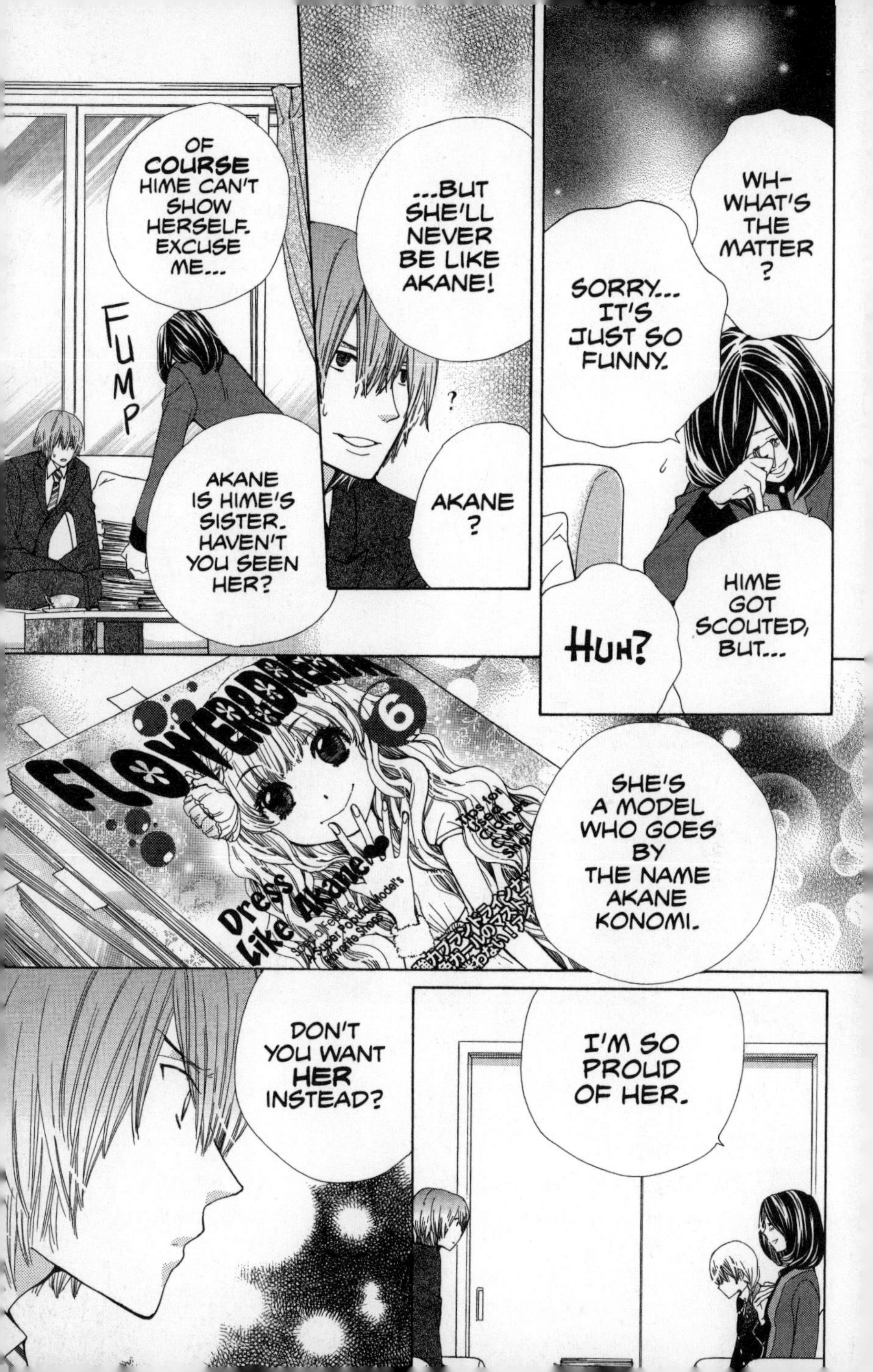
WH- WHAT'S THE MATTER?
SORRY... IT'S JUST SO FUNNY.
HIME GOT SCOUTED, BUT...
HUH?
...BUT SHE'LL NEVER BE LIKE AKANE!
AKANE?
AKANE IS HIME'S SISTER. HAVEN'T YOU SEEN HER?
OF COURSE HIME CAN'T SHOW HERSELF. EXCUSE ME...
FUMP
SHE'S A MODEL WHO GOES BY THE NAME AKANE KONOMI.
6
Dress Like Akane!
I'M SO PROUD OF HER.
DON'T YOU WANT HER INSTEAD?

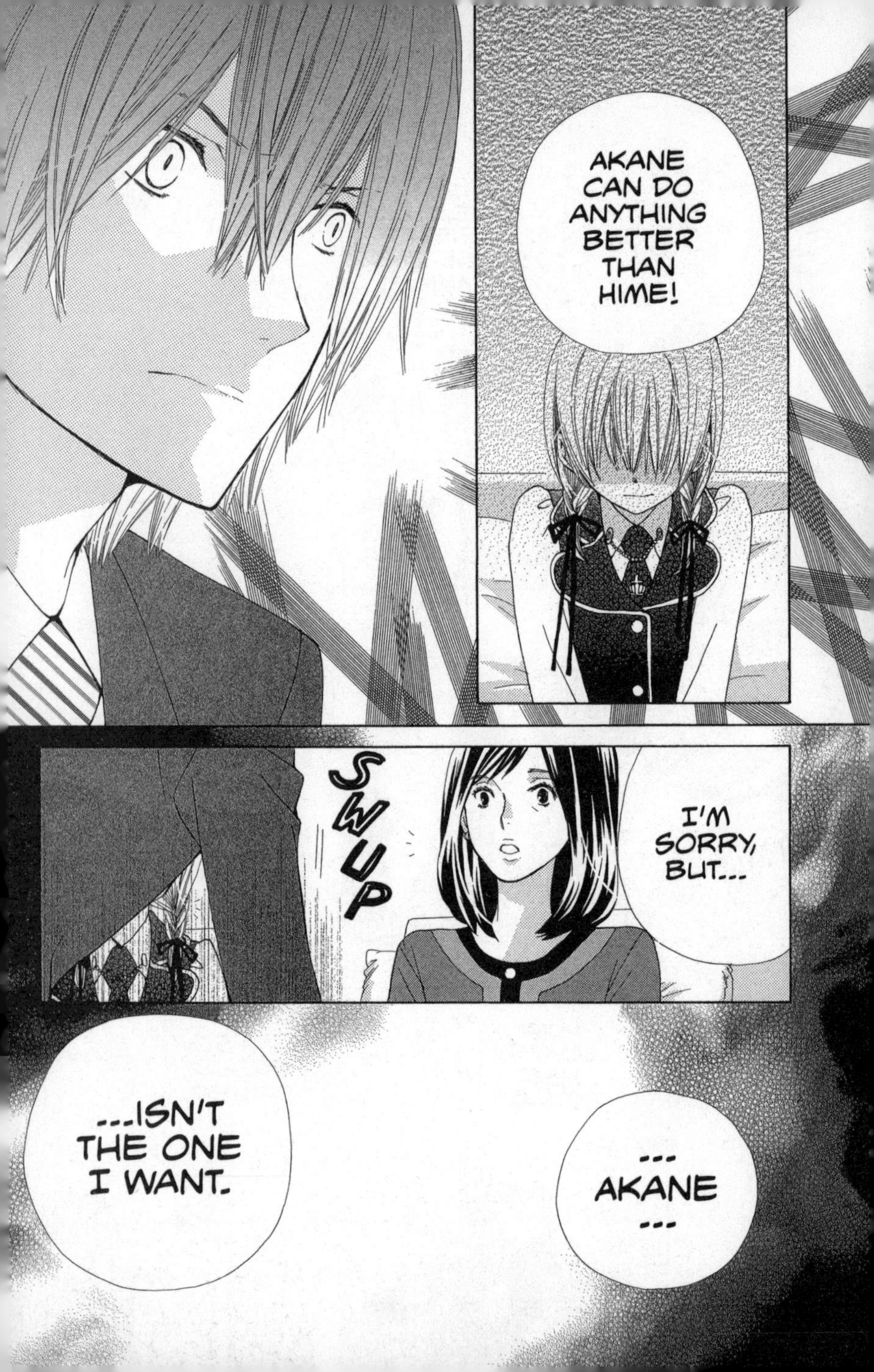
AKANE CAN DO ANYTHING BETTER THAN HIME!
I'M SORRY, BUT...
SWUP
...AKANE...
...ISN'T THE ONE I WANT.

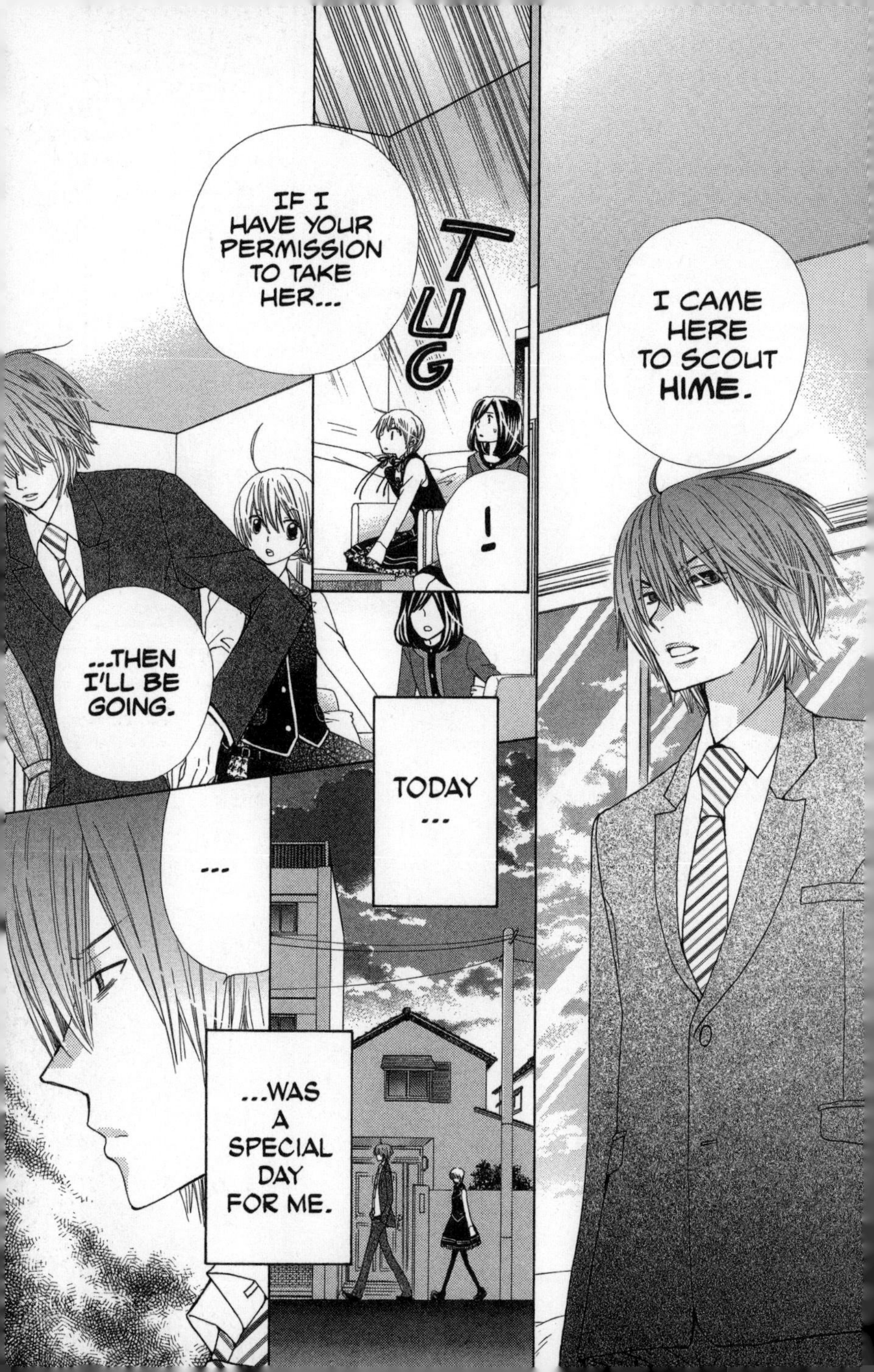
I CAME HERE TO SCOUT HIME.
IF I HAVE YOUR PERMISSION TO TAKE HER...
TUG
!
...THEN I'LL BE GOING.
TODAY...
...WAS A SPECIAL DAY FOR ME.
...

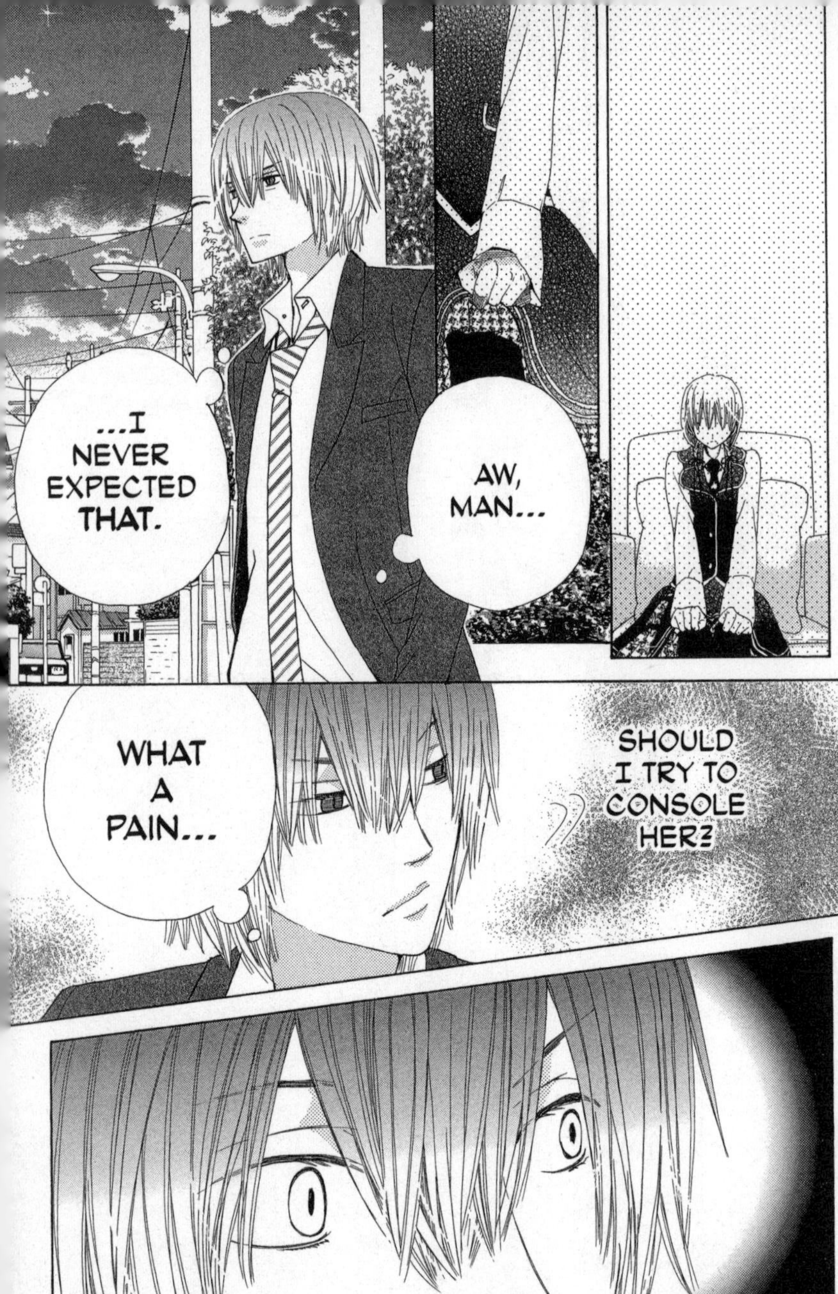
AW, MAN...
...I NEVER EXPECTED THAT.
SHOULD I TRY TO CONSOLE HER?
WHAT A PAIN...

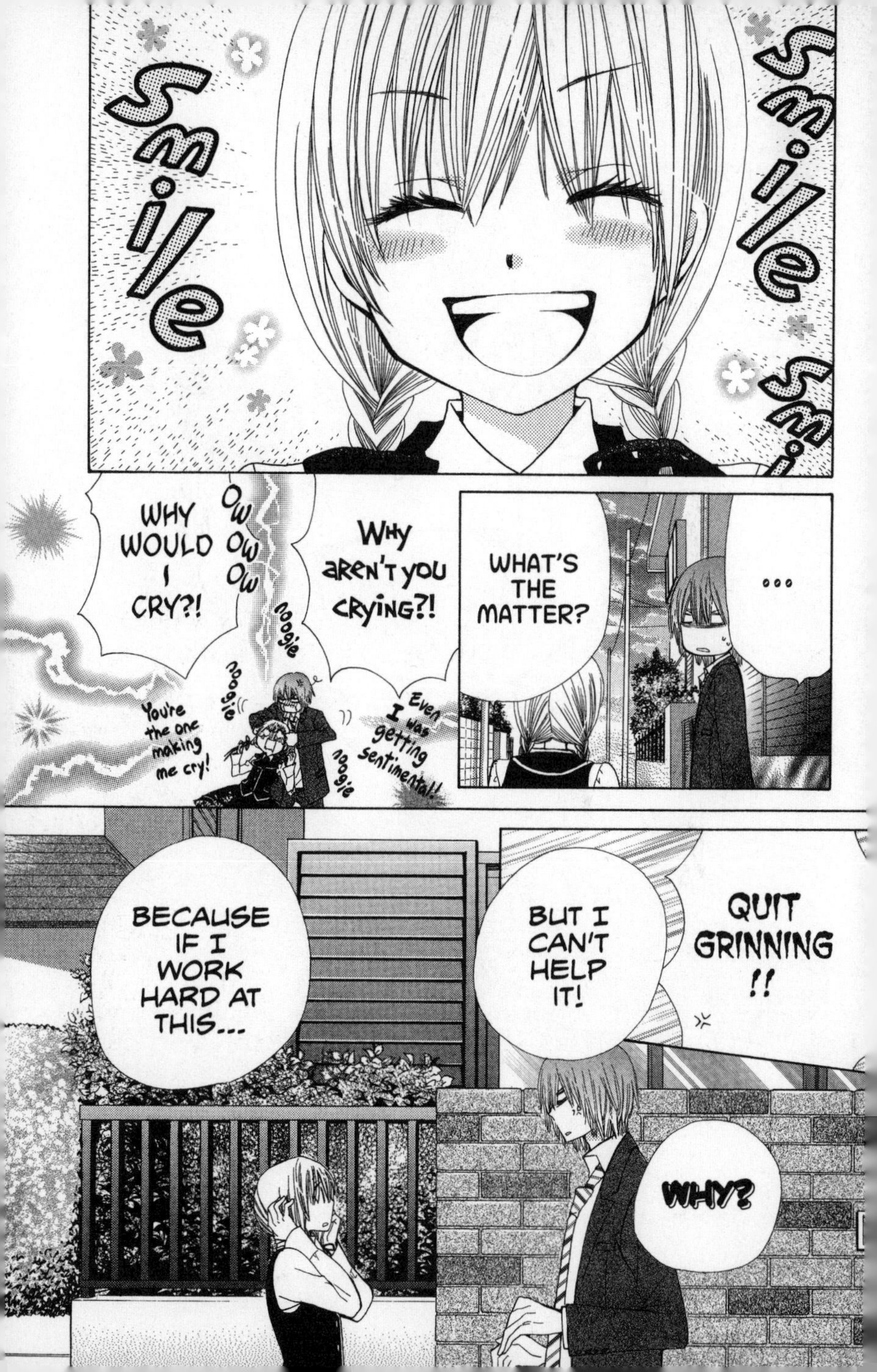
Smile
Smi
Smile
...
WHAT'S THE MATTER?
Why aren't you crying?!
WHY WOULD I CRY?!
OW OW OW
noogie
noogie
Even I was getting sentimental!
noogie
You're the one making me cry!
QUIT GRINNING!!
BUT I CAN'T HELP IT!
WHY?
BECAUSE IF I WORK HARD AT THIS...

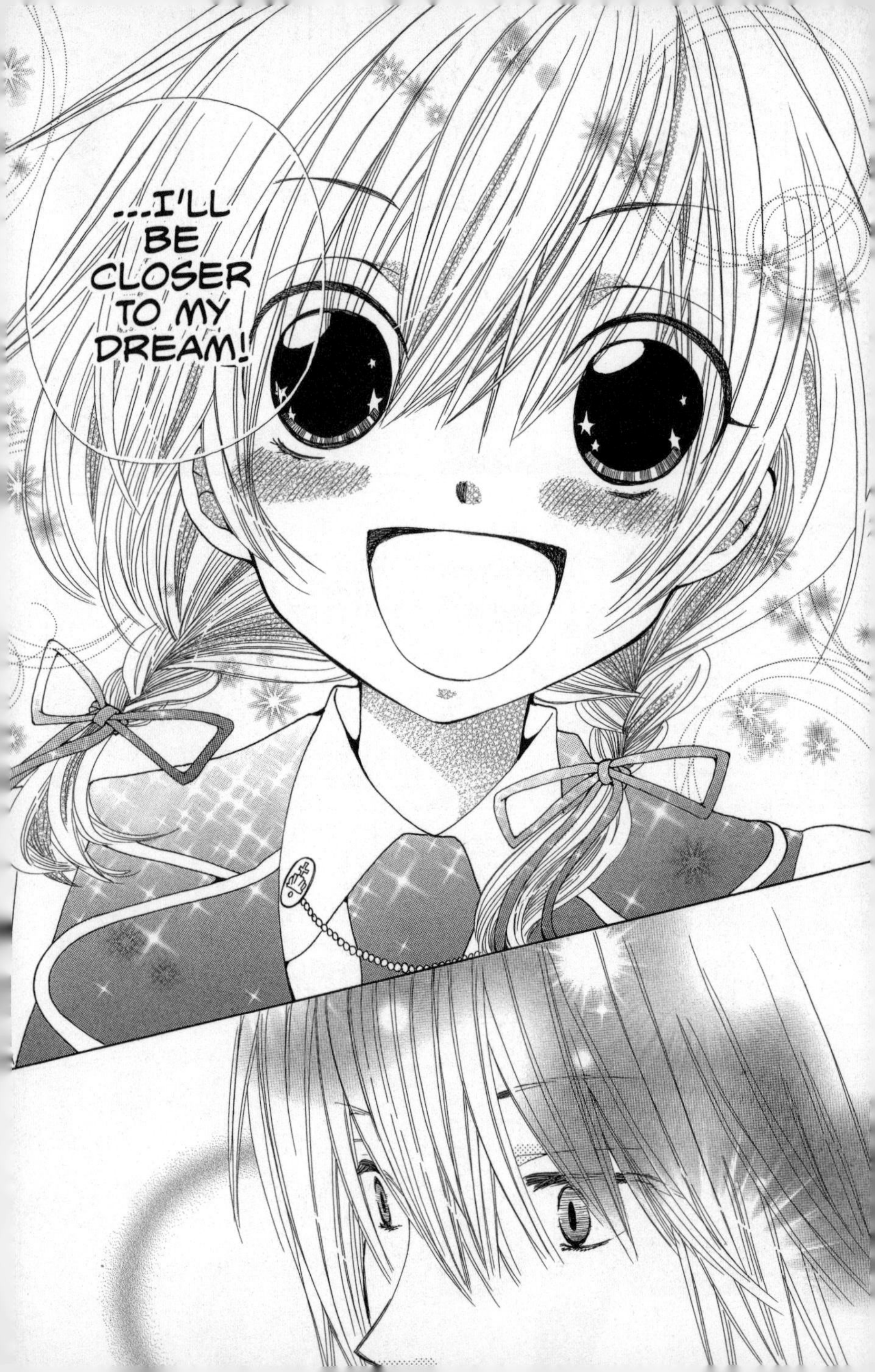
...I'LL BE CLOSER TO MY DREAM!

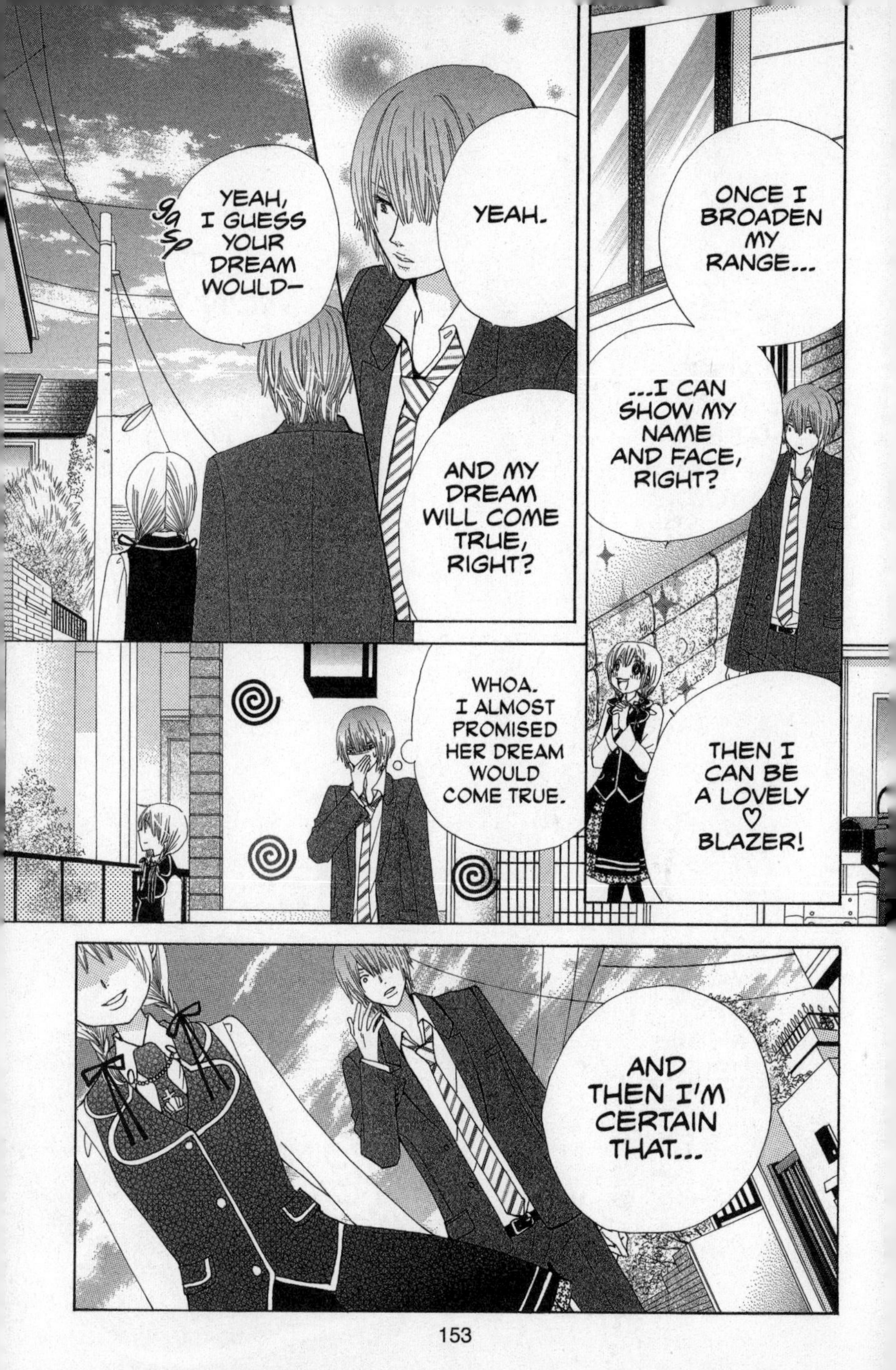
ONCE I BROADEN MY RANGE...
...I CAN SHOW MY NAME AND FACE, RIGHT?
YEAH.
AND MY DREAM WILL COME TRUE, RIGHT?
YEAH, I GUESS YOUR DREAM WOULD—
gasp
THEN I CAN BE A LOVELY ♡ BLAZER!
WHOA. I ALMOST PROMISED HER DREAM WOULD COME TRUE.
AND THEN I'M CERTAIN THAT...

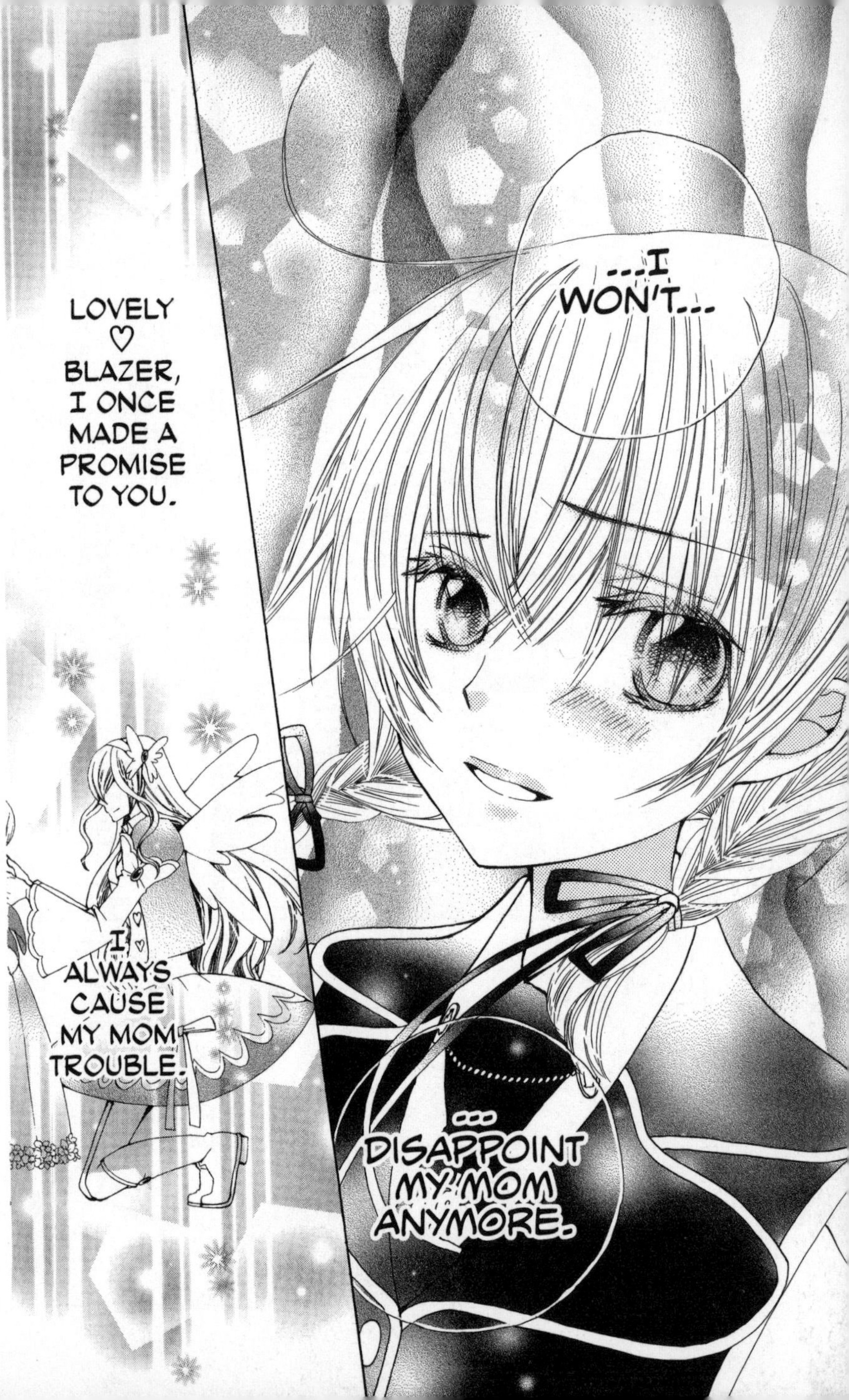
...I WON'T...
...DISAPPOINT MY MOM ANYMORE.
LOVELY ♡ BLAZER, I ONCE MADE A PROMISE TO YOU.
I ALWAYS CAUSE MY MOM TROUBLE.

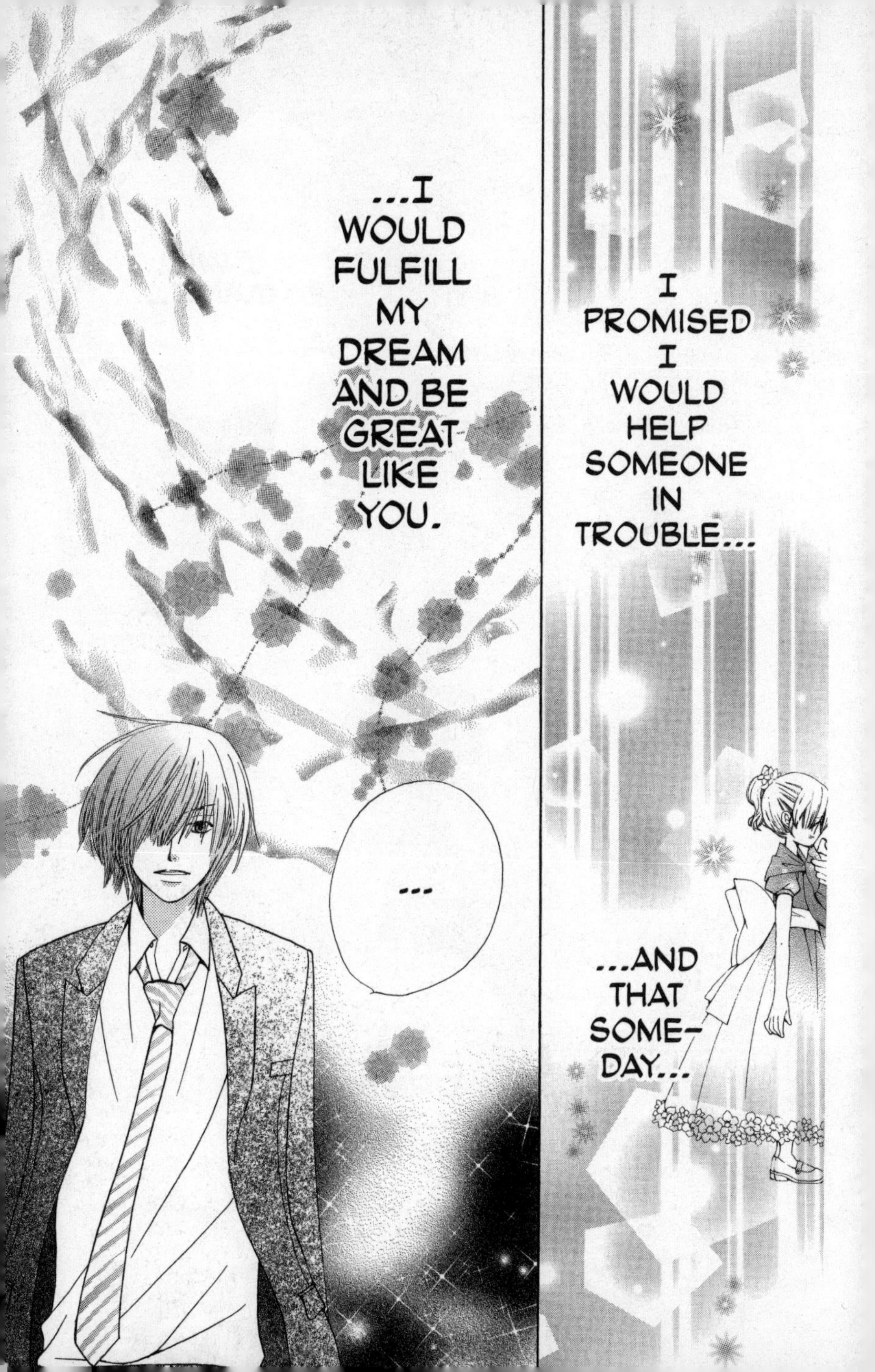
I PROMISED I WOULD HELP SOMEONE IN TROUBLE...
...AND THAT SOME-DAY...
...I WOULD FULFILL MY DREAM AND BE GREAT LIKE YOU.
...

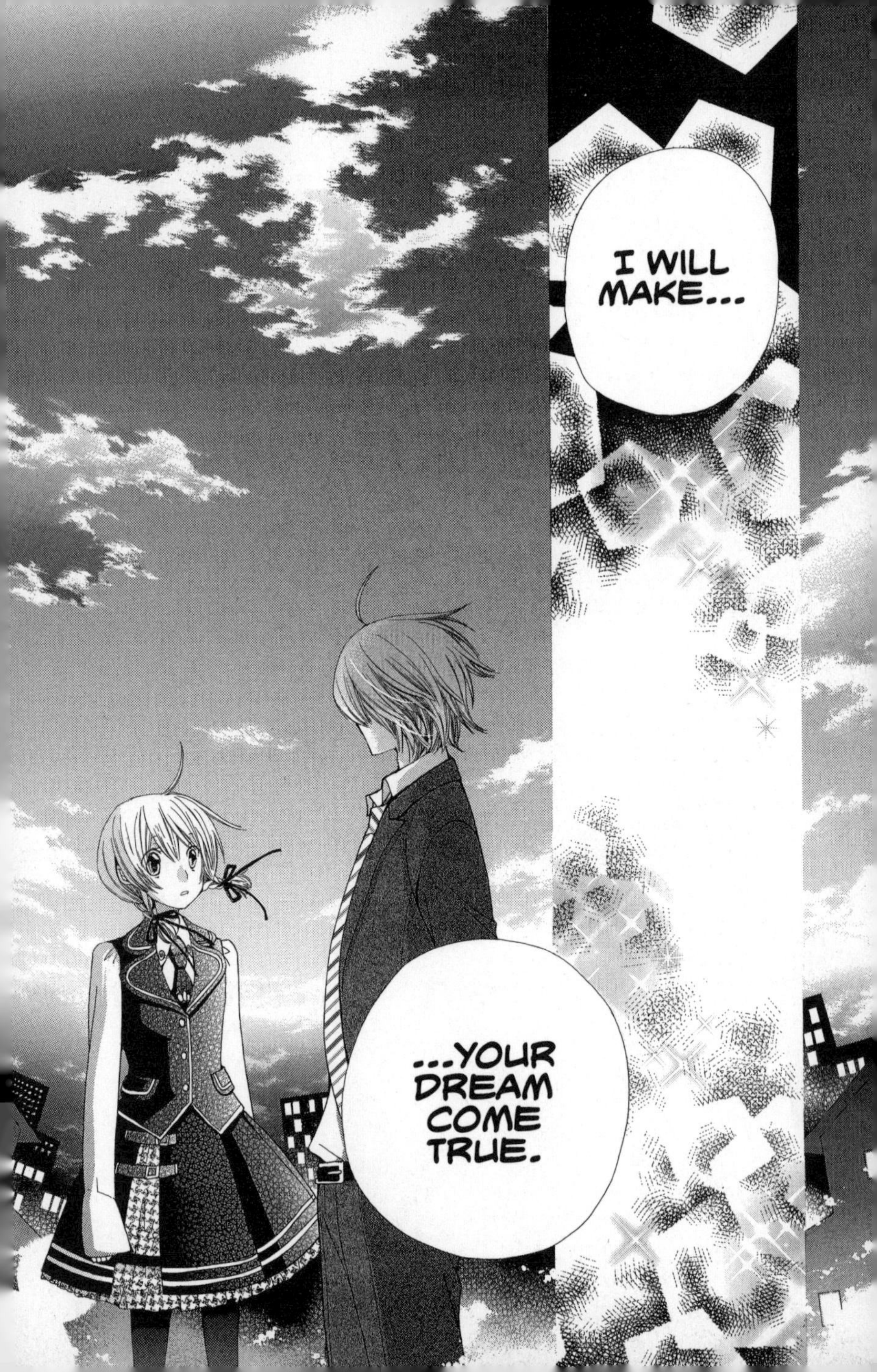
I WILL MAKE...
...YOUR DREAM COME TRUE.

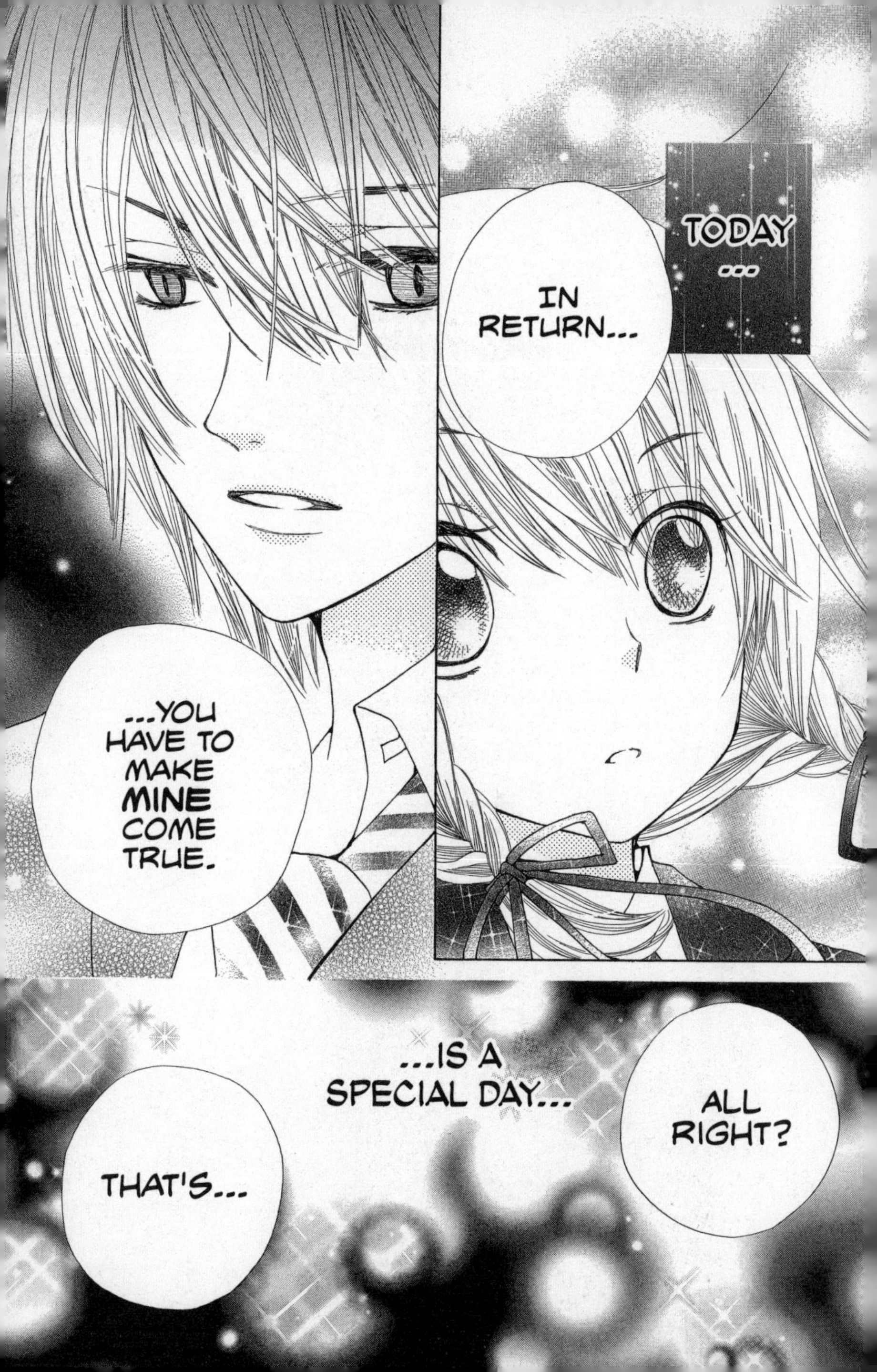
TODAY ...
IN RETURN...
...YOU HAVE TO MAKE MINE COME TRUE.
ALL RIGHT?
...IS A SPECIAL DAY...
THAT'S...

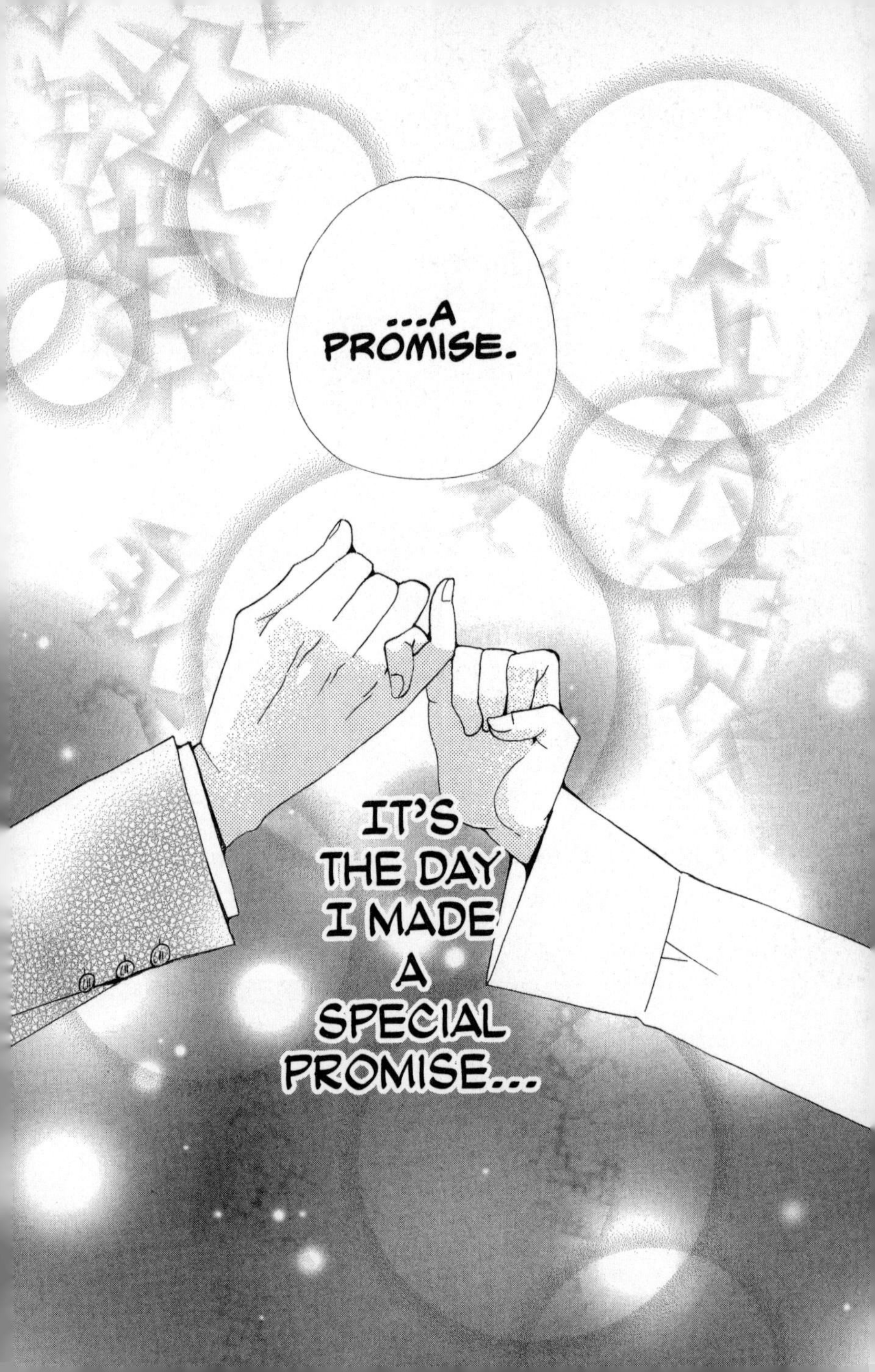
...A PROMISE.
IT'S THE DAY I MADE A SPECIAL PROMISE...

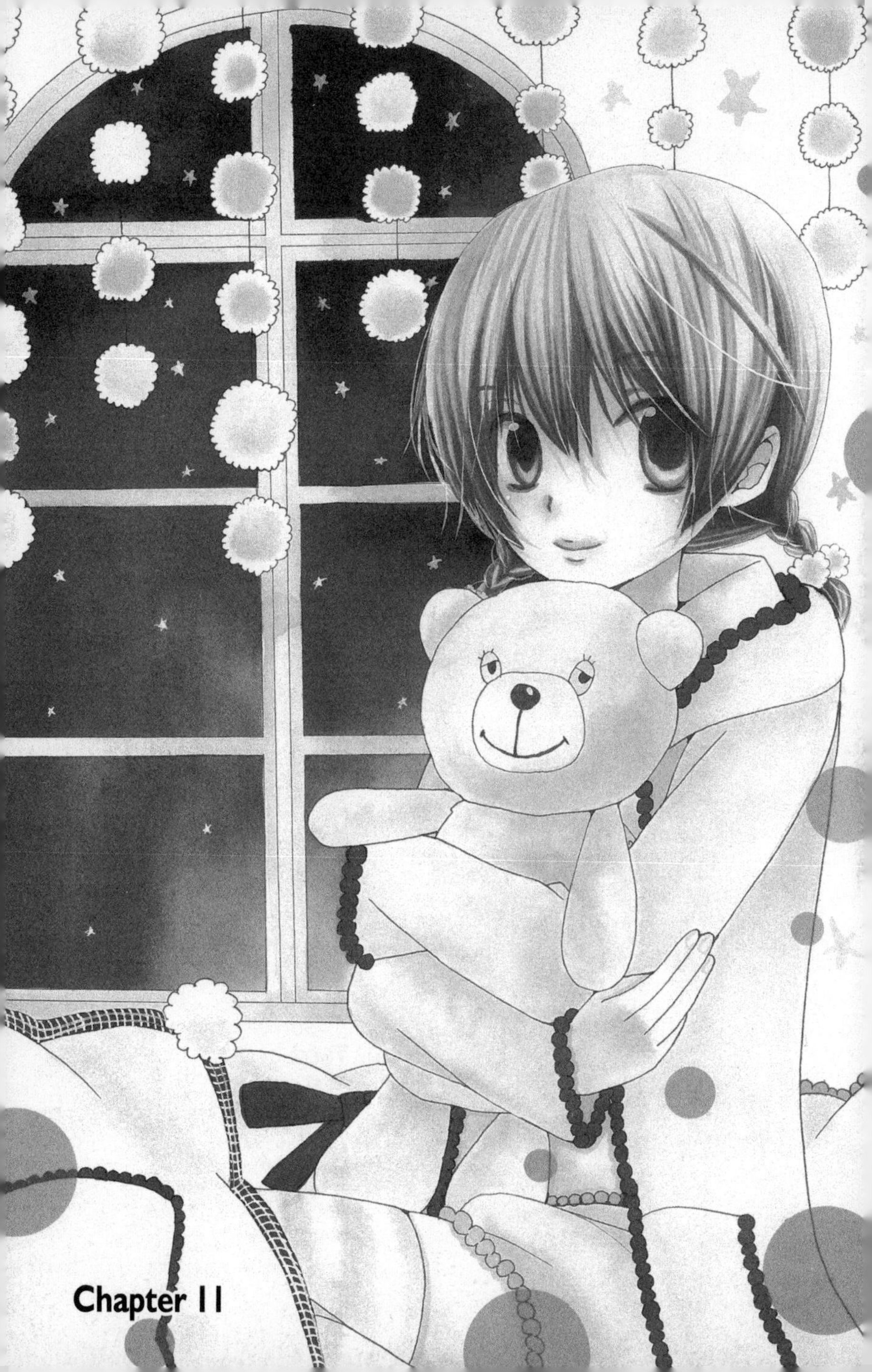

Chapter 11

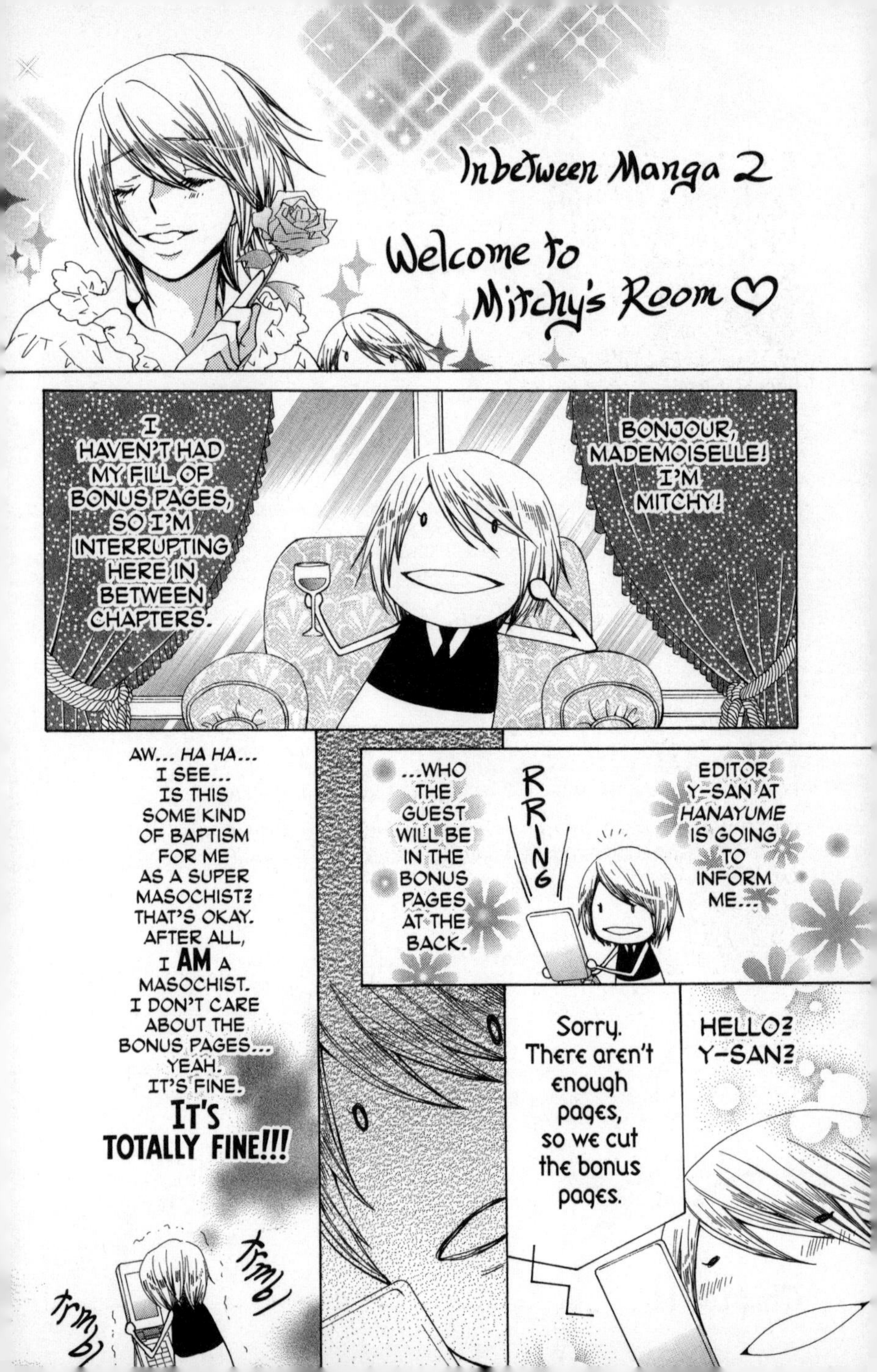
Inbetween Manga 2
Welcome to Mitchy's Room ♡
BONJOUR, MADEMOISELLE! I'M MITCHY!
I HAVEN'T HAD MY FILL OF BONUS PAGES, SO I'M INTERRUPTING HERE IN BETWEEN CHAPTERS.
EDITOR Y-SAN AT HANAYUME IS GOING TO INFORM ME...
RRING
...WHO THE GUEST WILL BE IN THE BONUS PAGES AT THE BACK.
HELLO? Y-SAN?
Sorry. There aren't enough pages, so we cut the bonus pages.
AW... HA HA... I SEE... IS THIS SOME KIND OF BAPTISM FOR ME AS A SUPER MASOCHIST? THAT'S OKAY. AFTER ALL, I AM A MASOCHIST. I DON'T CARE ABOUT THE BONUS PAGES... YEAH. IT'S FINE. IT'S TOTALLY FINE!!!
trmbl
trmbl

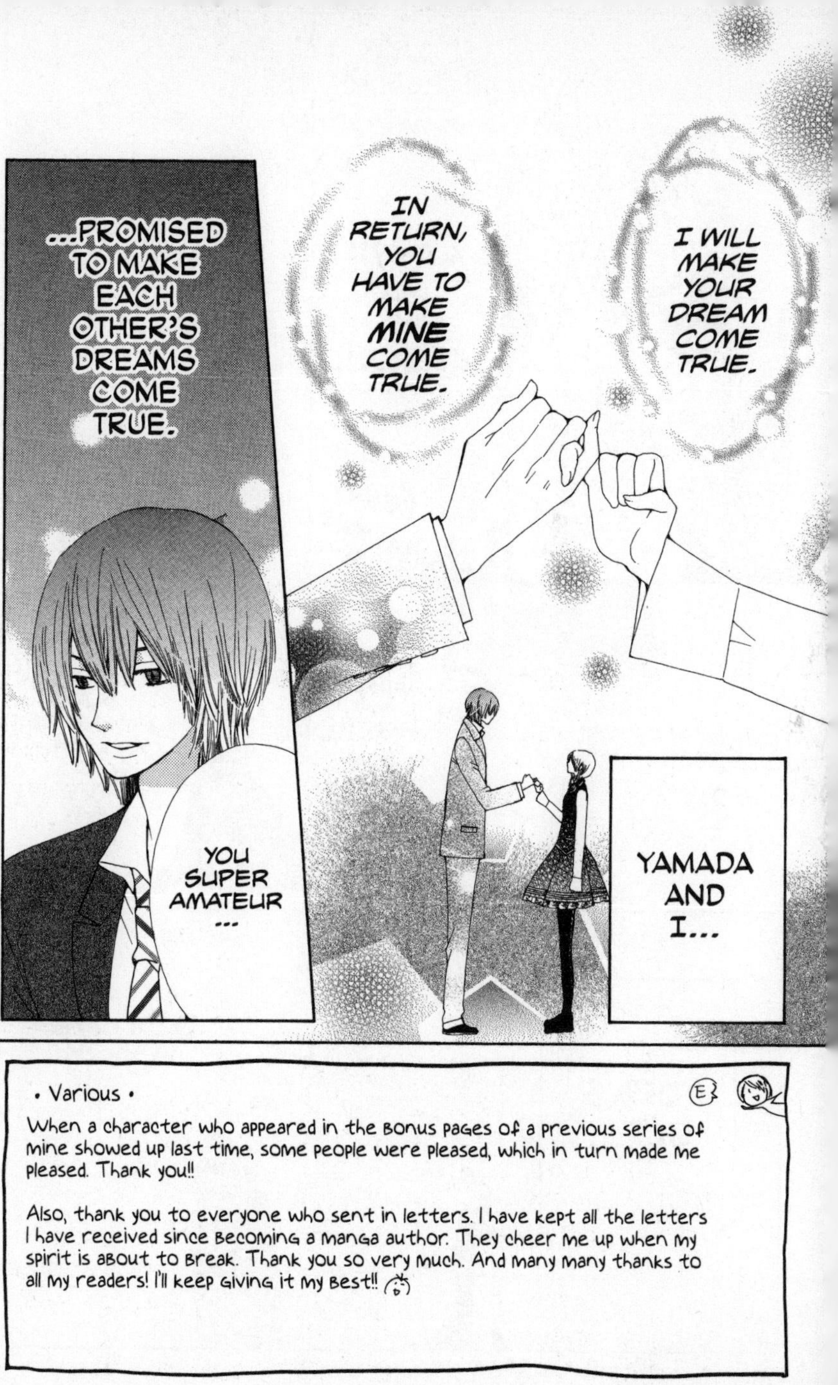
I WILL MAKE YOUR DREAM COME TRUE.
IN RETURN, YOU HAVE TO MAKE MINE COME TRUE.
YAMADA AND I...
...PROMISED TO MAKE EACH OTHER'S DREAMS COME TRUE.
YOU SUPER AMATEUR...

• Various •

When a character who appeared in the bonus pages of a previous series of mine showed up last time, some people were pleased, which in turn made me pleased. Thank you!!

Also, thank you to everyone who sent in letters. I have kept all the letters I have received since becoming a manga author. They cheer me up when my spirit is about to break. Thank you so very much. And many many thanks to all my readers! I'll keep giving it my best!!

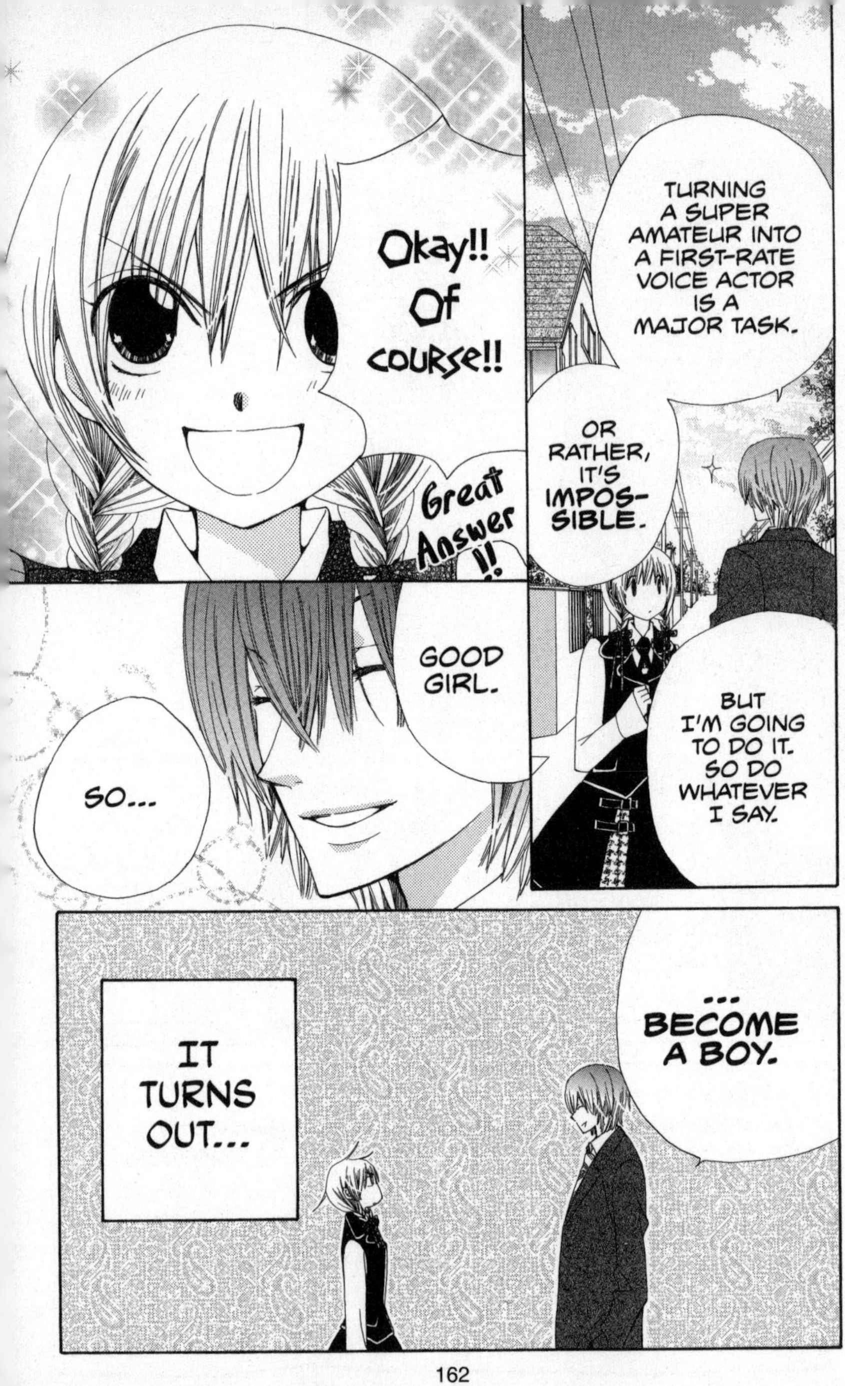
TURNING A SUPER AMATEUR INTO A FIRST-RATE VOICE ACTOR IS A MAJOR TASK.
OR RATHER, IT'S IMPOSSIBLE.
BUT I'M GOING TO DO IT. SO DO WHATEVER I SAY.
Okay!! Of course!!
Great Answer!!
GOOD GIRL.
SO...
...BECOME A BOY.
IT TURNS OUT...

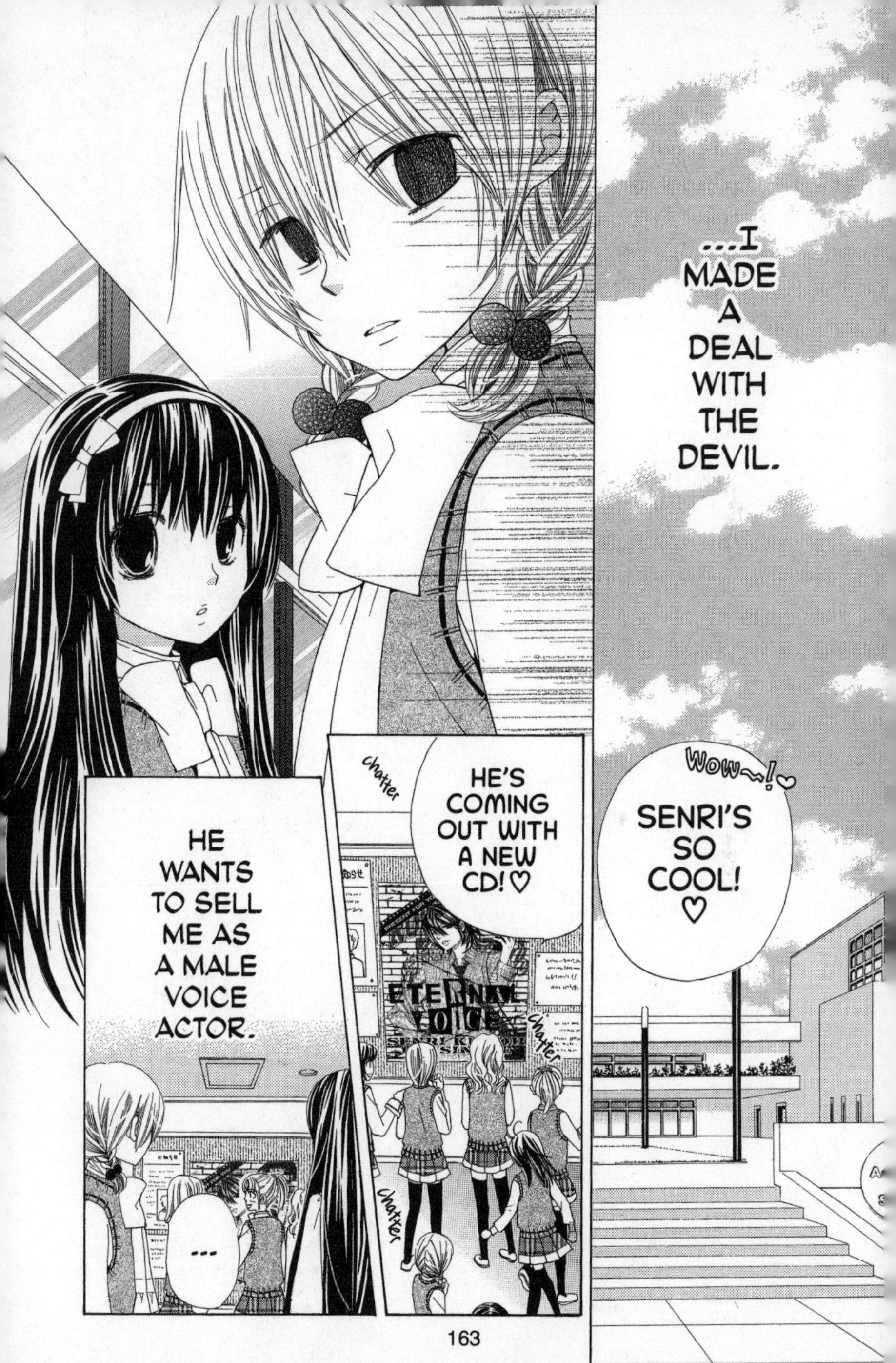
...I MADE A DEAL WITH THE DEVIL.
Wow~!♡
SENRI'S SO COOL! ♡
chatter
HE'S COMING OUT WITH A NEW CD! ♡
chatter
chatter
HE WANTS TO SELL ME AS A MALE VOICE ACTOR.
...

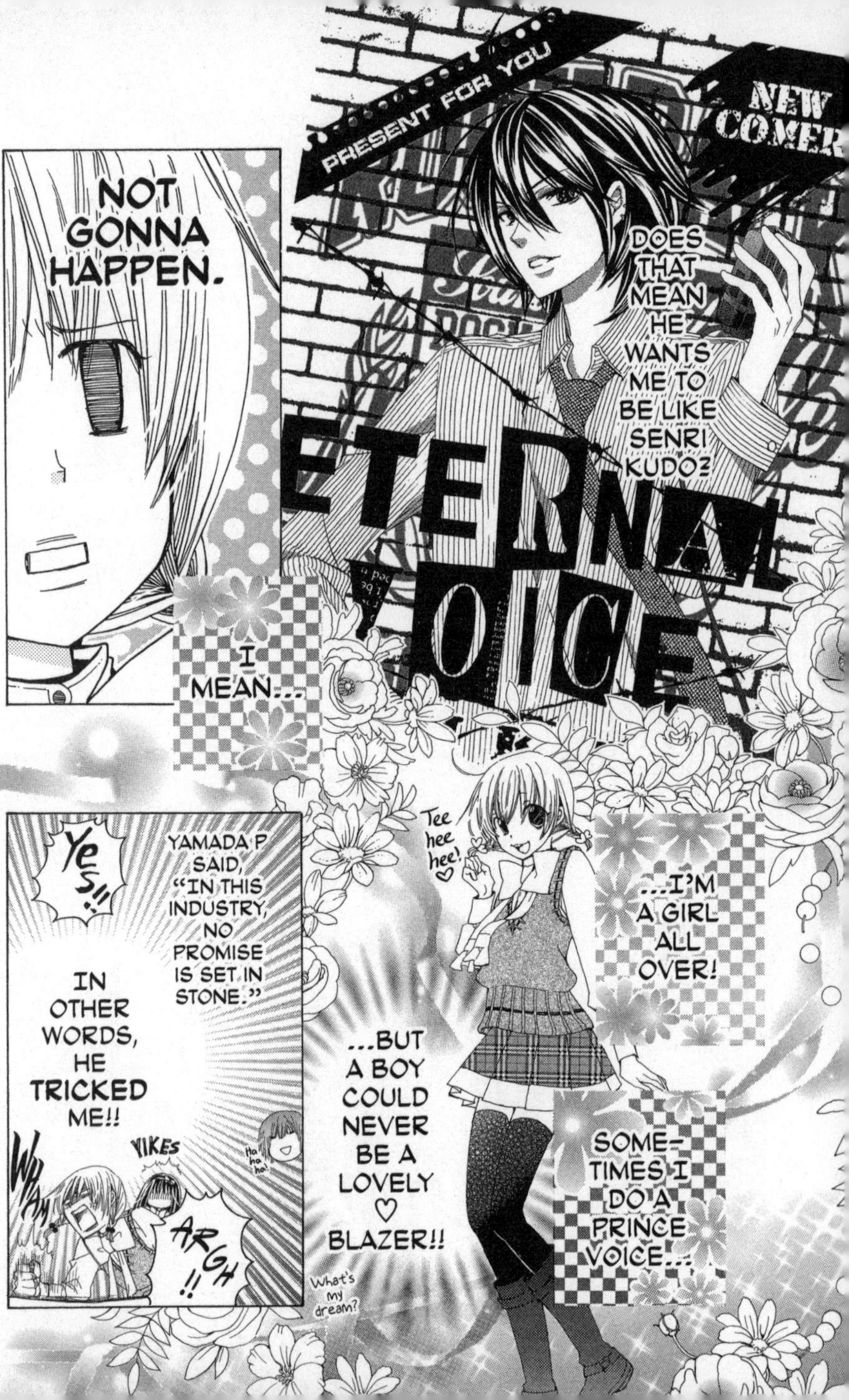
NEW COMER
PRESENT FOR YOU
DOES THAT MEAN HE WANTS ME TO BE LIKE SENRI KUDO?
NOT GONNA HAPPEN.
ETERNAL VOICE
I MEAN...
...I'M A GIRL ALL OVER!
Tee hee hee! ♡
SOME-TIMES I DO A PRINCE VOICE...
...BUT A BOY COULD NEVER BE A LOVELY ♡ BLAZER!!
What's my dream?
Yes!!
YAMADA P SAID, "IN THIS INDUSTRY, NO PROMISE IS SET IN STONE."
IN OTHER WORDS, HE TRICKED ME!!
Ha ha ha!
YIKES
WHAM
ARGH!!

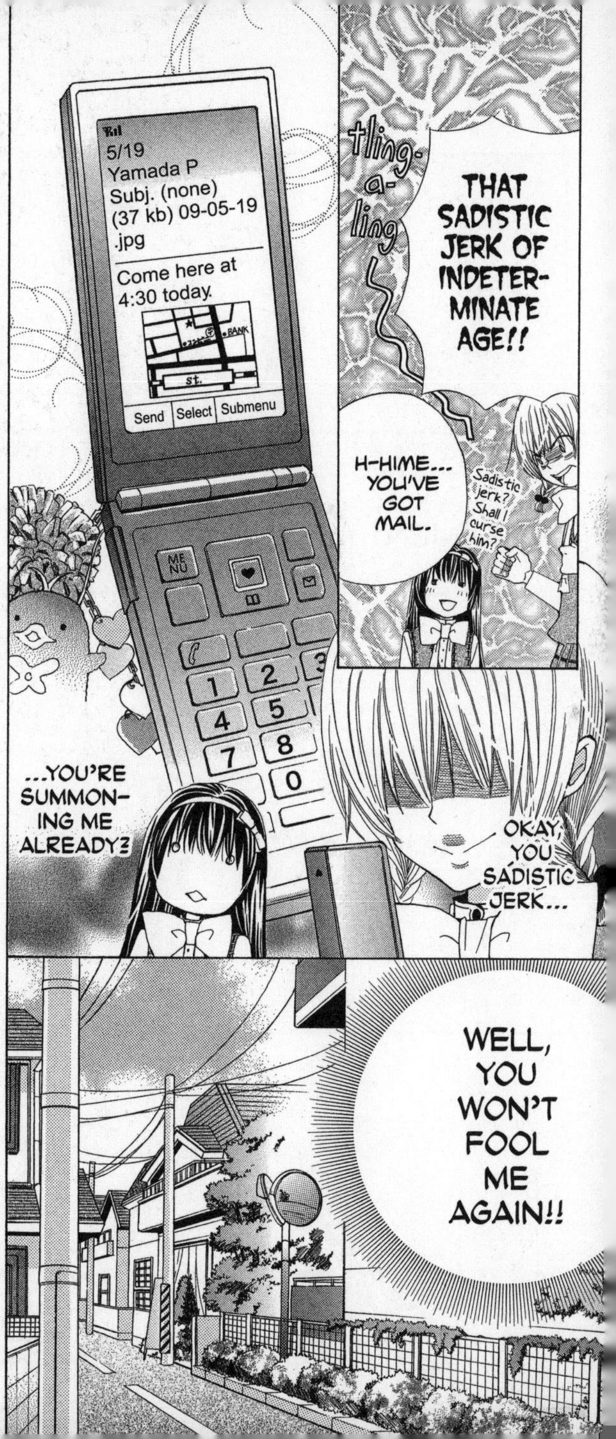
tling-a-ling
THAT SADISTIC JERK OF INDETERMINATE AGE!!
H-HIME... YOU'VE GOT MAIL.
Sadistic jerk? Shall I curse him?
OKAY, YOU SADISTIC JERK...
5/19
Yamada P
Subj. (none)
(37 kb) 09-05-19 .jpg
Come here at 4:30 today.
BANK
st.
Send
Select
Submenu
MENU
...YOU'RE SUMMONING ME ALREADY?
WELL, YOU WON'T FOOL ME AGAIN!!

6

• Various •

Thank you for reading all this way! The request and sidebar illustrations this time were Kitten Hime & Senri, a monster (?) series, Senri playing with cats, and Hime with a different hairstyle! Thank you!! If you've got any more requests, I'm counting on you! ♡

Thanks! ♡

And thanks to all the readers, my editor, my assistants, everyone who helped with composition and research, my family, and my friends!! Thank you so very, very much!!

Here's hoping we all meet again in Volume 3!!

♡ Let me hear your thoughts! ♡

Maki Minami
c/o Shojo Beat
P.O. Box 77010
San Francisco, CA
94107

南マキ
Maki Minami

From the bottom...
...of my heart!

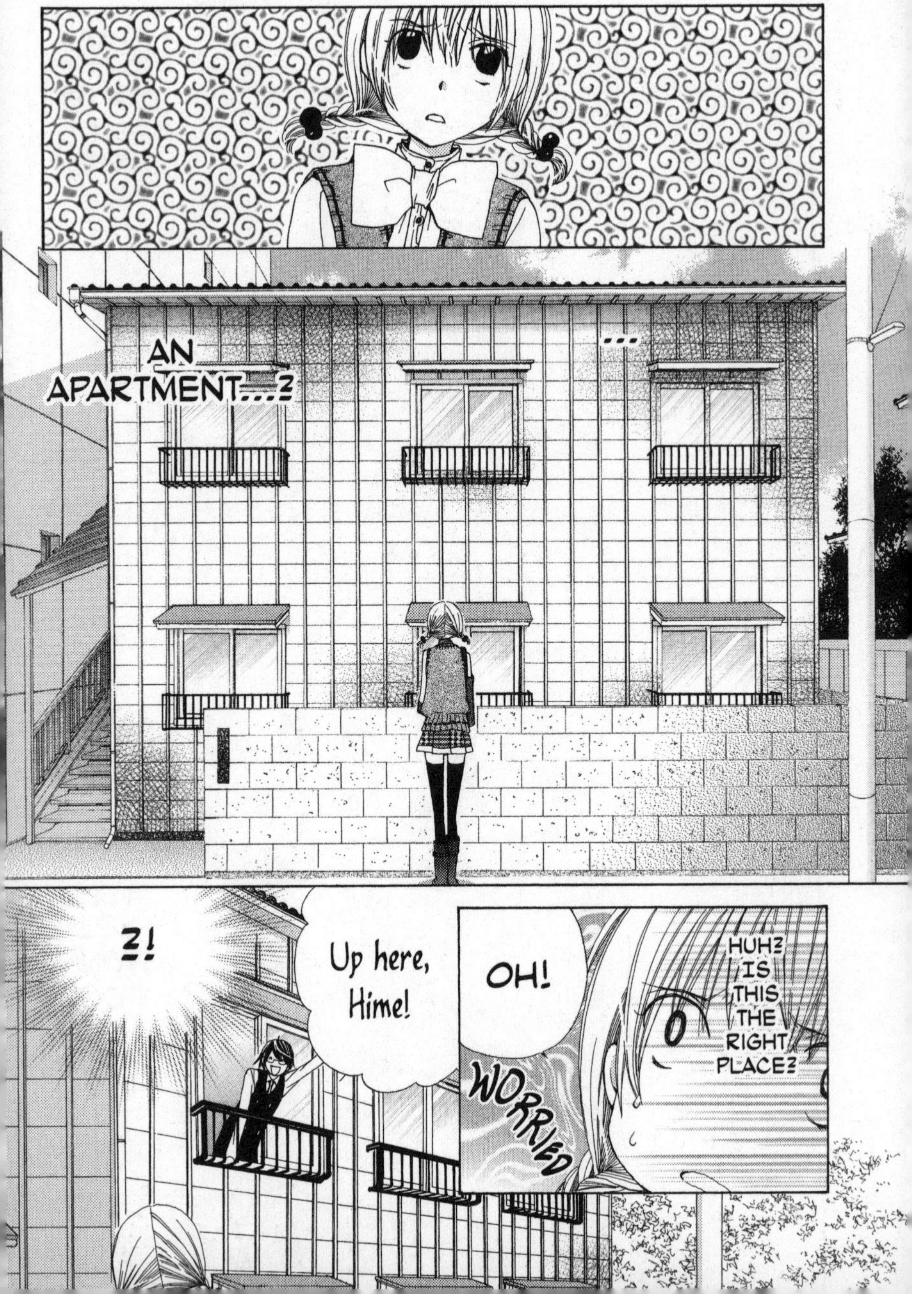
...
AN APARTMENT...?
HUH? IS THIS THE RIGHT PLACE?
OH!
WORRIED
Up here, Hime!
?!

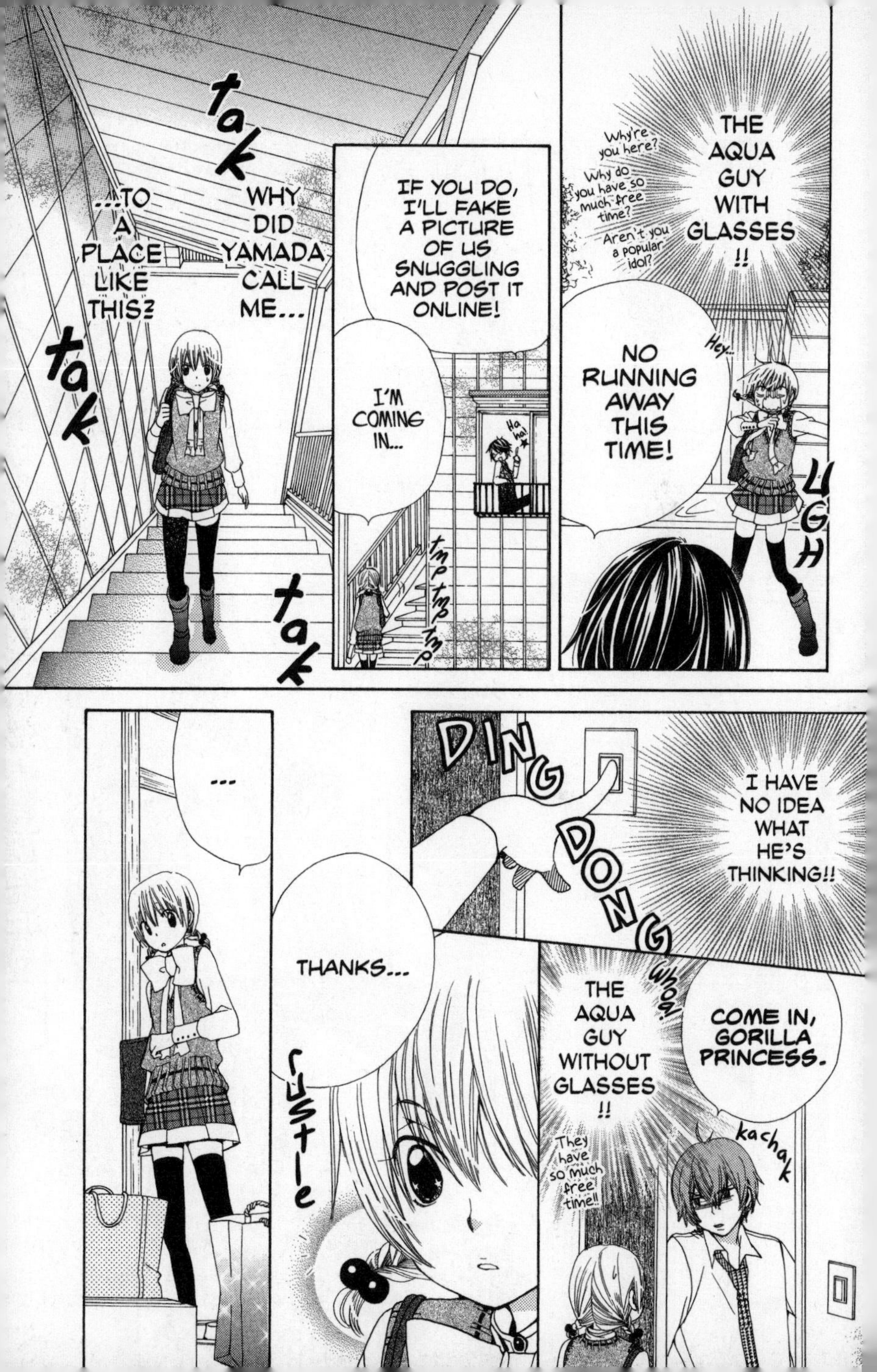
THE AQUA GUY WITH GLASSES!!
Why're you here?
Why do you have so much free time?
Aren't you a popular idol?
Hey...
NO RUNNING AWAY THIS TIME!
UGH
IF YOU DO, I'LL FAKE A PICTURE OF US SNUGGLING AND POST IT ONLINE!
Ha ha!
I'M COMING IN...
tmp tmp tmp
tak
WHY DID YAMADA CALL ME...
...TO A PLACE LIKE THIS?
tak
tak
DING DONG
I HAVE NO IDEA WHAT HE'S THINKING!!
COME IN, GORILLA PRINCESS.
kachak
THE AQUA GUY WITHOUT GLASSES!!
whoa
They have so much free time!!
THANKS...
rustle
...

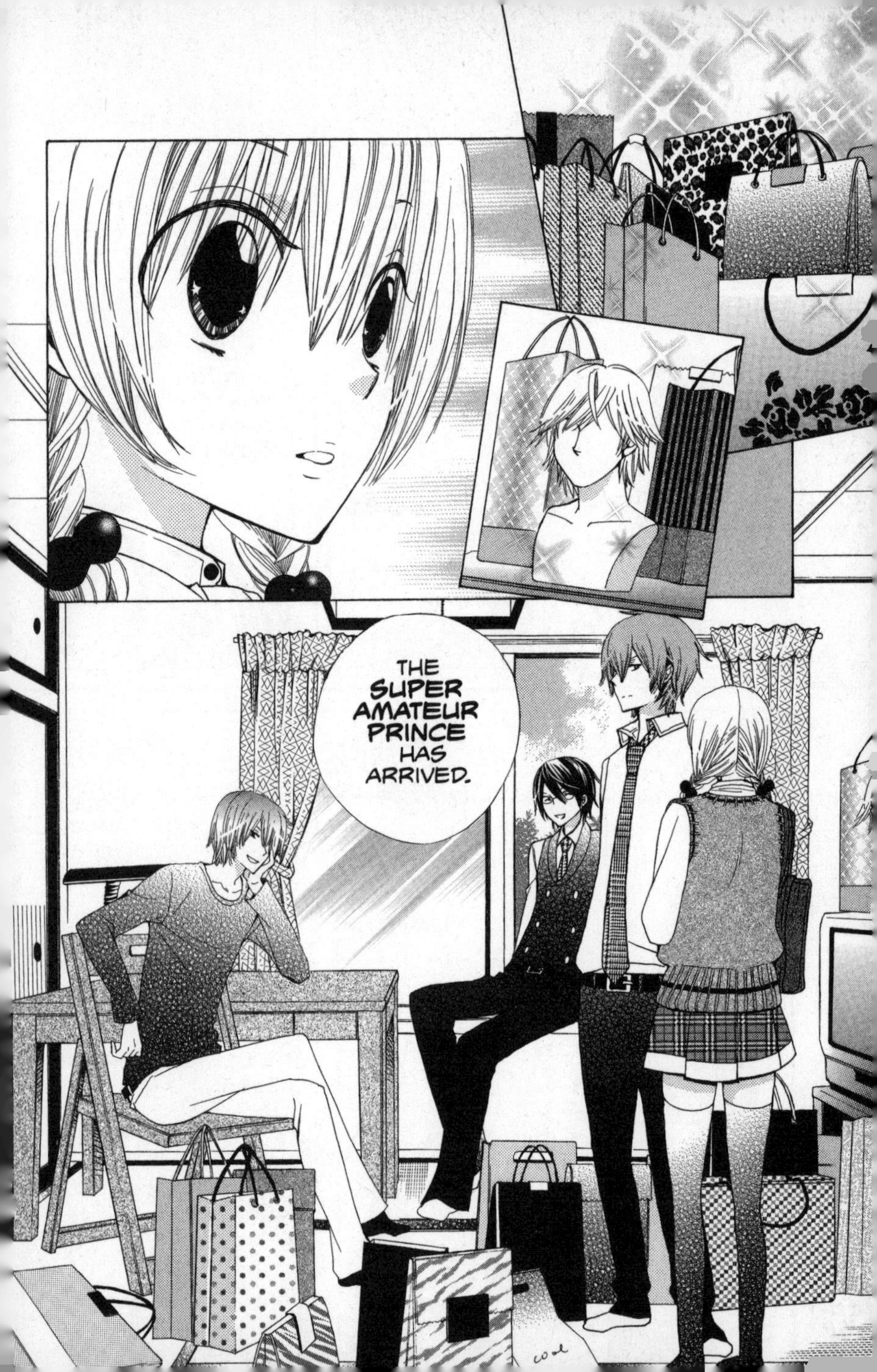
THE SUPER AMATEUR PRINCE HAS ARRIVED.

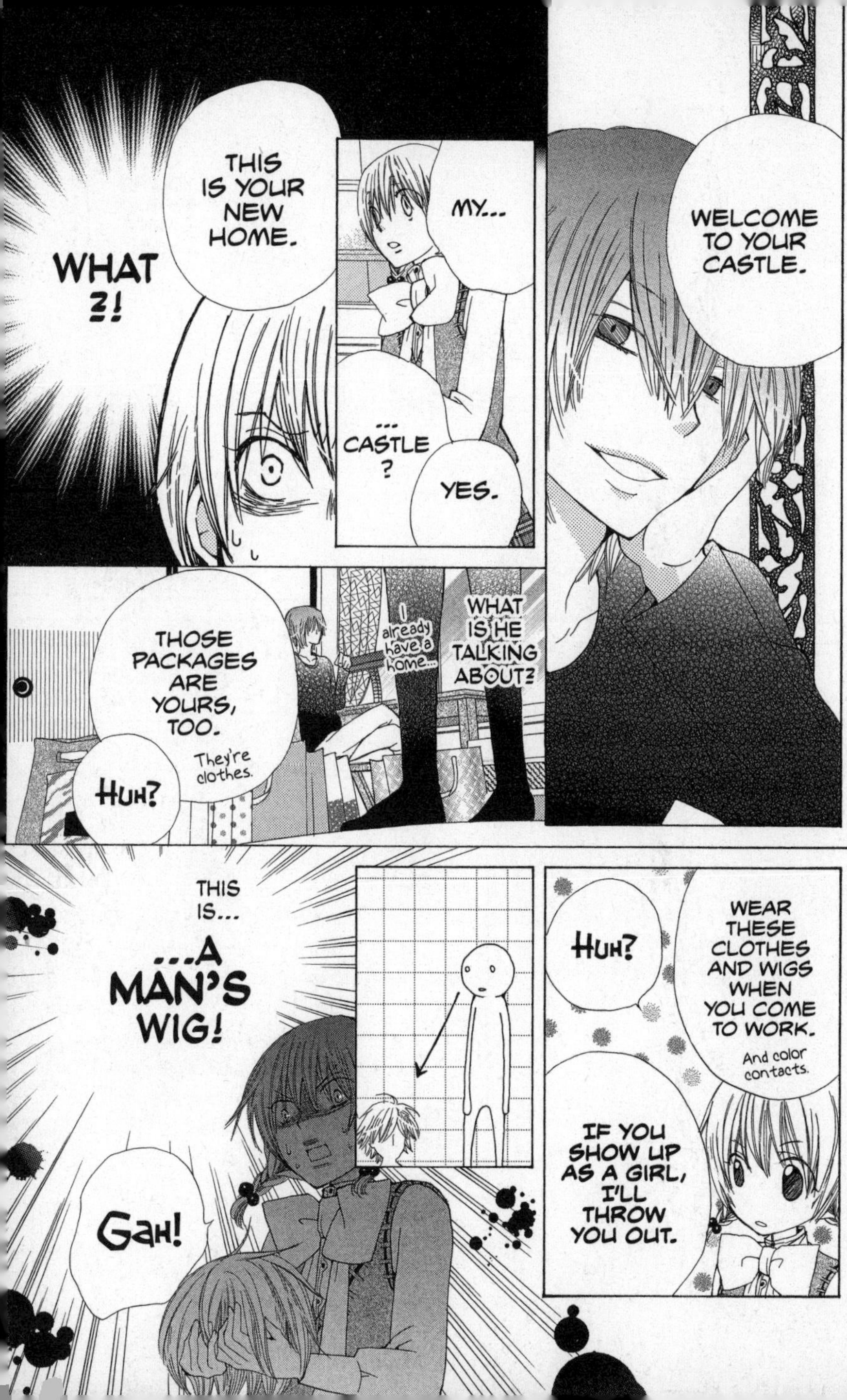
WELCOME TO YOUR CASTLE.
MY...
...CASTLE?
YES.
THIS IS YOUR NEW HOME.
WHAT?!
WHAT IS HE TALKING ABOUT?
I already have a home...
THOSE PACKAGES ARE YOURS, TOO.
They're clothes.
HUH?
WEAR THESE CLOTHES AND WIGS WHEN YOU COME TO WORK.
And color contacts.
HUH?
IF YOU SHOW UP AS A GIRL, I'LL THROW YOU OUT.
THIS IS...
...A MAN'S WIG!
GAH!

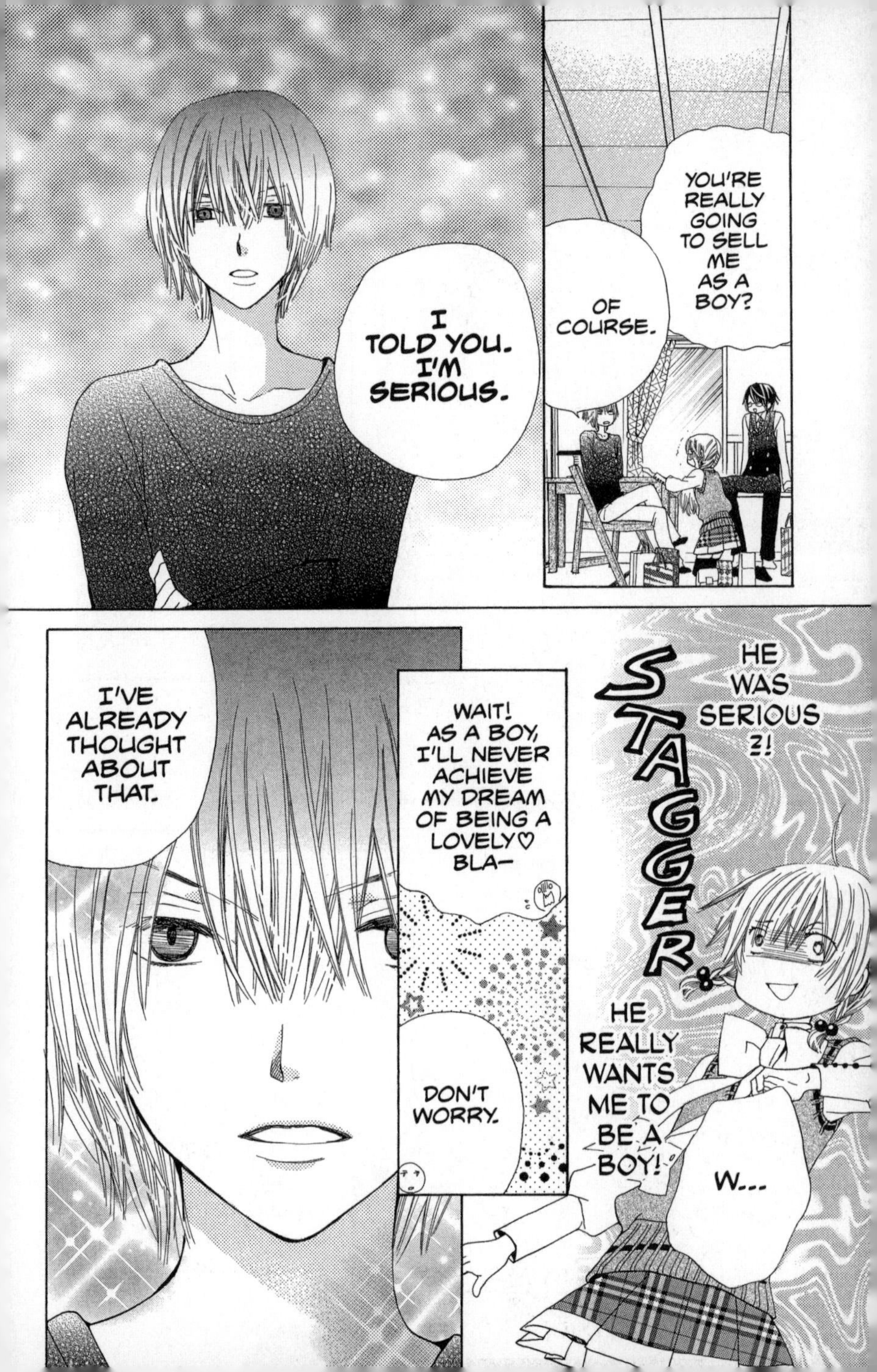
YOU'RE REALLY GOING TO SELL ME AS A BOY?
OF COURSE.
I TOLD YOU. I'M SERIOUS.
HE WAS SERIOUS?!
STAGGER.
HE REALLY WANTS ME TO BE A BOY!
W...
WAIT! AS A BOY, I'LL NEVER ACHIEVE MY DREAM OF BEING A LOVELY♡ BLA—
DON'T WORRY.
I'VE ALREADY THOUGHT ABOUT THAT.

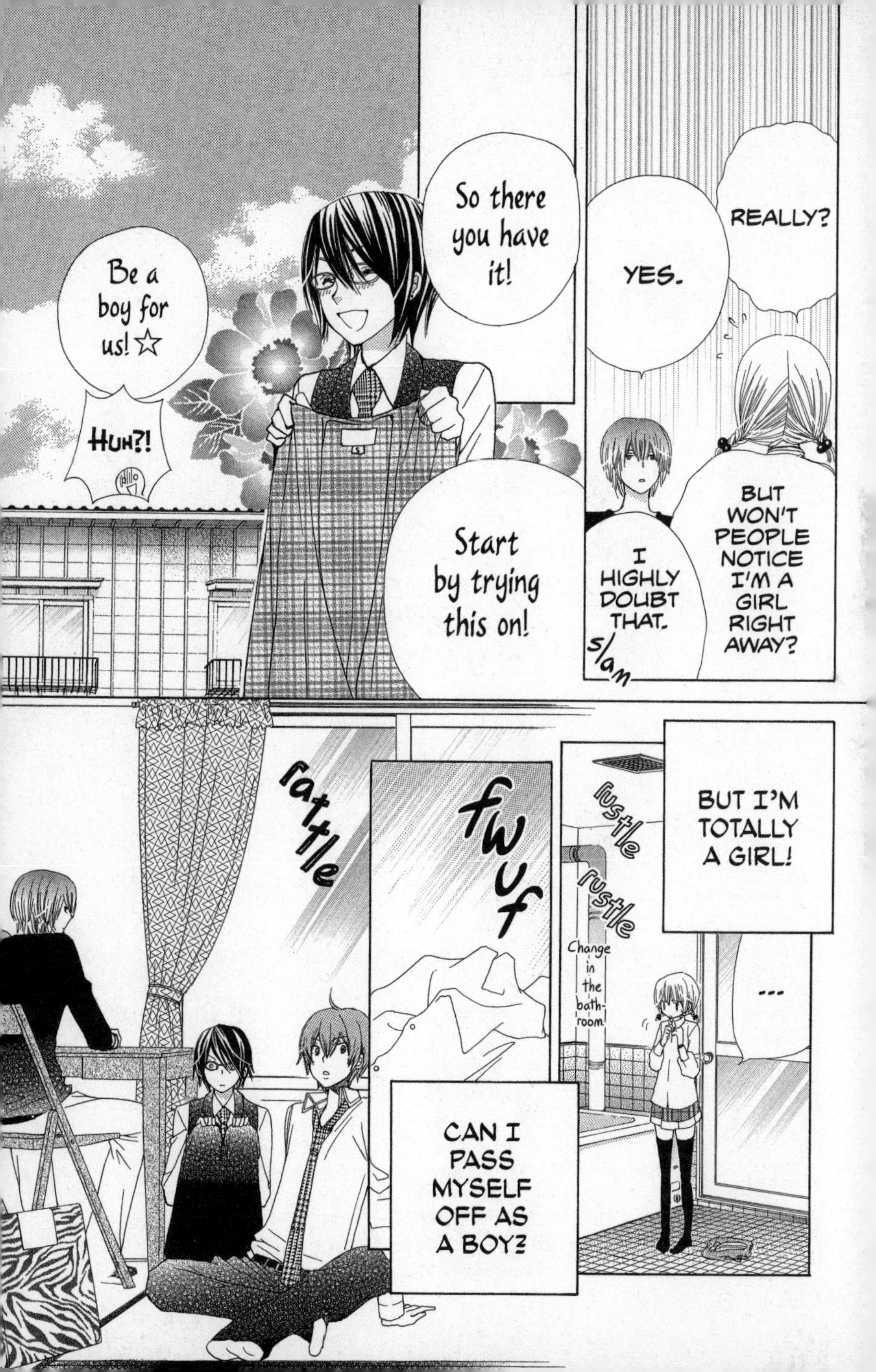
REALLY?
YES.
BUT WON'T PEOPLE NOTICE I'M A GIRL RIGHT AWAY?
I HIGHLY DOUBT THAT.
slam
So there you have it!
Be a boy for us! ☆
HUH?!
Start by trying this on!
BUT I'M TOTALLY A GIRL!
rustle
rustle
Change in the bathroom!
...
fwuf
rattle
CAN I PASS MYSELF OFF AS A BOY?

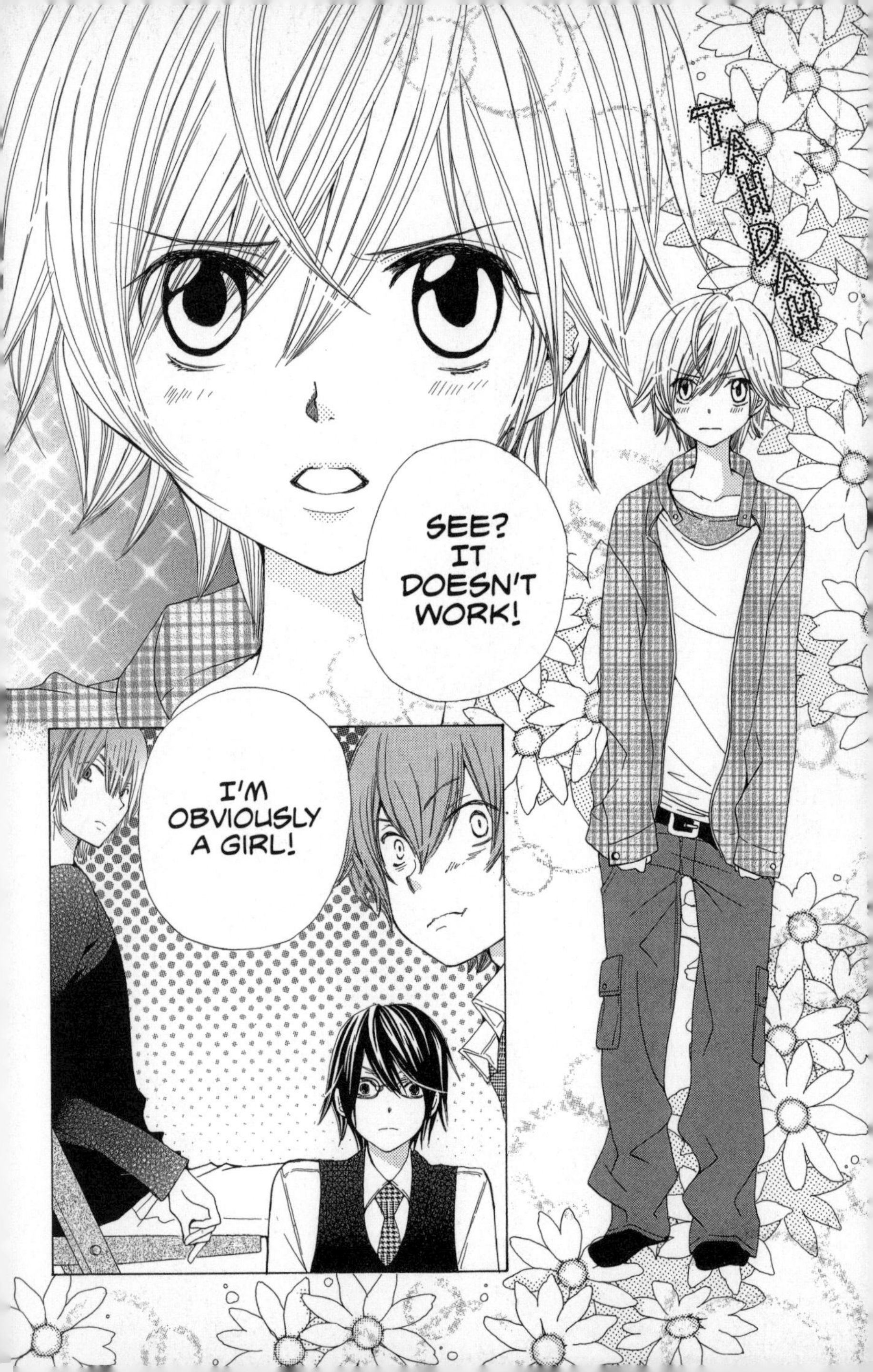
TA-DAH
SEE? IT DOESN'T WORK!
I'M OBVIOUSLY A GIRL!

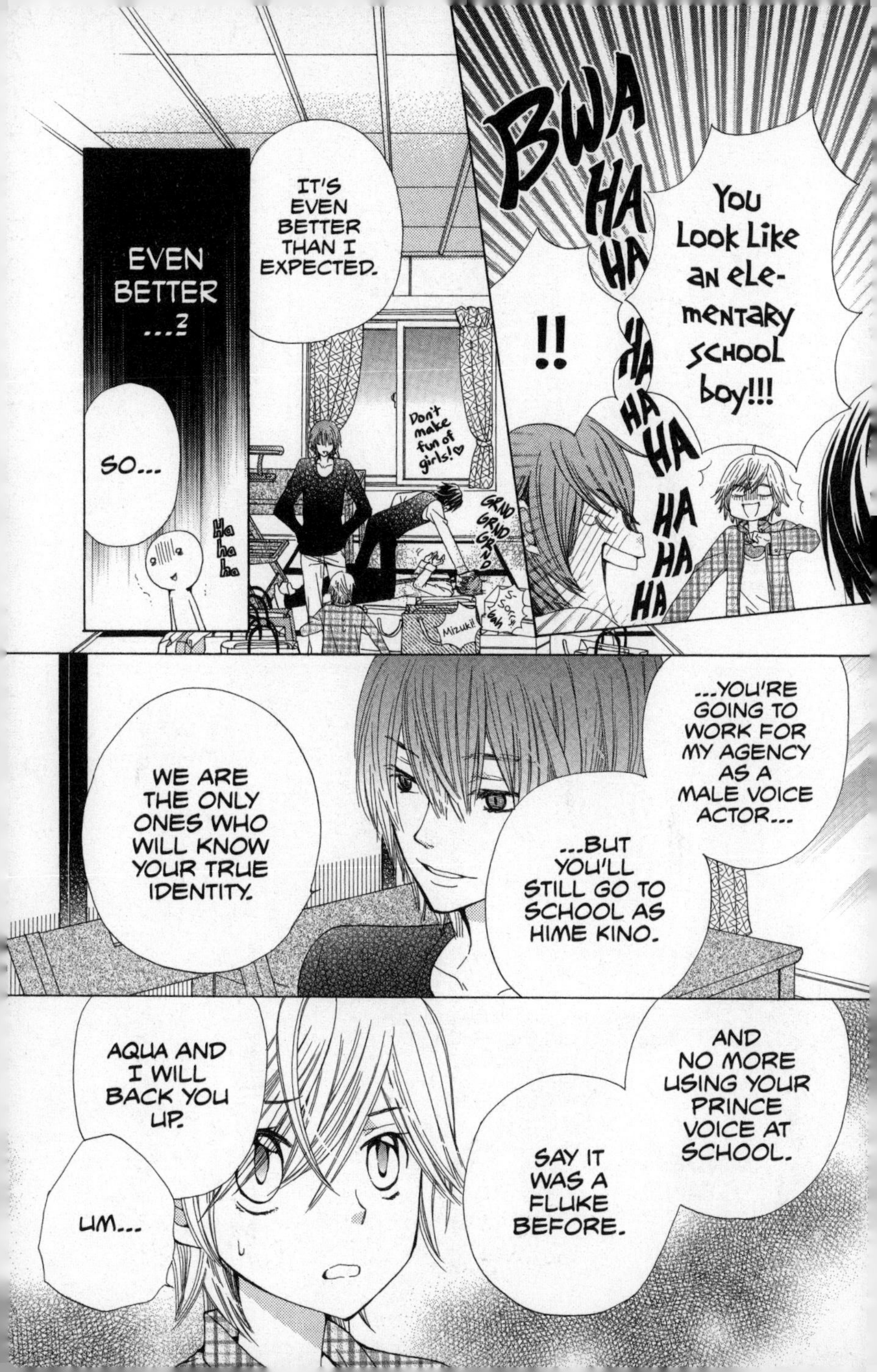
BWAHAHAHAHAHAHAHAHAHAHA
You look like an elementary school boy!!!
!!
IT'S EVEN BETTER THAN I EXPECTED.
EVEN BETTER ...?
SO...
Ha ha ha
Don't make fun of girls!♥
GRND GRND GRND
S-Sorry!! Waah
Mizuki!
...YOU'RE GOING TO WORK FOR MY AGENCY AS A MALE VOICE ACTOR...
...BUT YOU'LL STILL GO TO SCHOOL AS HIME KINO.
WE ARE THE ONLY ONES WHO WILL KNOW YOUR TRUE IDENTITY.
AND NO MORE USING YOUR PRINCE VOICE AT SCHOOL.
SAY IT WAS A FLUKE BEFORE.
AQUA AND I WILL BACK YOU UP.
UM...

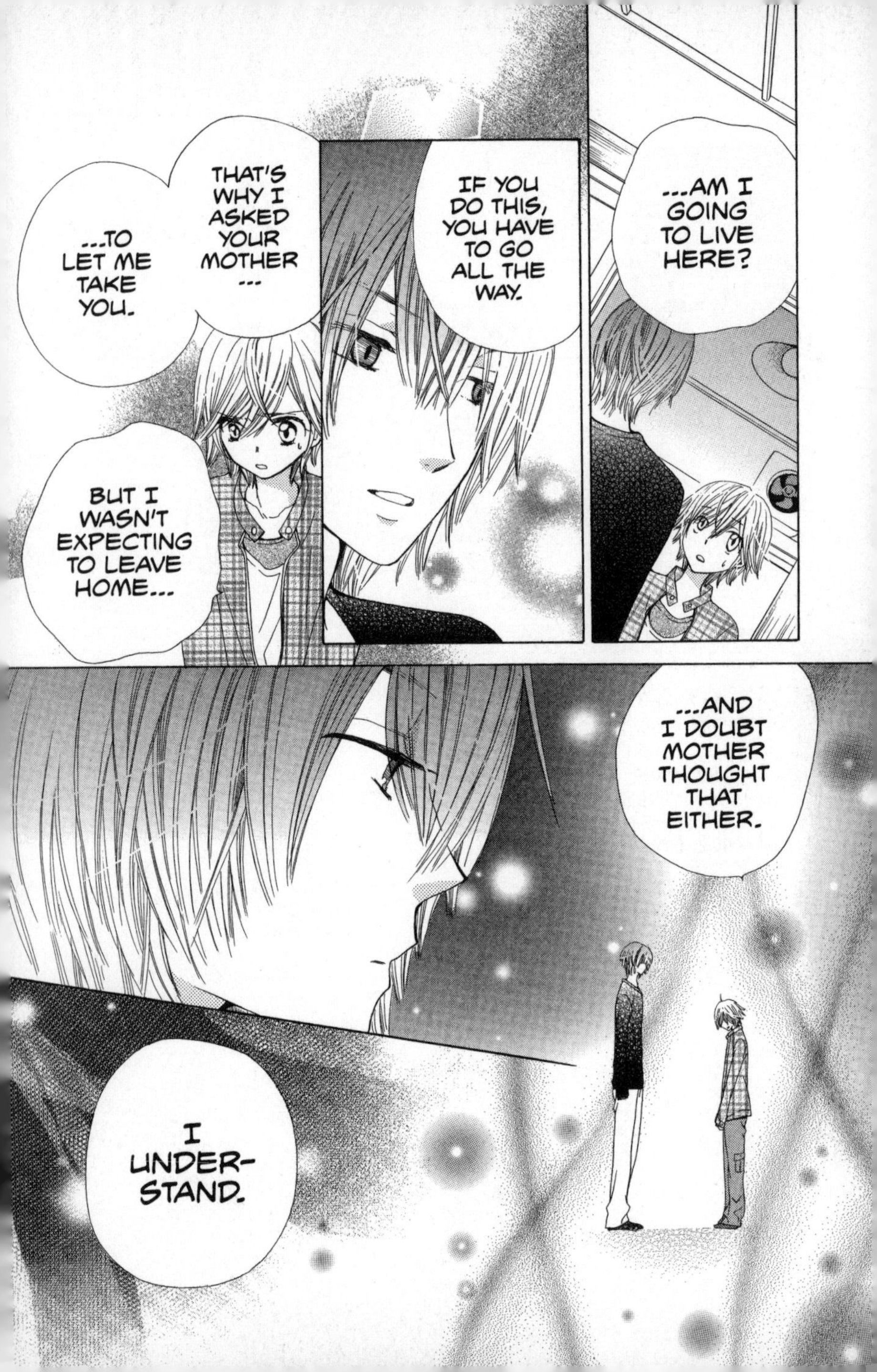
...AM I GOING TO LIVE HERE?
IF YOU DO THIS, YOU HAVE TO GO ALL THE WAY.
THAT'S WHY I ASKED YOUR MOTHER ...
...TO LET ME TAKE YOU.
BUT I WASN'T EXPECTING TO LEAVE HOME...
...AND I DOUBT MOTHER THOUGHT THAT EITHER.
I UNDER-STAND.

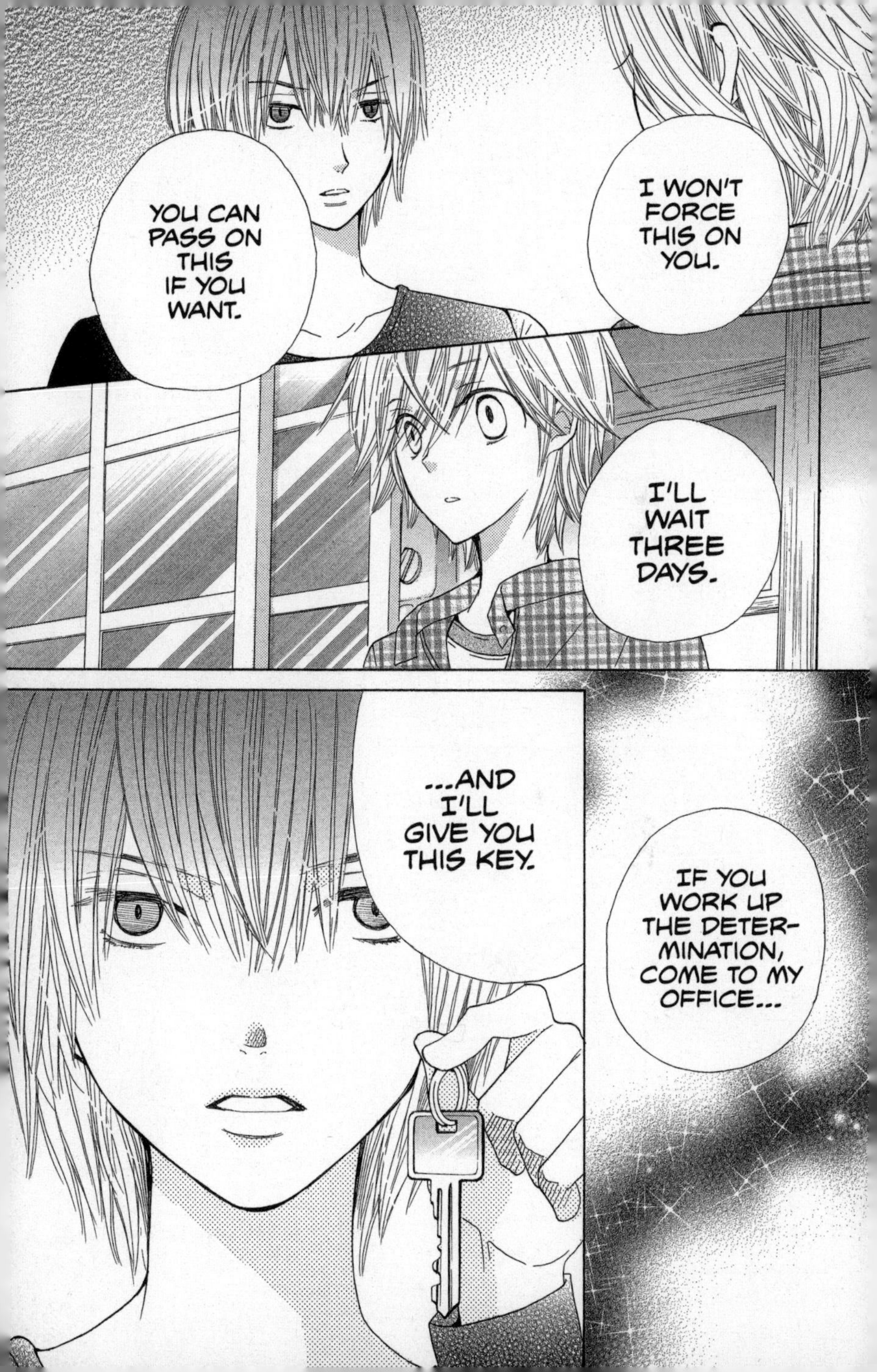
I WON'T FORCE THIS ON YOU.
YOU CAN PASS ON THIS IF YOU WANT.
I'LL WAIT THREE DAYS.
IF YOU WORK UP THE DETER- MINATION, COME TO MY OFFICE...
...AND I'LL GIVE YOU THIS KEY.

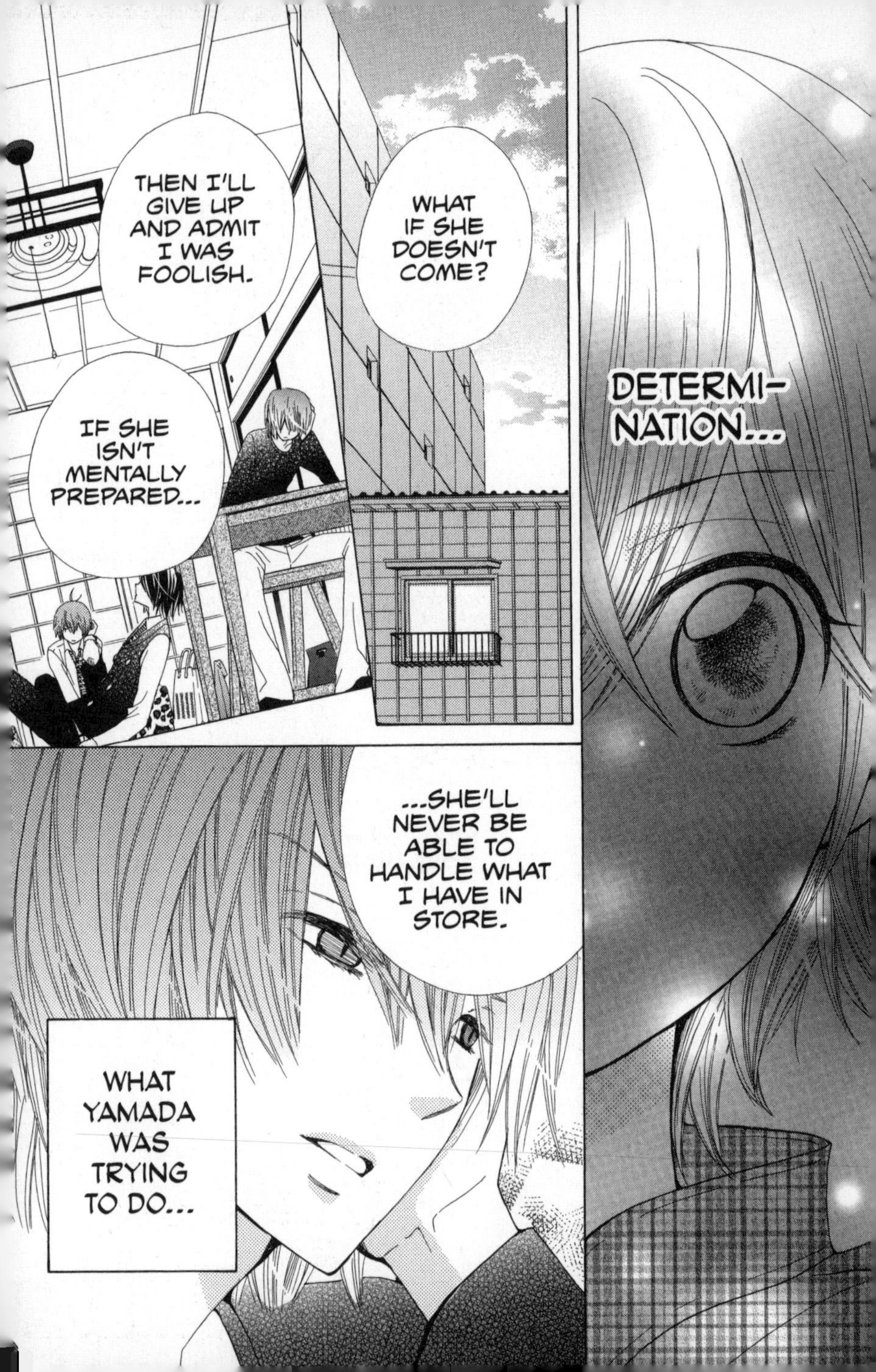
DETERMI-
NATION...
WHAT IF SHE DOESN'T COME?
THEN I'LL GIVE UP AND ADMIT I WAS FOOLISH.
IF SHE ISN'T MENTALLY PREPARED...
...SHE'LL NEVER BE ABLE TO HANDLE WHAT I HAVE IN STORE.
WHAT YAMADA WAS TRYING TO DO...

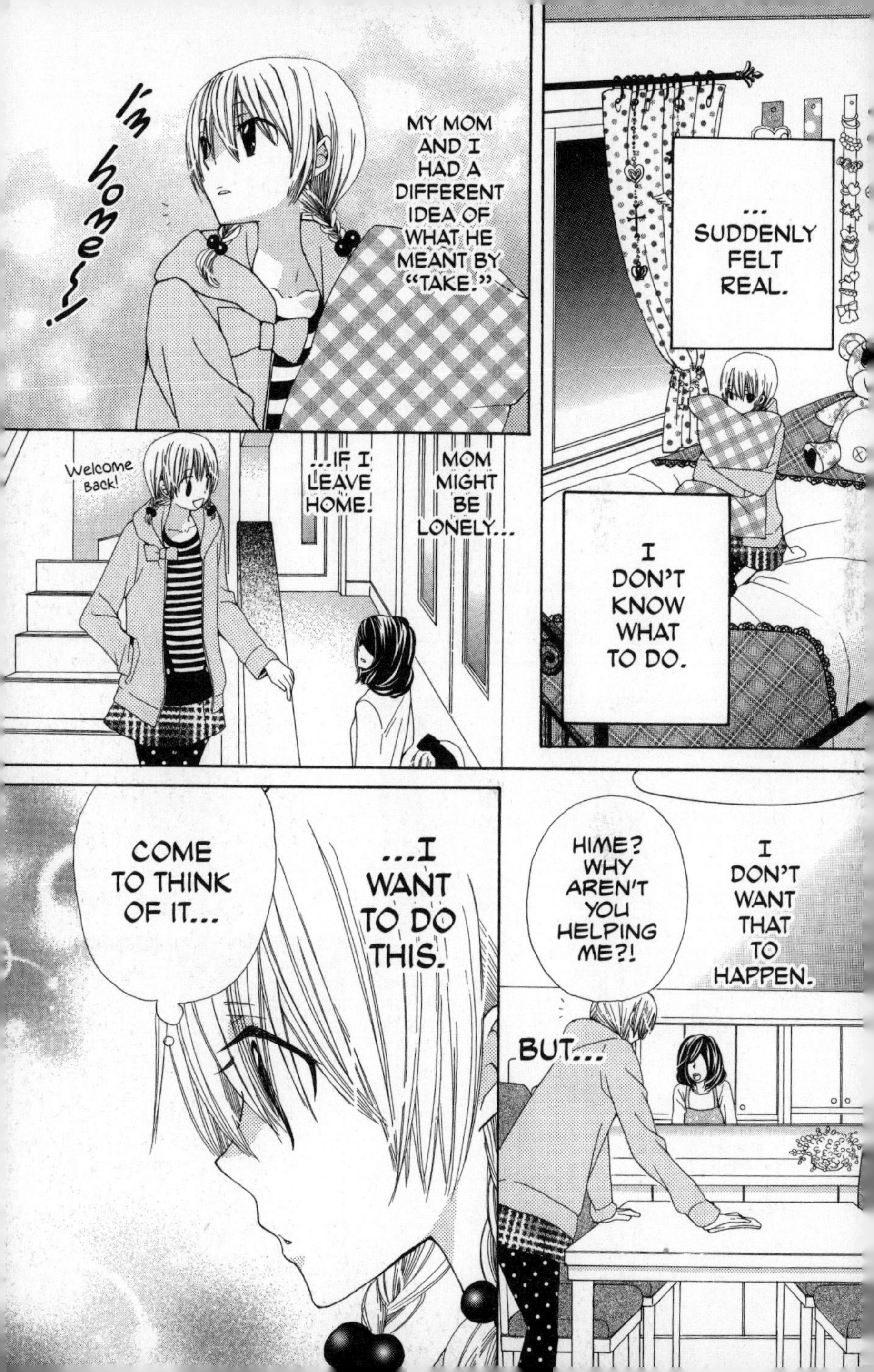
...SUDDENLY FELT REAL.
I DON'T KNOW WHAT TO DO.
MY MOM AND I HAD A DIFFERENT IDEA OF WHAT HE MEANT BY "TAKE."
I'm home~!
MOM MIGHT BE LONELY...
...IF I LEAVE HOME.
Welcome Back!
I DON'T WANT THAT TO HAPPEN.
HIME? WHY AREN'T YOU HELPING ME?!
BUT...
...I WANT TO DO THIS.
COME TO THINK OF IT...

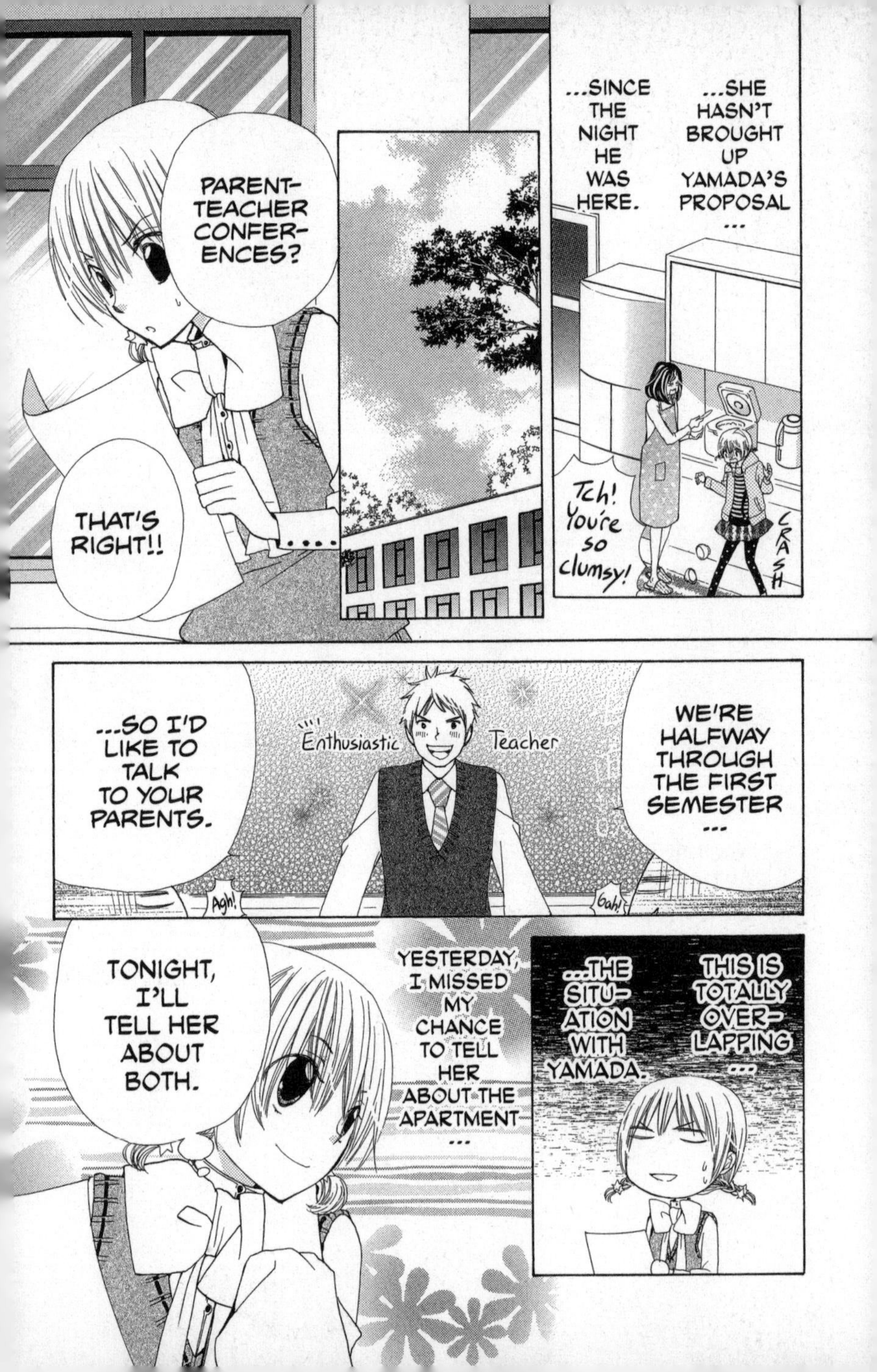
...SHE HASN'T BROUGHT UP YAMADA'S PROPOSAL ...
...SINCE THE NIGHT HE WAS HERE.
Tch! You're so clumsy!
CRASH
PARENT-TEACHER CONFERENCES?
THAT'S RIGHT!!
....
WE'RE HALFWAY THROUGH THE FIRST SEMESTER ...
Enthusiastic Teacher
...SO I'D LIKE TO TALK TO YOUR PARENTS.
Gah!
Agh!
THIS IS TOTALLY OVER-LAPPING ...
...THE SITU-ATION WITH YAMADA.
YESTERDAY, I MISSED MY CHANCE TO TELL HER ABOUT THE APARTMENT ...
TONIGHT, I'LL TELL HER ABOUT BOTH.

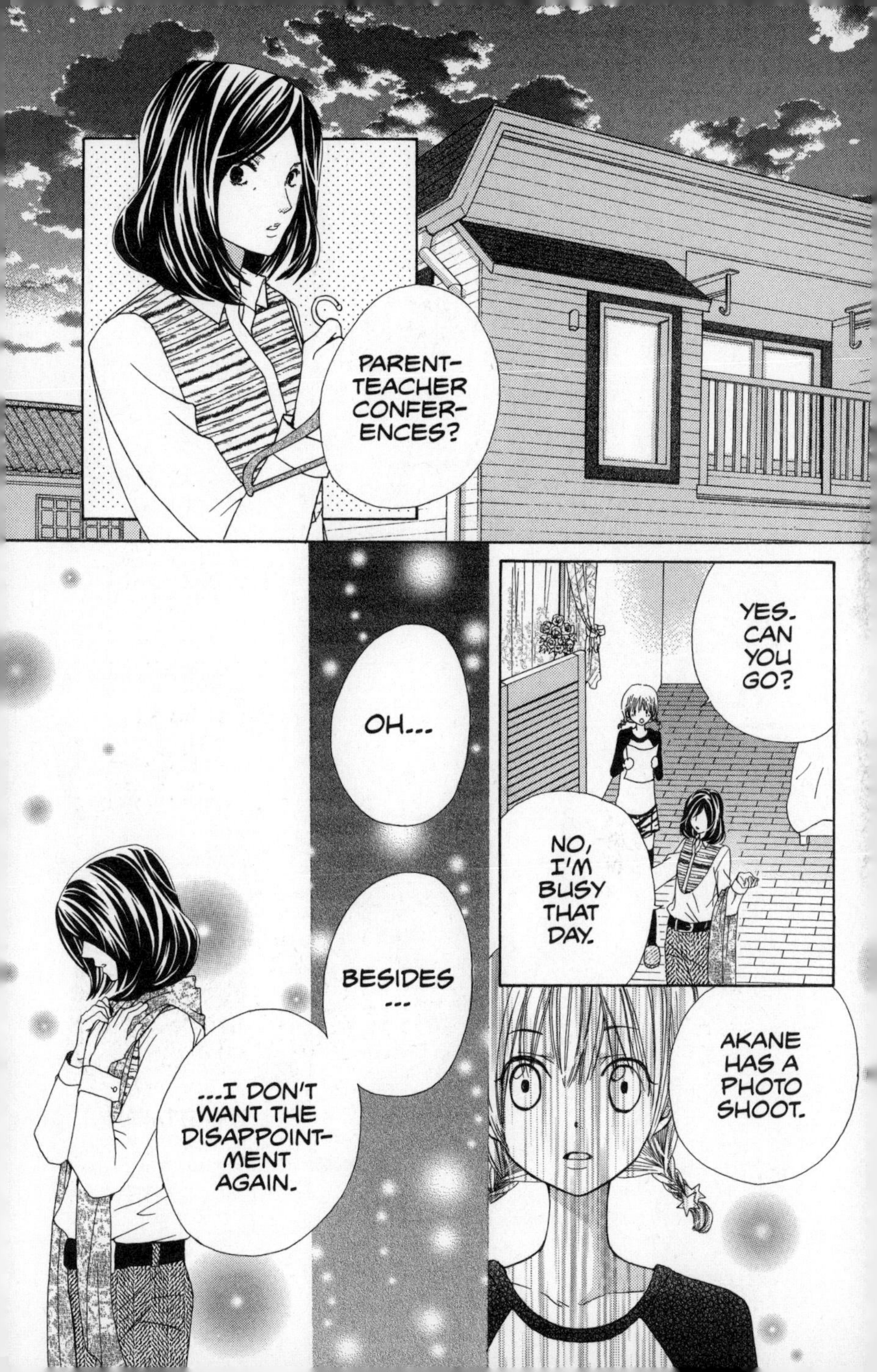
PARENT-TEACHER CONFERENCES?
YES. CAN YOU GO?
NO, I'M BUSY THAT DAY.
AKANE HAS A PHOTO SHOOT.
OH...
BESIDES...
...I DON'T WANT THE DISAPPOINTMENT AGAIN.

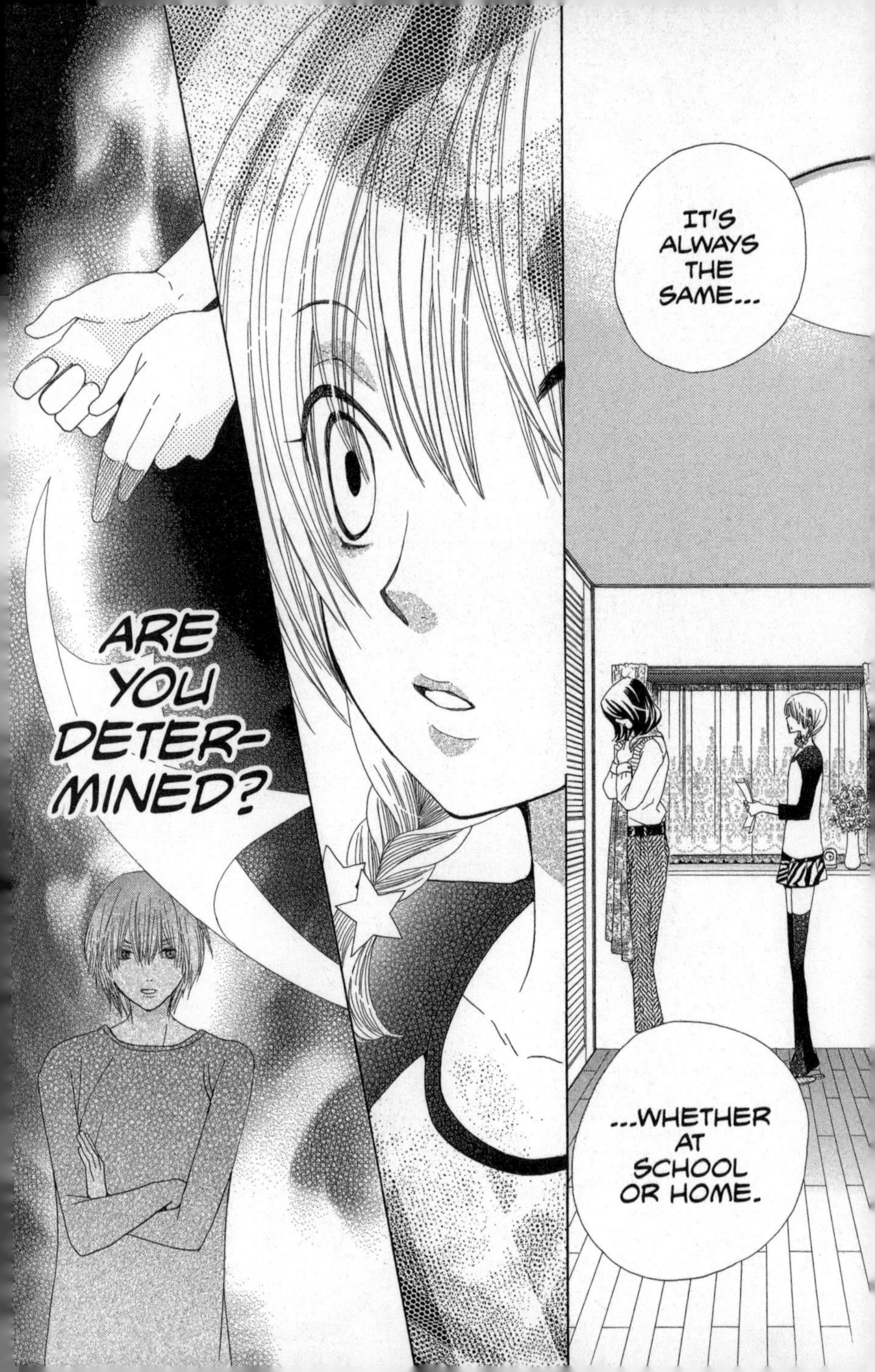
IT'S ALWAYS THE SAME...
...WHETHER AT SCHOOL OR HOME.
ARE YOU DETER-MINED?

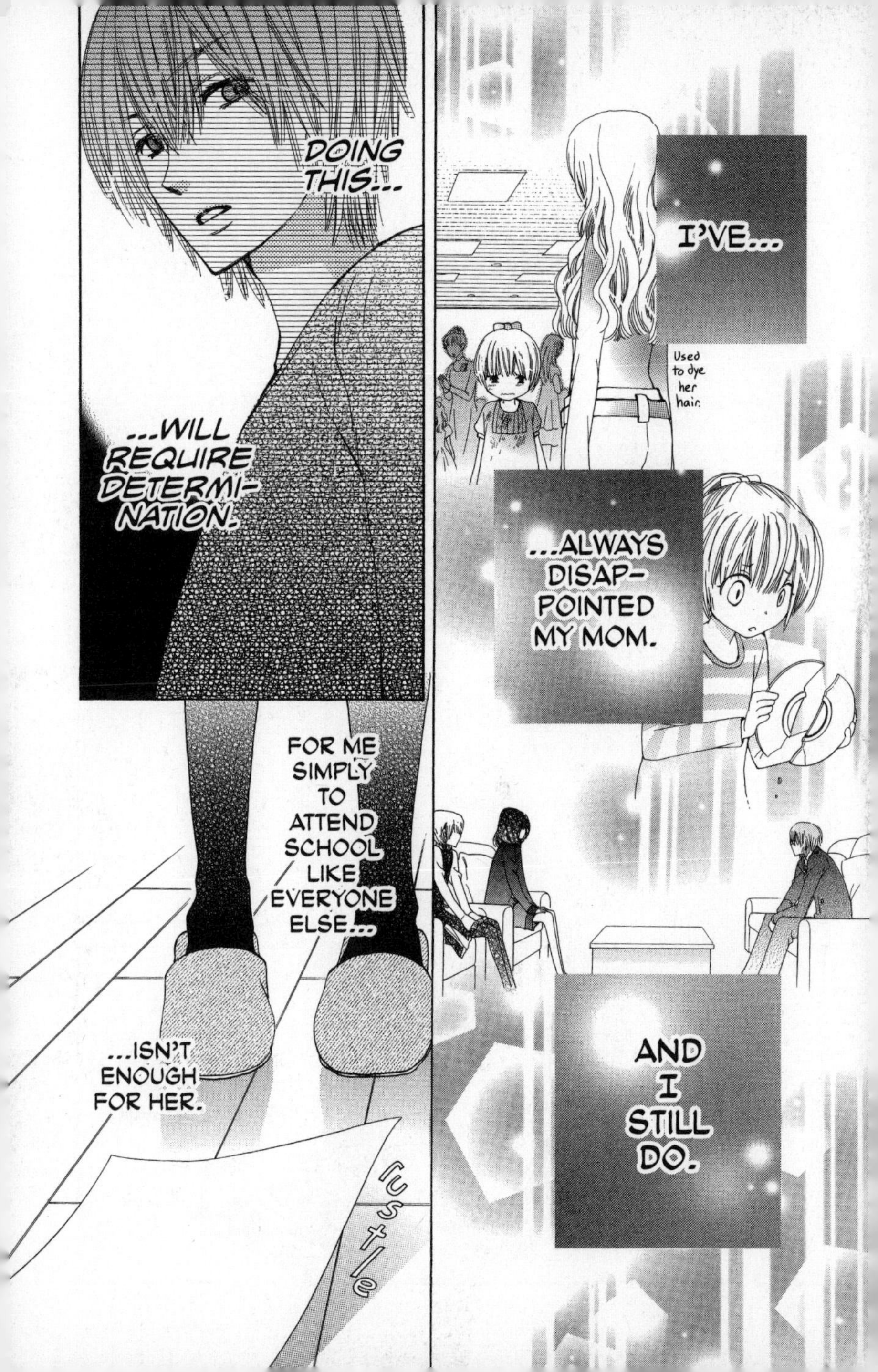
I'VE...
Used to dye her hair.
...ALWAYS DISAPPOINTED MY MOM.
AND I STILL DO.
DOING THIS...
...WILL REQUIRE DETERMINATION.
FOR ME SIMPLY TO ATTEND SCHOOL LIKE EVERYONE ELSE...
...ISN'T ENOUGH FOR HER.
rustle

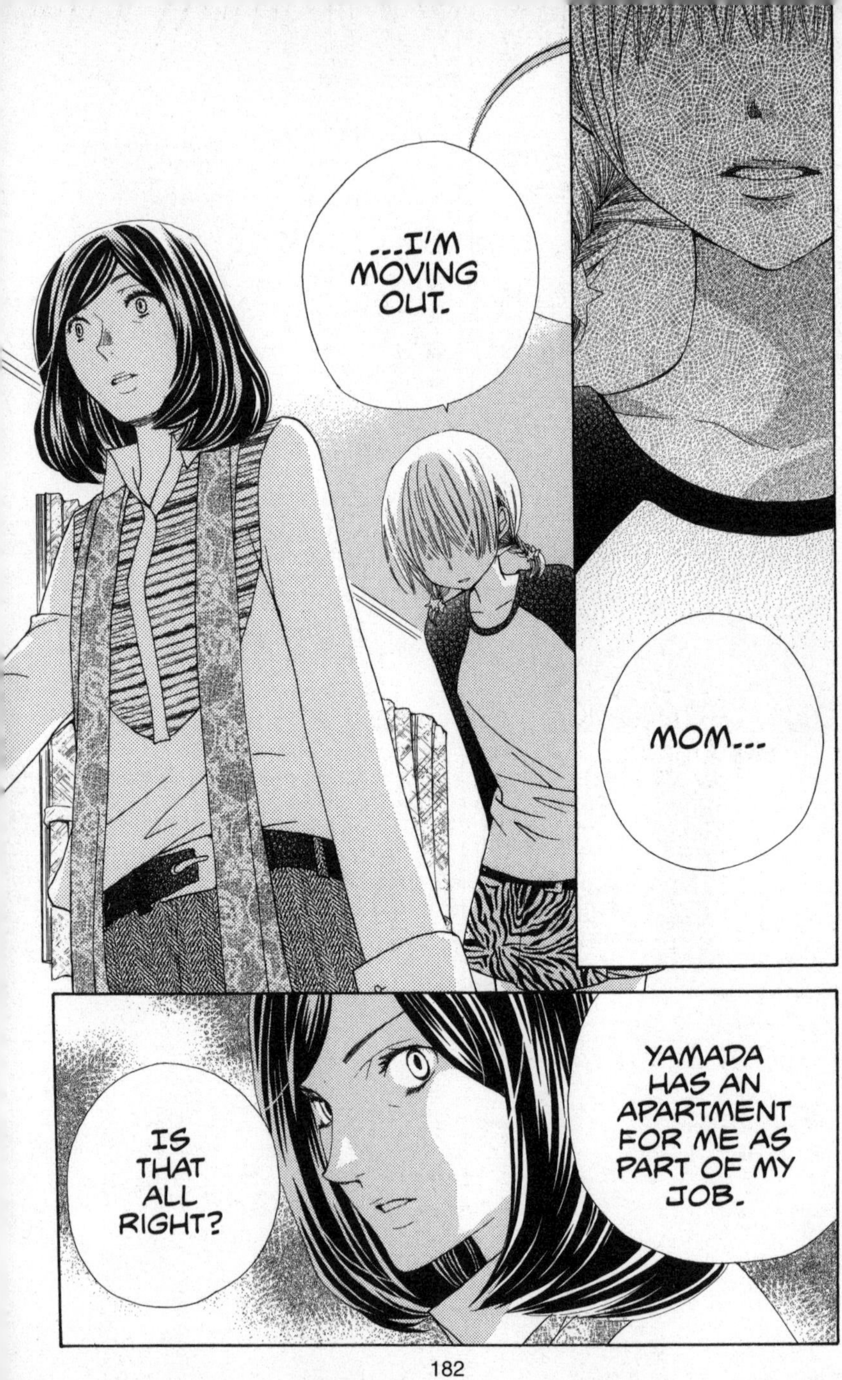
MOM...
...I'M MOVING OUT.
YAMADA HAS AN APARTMENT FOR ME AS PART OF MY JOB.
IS THAT ALL RIGHT?

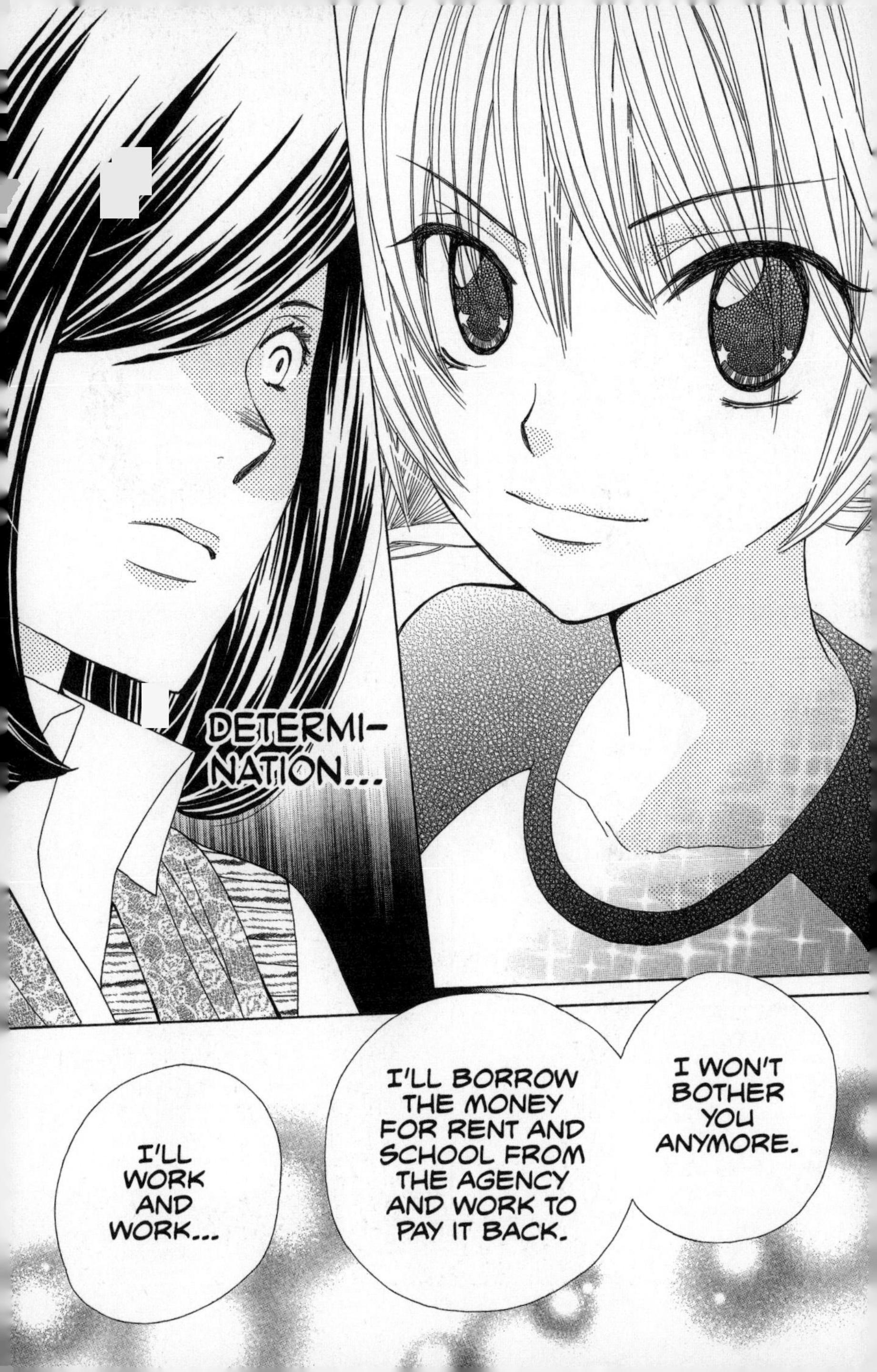
DETERMINATION...
I WON'T BOTHER YOU ANYMORE.
I'LL BORROW THE MONEY FOR RENT AND SCHOOL FROM THE AGENCY AND WORK TO PAY IT BACK.
I'LL WORK AND WORK...

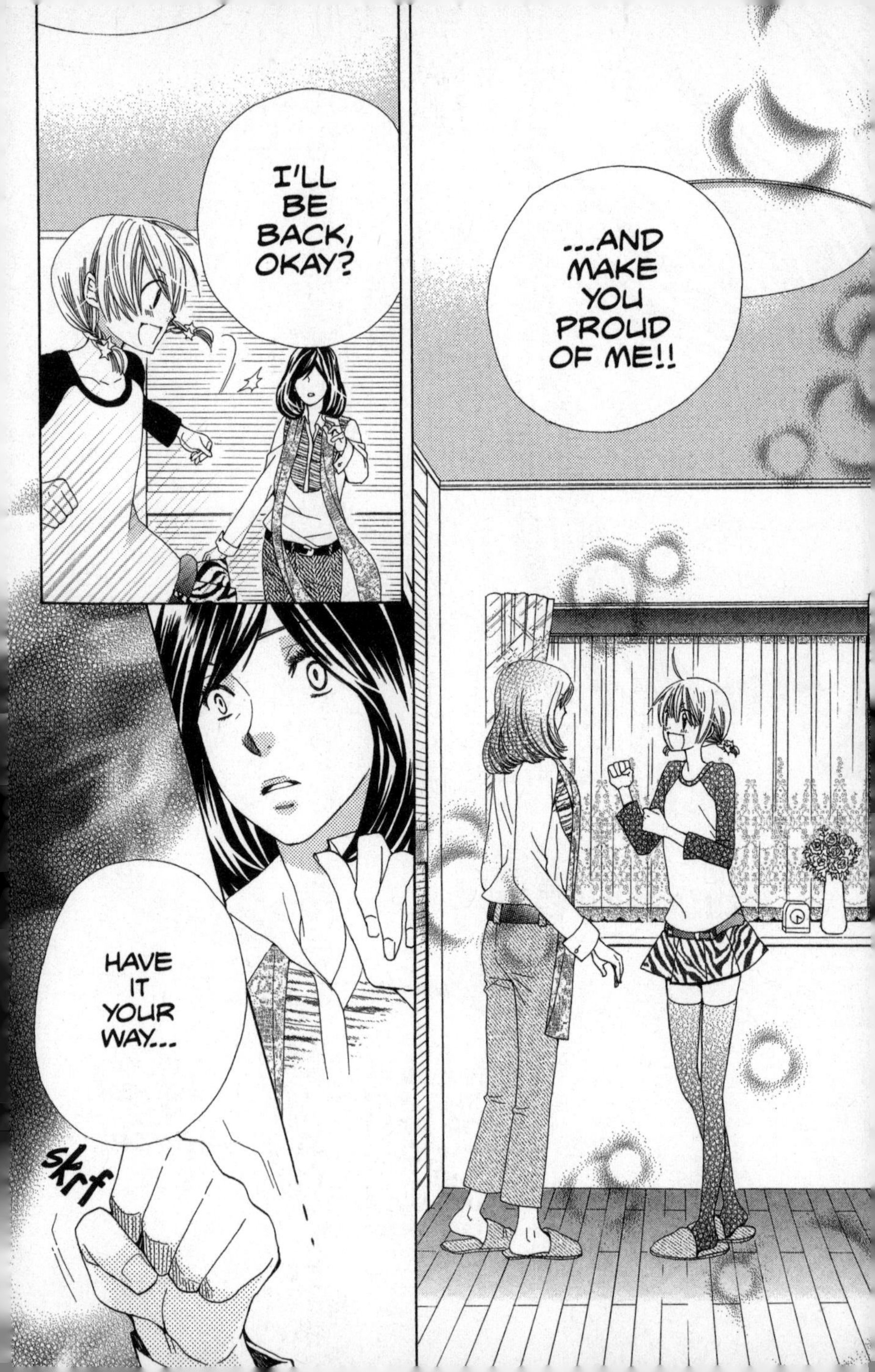
I'LL BE BACK, OKAY?
HAVE IT YOUR WAY...
skrf
...AND MAKE YOU PROUD OF ME!!

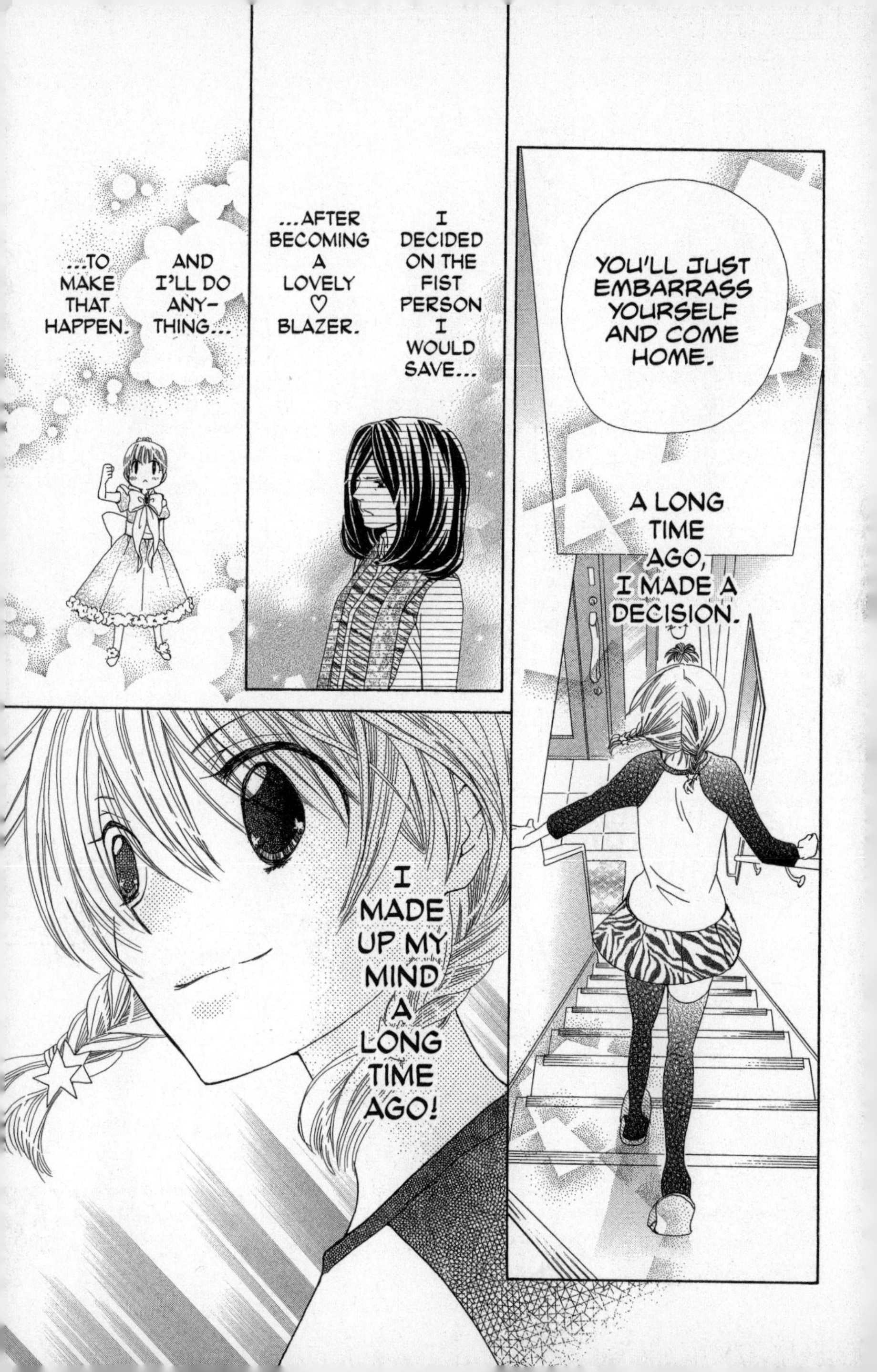
YOU'LL JUST EMBARRASS YOURSELF AND COME HOME.
A LONG TIME AGO, I MADE A DECISION.
I DECIDED ON THE FIST PERSON I WOULD SAVE...
...AFTER BECOMING A LOVELY ♡ BLAZER.
AND I'LL DO ANY-THING...
...TO MAKE THAT HAPPEN.
I MADE UP MY MIND A LONG TIME AGO!

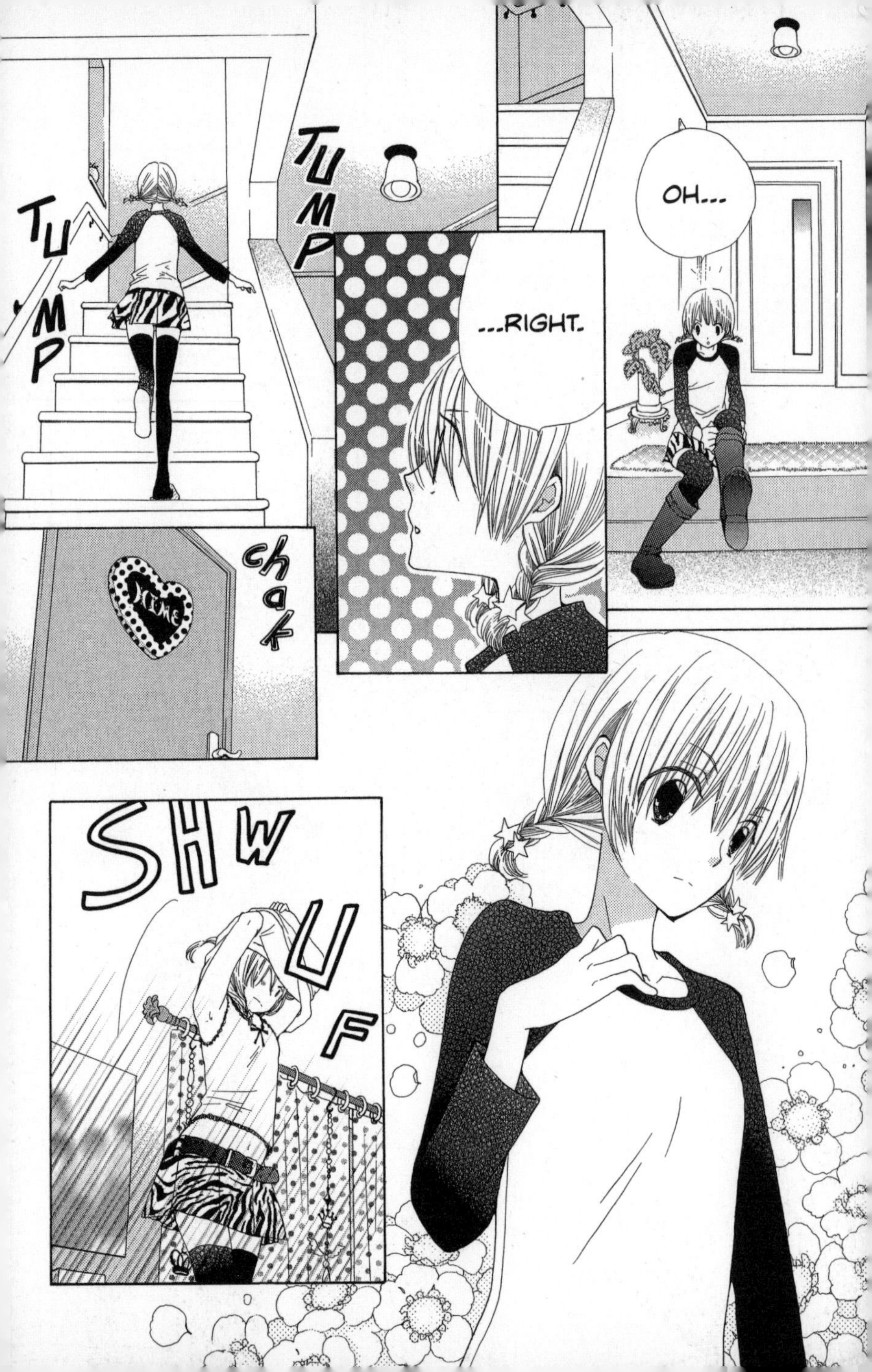
OH...
...RIGHT.
TUMP
TUMP
TUMP
TUMP
chak
SHWUF

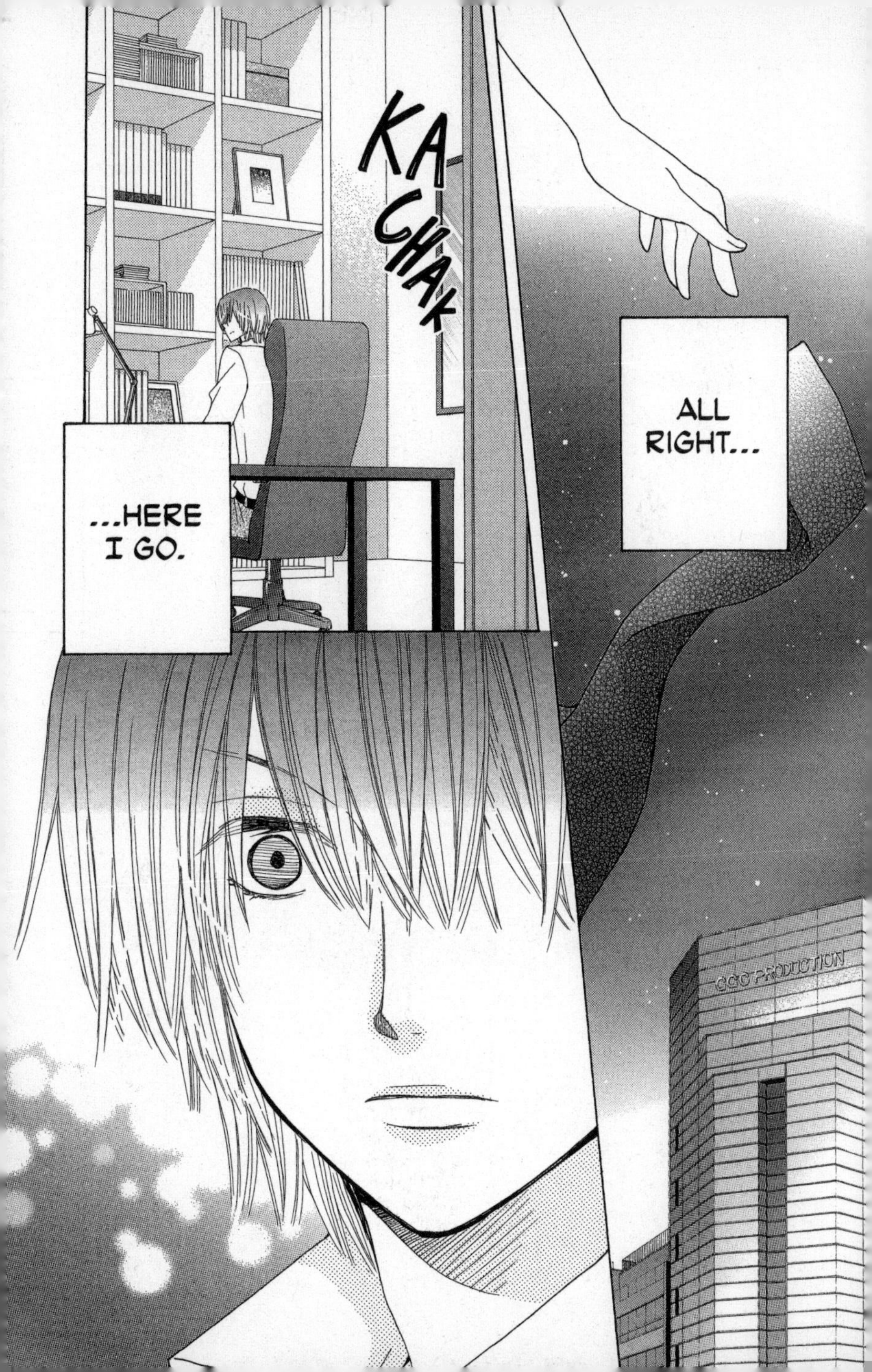
ALL RIGHT...
PRODUCTION
KACHAK
...HERE I GO.

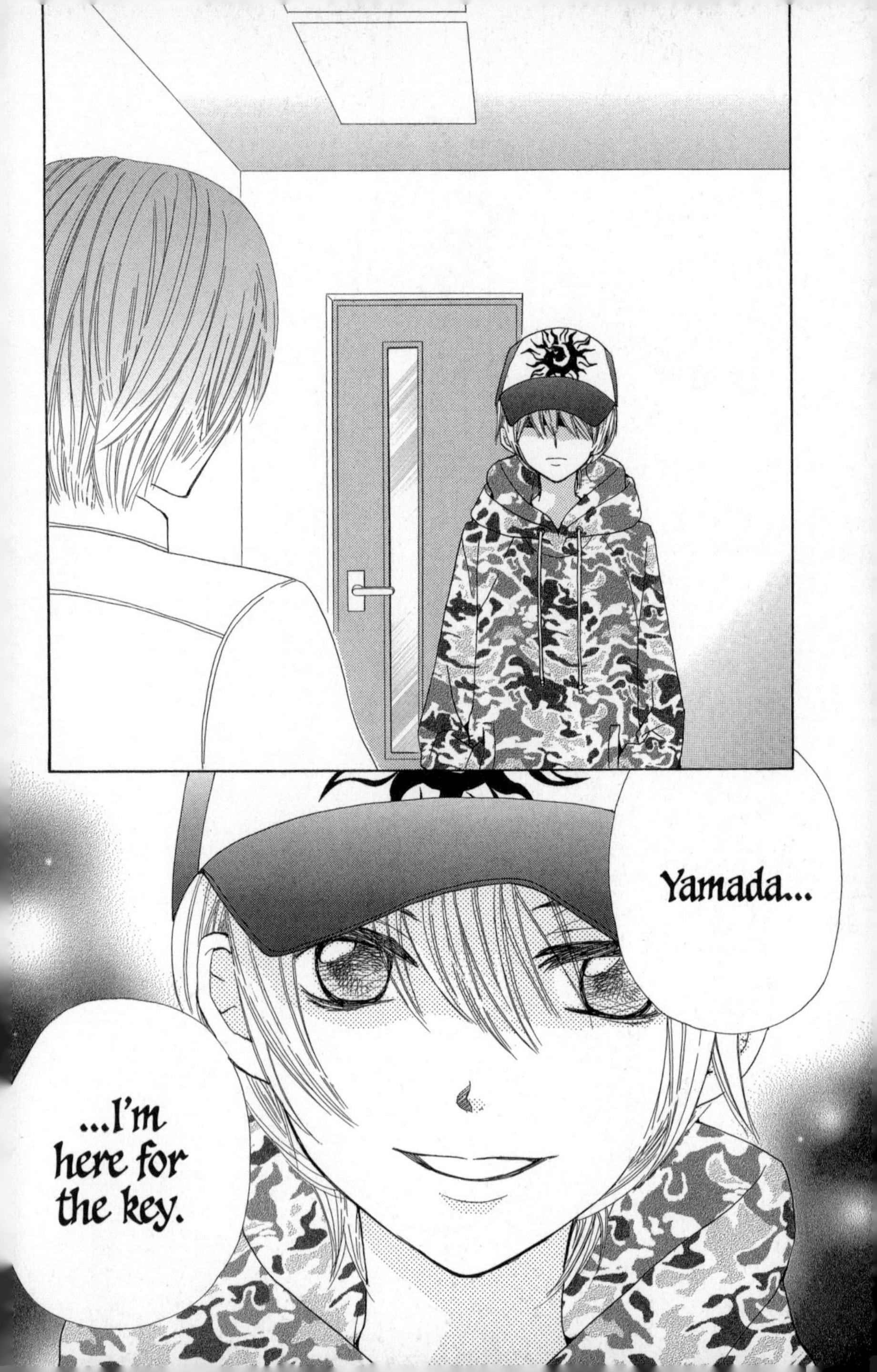
Yamada...
...I'm here for the key.

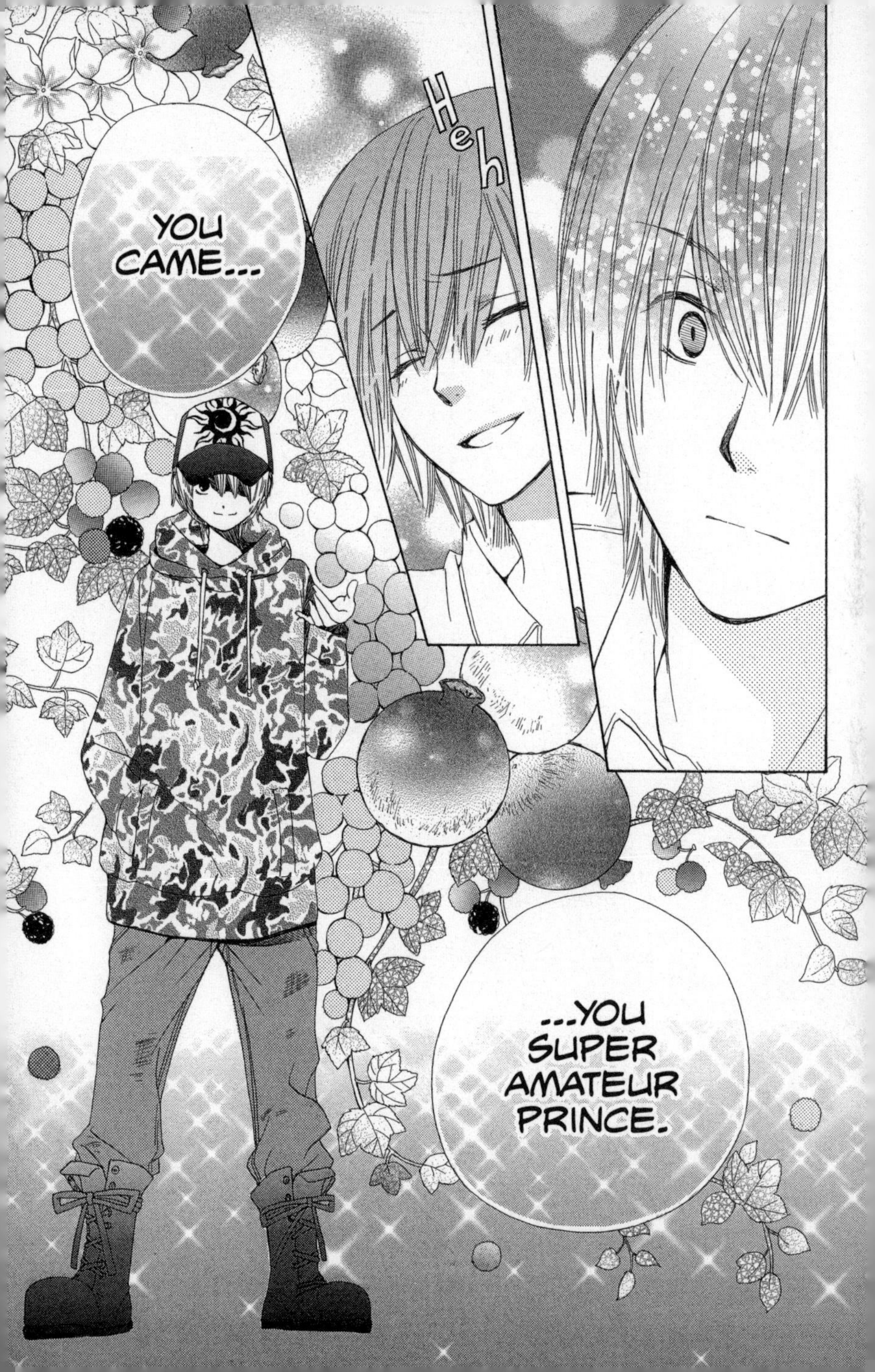
Heh
YOU CAME...
...YOU SUPER AMATEUR PRINCE.

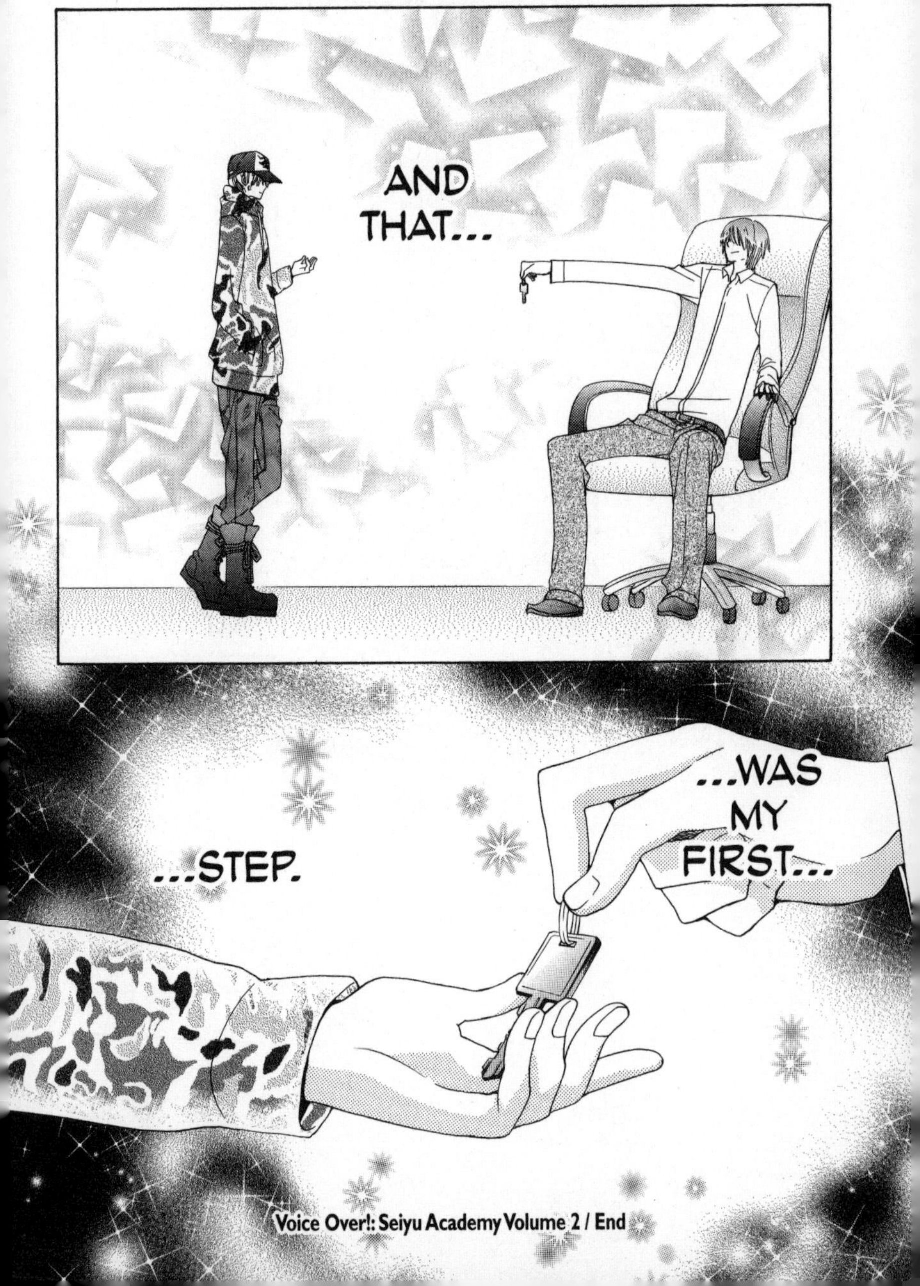
AND THAT...
...WAS MY FIRST...
...STEP.

Voice Over!: Seiyu Academy Volume 2 / End

Voice Over!
Seiyu Academy

End Notes

Page 5, panel 1-2: Mabo don
Similar to *mapo* tofu (spicy sauce with ground meat and tofu), but served on top of a bowl of rice (*don*).

Page 45, panel 3: Punta Sugawara
A spoof on popular yakuza movie actor Bunta Sugawara, who has also done voice acting for anime.

Maki Minami is from Saitama Prefecture in Japan. She debuted in 2001 with *Kanata no Ao* (Faraway Blue). Her other works include *Kimi wa Girlfriend* (You're My Girlfriend), *Mainichi ga Takaramono* (Every Day Is a Treasure), *Yuki Atataka* (Warm Winter) and *S•A*, which was published in English by VIZ Media.

VOICE OVER!
SEIYU ACADEMY
VOL. 2
Shojo Beat Edition

STORY AND ART BY
MAKI MINAMI

TECHNICAL ADVISORS
Yoichi Kato, Kaori Kagami, Ayumi Hashidate,
Ayako Harino and Touko Fujitani

Special Thanks
81produce
Tokyo Animator College
Tokyo Animation College

English Translation & Adaptation/John Werry
Touch-up Art & Lettering/Sabrina Heep
Design/Yukiko Whitley
Editor/Pancha Diaz

SEIYU KA! by Maki Minami
© Maki Minami 2010
All rights reserved.
First published in Japan in 2010 by HAKUSENSHA, Inc., Tokyo.
English language translation rights arranged with
HAKUSENSHA, Inc., Tokyo.

Printed in the U.S.A.

Published by VIZ Media, LLC
P.O. Box 77010
San Francisco, CA 94107

10 9 8 7 6 5 4 3 2 1
First printing, December 2013

www.viz.com　　www.shojobeat.com

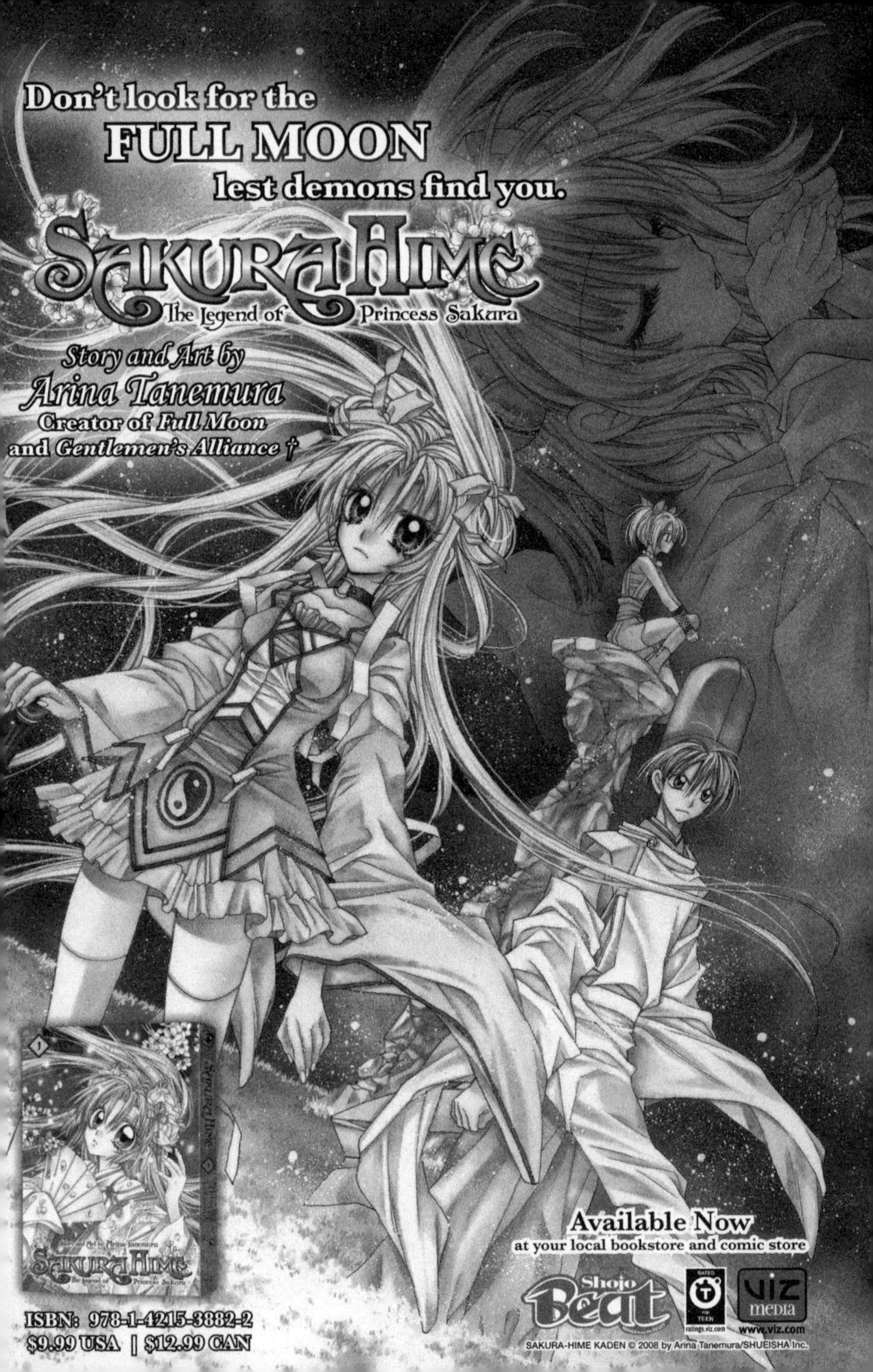
Don't look for the
FULL MOON
lest demons find you.
SAKURA HIME
The Legend of Princess Sakura
Story and Art by
Arina Tanemura
Creator of Full Moon
and Gentlemen's Alliance †
Available Now
at your local bookstore and comic store
ISBN: 978-1-4215-3882-2
$9.99 USA | $12.99 CAN
Shojo Beat
RATED T FOR TEEN
ratings.viz.com
VIZ media
www.viz.com
SAKURA-HIME KADEN © 2008 by Arina Tanemura/SHUEISHA Inc.

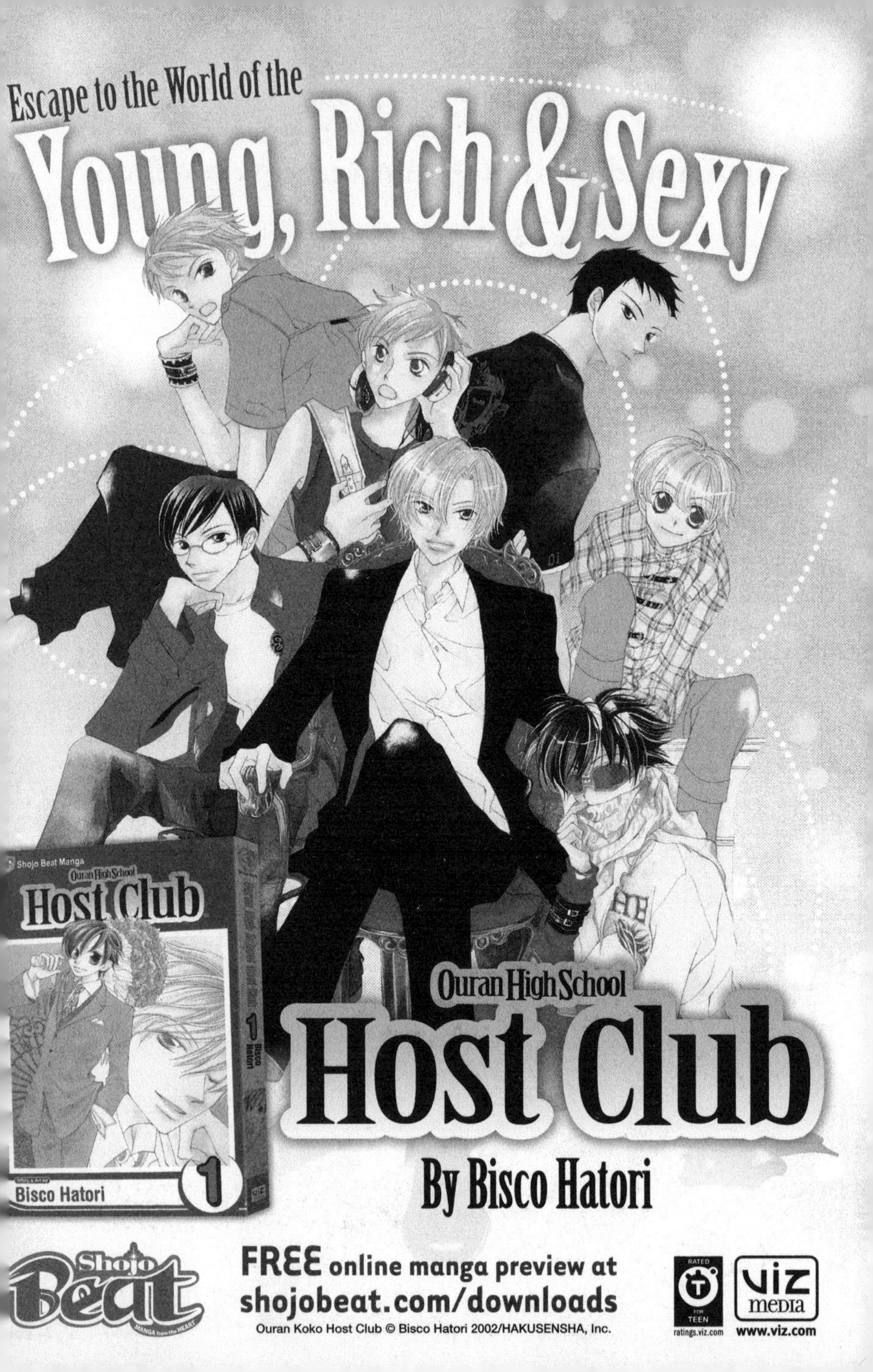
Escape to the World of the
Young, Rich & Sexy
Shojo Beat Manga
Ouran High School
Host Club
Bisco Hatori
1
Ouran High School
Host Club
By Bisco Hatori
Shojo Beat
FREE online manga preview at
shojobeat.com/downloads
Ouran Koko Host Club © Bisco Hatori 2002/HAKUSENSHA, Inc.
RATED
FOR TEEN
ratings.viz.com
VIZ media
www.viz.com

VIZMANGA

Read manga anytime, anywhere!

From our newest hit series to the classics you know and love, the best manga in the world is now available digitally. Buy a volume* of digital manga for your:

- iOS device (**iPad®, iPhone®, iPod® touch**) through the **VIZ Manga app**
- Android-powered device (**phone or tablet**) with a browser by visiting VIZManga.com
- **Mac or PC computer** by visiting VIZManga.com

VIZ Digital has loads to offer:

- 500+ ready-to-read volumes
- New volumes each week
- FREE previews
- Access on multiple devices! Create a log-in through the app so you buy a book once, and read it on your device of choice!*

To learn more, visit www.viz.com/apps

*** Some series may not be available for multiple devices. Check the app on your device to find out what's available.**

Aiwo Utauyori Oreni Oborero! Volume 1 © Mayu SHINJO 2010
DEATH NOTE © 2003 by Tsugumi Ohba, Takeshi Obata/SHUEISHA Inc.
NURARIHYON NO MAGO © 2008 by Hiroshi Shiibashi/SHUEISHA Inc.

RATED T+ FOR OLDER TEEN ratings.viz.com

viz media viz.com/apps

This is the last page.

In keeping with the original Japanese comic format, this book reads from right to left—so action, sound effects, and word balloons are completely reversed. This preserves the orientation of the original artwork—plus, it's fun! Check out the diagram shown here to get the hang of things, and then turn to the other side of the book to get started!